Living & Working in
SWITZERLAND

● A Survival Handbook ●

David Hampshire

Survival Books ● Bath ● England

First published in 1988
Fourteenth edition published 2013

Survival Books Limited
Office 169, 3 Edgar Buildings, George St, Bath, BA1 2FJ, United Kingdom
☎ +44 (0)1935-700060, ✉ info@survivalbooks.net
🖥 www.survivalbooks.net

British Library Cataloguing in Publication Data
A CIP record for this book is available
from the British Library.
ISBN: 978-1-909282-63-6

Printed and bound in Singapore by International Press Softcom Limited

Acknowledgements

M y sincere thanks to all those who contributed to the successful publication of this 14th edition of *Living and Working in Switzerland* and the previous editions of this book. I would particularly like to thank Dianne Hauptli for research and updating; Peter Read for editing and further research; David Woodworth for proof-reading; Di Bruce-Kidman for desktop publishing, photo selection and cover design; and Jim Watson for the illustrations, cartoons and maps. Also a special thank you to the many photographers (listed on page 310) – the unsung heroes – whose beautiful images add colour and bring the country to life.

Finally a big thank you to the advertisers, without whose support it would be difficult to produce books in colour without them being prohibitively expensive.

R E V I E W S

Swiss News

"Rarely has a 'survival guide' contained such useful advice – This book dispels doubts for first time travellers, yet is also useful for seasoned globetrotters – In a word, if you're planning to move to the US or go there for a long term stay, then buy this book both for general reading and as a ready reference."

Living France Magazine

"If I were to move to France, I would like David Hampshire to be with me, holding my hand every step of the way. This being impractical, I would have to settle for second best and take his books with me instead!"

Reader (Amazon)

"I read most of the books available on this subject before migrating to Australia, so I feel confident enough to say that although this guide is sometimes exhausting... if you pick out the information which is relevant to you the information is golden."

The Riviera Reporter

"Let's say it at once. David Hampshire's Living and Working in France is the best handbook ever produced for visitors and foreign residents in this country; indeed, my discussion with locals showed that it has much to teach even those born and bred in l'Hexagone. It is Hampshire's meticulous detail which lifts his work way beyond the range of other books with similar titles. This book is absolutely indispensable."

ICI (Switzerland) AG

"We would like to congratulate you on this work: it is really super! We hand it out to our expatriates and they read it with great interest and pleasure."

Important Note

S witzerland is a diverse country with many faces. It has four national languages, both federal and cantonal laws, a variety of religions and customs, and continuously changing rules and regulations – particularly with regard to foreigners.

Always check with an official and reliable source (not always the same) before making any major decisions or taking an irreversible course of action. Don't, however, believe everything you're told or read, even, dare I say it, herein!

To help you obtain further information and verify data with official sources, useful addresses and references to other sources of information have been included in all chapters, and in Appendices A to C. Important points have been emphasised throughout the book, some of which it would be expensive or foolish to disregard. **Ignore them at your peril or cost.**

NOTE

Unless specifically stated, the reference to any company, organisation or product in this book doesn't constitute an endorsement or recommendation. None of the businesses, products or individuals listed have paid to be mentioned (apart from the advertisers).

Contents

9. EDUCATION

9. EDUCATION — 103

12. HEALTH   163

13. INSURANCE   173

14. FINANCE   189

15. LEISURE
211

16. SPORTS
221

17. SHOPPING
243

Author's Notes

♦ Frequent references are made in this book to the European Union (EU), which comprises Austria, Belgium, Bulgaria, Cyprus, the Czech Republic, Denmark, Estonia, Finland, France, Germany, Greece, Hungary, Ireland, Italy, Latvia, Lithuania, Luxembourg, Malta, the Netherlands, Poland, Portugal, Romania, Slovakia, Slovenia, Spain, Sweden and the UK. The European Economic Area (EEA) includes the EU countries plus the European Free Trade Association (EFTA) countries of Iceland, Liechtenstein and Norway – plus Switzerland. (Switzerland is a member of EFTA, but isn't a member of the EEA.)

♦ All times are shown using the 12-hour clock; times before noon are indicated by the suffix 'am' and times after noon by 'pm'.

♦ Unless otherwise stated, all prices quoted are in Swiss francs (CHF) and include VAT. They should be taken as estimates only, although they were mostly correct at the time of publication and fortunately don't change overnight in Switzerland. See 🖥 www.xe.com for conversion rates.

♦ His/he/him also means her/she/her (please forgive me ladies). This is done to make life easier for both the reader and the author, and isn't intended to be sexist.

♦ British English and spelling is used throughout the book. Names of Swiss towns and foreign words are generally shown in their English spelling, e.g. Basle (Basel), Berne (Bern), Geneva (Genève), Lucerne (Luzern) and Zurich (Zürich).

♦ Warnings and important points are printed in **bold** type.

♦ The following symbols are used in this book: ☎ (telephone), 🖥 (Internet) and ✉ (email).

♦ Lists of **Useful Addresses, Further Reading** and **Useful Websites** are contained in **Appendices A, B** and **C** respectively.

♦ For those unfamiliar with the metric system of **Weights & Measures**, conversion tables are included in **Appendix D**.

♦ Maps showing the cantons, a physical map and communications (airports, rail, road) are included in **Appendix E**.

Introduction

Whether you're already living or working in Switzerland or just thinking about it – this is **THE BOOK** for you. Forget about those glossy guide books, excellent though they are for tourists; this book was written especially with you in mind and is worth its weight in Emmental cheese (and not just the holes!). Furthermore, this fully revised and updated 14th edition is printed in colour. *Living and Working in Switzerland* has been written to meet the needs of anyone wishing to know the essentials of Swiss life – however long your intended stay, you'll find the information contained in this book invaluable.

In contrast to the wealth of information provided by Switzerland Tourism, reliable and up-to-date information specifically intended for foreigners living and working in Switzerland isn't so easy to find – particularly in English. Our aim in publishing this book was to help fill this void and provide the comprehensive, practical information necessary for a relatively trouble-free life. You may have visited Switzerland as a tourist, but living and working there's a different matter altogether. Adjusting to a different environment and culture and making a home in any foreign country can be a traumatic and stressful experience – and Switzerland is no exception.

Living and Working in Switzerland is a comprehensive handbook on a wide range of everyday subjects and represents the most up-to-date source of general information available to foreigners in Switzerland. It isn't, however, simply a catalogue of dry facts and figures, but a practical and entertaining look at life. Adjusting to life in a new country is a continuous process, and although this book will help reduce your novice phase and minimise the frustrations, it doesn't contain all the answers (most of us don't even know the right questions to ask!). What it will do, however. is help you make informed decisions and calculated judgements, instead of uneducated guesses and costly mistakes. **Most importantly, it will help save you time, trouble and money, and repay your investment many times over.**

Although you may find some of the information a bit daunting, don't be discouraged. Most problems occur only once and fade into insignificance after a short time (as you face the next half a dozen …). Most foreigners in Switzerland would agree that, all things considered, they love living there. A period spent in Switzerland is a wonderful way to enrich your life, broaden your horizons, and, with any luck (and some hard work) you may even make your fortune. I trust this book will help you avoid the pitfalls of life in Switzerland and smooth your way to a happy and rewarding future in your new home.

Viel Glück/Bon courage!

David Hampshire
December 2012

1.

FINDING A JOB

Finding a job in Switzerland isn't as difficult as official Swiss policy may lead you to believe, although obtaining a permit can prove a problem if you aren't an EU/EFTA national. The European Union (actually the European Economic Area/EEA, which comprises the EU countries plus the EFTA countries) and Switzerland have a bilateral agreement that allows the free movement of people and removes the need for permits (there are no work permit quotas for most EU nationals).

Switzerland's economic success is largely dependent upon the influx of foreign labour, and foreigners are found in almost every walk of life. Many companies have a sizeable foreign labour force and foreigners fill almost half the top positions at the 25 largest Swiss companies (including two-thirds of the companies quoted on the Swiss stock exchange). Foreign employees in Switzerland number over 1.25m or some 30 per cent of the workforce.

> In addition to resident foreigners, over 200,000 people cross the border each day to work in Switzerland.

At the end of 2011, over 85 per cent of Switzerland's permanent resident foreign population was of European origin, with some two-thirds of the foreign workforce from EU-15 or EFTA countries. Italians, Germans and Balkan countries each comprise around 16 per cent of the foreign workforce, followed by the Portuguese with around 13 per cent. Almost a quarter of foreign residents were born in Switzerland and belong to second (called *Secondos*) or third-generation families. Some 30 per cent of resident Italians but only around 6 per cent of Germans were born in Switzerland. Almost half of the foreign resident population have been in Switzerland for over 15 years and around 90 per cent of Italian and Spanish residents have permanent resident status.

The employment of foreigners, albeit an economic necessity, is something of a political hot potato. The Swiss generally live and work harmoniously with their foreign 'guests', although there's a vociferous minority who would like to see the number of foreign workers drastically reduced. During the last 30 years they've gained sufficient support to stage a number of national referendums in an attempt to reduce the resident foreign population. All have been defeated but they've served to strain relations between some Swiss and resident foreigners.

Most positions held by foreigners fall into two main categories: seasonal jobs for less than a year and permanent staff positions. Seasonal workers include hotel and catering staff, building and construction workers, factory hands, farm workers, and many people in the tourist industry. Such jobs are available throughout Switzerland and aren't usually difficult to find. Permanent jobs are generally reserved for senior managers, professionals and specialists (e.g. computer experts and engineers), and require annual residence permits. Residence permits are also required by au pairs, students and trainees.

Labour relations in Switzerland are excellent and there are fewer strikes than in any other industrialised country. Increased global competition has meant that a large number of companies have streamlined (i.e. reduced) their workforces over the last few years and many have moved their production and research facilities abroad to reduce costs. However, Switzerland has one of the lowest unemployment rates in Europe – a 'jobless Swiss' used to be an oxymoron – in October 2012 the rate was 2.8 per cent (5.3 per cent in Geneva and 3.2 per cent in Zurich), slightly lower than the average of 3.3 per cent for 2011.

SWITZERLAND & THE EUROPEAN UNION

Despite being surrounded by European Union (EU) countries and being a 'currency island' (all its neighbours use the Euro, except Liechtenstein, which uses the Swiss franc), Switzerland is the only Western European country that isn't a member of the EU or European Economic Area (EEA) – the EU plus the EFTA countries minus Switzerland. The Swiss have twice voted in referenda against joining these entities – the first time in 1992, when they voted against joining the EEA, and in 2001, when they decided not to join the EU by a majority of 77 per cent. The referendum results highlighted a split between the Swiss Germans and Swiss French over Switzerland's future; French-speaking Swiss tend to be in favour of joining the EU, while German-speakers are generally against it.

In 2006, the Swiss Parliament decided to keep open the country's invitation to join the EU, but another referendum isn't expected any time soon. Surveys show that currently around a third of the Swiss population is in favour of EU membership, one-third is against, and the remaining third undecided. Meanwhile, the EU remains open to Swiss membership and undoubtedly the topic of European integration and EU membership will dominate Swiss politicians' thinking for the foreseeable future.

In spite of the referendum and survey results, there remains a mood for change in the country and the numerous bilateral agreements between Switzerland and the EU demonstrate a firm commitment to co-operation – one of the most important of these being the agreement on the free movement of EU citizens in Switzerland and vice versa.

> Switzerland and the EU are dependent on one another – Switzerland is one of the EU's most important export markets and its second-largest supplier after the US, and over one million EU citizens work in Switzerland.

SEASONAL JOBS

The majority of seasonal jobs in Switzerland are in the tourist industry, most lasting for the duration of the summer or winter tourist seasons, i.e. April to October and December to April respectively. To work in a seasonal job you need to obtain a (non-renewable) L permit, which are usually issued for a maximum of 12 months.

Although salaries are higher in Switzerland than in most other countries, you're expected to work hard and for long hours, particularly in hotels and restaurants in winter resorts (summer is generally more relaxed). Many businesses must survive for a whole year primarily on their winter earnings and employers expect everyone to earn their keep. Language fluency is required for all but the most menial and worst paid jobs, and is at least as important as experience and qualifications (not that language proficiency alone will get you a well paid job). The local language in Switzerland may be French, German or Italian, depending on the area (see **Languages** on page 29). Fortunately, there's a great sense of camaraderie among seasonal workers, which goes a long way towards compensating for the often boring and hard work (the Swiss francs also help).

If accommodation isn't provided with a job, it can be expensive and difficult to find. Ensure that your salary is sufficient to pay for accommodation, food and other living expenses, and hopefully also allow you to save some money (see **Cost of Living** on page 189). Seasonal jobs include the following:

Year Round Jobs

Bars & Clubs

Jobs in bars and clubs are available throughout Switzerland. English- and Irish-style pubs in many towns often hire native English-speaking bartenders and waiters to add a touch of authenticity (although they're often married to a Swiss, unless it's a seasonal job). Winter resorts have clubs and discotheques requiring disc jockeys, particularly those with a collection of up-to-date dance music. Jobs for disc jockeys are also advertised in British music newspapers. Casino staff, including croupiers, are also required in casinos throughout Switzerland.

Couriers & Resort Representatives

A courier's or resort representative's duties include ferrying tourist groups back and forth from airports, organising excursions and social events, arranging ski passes and equipment rental, and generally playing the role of Jack (or Jill) of all trades. A job as a courier is demanding and requires resilience and resourcefulness to deal with the chaos associated with the package holiday business. The necessary requirements include the ability to answer many questions simultaneously (often in different languages), and to remain calm, charming and humorous under extreme pressure. Lost passengers, tickets, passports and tempers are everyday occurrences. It's an excellent training ground for managerial and leadership skills, pays well, and often provides opportunities to supplement your earnings.

Couriers are required by many local and foreign tour companies in both winter and summer resorts. Competition for jobs is fierce and local language ability is always required, even for employment with British tour operators. Most companies have age requirements, the minimum usually being 21, although many companies prefer employees to be a few years older. The majority of courier jobs in Switzerland are available during the winter ski season with British ski-tour companies and school ski-party organisers.

A good source of information is ski magazines, which contain regular listings of tour companies showing who operates in which resorts. It's wise to find out the type of clients you're likely to be dealing with, particularly if you're allergic to children or yuppies (young urban professionals – similar to children but more immature). To survive winter in a ski resort, it helps if you're a keen skier or a dedicated learner, otherwise you risk being bored to death by ski bums.

Some companies, such as Club Méditerranée (Club Med), operate both summer and winter hotels and camps in French-speaking Switzerland (employees are required to speak good French). For information, contact Club Méditerranée, France (⌨ www.clubmedjobs.com). A variety of staff are required for summer and winter camps, which are organised for both adults and children. One such organisation is My Swiss Camp (⌨ www.myswisscamp.com, ✉ jobs@haut-lac. com), which hires seasonal workers year-round, including chalet girls, cooks, kitchen staff, ski instructors, sports supervisors, English teachers, etc. An excellent website for winter jobs is Snowsports (⌨ www.snowsports.ch – choose the French or German language at the top-right of the page then Services and offres d'emploi/jobbörse).

See also **Voluntary Workers** below.

Hotels & Restaurants

Hotels and restaurants are the largest employers of seasonal workers, with jobs available at all levels from managers to kitchen hands. Experience, qualifications and language fluency are required for all the best and highest paid positions, but a variety of jobs are available for the untrained and inexperienced. These include chambermaids, waiters and waitresses, cleaners, dishwashers, handymen, porters, messengers, drivers, kitchen assistants and MBOs (muscle-bound oafs).

The standards required by Swiss employers are high, and hard work and long hours are demanded, although the pay is usually good. The minimum monthly wage for employees in the hotel/restaurant industry is around CHF 3,300 (less in mountain regions and during the probation period) and a 13th month's salary (see page 34) is paid to most full-time employees – but not to seasonal workers. Employees in hotels are usually provided with full board and you should avoid any job that doesn't include it, as the cost can be prohibitive. Reductions from gross salaries for board and lodging and compulsory insurance amount to some 50 per cent.

Official working hours vary between 44 and 48 per week depending on the job, or around nine to nine-and-a-half hours per day. Your contract will state the maximum number of working hours per week; normal working hours should be a maximum of 45 per week, although in reality this may be the minimum. You're entitled to two free days each week and four weeks' paid holiday per year (around one-and-a-half days per month). Between Christmas and New Year you may be expected to work 12 hours a day, seven days a week, for which you'll usually receive time off in January. Most jobs include a two-week trial period with a notice period of three days, after which the notice period is one month.

Waiters and waitresses are expected to provide their own 'uniform' and wallet and a cash float of around CHF 200. The salary is often on a commission basis, where you're paid a percentage of your takings (plus tips – unless all your customers are Swiss!). Aprons, hats and oven gloves are normally provided for kitchen staff, plus a free laundry service for working clothes and uniforms. Other dress requirements vary according to the job; for example waiters require black trousers and shoes, white shirts and possibly jackets, while waitresses require black skirts, shoes and stockings, white blouses and possibly small aprons.

In addition to jobs in Swiss hotels and restaurants, jobs are also available in hotels and chalets operated by British and other foreign tour operators, where local language ability may be unnecessary. Work is generally easier and the atmosphere more relaxed, but salaries are usually lower than those paid by Swiss-run hotels, and may even be less than the minimum wage.

Many agencies and a number of trade newspapers are available in Switzerland to help you find a job in a hotel or restaurant. Union Helvetia is the official Swiss union for hotel and restaurant staff, and anyone who has training or qualifications in the hotel and catering trades can become a member. Union Helvetia publishes an official rule book (*Obligationenrecht*, *droit des obligations*) for employers and employees and a list of official minimum salaries for all jobs, plus a weekly newspaper, *Expresso*, listing job vacancies. It's available from news kiosks in Switzerland or on subscription from the Hotel & Gastro Union (☎ 041-418 22 22, 🖥 www. hotelgastrounion.ch).

The Swiss Hotel Association (*Schweizer Hotelier-Verein, Société Suisse des Hôteliers*) publishes a newspaper, *Hotel + Tourismus Revue*, which usually contains more job vacancies than the *Expresso* newspaper. It's also available from news kiosks (on Thursdays) or on subscription from *Hotel + Tourismus Revue* (☎ 031-370 41 11, 🖥 www.htr.ch). Both *Expresso* and *Hotel + Tourismus Revue* contain articles in French and German. Like Union Helvetia, the Swiss Hotel Association has its own employment agency and publishes a standard employment contract for hotel and restaurant staff, in use throughout the country. Another weekly newspaper advertising job vacancies for hotel and restaurant staff is *Schweizer Gastronome* (🖥 www.gilde.ch – French/German only).

Besides answering advertisements and visiting agencies, you could try contacting Swiss hotel and restaurant chains directly.

Manual Workers

Jobs for manual workers are usually available throughout Switzerland, mostly in the construction and farming industries. The minimum salary in the construction industry for an unskilled worker is around CHF 4,000 per month, but can be higher depending on the actual job and your experience. Jobs are also available for cleaners and general labourers in hospitals, factories, warehouses and large hotels. Farmers often require extra labourers, particularly in the spring and autumn to help with the fruit, vegetable and grape harvests. Farming jobs entail hard physical work, usually for around 12 hours a day, six days a week, for a low salary.

One of the most popular jobs is grape picking, e.g. in the cantons of Valais and Vaud. Lasting

for around eight to ten days in early October, the work is hard and the salary is around CHF 50 per day plus accommodation and meals. Even for this kind of work it may be important to have some knowledge of the local language.-

Unfortunately the worst abuses of seasonal workers' rights occur in the farming industry, particularly in the Geneva area, where complaints include low pay, long hours, inadequate living conditions and unpaid social benefits. If you're a seasonal worker from a country with a bilateral insurance agreement with Switzerland, the Swiss government doesn't repay federal social security payments (OASI/DI) when you leave Switzerland. Therefore there's a temptation for dishonest employers to deduct the OASI/DI payment from your salary and not declare it, particularly as you're unlikely ever to claim a Swiss pension.

The Swiss are continually digging tunnels, building and repairing bridges and roads, and constructing office blocks and shopping centres – and it's mostly foreigners who do the manual work. Enquire at building sites in Switzerland – the bigger the site, the better your chance of success. In summer, jobs may be available in ski resorts installing new ski lifts, snow-making machinery, and building chalets and hotels. Enquire at local lift operating companies, estate agents and construction companies.

If you have experience or training in the building industry, e.g. as a bricklayer or carpenter, you should be able to command a higher salary, even without local language fluency.

> Outdoor jobs in the building and construction industries are usually restricted to the warmer months, as trying to find your shovel under two metres of snow can be a handicap in winter.

Sports Instructors

Instructors are required for a variety of sports, including canoeing, diving, golf, gymnastics, hang-gliding, horse riding, mountaineering, parachuting, rock-climbing, sailing, squash, subaquatic sports, swimming, tennis and windsurfing. Whatever the sport, it's probably played and taught somewhere in Switzerland. Most jobs for sports instructors are available in summer, as winter sports vacancies are generally filled by the Swiss (for information regarding **Ski Instructors & Guides**, see below). However, if you're a qualified winter sports instructor, you can contact Swiss resorts or sports organisations for information about vacancies. You may require an officially recognised qualification to teach some sports, for example a life-saving certificate to teach swimming or a sailing instructor's certificate to teach sailing.

Voluntary Work

Voluntary work is primarily to enable students and young people to visit Switzerland for a few weeks or months to learn about the country and its people at first hand. Voluntary work is, of course, unpaid, although meals and accommodation are normally provided and a small amount of pocket money may be paid. This, however, may be insufficient for expenses such as entertainment and drinks, therefore you need to ensure that you bring enough money with you. The usual visa regulations apply to voluntary workers and your passport must be valid for at least a year. You'll be informed whether you need a visa when you apply (a work or residence permit isn't required).

Various kinds of voluntary work are available, including those listed below.

Farm Work

Voluntary farm work is usually available from March to October (mainly in German-speaking areas) and is organised by the Swiss Farm Work Association. You must be aged between 16 and 25 with a basic knowledge of German or French (depending on the area) and be prepared to work for a minimum of two weeks and a maximum of eight. It certainly isn't a holiday, as the work is usually strenuous and the hours long, for six days a week (Sundays are free!). Officially the maximum hours are 48 hours per week, although more may be expected. Work may be in the fields, farmyard, farmhouse or farm garden. For this you're paid at least CHF 20 a day (those aged over 18), plus board and lodging, and are insured against accidents. You must have your own medical insurance, carry a European Insurance card, and must pay for your own journey to and from the farm.

Many farms are in remote mountain areas, where living and working conditions may be primitive and there's little social life. If you enjoy a hectic social life and companionship, this isn't the job for you. Friends applying together aren't usually placed with the same farmer, as most farms are small and farms cannot usually accommodate more than one person. Application forms are available from Agriviva (☎ 052-264 00 30, 🖳 www.agriviva.ch). Registration (the fee is CHF 40/25 Euro) should be made at least four weeks before you wish to start work (you can apply online).

> Farm jobs include work on organically run farms, in return for which you receive free meals and accommodation (but no expenses). A year's membership and a list of participating farms costs CHF 20 from WWOOF Switzerland, Postfach 59, CH-8124 Maur (💻 http://zapfig.com/wwoof). You must send a copy of your passport with your payment and a letter explaining why you want to become a WWOOF volunteer.

General

There are organisations that require volunteer workers such as camp counsellors or to help on projects such as restoring hiking trails. Workcamps Switzerland (☎ 043-317 19 30, 💻 www.workcamp.ch) offers volunteers assignments, mostly in the summer months, but their website also lists international projects. There's a registration fee for Swiss workcamps of around CHF 150.

Winter Jobs

A seasonal job in a ski resort can be a lot of fun and very satisfying. You'll get fit, learn or improve a language and make friends, and may even save some money; all in addition to living in one of the most beautiful countries in the world. However, although a winter job may be a working holiday to you (with lots of skiing and little work), to your employer it's exactly the opposite! In general, hotel and restaurant staff work much harder in ski resorts during winter than in summer, when life is more relaxed. Some hotel and restaurant employers even forbid their employees to ski (although this is rare), particularly key personnel (e.g. chefs) over the Christmas and New Year period.

Ski resorts require an army of temporary workers to cater for the annual invasion of winter sports enthusiasts. Besides jobs in the hotel and restaurant trades already described, a variety of generally well paid winter jobs are available, some of which are described below. Usually the better paid the job, the longer the working hours and the less time off there is for skiing. Employment in a winter resort may entitle employees to reduced public transport fares and a discounted ski pass.

Seasonal workers in the tourist industry aren't covered by unemployment insurance, unlike, for example, workers in the construction industry. In a bad season, with little or no snow, you can therefore find yourself without work or money. Ski lift operators and others directly dependent on snow conditions for a living, should watch the weather forecast closely and pray for lots of snow. Even if you work in a hotel or restaurant, your contract can be cancelled or cut short when business is bad.

Chalet Girls

Hundreds of chalet workers (most are female, but males are also eligible) are required each winter to look after the everyday comforts of guests in holiday chalets and private hotels, many run by British and other foreign tour operators. The job of a chalet worker entails hard work, generally offers low pay (as little as half the rate paid by Swiss hotels) and requires a variety of skills and experience. You must usually be able to cook to a high standard or have experience of catering for parties; do shopping, housekeeping and laundry; deal with obstreperous clients; and generally be a Jill of all trades.

Nevertheless, once you get over the initial shock, you'll probably find the job satisfying and challenging, and it allows plenty of time off for skiing. One thing for sure, you won't have time to be bored. You'll also have to fight off the attentions of hordes of men and survive numerous late-night parties – it's a tough job but someone has to do it! A limited number of chalet workers are required in summer.

Ski Instructors & Guides

Jobs as ski instructors in Switzerland are almost impossible to obtain unless you've passed the Swiss ski instructors' examinations, although some resorts accept foreign qualifications, e.g. the advanced British Association of Ski Instructors (BASI) qualification or equivalent. Experience and local language fluency are also required. Jobs as ski companions, ski instructors for children and ski guides with foreign tour operators are easier to find. However, in some resorts local ski instructors are hostile towards ski guides, particularly as there's often only a thin dividing line between guiding and instructing, and as a result guide jobs have been reduced.

The Ski Club of Great Britain (SCGB, 💻 www.skiclub.co.uk) has representatives in many resorts, whose job is to take members on skiing excursions but not to teach them. Swiss resorts usually (wisely) allow British and other foreign school parties to be taught by qualified foreign instructors. To teach children, the lowest BASI qualification or equivalent may be sufficient.

If you work as a ski guide or instructor and an accident occurs through your negligence

(for example one of your customers falls down a precipice), you may be liable for damages, therefore you should ensure that you have liability insurance.

An excellent website for skiing jobs is Snowsports (🖳 www.snowsports.ch – choose French or German at the top-right of the page then 'Services' and '*offres d'emploi/jobbörse*'). You must speak a minimum of two languages, e.g. French or German and English.

⚠ Caution

Working as an unofficial instructor without a permit or qualifications is strictly illegal.

Ski Technicians

A ski technician's job entails fitting and maintaining skis, bindings and boots. Although some employers require previous experience, many ski rental shops provide training, and courses are available in some countries. Besides doing the round of resort shops, contact tour companies and large luxury hotels, as they often have their own ski hire and service shops. Local language ability is usually required, although it may depend on the employer and his clientele.

PERMANENT POSITIONS

Permanent positions in Switzerland require an annual residence permit (see **B Permit** on page 48). Most permanent positions require special skills, qualifications and experience, which are usually more important than the ability to speak fluent French, German or Italian. In fact, you may not be expected to speak the local language at all if your mother tongue is English. This is often the case when you're employed by an American or British company, or work in a high-tech field where English is an important language spoken fluently by your colleagues. If you need to speak (or learn) the local language, you'll be informed at your interview, and when necessary, language tuition may be subsidised or paid for by your employer.

There's often a huge difference between working for a Swiss or foreign company employing many other English-speaking foreigners, and working for a company where you have few or no English-speaking colleagues. You will, of course, learn the local language much more quickly working with colleagues who don't speak English. However, you may find – as many other foreigners do – that the working environment and general lack of camaraderie, warmth and friendliness, isn't to your liking. The Swiss don't generally mix socially with their colleagues and this may even exclude the occasional drink after work.

Foreign qualifications are recognised in many trades and professions, provided the length of training and syllabus was similar to those required for the equivalent Swiss qualification. Under bilateral treaties between Switzerland and the EU, Switzerland now recognises most EU-based diplomas and qualifications – even for formerly excluded professions such as teachers, barristers, lawyers, doctors, dentists, pharmacists and veterinarians. For non-EU citizens, restrictions remain but a non-EU foreigner entitled to live in Switzerland – for example as a result of long-term residence or marriage to a Swiss citizen – may be able to study or pass a Swiss examination entitling him to work in a restricted field. Regulations may also be relaxed by individual cantons when there's a shortage of qualified Swiss staff.

When applying for a job, you should provide copies of all qualifications and references, as these tend to impress Swiss employers and may also influence the authorities when deciding whether to grant a permit.

JOB APPLICATIONS

How you apply for a job depends largely on whether it's a seasonal or permanent position:

Seasonal Jobs

Apply for jobs as early as possible, for example March for summer jobs and June or July for winter jobs. For summer jobs in mountain resorts, you should apply in March or April. If you apply too early, the worst that can happen is that you'll be told to apply again later. The latest dates for applications are usually the end of September for winter jobs and the end of April for summer jobs. In some resorts, the summer season starts in spring (April), with staff being recruited in January. Don't put all your eggs in one basket – the more job applications you make, the better your chances of success.

Many jobs require local language fluency (see **Languages** on page 29); therefore if you apply for a job in writing, it's best to write in the local language – but obtain help if you aren't fluent. You can brush up your language ability after you've secured a job, but it isn't advisable to exaggerate your language ability, experience or qualifications in a letter. If you're offered a job on the basis of non-existent qualifications, you'll soon be found out and risk being fired. A good knowledge of the local language helps when dealing with local officials. For seasonal jobs, German is more advantageous than French, as the majority of jobs are in German-speaking resorts.

When applying for a job requiring experience, don't forget to provide your CV/resumé and copies of qualifications and references (see **Job Applications** below).

☑ SURVIVAL TIP

Always ask for a written job offer and a contract, and steer clear of employers who won't provide them (see Illegal Working on page 28). An official job entitles you to accident insurance, unemployment benefits, and in particular, official protection from exploitation.

Writing unsolicited letters for jobs is a hit-and-miss affair and is usually the least successful method of securing employment. An employer who doesn't know you from Adam (or Eve) may be unwilling to risk employing you because if you don't turn up he's left in the lurch. If you're really serious and can afford the journey, it may be worthwhile visiting prospective employers for an interview before the season starts.

Your best chance of obtaining a seasonal job may be to apply in person, particularly when looking for a winter job close to the start of the ski season. Success is often simply a matter of being in the right place at the right time, although you can give lady luck a helping hand by your

persistence and enterprise. Make an effort to look presentable, as Swiss employers expect a high standard of dress and cleanliness; hair must usually be short (except for women) and tidy, and beards aren't usually permitted. When looking for a job in person, try the following methods:

♦ Call on prospective employers, but avoid calling at hotels and restaurants during meal times.

♦ Ask prospective employers if they know of anyone looking for staff and leave your name and an address and a telephone number (if possible) where you can be contacted (a mobile phone is handy).

♦ Check wanted boards or place an advertisement on local notice boards, for example in a Migros or Co-op supermarket, or on the notice boards of expatriate clubs, churches and other organisations.

♦ Look in local newspapers or place an advertisement in the 'Jobs Wanted' section.

♦ Ask at tourist offices as many keep lists of job vacancies from September onwards for the coming winter season. Lists are regularly updated and the service is free.

♦ Ask other foreign workers.

If you're an English speaker, the best winter resorts to try are those with a large number of American and British skiers, which include Arosa, Champéry, Crans-Montana, Davos, Engelberg, Grindelwald, Gstaad, Klosters, Les Diablerets, Leysin, Saas Fee, St. Moritz, Verbier, Villars, Wengen and Zermatt. However, don't neglect the many smaller resorts; although jobs may be scarcer, there's less competition from other job hunters, who tend to focus on the major resorts.

Don't worry if you miss the start of the season, as jobs often become vacant at short notice to replace those who become sick or homesick, are injured or sacked – or who run off with a ski instructor. Don't forget to take enough money to see you through the job-hunting period. Allow at least two weeks and bear in mind that the cost of living (see page 189) is high in Switzerland.

Depending on your nationality, after you've found a job you may need to return to the nearest border point with your 'assurance of a residence permit' for a health check. When leaving a job at the end of the season, it's advisable to ask for a reference if one isn't provided automatically, particularly if you intend to look for further seasonal work.

If you need a visa to enter Switzerland as a visitor (see **Chapter 3**), you'll be unable to find a job on the spot as the work visa must be issued by an embassy abroad.

Permanent Positions

There are various ways to find a permanent position in Switzerland, including the following:

◆ Use the internet, which is the most popular option among Swiss job hunters. There are numerous websites devoted to job-hunting in Switzerland, many of which are available in English, such as 🖳 www.jobs.ch, www.stellen.ch and www.topjobs.ch, but note that some job descriptions are only in French or German. Some sites specialise in English-speaking positions, such as : www.jobsingeneva.com and www.jobsinzurich.com. Positions advertised on the internet often invite candidates to apply online, but many Swiss companies (as well as the post office!) prefer traditional job applications sent by post. Note that in Switzerland it isn't unusual for job ads to include age restrictions and Swiss companies sometimes advertise for C permit holders (see page 48) or Swiss nationals only.

◆ Obtain copies of Swiss newspapers – or access them online (see 🖳 www.onlinenewspapers.com) – most of which contain a positions vacant (*Stellenanzeiger/Stellenmarkt, offres d'emploi*) section on certain days. Outside Switzerland,

Swiss newspapers may be available from international news agencies. When the ability to speak English is paramount, a position may be advertised in English.

◆ Apply to American, British and other multinational companies with offices or subsidiaries in Switzerland, and make written applications directly to Swiss companies. The 2,000 largest Swiss companies are listed in *Top 2012*, published annually by HandelsZeitung Fachverlag (☎ 043-444 51 11, 🖳 www.handelszeitung.ch) and also available on CD. Many of the companies listed advertise jobs on their websites. When writing job application letters, you should address them to the personnel department manager (*Personalabteilungsleiter, Chef de Service du Personnel*). Include your CV/resumé and copies of references and qualifications with your letter. If possible, offer to attend an interview in Switzerland and state when you're available.

◆ Apply to international recruiting agencies acting for Swiss companies, which mainly recruit executives and key personnel, many of which have offices worldwide. A Swiss company may appoint a sole agent to handle recruitment in a particular country.

◆ Contact employment agencies in Switzerland. Some agencies specialise in certain fields, for example the computer or catering industries. Note that the Swiss labour exchange doesn't help foreigners find employment unless they're already resident in Switzerland. Swiss employment agencies are unable to apply for residence permits on your behalf and only a bona fide Swiss employer can do this. Many Swiss agencies find positions only for Swiss citizens or for foreigners with a B or C permit (see **Chapter 3**).

◆ If you're a member of a recognised profession, you can place a 'position wanted' advertisement in a Swiss professional or trade newspaper or magazine. Publicitas AG (☎ 0844-84 84 40, 🖳 www.publicitas.ch) can help you find the most appropriate publication.

◆ Apply in person to Swiss companies. This method is often successful but doesn't usually shorten the time required to process a job application and obtain a residence permit.

◆ Ask friends or acquaintances working in Switzerland if they know of an employer seeking someone with your experience and qualifications.

WRITTEN APPLICATIONS

In Switzerland, a written job application should include the following: a cover letter, a CV/resumé (with a photo), copies of all your education and training certificates and diplomas, and previous work references (if applicable). Your cover letter should be typed (unless a prospective employer specifically requests you submit a hand-written cover letter) and no longer than one A4 page. Your CV/resumé should be kept simple and precise, and must include your first and last name, address, phone number, age, nationality and civil status (married, single, divorced, etc) – and you should also include a recent photo. It should include your educational background, your professional and occupational experience, your skills, main interests and hobbies, plus the names and addresses of referees (people who can be contacted to give you a reference). Advice (in English) about the application process is available from www.jobs.ch (under TIPS).

WORKING ILLEGALLY

It isn't uncommon in Switzerland for foreigners to work without a work permit, although the number of illegal workers in Switzerland has fallen considerably since measures were taken to address the problem. The illegal labour market (termed the black economy) thrives because employers are often unable to obtain permits for non-EU foreigners, many of whom are willing to risk the consequences for the high wages on offer. Some unscrupulous employers use illegal labour simply to pay low wages for long hours and poor working conditions (Geneva is the black economy's worst canton). An employer may also be reluctant to pay for an employee's permit, particularly when he may need him for a short period only.

⚠ Caution

It's strictly illegal to work in Switzerland without a permit.

If you're tempted to take a job without a permit you should be aware of the consequences, as the black economy is a risky business for both employers and employees. An employer faces a fine of up to CHF 30,000 and repeat offenders can be fined up to CHF 1m (!) under a new law that came into effect in 2008. Companies found employing people without a permit are black-listed for one to five years and receive no state financial aid or contracts.

An individual caught working without a permit is usually fined and deported and may be refused a permit in future. You can even be black-listed (this also applies to those sacked for serious offences) or deported and your passport stamped so that you're unable to re-enter Switzerland. If you're caught working illegally, even for a few days while waiting for a permit to be issued, you can be fined and your permit application may be revoked.

Employees without permits have no entitlement to federal or company pensions, unemployment pay, health or accident insurance (e.g. when skiing), and no legal job protection.

SALARIES

It can be difficult to determine the salary you should get in Switzerland, as they aren't usually quoted in job advertisements and are kept strictly confidential – the Swiss don't like to discuss money, which simply confirms that they've got heaps of it! Usually salaries are negotiable and it's up to you to ensure that you receive the level of salary and benefits commensurate with your qualifications and experience. Minimum suggested salaries exist in all trades and professions, but there's no minimum wage in Switzerland.

Age is usually a major consideration with many Swiss companies, and seniority and experience are favoured by most Swiss employers (unless you're over 50). Many employers, particularly larger companies, are reluctant to pay a young person (e.g. below 30) a top salary, irrespective of his qualifications and experience. If you have friends or acquaintances working in Switzerland or who have worked there, ask them what an average or good salary is for your particular trade or profession. Various online forums discuss salaries in detail, for example English Forum (🖥 www.englishforum.ch).

Surveys consistently show that Swiss salaries are among the highest in the world, particularly those of managers and executives, and that the Swiss also have the highest net pay after the deduction of taxes and social security contributions. A professional or top manager usually earns well over CHF 100,000 per year and top executives from CHF 250,000, plus cash bonuses and non-cash compensation such as stock options and allowances. A top executive can earn at least 40 times that of the lowest paid worker, one of the highest salary differentials in the world. This is a controversial subject in

Switzerland – as it is in many other countries – and the Swiss (on low salaries!) are outraged by exorbitant executive salaries.

Salaries of both skilled and unskilled workers can be twice as high in Switzerland as in other European countries (but the cost of living is also much higher). Starting salaries with many large Swiss companies may, however, be lower than the national average. Salaries paid by some foreign (e.g. American) companies tend to be, on average, higher than those paid by Swiss companies, partly because many staff are specialists, managers and executives imported from abroad. Salaries are slightly higher in large than in small companies and organisations, although there's virtually no difference between the salaries of Swiss and non-Swiss employees.

Your working hours (see page 35) may be longer than in other countries and should be taken into account when negotiating your salary (an extra two hours a week adds up to around two and a half weeks a year!). In recent years, salary increases have been low and often below the rate of inflation (salaries have largely stagnated in the last decade).

Some employers may underestimate the cost of living in Switzerland, particularly the cost of housing, which can be astronomical. On average, the cost of living (see page 189) is much higher than in other developed countries, although the gross earnings and purchasing power of the Swiss are among the highest in the world. Income tax and pension contributions are progressive; the higher your income, the higher your pension and income tax payments (see **Chapters 13 & 14** respectively). They are, however, lower than in most other countries.

Women make up 45 per cent of the Swiss workforce and around 60 per cent of Swiss women aged between 15 and 64 are employed – one of the highest proportions

in Europe. However, over 55 per cent of women work part-time, compared with less than 10 per cent of men. Since 1981, employers in Switzerland have been legally required to pay equal wages to men and women doing the same job. Nevertheless, women's salary levels are (on average) around 15 per cent lower than men's (or around 10 per cent for professionals and managers), an inequality not entirely accounted for by their different occupations, and foreign women may earn less than Swiss women.

As in most countries, although there may be no official discrimination, in practice this isn't always so. Professional women are rarer in Switzerland than in many other developed countries and women often find it difficult to reach the top ranks of their profession, while only a small proportion are managers or executives – Switzerland has a concrete rather than a glass ceiling where career women are concerned! Swiss women have held a few one-day strikes to highlight salary inequalities, although they aren't well supported.

Married women usually face more discrimination in the workplace than single women, although it's no worse than in most other developed countries. Swiss employers must pay the salary of a female employee during pregnancy when she's absent from work, provided that she intends to return to work after giving birth (see **Pregnancy & Confinement** on 37). However, as no crèche service is provided by most companies in Switzerland, this is often difficult.

A useful guide to salaries and the cost of living is contained in a booklet entitled Living and Working in Switzerland, published in English by the Federal Department of Foreign Affairs (☎ +41-800-247-365, 💻 www.swissemigration. ch). See also the official Swiss comparison of average gross annual wages of full-time employees, between Switzerland and EU countries (💻 www.bfs.admin.ch/bfs/portal/ en/index/themen/03/04/blank/key/ lohnstruktur/interloehne.html and the salaries quoted on the Payscale website (💻 www. payscale.com/research/ ch/country=switzerland/ salary).

Every three years (the last was 2012) the United Bank of Switzerland publishes a free booklet (in English) entitled *Prices and Earnings Around the World*, which compares Swiss salaries with those of many other countries (it can be ordered from 🖳 www.ubs.ch).

CONTRACT JOBS

Contract jobs, usually for a limited period, are available through many foreign and Swiss employment agencies specialising in freelance work. Most contract positions are for specialists in the computer, engineering and electronics fields. A number of agencies in Switzerland specialise in supplying contract staff to major companies and many post lists of day labourers required in their windows. Foreign employees of a foreign company who are living in Switzerland and working temporarily for a Swiss employer require a work permit, which must be obtained by the Swiss employer (unless employment is for a brief period only).

SELF-EMPLOYMENT

Non-EU citizens require a C permit (*Niederlassungsbewilligung*, *permis d'établissement* – see page 48) to be self-employed. It's therefore virtually impossible for non-EU nationals to emigrate to Switzerland to become self-employed or to start a business (unless you have millions of francs and are going to create jobs and exports). There are sometimes exceptions in the fields of music and art, and in professions where Swiss nationals don't usually qualify, for example translating or writing in a non-Swiss language. Non-EU citizens married to Swiss nationals with a B permit may be allowed to be self-employed, although this is unusual.

EU citizens can be self-employed in Switzerland but must register with the authorities and obtain a work permit. This is usually granted if the self-employed person can prove that he has set up successfully and can make a living from his trade.

Non-resident foreigners who wish to establish a business in Switzerland may be able to negotiate a favourable tax deal with the cantonal authorities, plus residence permits for the owner and his family.

TRAINEES

Switzerland is a participant in an international trainee (*Praktikant*, *stagiaire*) programme designed to give young people the opportunity for further education and occupational training, and to enlarge their professional experience and knowledge of languages. The programme has exchange agreements with Argentina, Australia, Bulgaria, Canada, the Czech Republic, Hungary,

Monaco, New Zealand, Philippines, Poland, Romania, Russia, Slovakia, South Africa and the US, as well as the original 15 EU countries.

Due to the new freedom of movement agreement, nationals of the 15 EU countries as well as Norway, don't need to apply for a permit. If you're aged between 18 and 35 (18 to 30 for Australia, Hungary, New Zealand, Poland and Russia) and have completed your vocational training (minimum of two years), you may be eligible for a position as a trainee in Switzerland. The trainee agreement covers all occupations except those normally barred to foreigners, and employment must be in the occupation in which you were trained. Permits are granted for a maximum of 18 months.

Under the trainee agreement, the granting of a residence permit doesn't depend on quotas or the employment situation. After a training period in Switzerland, a non-EU trainee cannot be re-employed by the same or another employer in Switzerland for a period of two to twelve months. This is to prevent people using the trainee programme as a back door to securing a permanent job in Switzerland. Information about the trainee programme can be obtained from the Bundesamt für Migration (Abteilung Arbeitsmarkt, Sektion Auswanderung und Stagiaires, ☎ 031-325 11 11, 🖳 www.bfm.admin.ch).

AU PAIRS

If you're aged between 18 and 25 (you don't have to be female) you're eligible for a job as an au pair in Switzerland. The au pair system provides you with an excellent opportunity to travel, learn a language and generally broaden your education by living and working abroad. The main aim of the system is to give you the opportunity to learn a foreign language in a typical family environment. The au pair employment conditions state that you must attend language classes for a minimum number of hours a week (around four) and be given sufficient time off to study at home. Evidence of attendance at a language course is mandatory.

> Foreign au pairs are contracted to work for up to 24 months (12 months for non-EU foreigners) since 1st January 2008; an extension isn't possible. EU au pairs can be aged between 17 and 30, with most au pairs in Switzerland coming from within Europe, particularly Scandinavian countries.

British au pairs are popular, but you should make sure that a family isn't just looking for an unofficial English teacher. Young people from Australia, Canada, Europe, New Zealand and the US are permitted to work as au pairs in Switzerland.

You must be prepared to do most kinds of housework and various duties associated with children, including the preparation of their meals, washing and ironing their clothes, cleaning and baby-sitting. You aren't, however, a general servant or cook, although extra services are often taken for granted. You also shouldn't be expected to look after physically or mentally handicapped children. Working hours are officially limited to a maximum of 30 hours a week (five hours a day, six days a week) plus a few evenings' baby-sitting, and include at least one full day off each week.

Minimum pay is set by the cantons and varies between CHF 700 and CHF 900, e.g. in canton Zurich it's CHF 700-800, depending on your age and the number of children you're supervising (you may have fun as an au pair, but you're unlikely to get rich unless you marry a wealthy Swiss). Due to the government cutting au pair permit quotas in recent years, some cantons run out early in the year, while others have stopped issuing au pair permits completely.

All meals and accommodation are provided and you have your own room with a lockable door. Your employer pays for your residence permit (if applicable), health and accident insurance, and your language study costs (although he can deduct 10 per cent of your salary for school and insurance) and he may pay your journey to and from Switzerland, although this isn't usual. If you don't have the required insurance (see **Chapter 13**), he should deduct insurance contributions from your pay. Check that this is the case or you'll be working illegally. If you're aged under 20, you have five weeks paid holiday per year and four weeks when aged over 20. On days off, you're paid around CHF 20 in lieu of board. You should obtain a statement of your precise duties, time off and salary in writing before your arrival in Switzerland.

You can find a position as an au pair through agencies both in Switzerland and abroad. The major au pair agency in Switzerland is Pro Filia (🖳 www.profilia.ch > Au-pair-Stellen), which has a number of offices in Switzerland. There are specialist au pair agencies in most European countries and in North America, which can help you find a job as an au pair in Switzerland. It's also possible to advertise for an au pair position in a local newspaper and jobs are also often advertised in tourist offices.

The au pair system has been uncharitably referred to as a mine-field of guilt-ridden mothers, lecherous fathers and spoilt brats. Your experience as an au pair will depend on your family (and yourself). If you're fortunate enough to work for a warm and friendly host family, you'll have a wonderful experience, lots of free time, and possibly holidays in both Switzerland and abroad. Many au pairs grow to love their children and families and form lifelong friendships. On the other hand, abuses of the au pair system are common in all countries and you may be treated as a servant or slave rather than a member of the family, and be expected to work long hours and spend most evenings baby-sitting. Many families employ an au pair simply because it costs only a fraction of the salary of a nanny. If you have any questions or complaints about your duties, you should refer them to the agency which found you your position (if applicable).

There are many families to choose from and you should never remain with a family if you're unhappy with the way you're treated.

LANGUAGES

An important consideration for anyone seeking employment in Switzerland is the local language, which varies with the area. Switzerland has four official languages: German, spoken by around 70 per cent of the population, French

(20 per cent), Italian (7 per cent) and Romansch (Rhaeto-Roman), which is spoken by around 35,000 people (0.5 per cent of the population) in the canton of Graubünden. The remainder are foreigners whose mother-tongue isn't one of the Swiss national languages. Although all official languages are equal in principle, this is often not the case in practice, and the German language and German speakers dominate many areas of public life, to the displeasure of the French-speaking Swiss. The cultural and linguistic division between the German and French-speaking Swiss cantons is referred to as the *Röstigraben* (the 'fried potato cake' divide). Italian is usually relegated to a distant third place (except in Ticino).

Although English could be called the *lingua franca* of Switzerland, most official publications, forms, warning signs, etc., are printed in French, German and Italian, and seldom in English. English is a mandatory subject in most state schools from the age of 13 or later and is widely spoken by the middle-aged and youths, although less so by the elderly and in rural areas. Nevertheless, it's an important business and commercial language, even within Switzerland. Some 15 per cent of all Switzerland's workforce uses English at work, with the German-speaking Swiss more likely to use it than French or Italian speakers. Wherever you work, you'll be inundated with forms, documents, memos and other communications written in the local language. Don't ignore them as some will be important. The same applies to private mail – don't throw it away unless you're sure it's junk.

☑ SURVIVAL TIP

Probably nothing will affect your lifestyle (and possibly your career prospects) in Switzerland more than your ability to speak the local language(s). In an emergency, being able to make yourself understood in a foreign language could make the difference between life and death.

Berne, Fribourg and Valais are officially bi-lingual and have both French- and German-speaking areas. Graubünden is tri-lingual, where (some) people speak German, Italian and Romansch. Some Swiss towns are totally bi-lingual and languages are even alternated during conversation (the Swiss are very democratic). In parliament, members are free to speak their mother tongue, which may explain why governmental decisions take so long (it's said that the Swiss get on so well because they don't understand each other). The problem of which language to use on stamps and currency is solved by using the Latin name for Switzerland, *Helvetia*.

See also **Language** on page 105 and **Language Schools** on page 116.

German

The language spoken in German-speaking areas of Switzerland is Swiss German (*Schwyzertüütsch, suisse allemand*). It bears little resemblance to the High German (*Schriftdeutsch/Hochdeutsch, bon allemand*) of parts of Germany, which is a foreign language to the Swiss – although not half as foreign as Swiss German is to Germans, let alone the French- and Italian-speaking Swiss! There are over 100,000 recorded Swiss German words and although many have their origin in High German, the Swiss have successfully managed to make them unrecognisable to anyone but themselves. To the casual listener, Swiss German sounds like someone trying to speak while gargling and is often described as 'not so much a language as a throat disease'. There are many dialects of Swiss German and sometimes inhabitants of neighbouring villages, let alone cantons, have trouble understanding each other.

Most native High German speakers are initially just as confused as other foreigners. Most Swiss German speakers do, however, speak High German (fairly) fluently and, when talking to foreigners, many attempt to speak it or at least will do so when asked. Note, however, that the Swiss don't particularly like speaking High German.

Even if you don't understand what the locals are saying, the written language in Switzerland is High German, therefore if you understand High German you'll at least be able to read the newspapers. Strictly speaking, Swiss German isn't a written language and it's never used in official communications (the most common usage is in advertising). Most people write Swiss German using completely arbitrary phonetic spelling and the Swiss cannot even decide how to spell *Schwyzertüütsch* (Swiss German). Nevertheless, there are a few children's books in Swiss German dialects and some poets and authors use it. (It's all a fiendish plot to prevent foreigners from understanding what's going on.) All cantons except those listed under French and Italian below are Swiss German-speaking (some are bi-lingual with French or Italian).

French

French is spoken in the cantons of Geneva, Jura, Neuchâtel and Vaud, in addition to the bi-lingual cantons of Berne, Fribourg and Valais. In French-speaking Switzerland (*Westschweiz, suisse romande*) the language is almost the same as in France, with few Swiss idiosyncrasies added. The accent is clear and good French is spoken, the purest in Neuchâtel, although the same claim is often made for the French of Geneva and Lausanne.

If you work in a French-speaking region, it's usually necessary to speak French at work. Social life in French-speaking areas of Switzerland can also be difficult without at least basic French, although in cities such as Geneva and Lausanne, English is widely spoken.

Italian

Standard Italian is spoken in the canton of Ticino and parts of Graubünden (as well as 'High Italian' and some local dialects). It would be almost impossible to work in Ticino without speaking Italian. Socially the language isn't such a problem, as Ticino is a popular tourist area where people are used to dealing with foreigners. German is widely spoken in Ticino, mainly due to the influx of German and Swiss German tourists and retirees.

Greifensee, Zurich

2.
EMPLOYMENT CONDITIONS

E mployment conditions (*Arbeitreglement, règlement de travail*) in Switzerland are largely dependent on cantonal laws, an employee's contract, and an employer's general terms. In general, foreigners are employed under the same working conditions as Swiss citizens. This usually means that salaries, fringe benefits and working conditions are among the best in the world. Employees hired to work in Switzerland by foreign (non-Swiss) companies and organisations may be offered even better terms and conditions (including higher salaries) than those provided by Swiss employers.

In certain industries there are General Labour Agreements (GLAs), which is a written convention between one or more employers or employers' associations and trade unions. It contains provisions on relations between employers and employees as well as provisions which are directed at the contracting parties of the GLA, such as a minimum wage.

EMPLOYMENT CONTRACTS

Under Swiss law a contract exists as soon as you undertake a job for which you expect to be paid. For many Swiss, their word is their bond (in mountain areas, contracts are often oral and sealed by a handshake); however, even if you're employed only part-time, you should insist on a written contract. You and your employer are obliged to abide by the rules and regulations set out in the Swiss law of obligation (*Schweizerisches Obligationenrecht, Droit d'obligation suisse*), a copy of which can be purchased from most bookshops.

There are usually no hidden surprises or traps for the unwary in a Swiss employment contract (*Arbeitsvertrag, contrat de travail*). Nevertheless, as with any contract, you should know exactly what it contains before signing it. If you aren't fluent in the local language, you should get an English translation (your language ability would need to be excellent to understand the legal

jargon that goes into some contracts). Swiss employers seldom provide foreigners with contracts in English, irrespective of the number of English-speaking staff employed.

In some trades or fields (e.g. agriculture, domestic, and hotel and restaurant jobs) standard employment contracts are drafted by cantonal governments or a professional body, based on collective labour contracts or legislation (which cover around half the workforce). These are usually applicable unless both employer and employee agree otherwise in writing. Employment contract disputes can be easily and inexpensively resolved by a court – for information, contact the Federal Commission on Migration/FCM (☎ 031-325 91 16, 🖥 www.ekm.admin. ch). The FCM also publishes information (in

French, German and Italian – unfortunately not yet in English) on a wide range of subjects.

Your employment contract may contain the following:

♦ the date from which it takes effect and to who it applies;

♦ your job title;

♦ the name of your department and manager;

♦ your main duties;

♦ how your department relates to other departments;

♦ your place(s) of work;

♦ your salary details, including a 13th month's salary and any agreed increases;

♦ confidentiality clauses and restrictions on private work;

♦ information about membership of a compulsory health fund (if applicable);

♦ medical examination requirement (if applicable);

♦ a clause stating that the contract is subject to a residence permit or permission to change jobs being granted by the cantonal authorities;

♦ details of probationary and notice periods;

When you sign a contract, you're also confirming your agreement with your prospective employer's general employment terms. Before signing the contract you should therefore obtain a copy of these and ensure that you understand them.

SALARY & BENEFITS

Your salary (*Salär/Gehalt*, *salaire*) is stated in your contract, where salary reviews, planned increases

and cost of living rises may also be covered. Only general points, such as the payment of your salary into a bank account and the date of salary payments, are usually included in an employer's general terms. If the salary payment day varies each month, your employer may provide you with a list of payment dates. Salaries are usually paid earlier in December.

Salaries in Switzerland are generally reviewed once a year around November/December, with pay rises (if applicable – you don't always get one!) taking effect from 1st January of the following year. Annual increases include a percentage to cover a rise in the cost of living, although if there's a decrease in the cost of living (which has happened in Switzerland!), your salary may be **reduced**.

13th Month's Salary & Bonuses

Most employers in Switzerland pay their employees' annual salary in 13 instalments and not 12: in December you receive, in effect, two months' salary (which helps pay your end-of-year bills, Christmas and New Year expenses, etc.), although sometimes you receive half in July and half in December. Note, however, that a 13th month's salary isn't a bonus but is, in effect, a delay in payment. When a 13th month's salary (*13. Salär*, *13ème salaire*) is paid it's stated in your employment contract. Some companies don't pay a 13th month's salary but compensate by paying a higher monthly salary. When negotiating your salary with a prospective employer, you should ask whether a 13th month's salary is paid, i.e. whether you should divide your annual salary by 12 or 13. In your first and last year of employment, your 13th month's salary is paid pro rata if you don't work a full calendar year.

Some employers operate an additional annual voluntary bonus (*Gratifikation*, *gratification*) scheme, based on each employee's performance or the employer's profits. If you're employed on a contract basis for a fixed period, you may be paid an end-of-contract bonus.

If you pay direct income tax, then you'll pay a higher overall rate of tax if your 13th month's salary and bonus are paid in the same month.

Allowances

In addition to your salary, you may be paid various allowances, including the following.

Area Allowance

If you're a civil servant employed by the federal government or a canton or community, you may receive an area allowance or weighting (*Ortzuschlag*, *allocation locale*), depending on the region where you work. The allowance, which may total a few thousand francs a year, is paid in monthly instalments with your salary.

Child Allowance

In Switzerland, parents receive a monthly child (or family) allowance (*Kinderzulage, allocations familiales*), which depends on the number and age of children. Child allowance is paid by your employer and varies from canton to canton (some only pay it if your home country has a social security agreement with Switzerland). The majority of cantons pay a fixed allowance for each child, while some cantons pay an increased allowance for the third and subsequent children (to encourage the Swiss to have more children). The cantons with the smallest population or lowest birth rates usually pay the highest child allowances.

The allowance is usually paid up to a child's 16th birthday (15 in Fribourg and Geneva) or until the age of between 18 and 25 when he remains in full-time education or occupational training. Registration is made by your employer and the allowance is usually paid to the family's main breadwinner (you can choose) in his or her monthly salary payment.

You can check the monthly child allowance for the canton where you work at ⌨ www.kinderzulage.ch (click on your canton's shield).

Around ten cantons also pay a birth allowance.

Expenses

Expenses (*Spesen, frais*) paid by your employer are usually listed in his general terms. These may include travel costs from your home to your place of work, usually consisting of a second-class rail season ticket or the equivalent cost, paid monthly with your salary. Companies without a staff restaurant or canteen may pay a lunch allowance or provide luncheon vouchers. Expenses paid for travel on company business or for approved training and education may be detailed in a separate document.

Travel & Relocation Expenses

Travel (*Reisespesen, frais de voyage*) and relocation expenses to Switzerland depend on your agreement with your employer and are usually included in your employment contract or the employer's general terms. If you're hired from outside Switzerland, your air ticket (or other travel costs) are usually booked and paid for by your employer or his agent abroad. In addition, you can usually claim any extra travel costs, for example the cost of transport to and from airports. If you travel by car to Switzerland, you can usually claim a mileage rate or the equivalent air fare cost.

Most Swiss employers pay your relocation expenses up to a specified limit, although you may be required to sign a contract which stipulates that if you leave the employer before a certain period elapses (e.g. five years), you must repay a percentage of your removal costs, depending on your length of service.

An employer may pay a fixed relocation allowance based on your salary, position and size of family, or may pay the total cost of removal. The allowance should be sufficient to move the contents of an average house (castles aren't usually catered for) and you must normally pay any excess costs yourself. If you don't want to bring your furniture to Switzerland or have only a few belongings to ship, it may be possible to purchase furniture locally up to the limit of your allowance. Check with your employer. A company may ask you to obtain two or three removal estimates when it's liable for the total cost.

Generally you're required to organise and pay for the removal yourself. Your employer usually reimburses the equivalent amount in Swiss francs after you've paid the bill, although it may be possible to get him to pay the bill directly or provide a cash advance.

> ### ☑ SURVIVAL TIP
>
> If you change jobs within Switzerland, your new employer may pay your relocation expenses when it's necessary for you to move house. Don't forget to ask, as he may not offer to pay (it may depend on how keen he is to employ you).

WORKING HOURS

Working hours (*Arbeitsstunden, heures de travail*) in Switzerland vary with the employer, your position and the industry in which you're employed, the average being around 41 hours per week. Under Swiss employment law, normal working hours should be a maximum of 45 hours per week. Employees in industry work around 40 hours per week, while workers in the service sector, such as banking, generally work slightly longer hours (around 42 per week). Employees in hospitals, catering and hotels, however, may work up to 60 hours per week, although the average is between 45 and 48. Whatever your working hours in Switzerland, they may be longer than you're used to working. Of the leading industrial nations, only the Japanese and Americans work longer hours than the Swiss.

The Swiss have voted against shorter working hours on a number of occasions. In 2002, an initiative to reduce the normal working week to 36 hours was rejected by almost 75 per cent of voters. Many Swiss believe their long working hours are partly responsible for their economic success, but most analysts reckon that, although the Swiss work longer hours than most other Europeans, they don't actually do more work! Some people (especially wives and mothers) can choose to work reduced hours, e.g. four days a week (usually Friday is the free day).

If a company closes between Christmas and New Year or on other unofficial holidays, employees must usually compensate by working around one hour extra each week. If applicable, this will be stated in your terms of employment. Your working hours cannot be increased above the hours stated in your contract or terms without compensation or overtime being paid.

It may come as an unpleasant surprise to some foreigners to discover that many Swiss employers (including most large companies) require all employees to clock in and out of work. Anyone caught cheating is liable to instant dismissal./

Flexi-time

Most Swiss companies operate a flexi-time (*Gleitzeit*, *horaire flexible*) system, which requires all employees to be present between certain hours, known as the core or block time (*Blockzeit*,

temps bloqué/heures de présence obligatoire). For example, from 8.30 to 11.30am and from 1.30 to 4pm. Block time can start as early as 7.30 or 8am, which isn't early by Swiss standards. Employees may make up their required working hours by starting earlier than the start of block time, reducing their lunch break (a minimum 30-minute lunch break is a legal requirement) or working later. Smaller companies may allow employees to work as late as they wish, provided they don't exceed the maximum permitted daily working hours stipulated by cantonal or federal governments.

Working hours for employees who work a flexi-time system are usually calculated on a monthly basis, during which time they may run up a credit or deficit, e.g. 15 or 25 hours. Hours can be compensated or increased in the following month(s) by working fewer or extra hours. Employees who work a flexi-time system may usually take a day or a half-day off work each month without the need to request 'permission', provided the hours are made up either beforehand or afterwards.

Note that some companies automatically cancel hours worked in excess of 15 or 25 hours if an employee doesn't take time off in lieu of hours worked (*Kompensation*, *compensation*) within a certain time limit – they never, however, forget about the hours you owe the company!

Because flexi-time rules can be quite complicated (it sometimes takes months to understand them), they may be contained in a separate set of regulations.

Overtime

Overtime (*Überstunden*, *heures supplémentaires*) payments may be made for extra hours worked, depending on company policy and your employment conditions. Most companies pay overtime only for work that's urgent and officially approved. Overtime is generally paid at the normal rate plus 25 per cent on weekdays and Saturdays, and plus 50 per cent on Sundays and public holidays. Companies must generally obtain permission from the cantonal authorities for employees to work on Sundays and official holidays (see **Sunday Working** below).

Sunday Working

In Switzerland there's a law against working on Sundays and official holidays unless absolutely necessary (some people would like it extended to the other six days of the week!). When necessary, an official form must be completed by your employer and approved by the cantonal authorities. The general Sunday working law even prohibits the glorious Sunday pastimes of car washing and gardening – if you're fortunate enough to have a garden, you may sit, but not work in it on a Sunday. Washing your clothes on a Sunday is also forbidden, at least in a communal washing machine, as is hanging out clothes to dry.

Sunday is a day of peace when the Swiss won't tolerate noise, e.g. electric drills, hammering or loud music (somebody ought to inform the church bell-ringers and shooting ranges). Sunday working laws may be less strict or less strictly observed in country areas, where farmers are permitted to work (for example during harvest) on Sundays.

Fines can be imposed for ignoring the Sunday working law, although as a foreigner you may just be given a warning (usually by your upstanding Swiss neighbours).

HOLIDAYS & LEAVE

Annual Holidays

Your annual holiday (*Ferien, congé/vacances*) entitlement depends on your profession, position and employer. Most Swiss companies allow four weeks annual holiday up to the age of 50, five weeks when over 50 and six weeks when aged over 60. Top managerial positions may offer additional annual holidays (but no time to take them!). The average number of paid holidays a year is around 23 days.

Before starting a job, check that your new employer will approve any planned holidays. This is particularly important if they fall within your probationary period (usually three months), when holidays aren't usually permitted.

Public Holidays

Public holidays (*Feiertage, jours fériés*) vary from canton to canton, depending on whether the predominant local religion is Catholic or Protestant. The following dates or days are public holidays in most Swiss cantons; those marked with an asterisk are Swiss national holidays.

There are also half-day public holidays in some cantons, e.g. Zurich, and Catholic cantons have more religious holidays.

If a public holiday falls on a weekend, there's no substitute weekday holiday unless the number of public holidays in a particular year falls below a minimum number. When a holiday falls on a Thursday or a Tuesday, many employees take the Friday or Monday (respectively) off to make a long weekend, although the extra day must come out of their annual holiday entitlement or time worked in lieu.

Many Swiss companies close down during Christmas and New Year, e.g. from midday or 4pm on 24th December until the 2nd or 3rd January. To compensate for this shutdown (and perhaps other company holidays), employees are required to work around one hour per week extra throughout the year.

Pregnancy & Confinement

Time off for sickness in connection with a pregnancy (*Schwangerschaft, grossesse*) is usually given without question but may not be paid without a doctor's letter.

Public Holidays	
Date	**Holiday**
*1st January	New Year's Day (*Neujahr, Jour de l'An*)
2nd January	St. Berchtold's Day (*Berchtoldstag, le 2 janvier*)
*March or April	Good Friday (*Karfreitag, Vendredi Saint*)
	Easter Monday (*Ostermontag, Lundi de Pâques*)
1st May	May Day (*Tag der Arbeit, Fête du Travail*)
May	Ascension Day (*Auffahrt, Ascension*) – Thursday 40 days after Easter
*June	Whitsuntide (*Pfingsten, Pfingstmontag, Pentecôte*) – Sunday and Monday, ten days after Ascension
*1st August	Swiss National Day (*Bundesfeiertag, Fête nationale*)
*25th December	Christmas Day (*Weihnachtstag, Noël*)
*26th December	Boxing Day (*Stefanstag, le 26 décembre*)

* those marked with an asterisk are Swiss national holidays.

Some companies pay a monthly allowance to pregnant women (pregnant men receive the Nobel Prize for medicine!). Around ten cantons pay a birth allowance of from CHF 600 to 1,500. In 2005, the Swiss introduced state maternity insurance which pays working mothers 80 per cent of their average salary for 14 weeks after giving birth. To qualify, women must have been insured for 9 months before the birth and gainfully employed for at least five months during this time. Benefits are paid by the Erwerbsersatzordnung (*Ausgleichskasse, Caisse de compensation*) – the fund that pays the salary of Swiss men when doing military service. The maximum amount paid is CHF 245 per day.

Pregnant and nursing mothers cannot be required to work overtime and cannot be given notice during their pregnancy or the 16 weeks after a birth unless this falls during the probation period, in which case she can be made redundant. You cannot (by law) return to work during the eight weeks after delivery and you can choose to stay at home for another eight weeks.

Sick Leave

You're usually required to notify your employer as soon as possible of sickness or an accident that prevents you from working. If you're away from work for longer than two or three days, you may be required to produce a doctor's certificate. The period is stated in your general terms of employment. Your salary insurance policy will determine how much money you receive while unable to work (see **Salary Insurance** on page 179).

Compassionate Leave

Most Swiss companies provide additional days off for moving house, your own or a family marriage, the birth of a child, the death of a family member or close relative, and other important events. Grounds for compassionate leave (*Sonderurlaub, congé spécial*) should be listed in your general employment terms.

INSURANCE

Accident Insurance

Accident insurance (*Unfallversicherung, assurance accidents*) is mandatory for all employees in Switzerland. Occupational accident insurance is paid by your employer and covers accidents or illness at work, and accidents that occur when travelling to and from work or when travelling on company business.

Private accident insurance contributions vary according to your employer from nothing (in a non-contributory scheme) to around 1.5 per cent of your gross monthly salary. For information, see page 184.

Federal Social Security

Swiss federal social security provides old age and survivors' insurance/OASI (*Eidgenössische Alters- und Hinterlassenenversicherung/AHV, assurance-vieillesse et survivants/AVS*) and disability insurance/DI (*Invalidenversicherung/IV, assurance d'invalidité/AI*), and contributions are obligatory for most employees in Switzerland. A flat rate of 5.05 per cent of your gross salary is deducted at source by your employer. For details see page 174.

Salary Insurance

Many companies provide salary insurance (*Salärausfallversicherung/Salärlosenversicherung, assurance perte de gain*) to cover periods of sickness or injury. The cost to employees varies from nothing to around 1 per cent of your gross monthly salary. For further information, see page 177.

Unemployment Insurance

Unemployment insurance (*Arbeitslosenversicherung, assurance chômage*) is compulsory for all employees of Swiss companies. You pay 1 per cent of your gross monthly salary, which is deducted by your employer. Payment may be included with your OASI/DI payments on your pay slip (total 6.05 per cent). For details see page 179.

Miscellaneous Insurance

Other insurance provided by your employer is listed in his general terms. It may include free life and health insurance when travelling outside Switzerland on company business. Some companies have compulsory health insurance schemes.

RETIREMENT & PENSIONS

Your employment conditions may be valid only until the official Swiss retirement age (*Ruhestand*, *retraite*), which is 64 for women and 65 for men. If you wish to continue working after you've reached retirement age, you may be required to negotiate a new employment contract (you should also seek psychiatric help).

Company Pension Fund

Membership of a company pension fund (*Berufliche Vorsorge/BVG*, *prévoyance professionelle/LPP*) is compulsory for all employees over the age of 17 earning over CHF 24,360 a year. The amount you pay varies from around 7 to 18 per cent of your gross monthly salary, depending on your age and your employer's pension fund. See page 177 for further information.

OTHER CONDITIONS

Education & Training

Education and training (*Schulung und Ausbildung*, *enseignement et formation*) provided by your employer should be stated in his general terms. This may include training abroad, provided it's essential to your job (although you may need to convince your employer). In addition to relevant education and training, employers must provide the essential tools and equipment for a job, which is, however, open to interpretation.

If you need to learn a language or improve your language knowledge to perform your job, the cost of language study is usually paid by your employer. If it isn't essential, some employers will pay only a part of the cost or nothing at all (one of the penalties of being an English speaker).

Employees who aren't of English mother-tongue may be paid to learn or improve their English when necessary for their job. An allowance may be paid for personal education or hobbies such as flower arranging, kite flying or break dancing, which aren't work related or of any direct benefit to your employer.

Acceptance of Gifts

Employees are normally forbidden to accept gifts (*Geschenkannahme*, *accepter des dons*) of more than a certain value (e.g. CHF 50) from customers or suppliers. Many suppliers give bottles of wine or small gifts at Christmas that don't breach this rule. (If you accept a bribe, make sure it's a big one and that your bank account is covered by Swiss secrecy laws.)

Changing Jobs & Confidentiality

Companies in a high-tech or highly confidential business may have 'competition restrictions' (*Konkurrenzklausel/Konkurrenzverbot*, *clause de non-concurrence*) regarding employees working for a competitor in Switzerland or elsewhere. You should be aware of these restrictions as they're enforceable by Swiss law, although it's a complicated subject and disputes must often be resolved by a court of law.

Caution

Swiss laws regarding industrial secrets and employer confidentiality are very strict. If you breach this confidentiality it may not simply be a matter of dismissal and perhaps subsequently having to leave Switzerland. You may also find yourself subject to criminal proceedings, resulting in a fine or even imprisonment. Keep our secrets secret is the byword of all Swiss companies – not just the banks.

If you wish to change jobs, you may be affected by permit restrictions. Note also that the Swiss don't generally change jobs often and some employers may think that you're unreliable if you change jobs more than 'a few times' during your lifetime (although this has changed in recent years, during which redundancies have become commonplace).

Other matters to take into account when changing jobs are:

♦ If you're a member of a company health fund (*Krankenkasse*, *caisse de maladie*), you may wish to transfer your family's health insurance to another health fund or health insurance company, as you'll no longer benefit from the (usually substantial) company discount.

♦ If you're moving to another Swiss company, your accrued company pension fund benefits will be transferred to a private pension fund account in your name. If you're leaving Switzerland the accrued benefits will be paid to you in full.

If changing jobs entails moving house within Switzerland, see **Chapter 20.**

Dismissal

Dismissal is usually legal only in exceptional circumstances, depending on your contract, although an employer can make you redundant for any number of reasons. For example, refusing to work, cheating or stealing from your employer, competing with your employer, insulting your employer or colleagues, assaulting your employer or a colleague, and drunkenness during working hours on your employer's premises (office parties excepted). Under normal circumstances, you cannot be fired in the first four weeks of an illness, during pregnancy or the 16 weeks after giving birth, or during compulsory military service.

Military Service

Salary payment during Swiss military service (*Militärdienst, service militaire*) and time off for military and civil defence duties are included in your employment terms. These are of no interest to foreigners, as they aren't liable for Swiss military service unless they become Swiss citizens or have dual nationality, haven't already served in a foreign army and are young enough to be eligible (see **Military Service** on page 261).

Part-time Job Restrictions

Restrictions on part-time employment (*Nebenarbeit, travail accessoire*) are usually detailed in your employment conditions. Most Swiss companies don't allow full-time employees to work part-time (i.e. moonlight) for another employer, particularly one in the same line of business. You may, however, be permitted to take a part-time teaching job or similar part-time employment (or you can write a book!).

Probationary & Notice Periods

For most jobs there's a probationary period (*Probezeit, période d'essai*), ranging from two weeks for seasonal workers to three months or longer for permanent employees. Seasonal workers or their employer can usually terminate their contract with a notice period (*Kündigungsfrist, délai de résiliation*) of three days during the probationary period. For permanent employees, notice can be given at the end of any week, with a notice period of one or two weeks. After the probationary period, an employment contract may be terminated by either party at the end of any month, when the contract notice period applies.

Your contract notice period depends on your employer, profession and length of service and is usually noted in your employment contract and general terms. If it isn't stated, the notice period is usually one month during the first year, two months during the second to ninth years, and three months from the tenth year of service. The notice period for many professions is three months and may be longer for executive or key employees, e.g. six months. Your notice period may be extended after a number of years' service.

If an employer goes bankrupt and cannot pay you, you can terminate your employment without notice. Other valid reasons for an employee not giving notice are assault or abuse of you or a colleague by your employer, and failure to pay (or persistent delay in paying) your salary.

Trade Unions

Switzerland has an excellent record of industrial peace and strikes are virtually unheard of. Although strike action isn't illegal, the Federal Council prohibits industrial action that affects the security of the state, external relations or the supply of vital goods to the country, which helps to explain the reliability of Swiss public transport.

There isn't a strong trade union movement in Switzerland, but some 40 per cent of private-sector employees work under collective agreements negotiated between employers and trade unions.

Travail Suisse (Hopfenweg 21, PO Box 5775, CH-3001 Berne, ☎ 031 370 21 11, 💻 www. travailsuisse.ch) is the umbrella organisation for several Swiss workers' unions.

3.
PERMITS & VISAS

Before making any plans to live or work in Switzerland, you must ensure that you have a valid passport (with a visa if necessary) and the appropriate documentation to obtain a residence permit.

The laws regarding work and residence permits for European Union and European Free Trade Association nationals (Iceland, Liechtenstein and Norway), which together comprise the European Economic Area (EEA), changed in 2002 when a bilateral treaty between Switzerland and the EU/EEA came into effect. There are now two distinct categories of foreigners living and working in Switzerland: EU/EFTA citizens, who in many ways have similar rights to Swiss citizens, and non-EU (called 'third-state') citizens, for whom it has become much more difficult to obtain work and/or residence permits.

The acronym EU is used to refer to both EU and EFTA nationals in this chapter, unless otherwise noted.

Foreigners entitled to live or work (or both) in Switzerland are issued with a residence permit (*Aufenthaltsbewilligung, autorisation de séjour*) called a 'foreigners' permit' (*Ausländerausweis, livret pour étrangers*). Although it isn't mandatory, it's advisable to carry your Swiss residence permit, passport or other official form of identification with you at all times within Switzerland.

Older children without residence permits should carry passports or identity cards to verify their age, for example to purchase reduced price public transport tickets and cinema tickets for age-restricted performances. Secondary school children are usually issued with a school identity or student card (*Schülerausweis/Studentenausweis, carte d'identité scolaire/carte d'étudiant*).

Foreigners working for international organisations in Switzerland (such as the United Nations) are issued with an identity card (*Identitätskarte, carte de légitimation*) and not a residence permit, and aren't subject to quotas or the same regulations as those employed by Swiss employers.

> **⚠ Caution**
>
> Any infringements concerning residence permits or registration of foreigners are taken very seriously by the Swiss authorities. There are penalties for breaches of regulations, including fines and even deportation for flagrant abuses.

Immigration is the responsibility of the Federal Office of Migration (☏ 031-325 11 11, 🖵 www.bfm. admin.ch), established on 1st January 2005, which publishes a number of documents (in English and other languages) for prospective immigrants.

VISAS

Some foreigners require a visa to enter Switzerland, whether as a visitor or for any other purpose. This includes most, so-called, third-state nationals – a term used by the Swiss authorities to refer to anyone who isn't a citizen of an EU or EFTA member country. **It doesn't mean nationals of third-world countries.** If in doubt, check with a Swiss embassy or consulate.

Visitors

If you aren't a national of a Schengen member country or a country on the Schengen visa-free list (see 🖵 http://switzerland.visahq.com/requirements), you'll need a Schengen visa (🖵 www.theschengenoffice.com/explained/schengen_visa.html), costing around €60, to visit Switzerland. This also allows you to travel freely within all Schengen countries for up to 90 days in a six-month period or 180 days a year.

Schengen visa holders aren't permitted to live permanently or work in Switzerland (or any Schengen member country), although business trips aren't considered to be employment. Foreigners who intend to take up employment or a self-employed activity in Switzerland (or any Schengen country) may require an employment visa (see below), even if they're listed on the Schengen visa-free list.

To extend a stay beyond three months without leaving Switzerland, you must apply to the local canton's 'alien's police' and be registered by your landlord with the local community if your stay exceeds three months. If you wish to establish temporary residence for longer than six months a year, you must apply at a Swiss embassy or consulate before coming to Switzerland.

Third-state (non-EU) nationals aren't permitted to visit Switzerland as tourists and seek employment, because applications for work permits are only considered when a non-EU national is outside Switzerland. However, you can visit Switzerland to meet prospective employers or attend interviews.

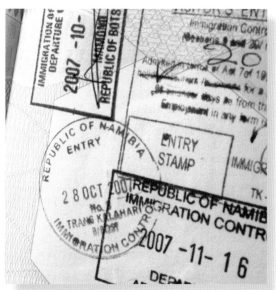

Employment Visas

If you need a visa for employment (*Einreisevisum zum Stellenantritt, visa d'entrée pour prise d'emploi*) in Switzerland, the procedure is as follows:

1. An offer of employment is sent to you by your prospective Swiss employer, stating your anticipated start date.

2. You take this with your passport to the Swiss embassy or consulate in your country of residence, where you'll be asked to complete a number of forms and provide passport photographs, which are sent to Switzerland for processing. Contact your nearest Swiss embassy or consulate, who will tell you what's required.

3. On receipt of your acceptance of the job offer, your prospective Swiss employer will apply to the cantonal alien's police for a residence permit.

4. When the application is approved, authorisation to issue the visa is sent to the nearest Swiss embassy or consulate in your country of residence. They will contact you and ask you to visit them with your passport, in which a visa is stamped permitting you to enter Switzerland to take up employment.

WORK PERMITS

EU Citizens

On 1st June 2002, a new permit system was introduced for most EU citizens under a bilateral agreement between Switzerland and the EU. This agreement applies to EU nationals from: Austria, Belgium, Cyprus, Denmark, Finland, France, Germany, Greece, Iceland (EEA), Ireland, Italy, Liechtenstein (EEA), Luxembourg, Malta, the Netherlands, Norway (EEA), Portugal, Spain, Sweden and the UK. Transitional measures apply to some member states, for example there are quotas for Bulgarian and Romanian nationals until 31st May 2016.

The agreement will eventually culminate in all EU citizens having complete freedom of movement within Switzerland and Swiss citizens within EU countries – scheduled to take effect from 1st June 2014, with the exception of Bulgaria and Romania (from 1st June 2019). Under the agreement, Swiss employers are no longer required to prove that they cannot find a Swiss person to do a job before employing an EU citizen, and employers aren't required to disclose salaries to the authorities.

In 2007, quotas for most EU work permits were suspended, although the Swiss authorities reserved the right to reintroduce quotas if the flow of workers from certain EU countries was overwhelming. This they did from 1st May 2012 when they introduced quotas (2,000 per year) and B permits for nationals of EU-8 member states: Estonia, Latvia, Lithuania, Poland, Slovakia,

Slovenia, the Czech Republic and Hungary. This measure (initially for one year) applies to those who come to Switzerland to become self-employed or who possess an employment contract valid for a year or more.

Companies registered in an EU country can send their employees to work in Switzerland for a maximum of 90 days per calendar year without obtaining a work permit. They must, however, register employees with the Federal Office for Migration (🖥 www.bfm.admin.ch) and provide the same conditions with regard to working time, salary and holidays as are mandatory for all employees in Switzerland.

For stays of up to 12 months and extendable for an additional six months, an L-EC/EFTA permit is issued, which can be transferred between employers and can be renewed if the employment continues or a new job is found after that time. L-EC permit holders can bring their families to Switzerland.

EU citizens with an employment contract for an unlimited term receive a B-EC/EFTA permit that's valid for five years, which allows employees to change jobs or cantons without any restrictions. If a B-EC/EFTA permit holder loses his job he can stay in Switzerland for the duration of the permit, provided he has sufficient funds to live and doesn't become dependent on social security. He can also claim unemployment benefits under the same conditions as a Swiss citizen, look for a new job or become self-employed. After five years a B-EC/EFTA permit is automatically converted to a C permit (*Niederlassungsbewilligung/permis d'établissement* – see **Settlement (C) Permits** below.

EU citizens wishing to work but not to be resident in Switzerland can obtain a G-EC cross-border permit.

EU citizens are allowed to bring their family members to Switzerland, including children or grandchildren aged under 21 who are financially dependent on the petitioner, as well as financially dependent parents and grandparents.

Non-EU Citizens

Non-EU citizens (and EU citizens who don't qualify under the new rules – see above) – officially termed 'third-state' nationals – must obtain a visa to work in Switzerland. Since the introduction of the Swiss-EU agreement it has become much more difficult for third-state nationals to obtain work permits and in general these are only available to highly qualified people with a higher education qualification and several years of work experience.

Before applying for an annual permit for a non-EU national, a Swiss employer must 'ensure that no resident Swiss or EU resident can do the equivalent job as that of the migrant they wish to bring into the country' and have previously advertised the job vacancy in Switzerland.

There are strict annual permit quotas in each canton, plus a federal government quota that can be used in exceptional circumstances. Each canton's quota is based on economic factors and manpower requirements in the canton. In deciding whether to grant a permit, the authorities consider the provision of essential services and supplies, economic necessity due to lack of personnel, and the promotion of commercial development. The authorities can usually exercise their discretion within the bounds of the law.

Each year the Federal Council fixes quotas for the number of non-EU nationals who may work in Switzerland. There are separate quotas in all cantons and your success in applying for a work permit varies according to the canton and often depends on the number of unemployed persons in a particular canton.

If an application for a permit is rejected, the reason is given to the prospective employer in writing, who will inform you of any right of appeal, the relevant appeal authority and any time restrictions that apply.

It can take up to three months for a non-EU national to obtain a residence permit to live or work in Switzerland – from the initial job application, interview and written job offer, until receipt of your permit approval. You must enter Switzerland within three months of the date of issue of your residence permit approval; if you're unable to take up employment within this period, you should inform your prospective employer so that he can apply for an extension.

Third-state nationals who are resident in Switzerland (or in any other Schengen country – see page 51) can travel freely to all Schengen member countries without a visa, simply by showing their Swiss residence permit (B, C or L) or Schengen ID card (issued to third-state nationals resident in Switzerland) and a valid travel document e.g. a passport.

In 2012, the quota for third-state nationals was 8,500 – 5,000 short-stay L permits and 3,500 annual B permits.

Employees of International Organisations

Foreigners employed in Switzerland by international organisations, such as the United Nations in Geneva, have a special status. They don't require a normal residence permit, but are issued with an identity card (*Identitätskarte, carte de légitimation*) obtained by their employer. Customs, immigration and housing regulations for employees of international organisations differ considerably from those of 'normal' permit holders (if the UN had to put up with the usual Swiss red tape, they would have gone elsewhere!).

There are some 30,000 international employees and their families registered in Switzerland.

RESIDENCE PERMITS

Swiss residence permits fall into a number of categories, as shown below.

Limited Validity (L) Permits

An 'L' permit (*Aufenthaltsbewilligung L, permis de séjour L*), issued in a purple cover, is for a limited period (*begrenzte Gültigkeit/limitierte Gültigkeit, durée limitée*), usually up to 12 months but can be extended for another 12 months. It's generally granted to students, trainees, au pairs and specialists employed by foreign companies working as 'consultants' with Swiss (or Swiss-based) companies. It's closely linked to the job for which it has been granted and, should this be terminated early, is revoked, whereupon the employee must leave Switzerland.

The validity of the permit is identical to the job contract, but may be renewed for less than 12 months provided the new quota hasn't been exhausted.

There are around 60,000 L permit holders (both EU and non-EU).

Annual (B) Permits

A 'B' permit (*Aufenthaltsbewilligung B, permis de séjour B/permis B*) is usually valid for one year and is renewable. It's generally issued only to qualified and experienced people in professions where there's a shortage of skilled labour, and to spouses of Swiss citizens. However, there are also B permits for those who establish companies in Switzerland and so called 'fiscal deal' permits for those wishing to live but not work in Switzerland. The latter require a minimum (high) net wealth and must spend at least 180 days a year in the country (see **Lump-sum Taxation** on page 203).

B permits (in a grey cover) are normally renewed annually on application, although this isn't an automatic entitlement. If you aren't an EU citizen, an application for the renewal of a B permit must be made by your employer, although it's your responsibility to ensure that your permit

is renewed. EU citizens can obtain the relevant renewal forms from their local authority. There are fees for the renewal of annual permits, usually paid by the permit holder.

Each canton has an annual quota for new B permits, i.e. excluding renewals of existing B permits. Non-EU holders of B permits may be restricted in their ability to change employers or professions in their first few years in Switzerland (see **Changing Jobs** on page 49).

There are some 500,000 B permit holders in Switzerland.

Settlement (C) Permits

A 'C' permit (*Niederlassungsbewilligung, permis d'etablissement/permis C*) entitles you to permanent residence and, although it may be reviewed from time to time, it can be renewed indefinitely provided the holder resides in Switzerland. C permits are issued (in a green cover) automatically to B permit holders after five or ten consecutive years as a resident in Switzerland. EU citizens (with the exception of those from Bulgaria, the Czech Republic, Estonia, Hungary, Latvia, Lithuania, Poland, Romania, Slovakia and Slovenia) and Canadian and US nationals qualify for a C permit after five years.

The qualification period for citizens of all other countries is ten years, although a C permit can be granted after five years if a foreigner is well integrated in Switzerland – the 'test' for this usually being that he masters the relevant language. The ten-year qualification period is also reduced to five years for a non-EU national married to a Swiss national.

C permits are also issued to stateless people and official refugees after five years, and to the families of C permit holders. Holders of C permits don't require permission to change jobs, change their cantons of residence or work, or become self-employed.

There are around 1.1m C permit holders in Switzerland.

Border Crossing (G) Permits

A 'G' permit (*Grenzgängerbewilligung, permis frontalier*) gives a person living in a neighbouring country the right to work in Switzerland (many people choose to live in a neighbouring country, where the cost of living is significantly lower, and commute to their jobs in Switzerland). The G Permit is issued for a period of five years, provided your employment contract is for a minimum of one year, otherwise it's valid for the duration of the job. (For EU nationals it's now called a G-EC permit.)

Unlike L, B and C permits, a G permit doesn't include residential rights in Switzerland. However, G permit holders are no longer required to return home daily but can do so weekly, which means that it's possible to work and stay in Switzerland from Monday to Friday and only return home at the weekends. If you live in Switzerland during the week, you must register with the local municipality where you live.

A G permit is renewed annually and cannot be converted into a B permit. There's no quota for G permits but positions must be advertised in Switzerland and companies must still satisfy the authorities that no equally qualified unemployed Swiss resident is available to fill a vacancy (before being permitted to hire a non-EU national).

The total number of G permit holders is around 225,000, most (99 per cent) held by EU nationals.

DEPENDANTS

The following entitlements and restrictions apply to the holders of residence permits:

◆ **L permit holders** – The families of L permit holders (including students and trainees) can be granted residence permits, although they

don't have an automatic entitlement. If a permit isn't granted, visits are limited to six months per year and shouldn't exceed three months at one time, with a month between visits. The 'visit only' rule isn't, however, always strictly enforced.

◆ **B permit holders** – Recent legislation has improved the situation for the families of 'B' permit holders: within five years of a permit holder starting work in Switzerland, the spouse and children up to 18 years of age can also move to Switzerland and the spouse and children aged 14 or older are automatically entitled to work permits. This also applies to spouses of international civil servants and members of diplomatic missions.

◆ **C permit holders** – There are no restrictions on the residence or employment of the families of a C permit holder.

◆ **Common-law & same-sex partners** – If you have a common-law partner or partner of the same sex, it may be possible for him or her to accompany you if you can prove that you've been living together for at least five years and you'll be living at the same address in Switzerland. It's usually easier if you have children and/or can provide good reasons for not getting married.

◆ **Dependants of Swiss nationals** – The foreign spouse of a Swiss citizen must have lived in Switzerland for five years and been married for three years before he or she can apply for Swiss citizenship, or have been married for six years and show 'a close relationship with Switzerland'.

Non-Swiss children with one Swiss parent must follow the normal immigration procedures for foreigners. They aren't, however, subject to quota restrictions, and there are no limitations on their freedom to live and work in Switzerland.

Note that Switzerland doesn't automatically recognise unmarried partners as family members for the purpose of residence permits.

PART-TIME WORKERS

Permits are required for all part-time occupations, with the exception of voluntary work, which comes under special regulations. This applies to all members of a foreigner's family living in Switzerland. A permit is required even for a part-time job for a few weeks, for example temporary work in the farming industry.

STUDENTS

Foreign students in Switzerland require a B permit (see above). Students first need to find accommodation and obtain a certificate from the educational establishment stating that they are full-time students. They then take the proof of accommodation and the certificate to the community office of the local town or area and apply for a residence permit in the normal way (see **Registration** on page 53).

Foreign students must prove that they can support themselves financially and show proof of adequate accident and health insurance – the authorities may also check that they're attending classes. With a student B permit, you're permitted to work a maximum of 15 hours a week. There are special regulations for students or trainees studying with international organisations. A period spent in Switzerland as a student doesn't count towards obtaining a C permit.

NON-EMPLOYED FOREIGN RESIDENTS

Foreigners wishing to live but not work in Switzerland (euphemistically called 'leisured foreigners' by the authorities) must apply for a residence permit from a Swiss embassy or consulate before arriving in Switzerland. Permits are normally issued only to those aged over 55 (i.e. pensioners) or those of independent means, particularly the very rich and famous. You're required to provide proof that you have private health insurance and sufficient assets or income to live in Switzerland, usually in the form of a statement from your bank.

Other information required may be a CV/ resumé, a statement of why you want to live in Switzerland, and the name of someone in Switzerland who will guarantee to look after you in an emergency. If you're a pensioner, you must have retired from all gainful employment. Regulations vary from canton to canton; contact the local cantonal authorities for local residence requirements.

PERMIT RENEWAL & CANCELLATION

If you're moving to a new community or leaving Switzerland permanently, you must complete a 'de-registration' (*Abmeldeung, déclaration de départ*) in your present community up to eight days before your departure, and (if applicable) register in your new community within eight days of taking up residence (if applicable).

B Permits

B permits are cancelled when any of the following occurs:

♦ the permit expires and isn't renewed;

♦ the permit holder leaves Switzerland;

♦ the permit holder has lived outside Switzerland for an uninterrupted period of six months without applying for leave of absence (see below);

♦ it can be assumed that the permit holder has left Switzerland, for example he has given notice of termination of employment or taken up employment abroad, even if he hasn't notified the Swiss authorities.

> ☑ **SURVIVAL TIP**
>
> If you're a B permit holder and live and work in different cantons, your residence permit won't be renewed by your canton of residence until your permission to work has been approved by the canton where you're employed.

C Permits

C permits are cancelled when any of the following occurs:

♦ the permit holder notifies the local authority of his permanent departure;

♦ the permit holder has lived outside Switzerland for an uninterrupted period of six months, without applying for leave of absence (see below).

Under certain circumstances, the B or C permit of the spouse of a permit holder can be cancelled when he or she is widowed or divorced.

LEAVE OF ABSENCE

If you plan to be absent from Switzerland for longer than six months and want to be sure of retaining your permit on your return, you can obtain an 'assurance of residence permit' (*Zusicherung der Aufenthaltsbewilligung/ assurance de l'autorisation de séjour*) if you're a B permit holder, or an 'authorisation of absence' (*Aufrechterhaltung der Niederlassungsbewilligung/ maintien de l'autorisation d'établissement*) if you're a C permit holder. The 'assurance of residence permit' for a B permit holder must be requested by your employer. It's granted for an absence of up to four years, provided your employer states that you'll return to his employment within this period.

If you're a C permit holder, you or your employer must request an 'authorisation of absence' from your cantonal authorities. It's granted for a maximum of three years, provided you can justify the necessity of your absence – for example study abroad, special education or training, or a special assignment for your employer.

CHANGING JOBS

The rules regarding changing jobs vary according to whether you're an EU national, whether you're married to a Swiss citizen and your type of residence permit. EU nationals can change professions and jobs with no permit restrictions. Non-EU L permit holders cannot change jobs without permission, and non-EU B permit holders aren't generally permitted to change jobs without permission until they've worked for a number of years in Switzerland. It's easier to change jobs within the same canton.

When you change jobs, you may have to resign from your present position before your prospective employer can apply for a new residence permit. Your new employer will need a copy of the letter from your current employer confirming your resignation. The authorities may also ask for an official letter (*Freigabe*, *libération*) from your present employer, stating that you've resigned voluntarily and that they don't object to your leaving. Your former employer must provide (by law) a reference (*Zeugnis*, *attestation*) in the local language and a salary statement (*Lohnausweis*, *certificat de salaire*) for tax purposes. Some companies will provide a reference in English on request.

A job offer doesn't guarantee that a residence permit application will be approved. This means, at least in theory, that changing jobs in Switzerland for non-EU nationals before they have a C permit (a permanent residence permit) can be a risky business. In reality, companies usually know when they can obtain a residence permit and wouldn't expect you to resign unless they were confident of receiving the permit approval, but take care. Check the notice period in your employment contract or conditions before resigning (see **Probationary & Notice Periods** on page ?? CH2) and whether there are any employment restrictions, e.g. with regard to working for a competitor.

Your resignation letter should be sent by registered post to reach your employer by the last working day of the month at the latest, or it can be presented personally to your employer, when a signed and dated receipt should be provided.

The Swiss don't generally change jobs very often and some employers may think that you're unreliable if you change jobs more than a few times during your lifetime (although this has changed in recent years, during which redundancies have become more commonplace). On the other hand, experienced and qualified foreigners with a C permit may find they can job-hop every few years when there are labour shortages.

Zurich

4.

ARRIVAL

O n arrival in Switzerland to take up employment or residence, there are a number of formalities that must be completed. These are described in this chapter, where you'll also find suggestions for finding local help and information and useful checklists.

SCHENGEN AGREEMENT

Switzerland is a signatory to the Schengen agreement, an open-border policy between 26 European countries. Switzerland officially became a member on 12th December 2008 and all land border controls between Switzerland and the other 24 member countries were removed (air border controls were removed in March 2009).

Other Schengen members are Austria, Belgium, the Czech Republic, Denmark, Estonia, Finland, France, Germany, Greece, Hungary, Iceland, Italy, Latvia, Liechtenstein, Lithuania, Luxembourg, Malta, the Netherlands, Norway, Poland, Portugal, Slovakia, Slovenia, Spain and Sweden. Bulgaria and Romania are planning to implement the agreement later, while Cyprus isn't a member due to the dispute over the Turkish occupied northern part of the island. The United Kingdom and Ireland also aren't members, but are signatories to the Schengen police and judicial cooperation treaty.

So-called third-world citizens who aren't on the Schengen visa-free list (see 🖥 http://switzerland. visahq.com/requirements) can download a free Schengen Visa application form via the UK Swiss embassy website (🖥 http://visaswitzerland.co.uk/ visaform.pdf). The visa costs €60 and allows you to travel freely between all Schengen member countries. Under the Schengen agreement, immigration checks and passport controls take place when you first arrive in a member country from outside the Schengen area, after which you can travel freely between member countries for a maximum of up to 90 days in a six-month period.

Schengen visa holders aren't permitted to live permanently or work in Europe (short business trips aren't usually considered employment). Foreigners who intend to take up employment or self-employed activity in Switzerland (or any Schengen country) may require a visa, even if their home country (nationality) is listed on the Schengen visa-free list.

Third-world nationals who are resident in Switzerland (or another Schengen country) can travel freely to all Schengen member countries without a visa, simply by showing their Swiss residence permit and passport (or other valid travel document). New third-world nationals resident in Switzerland receive a Schengen ID card.

For further information, see the Federal Department of Foreign Affairs website (🖥 www.eda.admin.ch/eda/en/home.html).

BORDER CONTROL

On arrival in Switzerland present your passport, Schengen visa and – if applicable – your 'assurance of a residence permit' (*Zusicherung der Aufenthaltsbewilligung, assurance d'autorisation de séjour et de travail*) document, to the immigration authorities at the frontier or airport. If driving, you may need to arrive at the border control during 'business' hours. For a list of all Swiss Federal Customs offices, locations and opening hours, see 🖥 www.ezv.admin.ch (under Services/List of Offices). If you have an entry visa (see **Chapter 3**) it will be cancelled by the immigration official.

Ask the immigration official to stamp your 'assurance of a residence permit' document to verify your date of entry. This isn't obligatory but, in the words of the Federal Office of Public Health, 'is strongly recommended'.

Foreigners from certain countries planning to work in Switzerland may be required to have a health check (usually consisting of an X-ray only) within 72 hours in order to detect contagious diseases. The health check is no longer required for nationals of EU countries, Australia, Canada, New Zealand and the US. When applicable, the health check is carried out at a designated Swiss clinic, after which you receive a stamp in your passport confirming that it has been completed.

CUSTOMS

When you enter Switzerland to take up residence, household or personal effects that you've used for at least six months can be imported without incurring duty or VAT. A complete list of the items being imported must be provided at the time of entry, together with a request for duty-free import (a form is provided). VAT (8 per cent) must be paid on any articles you've used for less than six months; itemised invoices should be provided. If your Swiss home is a second home, you must usually pay VAT on all imports except clothes and other exempt items (you may be granted an exemption if your home country grants reciprocal rights to Swiss nationals). You'll also require the following:

♦ an inventory of all goods to be imported. Articles which don't fulfil the duty-free conditions should be itemised at the end of the list as 'goods for normal customs clearance'.

♦ your Swiss residence permit or assurance of a residence permit (see **Chapter 3**);

♦ the official foreign registration certificate for cars, motorcycles, motorboats and aeroplanes, as well as the sales receipt if available;

♦ a contract for the lease or purchase of a property or other proof of accommodation;

♦ a photocopy of the passports of everyone taking up residence in Switzerland;

♦ a completed form 18.44 (declaration/ application for clearance of household effects), available from the Swiss Federal Customs Administration (Eidgenössische Zollverwaltung/ EZV) website (💻 www.ezv.admin.ch – follow links to *Dienstleistungen, Publikationen und Formulare bestellen*, and *Übersiedlungs- und Erbschaftsgut*; the form includes instructions in English).

If you import a car duty-free and sell it in Switzerland within one year of your arrival, you're required to inform the customs authorities at the location where it was imported and pay import taxes, which are calculated on the age, value and sale price of a vehicle.

If you plan to enter Switzerland with a foreign-registered car and household effects (for example on a trailer), it's advisable to enter via a major frontier post, as smaller posts may not be equipped to deal with you unless they're informed of your arrival in advance. Note also the following:

♦ Switzerland has no currency restrictions (the Swiss love all money).

♦ A licence is required to import guns and ammunition.

♦ There are restrictions on the type and quantity of plants and bulbs that may be imported.

Information regarding the importation of cars can be found on page 135, pets on page 263 and duty-free allowances (e.g. alcohol and tobacco) on page 251. Information about Swiss customs regulations is contained in a leaflet entitled *Customs Regulations for Travellers Domiciled Abroad*, available from customs offices, Switzerland Tourism offices or the Head Customs Office, (*Eidgenössische Zollverwaltung/EZV, Administration fédérale des douanes/AFD,* ☎ 031-322 65 11, 💻 www.zoll.admin.ch). The customs office also provides information regarding the importation of special items.

MOTORWAY TAX

On entering Switzerland you may be asked whether you intend to use Swiss motorways, particularly if you enter via Basle or Geneva, and if you answer yes you must pay an annual motorway tax of CHF 40 on the spot. This tax is payable in addition to Swiss road tax (see page 144) and is applicable to all motor vehicles (including motorcycles) under 3.5 tonnes using Swiss motorways, whether Swiss or foreign-registered.

On payment of the tax, you're given a sticker (*vignette*) which must be affixed to your windscreen on the left-hand side (top or bottom) or centre top. The *vignette* isn't transferable between vehicles and tears to pieces if you attempt to remove it (unless you know how!). If you have a trailer or caravan, it requires an additional *vignette*. Vehicles weighing over 3.5 tonnes are subject to a 'heavy vehicles' tax which is payable daily, monthly or annually (a 10-day pass is available for those who visit Switzerland frequently for periods of one or two days).

There's a proposal to increase the motorway tax by 150 per cent to CHF 100 per year, which – if passed – is expected to come into effect in 2014 or 2015, or when reserves for the upkeep of Swiss motorways drop below one CHF 1bn.

If you don't buy a *vignette* and are subsequently discovered driving on a motorway, you're fined CHF 100 and must also pay the road tax on the spot. It is, of course, possible to drive around Switzerland without using motorways, but (very) time consuming. In fact, the motorway tax is a small price to pay for the convenience of using some of the finest roads in Europe, particularly when you consider that there are no road tolls in Switzerland. To put it into perspective, the annual Swiss motorway tax is less than the price of around one day's motoring on French, Italian or Spanish motorways!

The *vignette* is valid for a calendar year, with a month's overlap at each end, e.g. 1st December 2009 to 31st January 2011 (although if you buy one in November, you must buy another in December for the following year!). It can be purchased in advance (although it's unnecessary) at Switzerland Tourism offices or from automobile associations throughout Europe. In Switzerland it's sold at border crossings, customs offices, post offices, garages, service stations and cantonal motor registries.

REGISTRATION

Within eight days of arrival in Switzerland and before starting work, you (and your family members) must register (*anmelden, s'annoncer*) with the local community (*Gemeinde, commune*) where you're living, even if you're in temporary accommodation, e.g. a hotel. This is done at your local community office (*Gemeindehaus, maison communale*) in country areas or an area office (*Kreisbüro, bureau d'arrondissement*) in cities. Cities and large towns often have an ominous-sounding 'residents' control' department (*Einwohnerkontrolle, contrôle des habitants*).

Switzerland has strict regulations regarding registration for a number of good reasons, the most important of which is that most residents pay taxes levied by their local community from their date of registration. Another is that each new resident foreign worker is deducted from his canton's annual permit quota. In any case, you must register in order to obtain your residence permit. If applicable, you must have a health check (see **Border Control** above) before you can register. Registration is obligatory for all residents, both foreigners and Swiss nationals.

At your community registration office you'll be asked to produce the following (as applicable):

♦ your passport (containing the border health check stamp, if applicable) and your spouse's and children's passports;

♦ your 'assurance of a residence permit' document, which will be retained by your community registration office;

♦ your property rental agreement (if applicable);

♦ proof of health insurance;

♦ your marriage certificate;

♦ birth certificates for each member of your family;

♦ two passport-size photographs (black and white or colour) for each member of your family up to 18 years of age (family members over 18 must present their own documents).

It's useful to have a supply of passport-size photos for all members of your family, for example for school ID cards, train and bus season tickets, ski passes and Swiss driving licences. Photographs are available from machines at most railway stations and in town centres.

You must complete a form that includes (vital) information such as your mother's and father's Christian names, and (for men) your mother's and wife's maiden names or (for women) you husband's mother's maiden name (make sure he knows this!). If you're divorced, separated or widowed, you should state this on the registration form, as you may be entitled to a small tax concession. You're also asked to state your religion (see **Church Tax** below).

Annual B permit applicants receive their permits within a few weeks via their employer or community.

If you're moving to a new community or leaving Switzerland permanently, you must complete a 'de-registration' (*Abmeldeung, déclaration de départ*) in your present community up to eight days before your departure, and register in your new community within eight days of taking up residence (if applicable). If you're a B permit holder and live and work in different cantons, your residence permit won't be renewed by your canton of residence until your permission to work has been approved by the canton where you're employed.

CHURCH TAX

When you arrive in Switzerland and register in your local community (see **Registration** above) you must complete a form asking you to state your religion. All communities in Switzerland levy a church tax (*Kirchensteuer, impôt ecclésiastique*) on members of the three main Swiss churches: Catholic, Old Catholic (Protestant) and Reformed. (Now you know why Swiss churches are in such excellent repair.) If you enter 'Protestant', for example, you're registered as a member of the relevant church and must pay church tax. Members of other religions such as the Church of England, Methodists and Baptists, should clearly indicate their religion on the application. If you aren't a member of any church, just enter 'NONE' as your religion. This is legal and will ensure that you're able to reclaim any church tax deducted from your salary (see below).

Most foreigners in Switzerland pay direct income tax (*Quellensteuer, impôt à la source*) and in most cantons church tax is deducted at source from your gross salary, often without your knowledge or permission. It doesn't appear on your pay slip or your annual salary statement (*Lohnausweis, certificat de salaire*) and many foreigners are unaware that they pay it.

☑ SURVIVAL TIP

If you pay direct income tax, in some cantons you automatically pay church tax, even, for example if you're registered as an atheist.

If you aren't registered as a member of an official Swiss church, you can reclaim your church tax every one to three years, via a form available from your community or by writing a letter to the relevant tax office. Enter your personal particulars and bank account information and attach a copy of your salary statement (*Lohnausweis, certificat de salaire*) for the period in question. Send the form to your canton's tax office (*Steueramt, Service des contributions*), the address of which is printed on the form. You'll be advised by letter when your money (excluding interest!) has been credited to your account, usually after six to eight weeks.

If you're wrongly registered as a member of a taxable religion, you can have your records officially changed and reclaim any tax paid, although you can reclaim church tax for a limited period only, for example the last three years. The procedure depends on the canton where you live and the religion under which you're registered. If you reclaim your church tax you cannot get married or buried by the church (without paying a huge fee) and it may affect your children's religious status, for example they may no longer receive religious instruction at school. Nevertheless, there are plenty of other churches only too happy to have you as a tax-free member, e.g. Anglicans, Baptists, Methodists, Pentecostals, the Salvation Army and others, not to mention any number of religious sects.

If you don't reclaim wrongly paid church tax, the three churches divide the spoils among themselves – the interest alone must be worth a Pope's ransom.

The amount of tax payable depends on your salary (church tax is calculated as a percentage of your basic tax value – see **Income Tax** on page 196), your community (parish), your canton tax rates and your religion, and can amount to several thousand francs a year if you earn a high salary.

EMBASSY REGISTRATION

Nationals of some countries are required to register with their local embassy or consulate, as soon as possible after arrival in Switzerland. Even if registration isn't mandatory or recommended, it's wise to do so in case of an emergency (when the embassy can contact you).

FINDING HELP

One of the biggest difficulties facing new arrivals in Switzerland is how and where to obtain help with day-to-day problems. This book was written in response to this need. However, in addition to the comprehensive information provided herein, you'll also require detailed local information. How successful you are in finding help depends on your employer, the town or area where you live (e.g. Geneva's and Zug's residents are better served than Zurich's), and your nationality, language proficiency and sex (women are better served than men through numerous women's clubs).

There's an abundance of general local information published in the Swiss national languages (French, German and Italian), although it usually isn't intended for foreigners and their particular needs, and there's little in English and other foreign languages.

You may find that your friends and colleagues can help, as they're often able to proffer advice based on their own experiences and mistakes – but take care as it may be irrelevant to your circumstances and needs.

Local Community

Your community is usually an excellent source of reliable information, but you'll probably need to speak the local language to benefit from it. Some companies may have a department or staff whose job is to help newcomers settle in or they may contract this task out to a relocation company. Unfortunately many employers in Switzerland seem totally unaware of (or uninterested in) the problems and difficulties faced by their foreign employees.

In the major cities, e.g. Geneva and Zurich, there are free advice centres for foreigners and most also provide useful websites for expats. The city of Zug website (🖳 www.stadtzug.ch) not only has an expat section in English, but supports the websites 🖳 www.zug4you.ch and www. thezugpost.ch, which provide local daily news in English with the goal of integrating the expat community into daily life. There's also a sister website (🖳 www.zurich4you.ch) for the canton of Zurich which provides expats with local news in English. In Geneva, Know-it-all (🖳 www.knowitall. ch) was launched in early 2010 and provides a wealth of information for the expat community in Geneva, Vaud and neighbouring France, while the Canton of Basle Office of Economic Promotion provides the Basel Area website (🖳 www. baselarea.ch) for expats. See also **Appendix C** (Useful Websites).

Women's Clubs

If a woman lives in or near a major town, she's able to turn to many English-speaking women's clubs and organisations for help. The single foreign male (who, naturally, cannot possibly have any problems) must usually fend for himself, although there are men's expatriate clubs in some areas and mixed social clubs throughout the country.

FAWCO

One of the best sources of information and help for women are the Swiss branches of the Federation of American Women's Clubs Overseas (FAWCO, 🖳 www.fawco.org) located in Berne, Basle, Geneva, Lausanne and Zurich. FAWCO clubs provide comprehensive information in English about both local matters and topics of more general interest. They can provide detailed information about all aspects of living in Switzerland including accommodation costs, school profiles, names of English-speaking doctors and dentists, shopping information and much more.

FAWCO clubs produce data sheets and booklets containing a wealth of valuable local information, and they also run libraries open to non-members. FAWCO publications can be purchased directly from FAWCO clubs or from local bookshops. Clubs organise a variety of social events, plus many day and evening classes, ranging from local cooking to language classes.

FAWCO run excellent orientation programmes for newcomers to Switzerland, open to both men and women, including non-members. See 🖳 www. fawcofoundation.org for information.

Other Sources

In addition to the above, there are numerous social clubs and other organisations for foreigners in Switzerland, whose members can help you find your way around. Many embassies and consulates provide information, particularly about clubs for their nationals, and many businesses (e.g. Swiss banks) produce booklets and leaflets containing useful information (see **Appendix A**). Bookshops and newsagents may stock useful publications (see **Appendix B** and also **Media** on page 288). Local tourist and information offices may also be of assistance.

Know-it-all passport

Know-it-all passport is a comprehensive English-language guide for the Geneva, Vaud and neighboring France areas. The current 2013/2014 (8th) edition contains over 750 pages, more than 50 chapters, a 27-page index, two bookmarks attached by ribbons, and maps of the area. The guide is published every two years.

First published in 1999, it has become THE reference book for anything you want to know from shopping, housing and education, to where to hold a birthday party, places to eat, night life, all about chocolate, and local information. It also includes information on winter activities, where to go for public transport and much more, including a chapter on Outing and Trips (54 pages) which is almost a book within a book.

For more information or to buy a copy, see 🖥 www.knowitall.ch.

CHECKLISTS

Before Arrival

The following checklist contains a summary of the tasks that should (if possible) be completed before your arrival in Switzerland:

◆ Obtain a visa, if necessary, for you and all your family members (see **Chapter 3**). Obviously this **must** be done before your arrival in Switzerland.

◆ If possible visit Switzerland to compare communities and schools, and arrange schooling for your children (see **Chapter 9**).

◆ Find temporary or permanent accommodation and arrange for shipment of your personal effects to Switzerland (see **Chapter 5**).

◆ Arrange health insurance for yourself and your family (see **Chapter 13**). This is essential if you aren't already covered by a private insurance policy and won't be covered automatically by your Swiss employer.

◆ Open a bank account in Switzerland and transfer funds (EU citizens can open an account with major Swiss banks from abroad, but US citizens may only be able to open an account if they're Swiss residents). It's best to obtain some Swiss francs before your arrival in Switzerland, which will save you having to spend time changing money on arrival.

◆ Collect and update personal records including medical, dental, schools, insurance (e.g. car insurance), professional and employment (including job references) records.

◆ Obtain an international driving permit, if necessary.

◆ Obtain an international credit card if you don't have one, which will prove invaluable during your first few months in Switzerland.

◆ Don't forget to bring all your family's official documents including birth certificates, driving licences, marriage certificate, divorce papers or death certificate (if a widow or widower), educational diplomas, professional certificates, job references, school records and student ID cards, employment references, medical and dental records, bank account and credit card details, insurance policies and receipts for any valuables. You will also need the documents necessary to obtain a residence permit (see **Chapter 3**) plus certified copies, official translations and numerous passport-size photographs (students should take at least a dozen).

After Arrival

The following checklist contains a summary of tasks to be completed after arrival in Switzerland (if not done before arrival):

◆ If applicable, on arrival at the Swiss border or airport, give your permit approval document and passport to the official for date stamping.

◆ If you're importing a car, complete a form for temporary importation. If you don't own a car, you may wish to rent one for a week or two until buying one locally. See **Chapter 11**.

◆ If necessary, visit a health clinic within 72 hours (three days) for a health check. If applicable, you'll usually be sent to an approved clinic by the border authorities.

◆ Open a bank account and give the details to your employer in order to receive your salary.

◆ Register at your community registration office within eight days of arrival.

◆ Register with your local embassy or consulate.

◆ Arrange schooling for your children (see **Chapter 9**).

◆ Arrange whatever insurance is necessary for you and your family (see **Chapter 13**) and **Car Insurance** (see page 142).

5.
ACCOMMODATION

I n many areas of Switzerland, finding reasonably priced accommodation is becoming increasingly difficult (if not impossible) and finding accommodation at almost any price isn't easy in the major cities. In the cantons of Basle-City, Geneva, Zug and Zurich there's an acute shortage of accommodation due to the lack of building land and high demand. House prices are high and rental costs can be astronomical, particularly in areas where rented accommodation is in high demand and short supply. For those on low incomes, including seasonal workers, students, pensioners, the young, single-parent and other low-income families, buying a home is impossible and even renting a decent home is too expensive. If you aspire to owning or renting a nice home, make sure that you salary will be sufficient to pay for it!

Housing accounts for around third or more of the average family's budget in Switzerland (there's an unwritten rule that rent shouldn't exceed more than a third of your monthly salary). Although the federal government subsidises the construction of low-cost housing for low-income families, invalids and pensioners, the growing lack of inexpensive rental accommodation is one of Switzerland's most urgent needs. Those earning high salaries are unlikely to be able to rent an inexpensive apartment.

This chapter contains information about buying property, renting accommodation, moving house, utilities and obtaining home help.

For comprehensive information about buying or renting property in Switzerland, see our sister publication *Buying or Renting a Home in Switzerland*.

LOCATION

Non-EU employees of Swiss companies must usually live in the canton where they work and which issued their residence permit, although this no longer applies to EU nationals. There are numerous beautiful areas to choose from in every canton, all within easy travelling distance of a town or city. When looking for a home, bear in mind the travelling time (particularly in winter

when it can increase significantly) and travel costs, for example to your place of work, shops and schools.

It may be possible for some foreign workers to live in one of Switzerland's neighbouring countries. However, if you don't live in Switzerland you aren't entitled to a Swiss residence permit and your employer must apply for a frontier crossing (*Grenzgänger, frontalier*) G permit (see page 46). Permission may depend on your nationality and whether you work for an international organisation.

If you decide to live outside Switzerland, you'll be subject to the laws of the country where you're resident, including, for example, registration with the local police, payment of taxes and car registration. Your rent and general living costs may be lower outside Switzerland, but the advantages may not be as clear-cut as they first appear, e.g. higher taxes.

Employees of international organisations aren't subject to the same regulations as those working for Swiss companies and there are generally no restrictions on where they may live in Switzerland.

RENTED ACCOMMODATION

For those who associate home ownership with prosperity, it will come as a surprise that most Swiss are surprisingly wedded to renting their homes – and unlike people in some other countries (e.g. France) it isn't common for Swiss to rent in the city where they work and buy a

property in the country. Most Swiss are generally content to rent – even when they can afford to buy – not least because tenants in Switzerland have considerable security and rents are usually reasonable compared to salaries. Nevertheless, the average Swiss family spends around 40 per cent of their income on housing.

In contrast with many other countries, rental units in Switzerland are well-built, usually fitted with all modern conveniences, and many developments offer a mix of rental and owner-occupied apartments (there are few rental 'ghettos'). There's little or no difference in quality between rental and owner-occupied units. Added to which there isn't a lot of property for sale, and very little in areas where most people want to live; buyers in Switzerland need a large deposit, there are few tax advantages and costs are high; and many Swiss consider owning property to be more of a liability than an asset.

It's now much easier for EU nationals working in Switzerland to buy property there, although most newcomers still rent for a period, which may be anything from a few months to a number of years – or even permanently. Whether you buy or rent will also depend on how long you're planning to stay, as many people don't consider it worthwhile buying if they're staying for less than five years. Even if you're set on buying, you usually need to rent for a period while looking for something to buy, and it's best not to be too optimistic about finding something suitable quickly, particularly in the major cities. Note also that even if you're planning to buy and don't need a mortgage, you won't be able to buy property until your Swiss permit is issued.

Don't underestimate the difficulty and time required to find a suitable long-term rental in Switzerland. When viewing property it's advisable to treat it as a job interview and dress accordingly – first impressions count!

Rented accommodation (*Mietwohnung, appartement à louer*) in Switzerland usually consists of an unfurnished apartment, although long-term furnished accommodation is becoming more common in the cities, but it's often very expensive. Unfurnished apartments are available in most areas, although in some regions and major cities accommodation is in short supply and expensive, and the situation has been exacerbated in recent years by the influx of foreign workers (notably Germans in the north and French in the Lake Geneva region) due to the relaxation of work permit regulations.

Rents in most of Switzerland are comparable with other European countries and cities, although there are regional variations. Rents are very high (and among the highest in the world) in Geneva, Lausanne, Zug and Zurich, due to excess demand, an acute shortage of accommodation and a vacancy rate of well below 0.5 per cent! There's a particularly shortage of rental properties in the middle to upper end of the market. The vacancy rate can, however, be slightly misleading, as the turnover of tenants is relatively high in Swiss cities (apparently a third of rental properties in Zurich city change tenants every year) and apartments become vacant every day, although they are snapped up quickly and therefore make little or no impact on the vacancy rate.

The market in the cantons of Basle, Geneva, Vaud, Zug and Zurich is distorted by the influx of international employees and company relocations, when incoming companies bring in dozens or even hundreds of employees each year. It can cost up to a million francs to settle a family of four for three to four years (which may be boosted by temporary housing costs or moving the family twice), therefore companies are willing to pay a premium for good housing that employees can move into immediately. The situation has worked its way down to the bottom and middle of the market, and in some cities it has become virtually impossible for essential workers (such as nurses and police officers) to find anywhere affordable to live.

In Geneva, an added problem is the wealth of diplomats and those working for international organisations, who have generous salaries compared to the local market, coupled with paying no local taxes and large housing allowances, which drives up the cost of housing at the upper end of the market. The acute shortage of housing in Geneva has forced many Swiss and EU citizens working there to live in neighbouring France, where property is 20-40 per cent cheaper and there's a lower cost of living (but higher taxes!). This has had the effect of pushing up housing costs in France – in some areas prices have doubled in recent years – and has inflamed local passions (since 2004, Swiss citizens haven't required a residence permit to live in France).

One of the biggest problems faced by newcomers is finding somewhere to live, and many people stay in temporary accommodation while looking for a long-term rental or somewhere to buy. Some companies have a human resources department to help new arrivals find a place to live or they may hire a relocation company (of which there are hundreds in Switzerland) to do this.

Non-residents are permitted to rent long-term in Switzerland, but they can only live there for a total of six months a year and a maximum of three months continuously.

Finding Accommodation

Finding a suitable rental at a price you can afford – and in an area where you would want to live – is difficult, and depends on the region, the type of property you're seeking and the local demand and how much you can afford to pay. If you're seeking a small two- or three-bedroom apartment, it's much easier to find something suitable than if you want a spacious four-bedroom detached house.

The chief sources of rental accommodation ads are local newspapers; the best days for advertisements are usually Wednesdays, Fridays and Saturdays. Apartments and houses for rent are also advertised (*Wohnungen zu vermieten, appartements à louer*) in free local newspapers, delivered in most areas along with copious 'junk' mail (Switzerland is a world leader in the production of junk mail, a major industry). There are numerous websites, e.g. 💻 www.homegate.ch, www.immoscout24.ch, www.immomarktschweiz.ch, www.anzeiger.ch and www.immostreet.ch, where you can usually subscribe to an email update which informs you about new property available in your chosen area. There are also free classified ad pages at 💻 www. xpatxchange.ch.

Advertisers may be private owners, property managers or rental agencies. Most advertisements include a telephone number, although some, particularly those for exclusive properties, provide a box number (*Chiffre Nr., chiffre No./sous chiffres*) and you must apply in writing. If you're interested in a property, apply as soon as possible and be prepared to inspect it at short notice – in major cities (particularly Geneva), an advertisement for a desirable apartment may attract over 100 replies.

Most towns have rental and estate agencies (*Immobilien, agences immobilières*) which are listed in local telephone directories. These usually charge a registration fee of around CHF 50 that's valid for three months – after signing a contract you must pay an additional fee. Fees vary from agency to agency, but are usually equivalent to a month's rent.

Apartments and houses for rent are also advertised on company bulletin boards, in company magazines and newspapers, and in official cantonal newspapers. Some communities publish a list of vacant accommodation in the community. You can insert a 'rental wanted' (*Mietgesuche, recherche un appartement/une maison*) advertisement in most newspapers and on bulletin boards in supermarkets, e.g. Migros and Co-op, churches, consulates and clubs (many also have newsletters where you can place a wanted ad). Finally don't forget to ask friends, relatives and acquaintances to help spread the word, particularly if you're looking in the area where you already live.

Fixtures & Fittings

Apartments usually include an oven (usually without a grill), a refrigerator, fitted kitchen units and sometimes a dishwasher or freezer. Kitchens are often tiny, even in many large houses. Apartments may have parquet (wooden) floors but carpets are rare. Larger apartments (from three bedrooms) usually have a second toilet and may have an en-suite shower room to the main bedroom, in addition to a separate family bathroom.

Unfurnished apartments usually have light fittings only in bathrooms, kitchens and occasionally hallways (most rooms just have bare wires). Fitted wardrobes in bedrooms are rare and curtain rails aren't provided unless they're built-in. A number of built-in linen cupboards and a cloakroom unit may be provided. The hot water supply is often shared and can run out during times of heavy use, although modern apartments usually have their own boilers(s).

A small storage room or pantry may be provided in an apartment and a lockable storage room in the cellar of the building, which doubles as the mandatory nuclear shelter (no joke), is usually included. Many apartment blocks also have a bicycle storage room. Luxury apartment blocks may have a communal sauna or heated swimming pool.

Most apartment blocks have a communal laundry room with a washing machine and tumble dryer and a separate drying room. Some apartment blocks have outside clothes lines where tenants may hang their clothes to dry. The sharing of washing machines can be most unsatisfactory for families, particularly in large apartment blocks; tenants may be allocated the use of the communal washing machine for only a few hours a week and at an inconvenient time. In larger, more expensive apartments, a personal washing machine and drier may be provided, which may be located in a private laundry/drying room. If you wish to buy your own washing machine and wash at your convenience, ensure that you have room to install it in your apartment and an appropriate power point (see **Electricity** on page 74) – and don't forget to ask your landlord for written permission!

Rental Costs

The cost of renting an apartment varies considerably according to its size, age, facilities and location. Rents (*Miete, location/loyer*) are high (especially in cities) and have risen rapidly in the last decade. In response to an increase in property speculation, a law was passed giving prospective tenants the right to know the rent paid by the previous tenant (so don't forget to ask). If your rent is increased sharply, you can usually have it reviewed independently; ask your community for information. Subsidised housing is available in some areas for low-income families, invalids and pensioners.

Rental costs used to be linked to mortgage interest rates and when the mortgage rate increased, landlords had the right to increase rents. Nowadays landlords have the right to increase rents at any time.

The number of rooms advertised excludes the kitchen (except in Geneva), bathroom and toilet, although the total area (stated in square metres) includes all rooms. Average rents for unfurnished apartments are shown in the table below.

The size (approx. m²) and rents shown above are only a guide and are for good quality new or renovated apartments, exclusive of extra costs (see below) and a garage (see below). Those that are classified as 'inexpensive' are generally older, smaller apartments or properties situated in rural or industrial areas, although these rents are around average for most of rural Switzerland. Nevertheless, most foreigners live in areas or cities where properties come under the 'moderate' or 'expensive' categories shown in the table. Properties in the expensive bracket are usually located in the most desirable areas, including the central area of cities. **Note that for apartments in renovated period buildings in major city centres and for luxury properties, the sky's the limit!**

An apartment with a patio (*Gartensitzplatz, terrasse*) is usually cheaper than a top floor

Rental Cost Guide

No. of bedrooms	Approx. m²	Monthly Rent (CHF)		
		Inexpensive	Moderate	Expensive
0 (studio)	30-40	500-750	650-850	850-1,200
1	50-60	750-1,000	1,000-1,300	1,400-2,000
2	75-90	1,000-1,500	1,250-1,750	1,750-2,500
3	90-120	1,250-2,000	1,500-2,000	2,000-3,000
4	120-150	1,500-2,000	2,000-2,500	2,750-4,000
5 or more	150+	2,000-3,000	2,500-3,500	4,000+

apartment, which may have a small balcony only. Generally the higher the floor, the higher the cost (you pay for the rarefied air). Top floor, penthouse or attic apartments (*Dachwohnung, un attique*) are the most expensive and are often fitted with an open fireplace (*Cheminée/avec cheminée*), considered a luxury in Switzerland – though lugging wood up several flights of stairs isn't a luxury.

Rents are highest in the cantons of Geneva, Zug and Zurich, and lowest in Jura, Neuchâtel and Valais. In some areas you can pay over CHF 10,000 per month for a furnished three- or four-bedroom house. It's possible to find cheaper, older apartments, but they're rare, generally smaller and don't usually contain the standard 'fixtures and fittings' of modern apartments, e.g. no central heating or double-glazing.

The Lease

When you find a suitable apartment, you need to sign a lease (*Mietvertrag, contrat/bail à loyer*) with the landlord or agent, which will be either for a fixed term or an indefinite period. If a fixed term is set, the lease expires without any need for notice of termination at the end of the term, but if the parties continue the agreement beyond the expiry of a fixed term lease, it becomes a lease for an indefinite duration.

Most leases are for a minimum of one year but for an indefinite period, with a notice period of three or four months (e.g. it's often four months in Lucerne and Zurich). If you want to leave without giving notice (or sufficient notice), as noted in your lease, you must find a replacement tenant (see **Terminating the Lease** below). In general, you sign a lease for between three and five years, with no notice period in the first year, and three or four months' notice period during each subsequent year. A rental property may only be sub-let by a tenant with the owner's agreement.

A landlord may try to get a tenant to sign a lease for a minimum number of years, e.g. three or five, with a notice period of one year, even after the first year of a lease. In this case the lease may have a progressive rent, for example, the first year's rent is CHF 3,000 per month, the second year is CHF 3,250 francs and the third year is 3,500 francs. This mostly applies to new-build properties. You can have a contract which allows three-month termination throughout the year or a rental agreement that allows termination at the end of any month excluding December – but it must be in the contract.

It's possible to terminate your lease at short notice, provided you find another tenant who's acceptable to your landlord to take over the lease, although this may be difficult unless the property is exceptional and in high demand.

A standard lease form is provided in most cantons, although you should take note of any added or deleted clauses or passages. Your lease should include details of when your rent and extra costs will be increased, if applicable. You must be notified of an unscheduled rent rise, e.g. due to a mortgage interest rate increase or an increase in the price index (inflation), by registered post at least three months **plus** ten days in advance, so that you can respond by cancelling your contract if you wish.

Before signing a lease you should check the following:

◆ whether there's a minimum or maximum limit on your tenancy period – this is usually negotiable;

◆ on which dates the lease can be terminated;

◆ what deposit is required (maximum three months' rent – box opposite);

◆ how many people may live in the apartment and whether you can sublet or share;

◆ what laundry facilities are provided and when they're available;

◆ if cable television is available and what channels;

- if satellite television is available or whether it's possible to install a dish;

- whether the telephone line is connected and how many points there are;

- if pets are allowed (you can be evicted if you keep a pet against your landlord's wishes);

- whether smoking is permitted;

- when the rent and extra costs are to be reviewed or increased;

- what the parking facilities are (particularly covered parking, in winter) and the cost, which may be covered in a separate agreement;

- what the house rules are (see below);

- any unusual rules or restrictions;

- whether there's a lift or a goods lift for furniture (some cantons' regulations require lifts in all new buildings with four or more floors).

If you rent a house (rather than an apartment), it's even more important to check the rules and regulations for tenants, because you may be responsible for the following if they're included in the lease:

- the gardens and grounds;

- the heating system maintenance, insulation, ordering fuel, etc.

- maintenance of the water supply;

- chimney-sweeping twice a year, which is compulsory for oil- and wood-burning systems (your landlord may pay for this).

Specific legal terms and conditions apply to renting a house or apartment as a 'family home', i.e. the primary residence of a married couple or family. In this case, both partners must sign the lease, and matters such as termination or a change in the terms are only valid if both partners sign. If a landlord wants to terminate a lease, notification must be made to both spouses separately. The landlord must be informed if a single tenant gets married, a couple are divorced or additional people wish to share an apartment. If you're sharing a home, you should have your name added to the lease, otherwise you have no legal rights. If a couple wish to terminate a lease, both must sign the termination letter.

Inventory & Condition

One of the most important tasks on moving into a new rental property is to complete an inventory and report on its condition (*Mängelliste*, *état des lieux*), which must be completed and checked in the presence of the landlord or agent. There's a handover at the start of the lease (*Übergabeprotokoll, état des lieux d'entrée*) and at the end of the lease when you leave (*Abgabeprotokoll, etat des lieux de sortie*). This includes the condition of fixtures and fittings, the cleanliness and state of the decoration (paintwork, plaster, floors, walls, etc.), and anything missing or in need of repair.

If you're renting a furnished apartment, the inventory will include all furnishings and equipment down to the last teaspoon. The apartment should be spotless when you move in, as this is certainly what your landlord will expect when you move out – see **Terminating the Lease** below.

The inventory form is provided by your landlord, and must be completed, signed and returned within 14 days of occupying your apartment. If you're taking over an apartment from the previous tenant, the landlord may arrange for the handover to be done when you're both present so that any problems can be sorted out on the spot. The inspection list should be as accurate and detailed as possible, as it's accepted as proof of any faults and deficiencies that existed when you moved in. If any problem isn't listed, you can be held responsible when you vacate the property. When the participants agree on the contents of the inspection list, it's signed by all parties, who each receive a copy.

You should inspect the apartment carefully over the first few days and check that all the equipment and electrical and plumbing installations are operating correctly. If you discover any problems, you should add them to the signed inventory report and return it to the landlord or agent within the time required (usually 14 days after the handover). If you find anything that isn't perfect you should take photographs to accompany the report. The landlord or agent must counter-sign it and return a copy to you for your records.

Bear in mind that if you agree to take over or buy anything from the previous tenant, e.g. you agree to buy or accept a fitted carpet, you'll have to dispose of it at your expense when moving out if the next tenant doesn't want it.

Note the reading on your meters (electricity, gas and water) and check that you aren't overcharged on your first bill. Most Swiss landlords are honest and won't try to cheat you, but it's better to be safe than sorry.

Note that it's important to have household and private liability insurance (see **Chapter 13**) in Switzerland, which may be required by your lease.

Terminating the Lease

You must generally give a minimum of three months' notice by registered letter (*Einschreiben Brief, lettre recommandée*) when you wish to terminate (*Kündigung, résiliation*) the lease of an apartment, which cannot usually be done in the first year of a lease. This applies to most contracts in Switzerland. Notice letters must be signed by both the husband and wife, where applicable (if a landlord wants to terminate a lease, he must notify both spouses separately), and you must receive confirmation from the landlord that he has received and accepted your termination.

☑ SURVIVAL TIP

Bear in mind that if you have a contract for the lease of a parking space or garage, this must be terminated separately.

The lease may usually be terminated only on the official dates listed in your lease, e.g. the end of March and September in canton Zurich (just twice a year), which applies to both parties. If it isn't terminated by either party, a lease is normally automatically extended for a further period, as stated in your lease. However, a landlord isn't permitted to terminate a lease without good reason and must use an official form provided by the cantonal authorities. Good reasons include the landlord requiring the property for his own family's use or when a property has been sold, in which case the new owners can effect an extraordinary termination of the tenancy under certain conditions.

The legally or contractually agreed periods of notice and due dates must be complied with and at least three months notice given. Tenants are entitled to be notified of the reason for the termination and a termination that isn't made in good faith can be contested before a conciliation board within 30 days. If a termination constitutes hardship for the tenant, e.g. financial or family difficulties or homelessness, an extension of the term of the tenancy can be applied for at the conciliation board.

A lease can be terminated with 30 days notice by the tenant if the landlord has failed to remedy any serious defects within a reasonable period of time. Similarly, the landlord can terminate the lease with 30 days notice if the tenant hasn't paid the rent, has seriously neglected or damaged the property, has used the property unlawfully (for example, to produce illegal drugs!), or has been officially warned for some other matter, such as persistent noise, and has failed to comply.

If you wish to terminate your lease outside the official dates, at short notice or in the first year of a lease, you must find a replacement tenant who's acceptable to your landlord. If you're given notice to vacate a property, you can find out about your rights and options from the cantonal Mieterverband (🖳 www.mieterverband.ch).

If you want to terminate a lease, you must do so in writing and send the letter to your agent or landlord by registered mail (*Einschreiben/Lettre recommandée*), which should reach the agent or landlord in good time, e.g. at least one day before the notice period deadline.

Cleaning & Redecoration

You're expected to leave your apartment spotlessly clean – as it was when you took it over – and the return of your deposit in full depends on this. Your landlord may even don white gloves to check that the oven is clean! One method of avoiding any problems is to employ professional cleaners, which most people consider well worth the money. You can find ads in local newspapers and *Yellow Pages* under 'Removal cleaning' (*Umzugsreinigung, nettoyage pour remise d'appartement*) or can surf the internet. Professional cleaning can be expensive, for example CHF 1,000 or more, depending on the size of your apartment. Charges vary from company to company, so shop around and don't

Alcohol

marks on wooden floors (resanding/polishing), carpet cleaning, and repainting woodwork.

Necessary repairs or replacements usually depend on the length of your tenancy; if you're a long-term tenant certain things may be overlooked, e.g. 'normal' wear and tear, although this is open to interpretation. Most items have an official life-expectancy (there's an official list called a *Lebensdauertabelle/Tableau paritaire des amortissements*) – even paintwork – and you're usually charged accordingly for renovation or replacement items when you vacate an apartment.

You will receive a copy of the inventory and condition report, which you and your landlord must sign, which verifies that the apartment is in an acceptable condition – or as otherwise noted – and that no further claims can be made.

You may wish to make a note of your electricity, water and gas meter readings and ensure that the telephone is disconnected. Finally, if applicable, ensure that your deposit is repaid (if paid – see box on page 64) with interest. Any deductions from your deposit should be accompanied by an itemised list of all work completed and a copy of the receipts.

pay the bill until the apartment has been cleaned to your landlord's satisfaction. You should have a 'handover acceptance guarantee' from the cleaning company.

> ### ☑ SURVIVAL TIP
>
> **Book well in advance as cleaning companies can be very busy, particularly around popular house moving dates.**

The cleaning of your apartment should include everything, including carpets (professional cleaning), floors, walls, paintwork, windows, oven, cupboards, bath/WC, lampshades, refrigerator, dishwasher, blinds, pipes and radiators; plus the garage, patio, balcony, storeroom, attic and basement, and the decalcification of taps (faucets). A cleaning company contract should include all of the above.

Your agent or landlord will inspect the property just before you vacate it and will expect it to be in the same state of cleanliness and repair as it was when you took it over. A new inventory and condition report (*Mängelliste/Abgabeprotokoll, état des lieux de sortie*) will be completed (see **Inventory & Condition** above) and compared with the one completed when you took over the property. The landlord will also collect the keys.

You must pay for any damage to fixtures and fittings and you may also be required to redecorate the apartment, depending on its condition when you moved in, how long you've lived there and the terms of your lease. Redecoration usually includes filling any holes in walls and repainting them, erasing excessive

BUYING PROPERTY

Buying property in Switzerland is an excellent long-term investment, particularly for anyone resident there, although capital growth is generally relatively low (around 6 per cent annually) by international standards, so you're unlikely to make a killing. A property purchase should be viewed as a long-term commitment rather than a quick way to turn a profit. Non-resident foreign buyers have traditionally been attracted to Switzerland by the country's low taxes and excellent quality of life. Low Swiss interest rates also help sustain demand from international buyers, despite the relatively high cost of property.

In recent years, Switzerland has experienced a wave of immigration from EU countries, which has considerably increased the demand for housing, particularly apartments, and although there has been a small increase in unemployment in the last few years this has had only a limited effect on the demand for housing. In the major cities (e.g. Basle, Geneva and Zurich), where demand for housing is highest – although mostly for rental properties – there's generally a shortage of homes and the supply is failing to keep pace with demand.

Property Purchase by Foreigners

The Swiss authorities have long placed restrictions on foreigners buying property in

Switzerland, although these have been relaxed in recent years, particularly for EU nationals. Under the Lex Koller law (1961 – named after the federal councillor who last amended it), there are restrictions on the purchase of real estate by non-EU foreigners and non-residents, although it's expected to be repealed in future and replaced by a more flexible arrangement which relies on local regulation.

The federal regulations regarding property purchase by foreigners depends on whether the buyer is a resident or non-resident and his nationality. The law varies from canton to canton and a permit may be necessary from the local cantonal authorities before a purchase can be granted. Authorisation is required irrespective of whether a property is already foreign-owned or the legal basis of the acquisition, e.g. purchase, barter, gift, inheritance, legacy, acquisition of assets and liabilities of a business, merger, de-merger, conversion of companies or asset transfer. A property purchase requiring authorisation becomes valid only after a permit has been obtained, although the contracted partners are still bound by the undertaking.

 Caution

Bear in mind that ownership of property in Switzerland doesn't entitle a foreign national to a residence permit.

Questions regarding specific cases must be addressed to the relevant cantonal authorities.

Swiss Nationals & EU Residents

Swiss nationals domiciled in Switzerland or abroad, including those with dual nationality, don't require authorisation to buy property in Switzerland, neither do residents of an EU member state who are resident in Switzerland with a B (annual residence) or C permit (permanent residence), or EU cross-border commuters with a G permit (*Grenzgängerbewilligung, permis frontalier*).

Nationals of other countries who hold a C permit and are domiciled in Switzerland; those working for embassies, consulates and international organisations; or for foreign railway, post and customs administrations based in Switzerland, also don't require authorisation. However, they must be able to prove they have been in Switzerland long enough to qualify for settlement (five or ten years, depending on their nationality).

The Swiss need have little fear that resident foreigners will buy up all their property, as very high property prices mean that most foreigners (and the average Swiss family) can only dream of owning their own home. In fact, many thousands of Swiss live outside Switzerland in what are ostensibly 'second' homes and commute to their jobs in Swiss cities such as Basle, Geneva and Zurich. Working foreign residents and their families comprise around 23 per cent of the Swiss population, but own just a few per cent of Swiss property (although some 5 per cent of Switzerland's total housing stock is foreign-owned).

Employees of international organisations and members of the diplomatic service enjoy more freedom in purchasing property than most other foreign residents. The regulations outlined here don't apply to these residents, who aren't included in the scope of this book.

Non-residents

Non-residents include all foreigners domiciled abroad and foreigners domiciled in Switzerland who aren't nationals of an EU member state and don't hold a C permit (permanent resident). Companies with their registered office abroad or companies with their registered office in Switzerland which are controlled by persons abroad, i.e. when more than one-third of a company's capital or voting rights are owned by non-residents, are also classified as non-resident.

Those who aren't, in principle, subject to authorisation are considered as non-residents if they wish to acquire property on behalf of persons abroad (called 'fiduciary transactions'). The transfer of property to a trust is also subject to authorisation if any trustees of the beneficiaries qualify as a person abroad.

A non-EU citizen with a Swiss spouse doesn't qualify to buy property unless he lives in Switzerland and has at least a B permit.

Property Prices

The cost of real estate in Switzerland is generally high, particularly in and around the major cities, where real estate is among the most expensive in the world. However, a slice of the Swiss good life needn't cost the earth, particularly if you're looking for an apartment in a rural area, where property can be surprisingly good value. If you wish to buy a house, it may be better to move to a rural area and commute to work by car or train. Despite the high prices, in most areas there isn't a lot of property for sale, as people rarely move house (it's too expensive) and buyers sometimes spend many months or even years looking for a house or apartment in a particular town or canton.

The cost of 'old' apartments in most areas is usually between CHF 4,000-6,000 per m², with the exception of period (pre-1945) properties in cities such as Geneva and Zurich, when the sky's the limit. You should generally expect to pay CHF 1,000-2,000 more per m² for a new apartment rather than an old one. The cost of new detached houses and luxury apartments is much higher than older properties, e.g. CHF 10,000-15,000 per m² for large properties – and that isn't even in a top area or town! The cost of real estate in the most desirable areas and major cities is very expensive; for example you can expect to pay CHF 45,000 per m² for a top-end property on Via Suvretta in St Moritz, one of the world's most exclusive addresses, and property in Zurich's Bahnhofstrasse has been sold for over CHF 250,000 per m².

Always check carefully what's included in the size as it's possible that the vendor or agent may include something such as a balcony, patio, parking space or storage room in the habitable area.

Prices vary considerably with the location – the most important factor – age, number of rooms and the size (m²) of a property. New properties tend to command higher prices, not least due to the higher rents that can be obtained. Holiday apartments and chalets are also expensive, not least because there are strict quotas and waiting lists which allow developers to demand high prices. For a simple studio without any special view, the minimum price is usually around CHF 125,000, while an average two-bedroom apartment costs around CHF 500,000 and a four-bedroom semi-detached or detached house at least CHF 800,000, although it can cost millions in an expensive region. In some 75 communities, you can expect to pay over CHF 1m for a new 'standard' apartment with four and a half rooms,

i.e. three bedrooms, living room, kitchen and bathroom(s).

The main features that add to the value of an apartment are a lift/elevator (not all apartment blocks have them), a fireplace and views. When buying an apartment, generally the higher the floor the more expensive it is (unless it's number 17, considered by many Swiss to be an unlucky number), as it will have more light, less road noise, better views and be more secure. A garage or parking space (see below) isn't usually included in the cost of an apartment and usually costs between CHF 25,000 and 50,000.

The approximate average price for apartments and houses is shown in the table below.

The size (approx. m²) and prices shown in the table are only a guide and are for good quality new or renovated apartments, excluding a garage. Extra large, spacious (*Grosszügig, spacieux*) apartments (with a much larger area than that shown in the table), penthouses and 'luxury' apartments may be much more expensive than the guide prices shown. The table also provides a rough guide to house prices (i.e. excluding apartments), but doesn't include detached houses, houses with a large plot of land, luxury and period houses, and houses situated in the central areas of cities.

Properties classified as 'inexpensive' are generally older, smaller apartments or properties situated in rural or industrial areas, although these prices are around average for most of Switzerland. However, most foreigners live in regions or cities where properties come under the 'moderate' or 'expensive' categories shown in the table. Properties in the expensive bracket are usually located in the most desirable areas, including the central area of cities. **Note that for apartments in renovated period buildings in**

Property Price Guide

No. of bedrooms	Approx. m²	Price (CHF)		
		Inexpensive	Moderate	Expensive
0 (studio)	30-40	100-150,000	125-175,000	150-200,000
1	50-60	200-250,000	250-350,000	350-450,000
2	75-90	300-400,000	400-550,000	550-750,000
3	90-125	400-550,000	550-650,000	650-850,000
4	125-150	550-650,000	650-750,000	750-1m+
5 or more	150+	600-700,000	700-800,000	1m+

major city centres and luxury properties, the sky's the limit!

Mortgages

Switzerland has a large and sophisticated mortgage (*Hypotheke, hypothèque*) market, which is the cornerstone of its flourishing banking system. The country's unique mortgage system features the highest per capita mortgage indebtedness in the world, interest rates which almost never vary more than 2 to 3 per cent, and the highest withholding tax rate of any country.

The major mortgage lenders in Switzerland are the large national banks and the cantonal banks, although mortgages are also provided by regional, co-operative and savings banks (all Swiss banks are generally allowed to grant mortgages). The high level of foreign deposits in Switzerland, coupled with a high rate of domestic savings and the small population, results in a high rate of per capita mortgage indebtedness. Because of the vast mortgage debt, the mortgage rate is the leading interest rate indicator in Switzerland and has traditionally been kept low thanks to the huge capital inflows into the country and interest rate cartels maintained by Swiss banks.

There's also a direct link between the mortgage interest rate and inflation, where the rate of inflation is increased markedly by minor mortgage rate increases which have a direct affect on rents, which are in turn included in the Consumer Price Index (CPI) used to calculate inflation. Rising interest rates push up rental rates, which then exert upward pressure on wages, which are also tied to the CPI, leading to what is commonly referred to as the 'price-wage spiral'. Therefore, the mortgage rate isn't just a leading interest rate indicator but is of major political importance, as it directly involves most Swiss and foreign residents, whether they're property owners, tenants or savers (the Swiss are the world's biggest savers).

Swiss regulations determine that rents for residential and business premises are dependent upon a reference interest rate (currently 3 per cent) set by the Swiss National Bank. The reference rate is based on the volume-weighted average interest rate of Swiss franc-denominated domestic mortgages held by banks in Switzerland, and is published quarterly. If the newly published reference rate doesn't correspond to the rate for variable-rate mortgages previously used for rental agreements, a landlord or tenant is entitled to call for the rent to be increased or decreased, as applicable.

The Purchase Process

Property conveyance must be done by a notary (*Notar, notaire*), whose primary role is to protect

the interests of the buyer. In any case, due to the complexities of Swiss property ownership laws, it would be almost impossible to find your way through the paper jungle without a notary. On completion of the purchase and registration of ownership, legal fees, land registry fees and a transfer tax (*Handänderungssteuer, droits de mutation*) totalling from 2.5 to 5 per cent of the purchase price, are payable to the notary. The sale of real estate doesn't incur VAT, although it's payable on materials and labour, e.g. if you're building your own home, and isn't refundable.

Take care before signing any legal papers in connection with buying property and have your lawyer and lender check all contracts.

EXTRA COSTS

Extra costs (*Nebenkosten/NK, charges/frais annexes*) or supplementary charges for services are payable in addition to the monthly rent of an apartment and are also payable by apartment owners. These usually total around 10 per cent of the rent, although it can be more – usually, the lower the rent the higher the extra costs are as a percentage of the rent. When a property is advertised, it's usually stated whether extra costs are included in the rent (usually a net figure is shown for the rent with extra costs shown separately). If there's no mention of extra costs in a lease (see below) it can be assumed that there aren't any, as when applicable they must be itemised in the lease.

Extra costs are usually paid along with the rent and include an estimated (*pauschal, comptes les frais annexes*) cost for communal expenses such as central heating, electricity, waste collection, water, chimney cleaning, caretaker (*Hauswart, concièrge*), cable television and maintenance. If the cost for a particular item, e.g. for heating, isn't measured individually for each apartment, then it will be split between all tenants in a building according to their apartment size (which isn't a good idea if you aren't a full-time resident). Costs depend on the actual apartment and its location in the building, and are detailed in your lease.

GARAGE OR PARKING SPACE

A garage or parking space (*Parkplatz, parking*) isn't usually included in the rent or purchase price of an apartment and must usually be rented or bought separately. A single lock-up garage or a parking space in an underground garage is usually available in modern apartment blocks, and costs from CHF 130 to 180 per month and an outside parking space from CHF 50 to 100. Most developments have adequate parking for both tenants and visitors (which is a legal requirement). If an apartment block has no parking spaces, it may be possible to rent one nearby, for example in the underground garage of a hotel or in a private car park. The rent varies considerably and can be anything from CHF 100 to 500+ (e.g. in central Geneva or Zurich) per month.

Note that sometimes you're required to rent a parking space as a condition of renting an apartment, whether you want it or not!

You must sign a separate lease for a garage if it isn't rented with your apartment. It's possible to rent a garage for the winter months only, although the lease may need to start and end on fixed dates, for example from 1st October to 1st April (see also **Termination** on page 65). A garage is useful, particularly in winter – unless of course you enjoy trying to find your car among the snow drifts – and it also keeps your car cool in summer.

Most property websites (see **Finding Accommodation** above) also contain advertisements for parking space rentals and sales.

HOUSE RULES

All apartment blocks have house rules (*Hausordnung, règlement d'immeuble*) – which apply whether you're an owner or tenant – some of which may be dictated by your local community

and enforceable by law, particularly those regarding noise and siesta periods. You should receive a copy on moving into your apartment; if you don't understand them you should have them translated.

House rules generally include the following (basically, anything that isn't compulsory is strictly forbidden!):

♦ Entrances, landings, stairwells, corridors and fire escape routes must be kept free of obstructions. It's prohibited to place objects in stairwells. You aren't permitted to leave footwear or items such as children's toys in public areas or outside your door in the stair well.

♦ The building and its surrounds must be kept clean and tidy at all times.

♦ A noise curfew between 10pm and 6am (times may vary). The Swiss generally take this very seriously, as most go to bed early and rise at the crack of dawn. They may hammer on your door, walls, floor or ceiling, or even call the police if you play music or hold a noisy party after 10pm. It may be forbidden to play a musical instrument for more than two hours a day.

♦ If you have a party you must warn your neighbours, but don't be surprised if it results in complaints about too much noise – even inviting your neighbours to a party doesn't always do the trick, as they've been known to call the police and complain about the noise as soon as they're back in their own apartments! Some apartment blocks have a party room.

♦ Absolutely no loud noise, e.g. drilling, banging in nails or playing loud music on Sundays and public holidays. Sunday is a day of rest, when working is forbidden by law.

♦ A siesta (*Mittagsruhe*, *sieste*), e.g. from noon to 1 or 2pm, during which time you mustn't make any loud noise. This is to allow young children and pensioners (and exhausted writers) an undisturbed afternoon nap.

♦ Small house pets such as birds in cages, guinea pigs and fish can usually be kept without permission, but written permission is usually required to keep cats, dogs, parrots or reptiles. If pets are allowed, it's forbidden to let them run wild in public areas (e.g. playgrounds) and owners must clean up after them.

♦ Non-smokers on stairs, in lifts or in other communal areas and rooms – some landlords will only rent to non-smokers.

♦ No installations (e.g. satellite dishes, flags, signposts, etc.) in communal rooms, on balconies or patios, or on the outside of the building without the written permission of the management.

♦ Flower boxes on balconies and window boxes must be secure. It's necessary to take care when watering and ensure that water doesn't drip onto the wall or the neighbours' windows, balconies or vehicles.

♦ Rubbish must be put in the rubbish containers provided and separated for recycling where possible. It's forbidden to put toxic substances and large objects in rubbish containers.

♦ Children are required to use play areas and are forbidden to play in cellars, on grass areas, in underground car parks or in other communal areas. Parents are required to tidy play areas after their children, e.g. put away toys.

♦ It may be forbidden to barbecue with charcoal on balconies.

♦ Hanging net curtains at your windows is compulsory in some apartments.

♦ Airing bedding, i.e. hanging it from windows, may be permitted only at certain times, which may be dictated by cantonal law.

♦ It's forbidden to park in the courtyard, on a path or on the grass. It's also prohibited to wash a car or motorcycle (unless there's a area set aside for this) or do any repairs on the property. Drivers must drive slowly when entering the car park or parking.

♦ Bicycles must be stored in the bicycle rack or in the bicycle room provided.

♦ Sunblinds must be rolled in at night and during rain and storms.

♦ Windows in the cellar, stairwells and roof must be kept closed during the cold winter months.

♦ If a roster exists for the use of the laundry room, you're only permitted to use it during your allotted times. Usually a laundry room can be used only between 7am and 9pm, Mondays to Saturdays. It's forbidden to use it on Sundays and national holidays. Machines must be cleaned after use.

☑ SURVIVAL TIP

No toilet flushing between 10pm and 6am; a request to gentlemen to 'please sit down when using the toilet between these hours' was even displayed in an expensive apartment block in Zurich (presumably with very thin walls).

♦ Airing a few times a day (two windows open on opposite sides to create a through draft), particularly in winter, for around five minutes (unless your apartment has an automatic air circulation system). When not airing, windows must be closed in winter and can be left in the semi-open position only during the summer months.

♦ The building entrance door and other entrance doors (e.g. cellar and garage entrances) must be kept locked between 10pm and 6am.

♦ Any damage to an apartment or the communal areas of the building must be reported to your landlord or the management ASAP.

You should take the house rules seriously, as repeated transgressions (e.g. making too much noise) can lead to a police fine or even eviction. (Your Swiss neighbours will usually be happy to point out any transgression of house rules!) Most of the above regulations are listed in the house rules of most apartment blocks.

If disputes between neighbours cannot be resolved between tenants or owners (e.g. complaints regarding noise or untidiness), tenants can call on the caretaker (*Hausmeister, concierge*) or house management (*Hausverwaltung, régie*) to mediate or make a decision. Together, the caretaker and management are responsible for the day-to-day running and organising repairs.

KEYS

You usually receive three keys to an apartment or house and two keys for the post box. You must ensure that you receive all the keys stated in the lease or inventory and the correct number – and check that they work! Note that with some locks, you need to pull up the handle to lock or unlock a door. Your house key may also fit your garage door (and everything else) or you may receive a garage remote control, although the doors to underground garages are normally opened with a key.

If you require extra keys you must pay for them. The locks fitted to most apartments and houses are usually of a high security type; keys have individual numbers and copies cannot be cut at a local hardware store. If you require additional keys you must ask your landlord or agent, who'll arrange for copies to be made and sent to you (along with the bill).

If you lock yourself out of your apartment (or car), there's usually a local locksmith on call day and night to help. Ask the telephone operator (☎ 1811) for the number. This service is, however, very expensive and it may be cheaper to break a window to gain entry to your apartment (difficult if you live on the 14th floor!). Whatever you do, don't call a locksmith out at night or at weekends – it could bankrupt you (stay with a friend). Your landlord or agent will have a copy of your house keys, but isn't permitted to enter the premises without your permission.

If you vacate your apartment for an extended period, it may be obligatory to notify your caretaker (*Hauswart/concierge*) and leave a key with him or with a neighbour in case of emergencies. If you don't have all the copies of your keys when you vacate an apartment, the barrel of a lock for which you've lost a key may need to be changed at your expense; if it's a 'pass' key for the main entrance to your building (and possibly the cellar, garage and laundry room), you could be charged for changing all the locks in the building and providing new keys for all the owners/tenants!

Most house keys are security keys and coded, and anyone finding a key can drop it in a post box

and the post office will send it to the company that made it. They in turn will return the key to you (or the landlord) along with a payment slip for CHF 25 to cover their costs and the finder's fee (they pay the finder a reward, if known).

If you're a habitual key loser, there are a number of companies that provide a key-return service, such as 🖥 www.keyfinder.ch. For CHF 6 per year (five-year contract CHF 30) they'll provide you with a coded tag which you attach to your key-ring. A message on the tag asks anyone finding the keys to drop them in the nearest post box. Return rates of over 90 per cent are claimed, including keys lost outside Switzerland.

REMOVALS

After finding an apartment, it normally takes just a few weeks to have your belongings shipped from within Europe – from anywhere else it varies considerably. If you're flexible about the date, it's cheaper to have your move done as a part load, rather than an individual delivery. If large items of furniture need to be taken in through an upstairs window or balcony, you may need to pay extra. Obtain a number of estimates in writing before committing yourself, as costs vary considerably. However, you should be wary of a company whose estimate is much lower than others. Some removal companies will promise anything to obtain a contract and increase the cost later, and many don't deliver on the planned date. Always use an established removal company with a good reputation. Check that a company uses its own

vans and staff, as some companies use sub-contractors, known in the trade as 'cowboys'.

For international house moves it's best to use a company that specialises in international removals. Try to use a removal company that's a member of an organisation such as the Federation of International Furniture Removers (FIDI, 🖳 www.fidi.com) or the Overseas Moving Network International (OMNI, 🖳 www.omnimoving.com). These, and some national removal companies, are usually members of an advance payment scheme that provides a guarantee: if a member company fails to fulfil its commitments to a client, the removal will be completed at the agreed cost by another company or your money will be refunded.

Make a list of everything to be moved and give a copy to the removal company. Don't include anything illegal (e.g. guns, bombs, drugs or pornography) with your belongings, as customs checks can be rigorous and penalties severe. Give your removal company a telephone number and address in Switzerland where you can be contacted, and ask a relative or friend to handle any 'problems' in the country from where your belongings are being shipped.

Be sure to fully insure your household contents during removal with a reputable insurance company. It isn't advisable to insure with a shipping company which carries its own insurance as it will usually fight every cent of a claim. In some countries most removal companies' insurance policies restrict their liability to a pittance, which also applies to goods held in storage. It's advisable to make a photographic or video record of valuables for insurance purposes.

If you need to make a claim, be sure to read the small print, as some companies require you to make claims within three or seven days. Any claims outside this period aren't considered! Send your claim by registered post. If you need to put your household effects into storage, it's imperative to have them fully insured against fire, as warehouses occasionally burn down (often as a result of arson). Note also that many warehouses have no fire alarms, sprinklers or fire-fighting equipment. It's better to be safe than sorry!

If you plan to transport your belongings to Switzerland personally, check the customs requirements in the countries you must pass through. To expedite customs formalities, it's advisable to inform Swiss customs of the date and approximate time of your arrival in Switzerland. If your household and personal effects are sent unaccompanied, the receiving freight company sends you a customs form to be completed and signed. In addition, they require a photocopy of your residence permit, a copy of the personal details' pages of your passport and proof of accommodation, e.g. a copy of a rental contract.

For removals within Switzerland, vans and trucks can be rented by the hour, half-day, or day (local rental companies are the cheapest). Some companies allow employees the use of a company vehicle free of charge. Many removal companies sell packing boxes in numerous sizes and rent or sell removal equipment (e.g. trolleys and straps) for those who feel up to doing their own house moving.

☑ SURVIVAL TIP

Make sure that the insurance covers your belongings for their true value and have the policy small print checked by an expert.

Bear in mind when moving home that everything that can go wrong often does, therefore allow plenty of time and try not to arrange your move to a new home on the same day as the previous owner is moving out. That's just asking for fate to intervene! Last but not least, if your Swiss home has poor or impossible access for a large truck, you must inform the shipping company (the ground must also be firm enough to support a heavy vehicle). If necessary, you can ask the local police to reserve a parking space for a removal truck when moving house (at a cost of around CHF 50).

The cost of moving your house contents from your previous country of residence to Switzerland may be paid for by your Swiss employer. You're officially allowed a day off work when moving house (provided you don't move every month!). See also **Customs** on page 52 and **Chapter 20**.

UTILITIES

Utilities include electricity, gas and water services (*Städtische Werke-Elektrizität, Gas und Wasser, centrale des services techniques: électricité, gaz, eau/services industriels*). This section also includes information about central heating, the cost of which may be included in your apartment's monthly charges (*Nebenkosten/NK, charges/frais immobiliers*).

Registration & Billing

You don't always need to apply to your local electricity, gas and water companies to have your supply connected and/or transferred to your name, which may be done automatically by your landlord or community, although a deposit (e.g. CHF 250) is required in some areas.

You're billed quarterly and can pay your bills by direct debit from a bank account. You may receive a single bill for your electricity, gas, water and sewerage, or separate bills. Meters are usually read every six months, so that the first bill in a six-month period (i.e. after three months) is an estimate, and the second bill contains an itemised list of your actual consumption and costs. If you think the estimate is wildly inaccurate, you can ask for an adjustment.

Electricity

The electricity supply in Switzerland is 220 volts AC, 10 amps maximum, with a frequency of 50 hertz (Hz). This is suitable for all electrical equipment with a power consumption of up to 2,200 watts. For equipment with a higher power consumption (e.g. oven, washing machine, dishwasher, etc.), a single or three-phase 380 volts AC, 20-amp supply is necessary.

A low-cost electricity rate is in operation from around 8pm to 6 or 7am, Mondays to Fridays, Saturday afternoons and all day on Sundays, depending on the area and the time of the year (good times to run a washing machine, dryer or dishwasher).

Converters & Transformers

Electrical equipment rated at 110 volts AC (for example from the US) without a voltage switch requires a transformer to convert it to 220 volts AC, which are available from electrical retailers in Switzerland. Some electrical appliances (e.g. electric razors and hair dryers) are fitted with a 110/220 volt switch. Check for the switch, which may be inside the casing, and make sure that it's switched to 220 volts before connecting it to the power supply.

Fuses, Plugs & Bulbs

ost apartments and all houses have their own fuse boxes, which may be of two types. Older houses may have screw fuses with a coloured disk, which when it isn't displayed indicates that the fuse has blown. These fuses, which have different amp ratings, can be purchased in electrical stores and supermarkets. The other type of fuse, found in newer houses and apartments, consists of a simple switch, which when a circuit is overloaded, trips to the OFF position. After locating and remedying the cause, simply switch it back to the ON position.

Switzerland has three different plug configurations with two, three or five contact

points (including the earth) and a 16-amp rating. Modern Swiss plugs are of the two- or three-pin or two-pin/earth socket type. Pins are round with a 4mm diameter, with live and neutral pins 2cm apart. Electric light bulbs are of the Edison screw type. Bayonet-fitting bulbs for British-type lamp fittings aren't available in Switzerland but can be purchased in France. As in EU countries, from 1st January 2010, only energy-efficient electric light bulbs have been sold in Switzerland.

 Caution

In most cantons, only a qualified electrician is allowed to install electrical wiring and fittings, particularly in connection with fuse boxes.

Gas

Gas is piped from Germany, the Netherlands and France to the major Swiss cities, but isn't used in many homes, although its use is rising and it now accounts for around 15 per cent of total energy consumption (mainly industrial). If you want to cook by gas, you may be able to find a house or apartment that has it, or you can buy a combined electric/gas cooker, where the gas is provided by gas bottles.

Water

Water is usually hard in Switzerland with a high calcium content, which means that you'll need a copious supply of decalcification liquid to keep your kettle, iron and other equipment and utensils clean. Stainless steel pots and pans stain quickly when used to boil water, and should be cleaned soon after use. Tap and shower filters must be decalcified regularly. You can have decalcification equipment installed (or a water softener) in your water system, which is rarely fitted as standard equipment in apartments. There are various systems available, most of which are expensive and not all are effective. Distilled water, or water melted from ice from your refrigerator or freezer, should be used in steam irons (mineral water is also okay).

Water rates are calculated by one of two methods. If your apartment has a water meter, you're billed for the amount of water you use. Otherwise, you pay a fixed rate according to the size of your house or apartment and possibly the number of taps. In Zurich, water costs around CHF 2.50 per cubic metre – there have been large increases in some areas in recent years.

In Switzerland, the left tap is always the hot water tap.

Security Measures

Before moving into a new home you should check where the main stop-valve or stopcock is located so that you can turn off the water in an emergency. If the water stops flowing for any reason, you should ensure that all the taps are turned off to prevent flooding when the supply starts again. In community properties, the tap to turn the water on or off may be located outside the building.

When leaving a property empty for an extended period, particularly during the winter when there's the possibility of freezing, you should turn off the main stopcock, switch off the system's controls and drain the pipes, toilets (you can leave salt in the toilet bowls to prevent freezing) and radiators. It's also recommended that you have your cold water tank and the tank's ball valves checked periodically for corrosion and to check the hoses on appliances such as washing machines and dishwashers. It can be very expensive to repair the damage if a pipe bursts, particularly if the leak goes undiscovered for a long time!

Central Heating

Most apartments in Switzerland have central heating (*Zentralheizung, chauffage central*), the cost of which is included in your extra costs (see above). Heating is usually switched on in the autumn and off in the spring by the caretaker or landlord, or it may be thermostatically controlled all year round (you can usually set the temperature in your own apartment and switch off individual radiators). In most apartment blocks, the cost of heating for the whole building is divided among tenants according to their apartment size, while in others radiators may be individually metered, so you pay only for the heating you use. All modern apartments have under-floor heating.

WASTE DISPOSAL

Switzerland produces around 700kg of waste per head of population annually, around half of which is recycled. The country has one of the highest rates of waste recycling in the world, and most Swiss religiously sort their rubbish (where there's muck, there's money!), which in many cases is obligatory. Recycling is a way of life in Switzerland, where there's a successful national campaign to reduce household waste under the slogan 'reduce, reuse and recycle' (see **Recycling** below). Large apartment blocks may have different coloured bins for different types of waste.

For non-recyclable waste, most apartments have large rubbish disposal bins in which rubbish must be deposited in special plastic bags (*Kehrichtsäcke, sacs à ordures*). In most communities, you must use only 'official' (taxed) bags, usually coloured and printed with the community name, sold in local stores and supermarkets (only at the checkout to prevent theft!). Regular rubbish bags aren't official and cannot be deposited in the rubbish disposal bins in most communities, unless they have a 'tax stamp' attached – in some areas, you must buy 'tax stamps' (sold at the town hall or other council offices), which are affixed to regular (non-taxed) rubbish bags before disposal. Rubbish is usually collected weekly.

Rubbish bags come in various sizes (e.g. 17, 35, 60 and 110 litres), each with a different tax, e.g. CHF 2.50 (35-litre) to CHF 6.50 (110-litre) each, which varies according to the community and/or canton. Waste deposited in these bags is usually restricted to materials that can be incinerated. If you use unofficial rubbish bags, they won't be collected and the local waste 'detective' may track you down and fine you, e.g. CHF 100.

The aim is to encourage recycling and avoid the unnecessary use of wrapping and packaging, which prompts most people to deposit unwanted packaging in supermarket bins specially provided for this purpose. It must be working, as since the tax was introduced, waste has been reduced by over 50 per cent in many areas. Some communities, however, charge residents an annual waste tax, e.g. CHF 30, irrespective of the amount of waste they generate.

In some communities you may need to buy a dustbin (trash can), which is usually emptied once a week.

Recycling

Many kinds of waste are recycled or reused in Switzerland – where recycling is a very serious business – and all major towns and cities have recycling centres. Most cities organise a home pick-up of certain recyclable waste and publish an annual recycling collection calendar – which may also be published online – and you may even be able to sign up to receive a text reminder the night before collections! There's a charge for the collection of some waste.

The following waste is recycled in most communities:

♦ Paper and cardboard should be tied in bundles with string and shouldn't include any plastic or metal, e.g. covers or bindings. Don't pack papers into paper or plastic bags for street pick-up as this isn't permitted. If you do it wrong it will be left and labelled 'not fit for collection'! Collection is organised by the community each month (for paper and cardboard), although in some communities there are no collections and it must be deposited in a special container or storage area.

♦ Large objects, for example, old furniture, carpets, skis and appliances, are collected periodically (e.g. once a month) in some areas (or on request), usually just after the official house moving dates (dates are announced in local newspapers). Second-hand 'junk' and furniture stores, often operated in aid of charities such as the Red Cross or Salvation Army, may collect old furniture free of charge.

♦ Bottles and glass should be deposited in bottle banks provided in all towns and villages. Bottle banks are divided into sections for green, brown and clear bottles. Their use may be restricted; for example, no deposits between 8pm and 7 or 8am and on Sundays and public holidays (or as listed). Some bottle banks are reserved for large bottles (0.5l or larger) of all colours, which are washed and reused. Switzerland is the world leader in glass recycling with an over 90 per cent recovery rate. There's a returnable deposit of CHF 0.30 to 0.50 on most one-litre glass bottles, so don't throw them away but return them to the store.

♦ Tin cans can be taken to collection areas or deposited in can-crunching machines. They should be washed and squashed flat after the label, lid and base have been removed, and should be deposited only in the specified container.

♦ Household cooking oils shouldn't be flushed down sinks as they clog the pipes. Most communities have oil bins and designated dumps for motor oil.

♦ Hazardous and toxic waste, such as chemicals, paints, thinners and varnishes, can be returned to the point of sale or taken to a hazardous waste collection point.

♦ Batteries should be returned to retailers, who must provide containers; or taken to a designated dump (some are recycled). Car batteries should be returned to a garage.

♦ Aluminium (e.g. cans, tops and frozen food containers) may be taken to collection areas. A magnet is built into containers for aluminium waste: if it's magnetic, it isn't aluminium.

♦ Vegetable or organic waste, including garden rubbish, may be collected and used as compost (designated green bins may be provided next to your housing rubbish bins) – or you can make your own compost heap if you have a garden.

♦ Old clothes are collected by charitable organisations, usually once or twice a year. You usually receive special bags (e.g. Tex-Aid in Zurich) by mail. In some communities, women's groups organise a clothes exchange once or twice a year and collect and sell nearly-new clothing for a small commission. Old shoes are collected by local shoe stores in

recycling machine

some towns and sent to third-world countries (opticians may also collect old spectacles for the same purpose).

♦ Unused medicines and poisons should be returned for disposal to a chemist (pharmacy) or to the shop where they were purchased.

♦ Old electronics products, computers, household appliances and tyres can be returned to the vendor, who must take them back (but may charge for the service); although when buying new appliances, such as a refrigerator, the vendor may take your old one away free of charge.

♦ Plastic (PET) bottles must be flattened and deposited at the PET bottle drop at the store where you bought them.

In communities with a recycling centre, there are sometimes collection bins for other types of waste, e.g. soft PVC, metal (other than that specified above), electrical apparatus, mineral items, books (which other people can take for free), and various other waste such as cork, broken flower pots, china, etc.

All communities publish instructions regarding what to do with different waste and a list of waste collection times and depots. Many large stores, e.g. the Co-op, Manor and Migros, have collection bins for aluminium, batteries, tins and certain types of bottles.

▲ Caution

The indiscriminate dumping of rubbish is strictly forbidden in Switzerland.

HOME HELP

The following pages contain information about the various types of home help available in Switzerland, which may be of particular interest to working parents. All the organisations mentioned below are listed in local telephone directories or registered with your local community.

Part-time

If you require part-time domestic help (*Putzfrau*, *femme de ménage*) there are various ways to find someone:

♦ Place an advertisement (*Inserat, annonce*) in your local newspaper. This is usually the cheapest way of finding help. Your community

may have a notice board (*Notizbrett*, *tableau d'affichage*) where you can place a free advertisement, and many stores and supermarkets, e.g. Migros and the Co-op, have a free or inexpensive notice board.

♦ Look under 'positions wanted' (*Stellengesuche*, *marché du travail*) in your local newspapers.

♦ Contact employment agencies (*Stellenvermittlungsbüro, bureau de placement*) listed in your local telephone directory. This is the most expensive way to find home help. Expect to pay a minimum of around CHF 25 per hour – twice as much if you use an agency. The advantage is that employees are usually vetted.

You must pay old age and survivor's insurance and accident insurance (see page 178) for a part-time domestic help.

Many communities provide families with a cleaning and general household service (including cooking) when the housewife (or househusband) is ill, which is cheaper if you're a member of a local housekeeping and nursing service association.

Full-time

There are regulations concerning the employment of full-time domestic helpers (*Diener/Dienerin*, *domestique*) in Switzerland. These include minimum salaries, maximum working hours, meal allowances, time off and paid holiday. Regulations are usually detailed in a booklet available from the cantonal authorities. Salaries may vary considerably according to the nationality, age and experience of domestic staff. If your help isn't a Swiss national (unlikely) and doesn't have a C permit, you must apply for work and residence permits and pay his or her pension and accident insurance. Tax must be deducted at source from the salary and all associated paperwork must be completed. Bringing a foreign servant with you to Switzerland is usually difficult (unless you're an ambassador!) and may be permitted only in exceptional circumstances upon proof of a special need.

Au Pairs

Regulations concerning the employment of au pairs vary from canton to canton. In some cantons priority is given to working mothers, while in others a mother must spend a minimum number of hours a week with the au pair, thus restricting her ability to work full-time. A permit for an au pair is issued for up to 18 months. Although families may hire a succession of au pairs, parents should take care that young children aren't unsettled by the frequent change of 'minder'. It may be better from your child's point of view to find a local person who will work for you for several years.

English-speaking families in Switzerland are unable to employ a Swiss or foreign au pair who wants to learn English. However, if one parent is a native German, French or Italian speaker, and the family speaks that language at home, they may be given permission to employ an au pair wishing to learn that language. For more information, see **Au Pairs** on page 29.

Baby-sitters

Some women's organisations, for example American Women's Clubs, have baby-sitting lists or circles (see **Appendix A**). The Red Cross (💻 www.srk.ch) runs a training and referral service in some areas. (It may even be worthwhile starting your own baby-sitting circle with other local couples.) Globesitters (💻 www.globesitters. org – in English and German) is an organisation that brings together families who need a nanny, au-pair, nurse or babysitter with those providing these services. It's free to sign up and families pay a fee to use services.

Alternatively you can use a baby-sitting agency (*Babysitter-Vermittlungsbüro, agence de babysitting*), which are found in major towns and cities. The hourly rate charged by baby-sitting agencies depends on the number of children to be cared for, and you must also pay for public transport for your baby-sitter to and from your home (if applicable). If this is unavailable, you must take him or her home yourself or pay for a taxi. In rural areas, some communities keep a list of local baby-sitters. You can also advertise for a baby-sitter in your local newspaper or on a supermarket notice board.

The cost of a baby-sitter varies from around CHF 15-20 an hour for a person found through word of mouth to more than double for someone from an agency. A qualified nurse can be hired from a nursing agency to look after children with special medical needs.

Many villages and towns run a child minding service (*Kinderhütedienst, garderie d'enfants*) which provides baby-sitting facilities during the day for working mothers, and some village women's groups take care of pre-school-age children one afternoon a week. Child minding services are also provided by 'day mothers' (*Tagesmütter, Mamans de jour/gardiennes d'enfants*), whose fees are from around CHF 10-15 per hour (sometimes calculated according to income and not a flat rate for all), plus meals. To take advantage of the 'day mother' child care programme, you must be a member of the Day

Mothers Association (fees are around CHF 100 per year). Placement fees are an additional CHF 100 (young children) to CHF 200 (babies). Children aged from three to five are usually accepted.

Many holiday resorts have nurseries where you can leave your children while you ski or hike and child-minding centres (*Kinderparadies, paradis des enfants*) are also provided by many shopping centres and large stores.

Playgroups & Day Care Centres

There are playgroups (*Spielgruppe, groupe de jeux/classe enfantine*) for children in all cities, but few in rural areas. Children usually need to be aged over three or at least be toilet trained to be accepted. Groups usually meet for two to three hours, several times a week.

Day care centres (*Kinderhort, crèche*) are also quite common and accept children of any age. Children are usually accepted on a part-time basis as often as required, although some centres provide full-time care only. They provide hot lunches, daytime sleeping facilities and outdoor activities. Fees are usually fixed, but are sometimes reduced for low-income families.

harbour, Geneva

POSTALE

6.
POSTAL SERVICES

There's a post office in most towns in Switzerland, although some smaller post offices have been closed in recent years. In addition to the usual post office services to be found in most countries, the Swiss post office provides a number of unique services, many of which are described in this chapter. In surveys, the Swiss postal service is consistently rated one of the world's best (if not the best) delivering some 15m letters, newspapers and magazines and half a million parcels a year; it's also the second-largest employer in Switzerland. Information (in English, French, German and Italian) about post office services is available online (🖥 www.post.ch).

All main post offices now include shops selling stationery items plus cameras, mobile phones, toys and books.

BUSINESS HOURS

Post office business hours in Switzerland vary enormously, for example the main post office in Zurich (Kasernenstrasse 95) is open continuously from 6.30am until 10.30pm, Mondays to Fridays and may also open on Saturdays. Smaller post offices in city suburbs and large towns usually open later, for example any time between 7.30am and 9am and usually close at midday, e.g. from between 11am and noon until 1.30 or 2pm.

Main post offices in major towns don't close for lunch and may provide limited services for urgent business outside normal business hours. The opening hours for all post offices can be found on the Swiss Post website (🖥 www.post.ch/en – enter the town under 'Locations and opening hours' on the right of the screen).

LETTER POST

Switzerland has a two-speed letter and parcel postal service: 'A' and 'B' class for domestic mail and 'Economy' and 'Priority' for international letters and parcels. 'A' class domestic mail is usually (around 99 per cent) delivered the day after posting and costs CHF 1 for items up to size B5 (250 x 176mm) and 100g; CHF 1.30 for items up to B5 and 101 to 250g; CHF 2 for items from size B5 to B4 (353 x 250mm) weighing up to 500g and CHF 4 for items weighing from 501g-1kg.

Delivery of 'B' class domestic mail takes two to three working days and costs CHF 0.85 for items up to B5 and 100g; CHF 1.10 up to B5 and 101-250g; and CHF 1.80 for items from B5 to B4 weighing up to 500g.

A class stamps have a screen printed on them to allow for automatic sorting and an *A Prioritaire* sticker is required for A class/Priority mail to European and overseas addresses. In most of Europe, international priority mail takes 2-3 days (3-7 days to the USA) and economy mail 4-7 days (7-15 days to the USA). Delivery times for international letters are shown on the Swiss Post website.

The cost of sending standard letters and postcards in Switzerland weighing up to 100g is shown in the table overleaf..

Letter Notes

Note the following when posting letters in Switzerland:

♦ Letters up to 50mm thick and up to 2kg can be sent within Switzerland for a surcharge of up to CHF 9. Larger letters are classed as parcels (see below).

♦ It's necessary to use an *A Prioritaire* or airmail (*Luftpost, par avion, via aerea*) label for Priority class international mail, although all letters to Western European countries are transported by air, including economy mail.

♦ Post for the blind weighing up to 7kg is delivered free.

♦ Letters sent with insufficient postage are usually delivered, but not by A-Post. If known,

			Price (CHF.)					
Size	Weight	Thickness	Switzerland		Zone 1 (Europe)		Zone 2 (Rest of World)	
			A	B	A	B	A	B
B6/B5 (incl. postcards)	Up to 20g	20mm	1.00	0.85	1.40	1.30	1.90	1.60
B6/B5	21 to 50g	20mm	1.00	0.85	2.60	2.20	3.80	2.80
B6/B5	51 to 100g	20mm	1.00	0.85	3.70	2.90	5.00	3.60

Cost of Sending Letters

In the above table, A is priority mail and B is economy.

the sender is sent a card showing the postage due plus a surcharge of CHF 0.50, to which he must affix stamps equal to the amount due and re-post (this actually functions well!). If you receive a letter with insufficient postage (and the sender is unknown), you're required to pay the postage due, either to the postperson or at your local post office (a collection form will be left – see **Mail Collection** below).

♦ Post boxes are yellow and are usually set into (or attached to) a wall. Post boxes near post offices and train stations are generally emptied the most frequently.

♦ There's one mail delivery a day (in the morning), including Saturdays (which is restricted to A class mail only).

♦ It's possible to send international letters and parcels by express (*Urgent*) mail to most western European countries. The fee (minimum CHF 50) depends on the size and weight of the letter or parcel. There are also a number of domestic express mail services offering guaranteed delivery and taking a maximum of two (City-Express) or five hours (Intercity-Express) or next day (Swiss-Express). If you receive an express letter, a sticker reading *Achtung!/Attention!* is affixed to your letter box or door, advising you of this. (Express mail has replaced the telegram service, which has been discontinued.)

♦ Aerogrammes (*Aerogramm, aérogramme*) are available from stationery stores or post office shops and don't include postage.

♦ Christmas surface mail should be sent by around 1st November for North America and

by 25th November for Europe. For other destinations enquire at a post office.

♦ All letters to Swiss addresses sent from outside Switzerland should have 'CH' (*Confederatio Helvetic* – Swiss stamps have 'Helvetia' written on them) before the town's post or zip code (*Postleitzahl/PLZ, numéro postal/NPA*), which is the European postal designation for Switzerland. A typical Swiss address is shown below; in German, street (*strasse*) may be abbreviated as *str.* and the house number is listed after the street name:

Heidi Schweizer
Hauptstr. 10
CH-3000 BERNE
Switzerland

All Swiss postcodes are listed in the pink section of Swiss telephone directories (see page 89). Postcodes are also available via the internet (💻 www.post.ch).

♦ A brochure showing how mail should be addressed is available from post offices. A green sticker may be attached to incorrectly addressed letters, asking you to inform your correspondent of your correct address (*Bitte richtige Adresse dem Absender melden, veuillez communiquer votre adresse exacte à l'expéditeur*).

♦ Parcels must not be tied with string (otherwise you'll be given scissors and sticky tape to re-seal it) and the address must be written in the upper right corner.

♦ A surcharge of CHF 5 is made for registered letters (*Eingeschriebener Brief/lettre*

recommandée) within Switzerland and CHF 6 for destinations outside Switzerland, plus the standard postage fee. The sender's address must be written on the back of registered letters. You receive a receipt for a registered letter or parcel. Proof of receipt (delivery) costs CHF 5, when a card is returned to the sender. Registered letters and packages can be insured. Insured registered letters and packages weighing over 1kg and with a value of over CHF 5,000 must be security sealed with wax/lead or special tape. The highest insured value for unsealed packages is CHF 5,000.

◆ Stamps (*Briefmarke*, *timbre*) can be purchased from post offices, stamp machines outside post offices, online, and from shops and kiosks selling postcards (*Postkarte*, *carte postale*). Books of five plain stamped postcards can be purchased from post offices. You can even create and print your own personalised postage stamps (🖥 www.webstamp-easy.ch).

◆ Special stamps are sold to celebrate Swiss National Day on 1st August (*Bundesfeiermarke, timbre de la fête nationale*) which have a surcharge, proceeds from which support Swiss social and cultural organisations. Other special charitable stamps are also sold occasionally (Pro Juventute, Pro Patria, Pro Natura, etc.). A magazine and brochures describing special stamps and first day covers is published for philatelists and available from main post offices.

For information about services for philatelists, see 🖥 www.post.ch/en. The website enables you to view and order stamps online (addresses are also provided for the six regional philatelist centres).

PARCEL POST

For standard domestic parcels (*Paket, paquet/ colis*) of any size, the postage depends on the weight, as shown by the examples in the table below.

Parcel Post Costs		
Weight	Class/Cost (CHF)	
	Economy	Priority
Up to 2kg	7	9
2 to 5kg	9	11
5 to 10kg	10	12
10 to 20kg	15	18
20 to 30kg	22	25

Priority parcels are delivered the next working day when posted before noon and economy parcels within two working days. International parcels may be sent by economy (delivery by rail in Europe and air elsewhere), priority (airmail, e.g. two to three days in Europe) and worldwide (courier). Airmail parcels, irrespective of the destination, take the same time to be delivered as airmail letters. A form must be completed when sending an international parcel weighing over 2kg.

The post office is strict regarding how parcels must be wrapped (see above) and how the address is written. A charge of CHF 3 for manual handling is charged for a parcel that isn't considered 'standard' (i.e. too small, too big, too thick, too thin). It's often worthwhile enquiring at a post office before sealing a parcel. A brochure is available from post offices describing how to pack goods.

Swiss post provides a TNT Swiss Post service which sends letters and packages weighing up to 30kg to over 200 countries. Each item has a barcode and can be tracked and traced online. This replaces the international post EMS (Express Mail Service). You can calculate the cost of sending a parcel via the Swiss Post website (🖥 www.post.ch). International couriers such as DHL, UPS and FED-EX also operate in Switzerland.

Parcels sent to addresses outside Switzerland must be accompanied by a customs declaration form. Parcels weighing up to 1kg and not more than 90cm in circumference require an international green customs form (CN22) and are sent at a small parcel postage rate. The value of such a parcel should generally not exceed

CHF 50. When sending an international parcel weighing over 1kg, special customs' forms must be completed. Parcels can be insured when they're sent by registered mail. Parcels sent within Switzerland can be registered for CHF 2.

Most post offices have scales and special post boxes for parcels – don't put letters in them and bear in mind that you don't receive a receipt when using a post box. For parcels to the US, check the latest regulations and/or restrictions with Swiss Post.

Cardboard boxes, called POST PACs, and padded 'jiffy' bags (*Luftpolster Couvert, enveloppe capitonée*) are available from post offices and most department and stationery stores. POST PACs are available in seven sizes (costing from CHF 2 to 4.70) and include sealing tape.

All domestic parcels have a barcode sticker affixed to enable them and you (see 🖥 www.post.ch/trackandtrace) to track parcels and check delivery times. You receive a receipt with a matching barcode sticker, which you should retain in case of late delivery, loss or damage.

MAIL COLLECTION

If the postperson calls with mail requiring a signature, payment of duty or excess postage when you aren't at home, he'll leave a collection form (*Abholungseinladung, avis de retrait*). Present this form with some identification (for example your Swiss residence permit, passport or driving licence) at your local post office, the address of which is shown on the form. The collection form includes the date and time when the item can be collected and when it will be returned to the sender if it isn't collected (usually after seven days). This is a good reason to inform the post office if you're going to be away from home for some time (see **Change of Address** below), as they'll hold your mail for a small fee.

You can receive mail via the main post office of any town in Switzerland through the international *poste restante* (*Postlagernd*) service. Post sent to a *poste restante* address is returned to the sender if it's unclaimed after 30 days. Identification is necessary for collection (see above).

You may be able to obtain a post office box at your local post office free of charge. If you do, all your mail will be stored there and the postperson will no longer deliver to your home (it may be quicker to pick it up than wait for the postperson). You can arrange to be informed when registered or express mail arrives.

CHANGE OF ADDRESS

If you're going to be away from your home for up to two months, you can ask the post office (five days in advance) to hold your mail for the sum of CHF 10. You can either collect it at the end of the period or the postperson will deliver it on the date specified. Your mail can also be redirected to a temporary address in Switzerland (via the internet, CHF 10 for two weeks, CHF 4 for each additional week) or abroad (CHF 30 for two weeks, CHF 10 for each additional week). For a permanent change of address, mail forwarding (arranged via the internet) costs CHF 30 within Switzerland and CHF 90 abroad.

All mail sent within Switzerland, including parcels, is redirected (excluding circulars, which are returned with your new address to the sender). Only cards and letters are redirected abroad. A temporary forwarding order must be completed at your local post office. The post office provides free (no stamp required) change of address cards in local languages if you're moving house within Switzerland.

Printed matter sent from abroad, e.g. magazines, newspapers and newsletters, won't

usually be forwarded and will be returned to the sender, possibly without your new address. You may be able to request that all mail is redirected, including mail from abroad, provided you're willing to pay for the service.

If a letter is unable to be delivered due to the wrong address, the addressee no longer being at the address or the redirection period having expired, it will be returned with a note stating this, i.e. 'moved; redirection period expired' (*Weggezogen; Nachsendefrist abgelaufen, A déménagé; Délai de réexpedition expiré*).

PAYING BILLS

In contrast with many other countries, personal cheques were never the most common way to pay bills in Switzerland (and are, in fact, no longer used). Most people used to pay their bills (except when paying in cash) via the post office giro service, although nowadays they are more likely to pay them online or via their bank. An orange or red giro payment form (*Einzahlungsschein, bulletin de versement*) is usually included with every bill you receive by mail. You can take the payment form to a post office and pay it in cash at the counter, pay it at your bank in a special business machine in the lobby (for example 'multimat' at UBS) or pay it online from your bank account (e-banking). If it's a regular bill (e.g. rent) you can give your bank a permanent bank payment (standing) order.

Payment forms produced by a computer include all the necessary details including your name and address, the payee's name and account number, and the amount due. If it's a non-computerised form you need to enter these details. If you're paying in person at a post office, post office payment forms must be completed in blue or black ink and in BLOCK CAPITALS. If you make a mistake you must complete a new form as you aren't permitted to make corrections. If you're paying via your bank (e-banking/bank business machines or a permanent payment order) then it doesn't matter if you make a mistake as you can correct it.

The left hand stub of the payment form is your receipt and is stamped by the post office clerk and returned to you when you pay bills at a post office.

General Information

The Swiss don't appear as anxious to be paid as creditors in most other countries. Don't

be surprised if you aren't billed for weeks, or even months after you've received a service or purchased something – they haven't forgotten you! You aren't normally required to pay in advance when you order goods and are rarely asked to pay a deposit. You are, however, expected to pay all bills when due. The payment date (*Fällig am . . ./Zahlbar bis . . ., payable le . . ./échéance . . .*) is usually stated on the bill accompanying the giro payment form, or the number of days within which you must pay the bill. Payment is usually due immediately or within 10, 30 or 60 days. Some creditors offer a discount for prompt payment or payment in cash.

If you don't pay a bill on time, you're sent a reminder (*Mahnung, rappel/sommation*) and may be charged interest. Usually only two reminders are sent, after which your creditor may take legal action if you don't pay within the specified period.

You may receive a giro cheque (*Auszahlungsschein, bulletin de paiement*) as a payment, for example for an income tax or road tax refund. This can be cashed at any post office on production of proof of identification (Swiss residence permit, passport or driving licence).

A giro cheque must usually be cashed within four to six weeks (the validity period is printed on the cheque).

When writing figures in Switzerland (or anywhere within continental Europe) the number seven should be crossed to avoid confusion with the number one, written with a tail and looking like an uncrossed seven to many foreigners. The date is written in the standard European style, for example 10th May 2013 is written 10/5/13 (not as in the US, 5/10/13).

7.
TELECOMMUNICATIONS

Among the various reasons for Switzerland's economic success are the many unfair advantages it has over other countries, one of which is that its telephones always work. In Switzerland you rarely get a bad or crossed line and the quality and range of services are second to none. Switzerland has one of the highest numbers of (fixed-line) telephones per head of population in the world and nearly every household has one. However, the number has fallen in recent years during which mobile phone use has increased sharply.

The Swiss telecommunications market has been open to competition since 1st January 1998, when state-owned Telecom PTT became Swisscom (an independent company), which still maintains the infrastructure.

Switzerland's mobile phone system, previously operated only by Swisscom, was opened to competition several years ago with the entry of Orange and Sunrise into the market. There are also 'dozens' of internet providers in the country. As a consequence of deregulation, telephone rates have tumbled in recent years, although Switzerland is still a high-priced market compared with other European countries and the US,

A list of emergency numbers is provided on page 91.

INSTALLATION & REGISTRATION

If you move into an old apartment, i.e. any apartment where you aren't the first occupant, a telephone line will usually have been installed but there'll be no telephone. A new apartment, however, may just have a few holes in the wall in preparation for the installation of telephone sockets.

Foreigners without a C permit (see **Chapter 3**) must usually pay a deposit before they can have a telephone line connected or installed. The deposit is returned with interest when you leave the country or obtain a qualifying permit, or may be repaid after one to two years if you pay your bills regularly (although you may need to request it).

To have a telephone line installed or connected, contact your nearest Swisscom office or ☎ 0800-800 800.

Line installation is usually quick and takes an average of around seven days (where a line is already installed, connection takes one or two days) and costs around CHF 45. When you've paid your deposit, Swisscom will arrange for the connection or installation to be completed at a convenient time. If your apartment doesn't already have a telephone socket(s) installed, then you need to pay additional installation costs.

Choosing a Phone Company

After initially registering with Swisscom, you can choose your phone service provider from a number of companies including Abalon (☎ 041-747 17 00, ⌨ www.abalonag.com), EconoPhone (☎ 0800-88 188, ⌨ www.econophone.ch – owned by Sunrise), Sunrise (☎ 0800-707 707, ⌨ www.sunrise.ch), TalkTalk (☎ 0800-300 250, ⌨ www.talktalk.ch), Tele2 (☎ 0800-242 424, ⌨ www.tele2.ch – owned by Sunrise), Vtx Datacomm (☎ 0800-883 883, ⌨ www.vtxnet.ch) and, of course, Swisscom (☎ 0800-800 800, ⌨ www.swisscom.com).

The line rental fee of CHF 25.35 per month for an analog line (EconomyLINE) or CHF 43.20 for an ISDN line (MultiLINE) must be paid either to Swisscom directly or can be paid to Sunrise or TalkTalk, if they are your provider, which saves you having to pay more than one bill. One way to avoid paying a line rental fee is to choose a cable company such as Cablecom (☎ 0800-660 800, ⌨ www.cablecom.ch), which has its own cable network (including super-fast fibre broadband), although it isn't available in rural areas. There are other cable phone companies such as Datazug in Zug (⌨ www.datazug.ch).

USING THE TELEPHONE

Using a telephone in Switzerland is much the same as in any other country. Telephone numbers consist of a three-digit area code, e.g. 044 for Zurich and 022 for Geneva, and a seven-digit subscriber number. Numbers are usually written as 044 123 45 67. An area code may cover a city or a much wider area. When dialling a number in Switzerland, even a number with the same area code, you must always dial the area code.

When dialling Switzerland from overseas, you dial the local international code (e.g. 00 from the UK), followed by Switzerland's international code (41), the Swiss area code without the first 0, e.g. 44 for Zurich, and the subscriber's number. See also **International Calls** below.

Service numbers (such as six-digit 0800 numbers) are toll-free numbers provided by companies and organisations. Numbers beginning with 156, 157 and 0900/0901/0906 are service numbers (or information lines) where calls can cost a flat fee, e.g. CHF 80, or are charged per minute (e.g. CHF 5) or have a basic charge, e.g. CHF 10, in addition to an extra charge per minute, e.g. CHF 5.

⚠ **Caution**

Be wary of using 'service numbers' and be aware that it can be difficult to know numbers are service numbers and how much calls cost. They include 'sex lines', for which there's no upper limit on charges! **If you have children it's advisable to bar calls to service numbers.**

Telephone Tones

Standard telephone tones, i.e. the strange noises you hear when you aren't connected to a subscriber, are provided to indicate the progress of calls. The following standard tones are used in Switzerland and are different from those used in some other countries:

♦ **Dialling tone:** A steady note is heard after you lift the receiver, indicating that the telephone is working and that you can start dialling.

♦ **Ringing tone:** A single note repeated at intervals means that the call has been connected and the number is ringing.

♦ **Engaged tone:** A short single note repeated at rapid intervals means that the number or all lines are busy.

♦ **Information tone:** A repeated sequence of three notes in rising pitch means that the party called cannot be reached on the dialled number. If you don't understand the recorded announcement following the tone, call the operator on 1811. If you dial a non-existent number, you receive a message informing you of this and telling you to check your telephone directory. If you dial a number that has changed, you'll hear a message stating the new number or that the number no longer exists. Call 1811 and ask for the subscriber's new number.

CHARGES

Since deregulation of the Swiss telecoms market and the proliferation of new companies, it has been difficult to compare rates, although you can do so in Allo (🖳 www.allo.ch) and Comparis (🖳 www.comparis.ch). However, comparisons sites may not accurately reflect the cost of calls as companies pay to be promoted on these websites – it's better to compare actual international call rates on providers' websites. It's important to compare rates, particularly when making international calls, when huge savings can be made by choosing the cheapest company.

When using a company other than Swisscom, the company will obtain your authorisation to inform Swisscom and connect you to their network (a prefix number isn't required). If you're using a telephone company other than Swisscom – apart from Sunrise and TalkTalk – you'll still receive a monthly (possibly every two months) bill from Swisscom for the line rental, plus a separate bill from your provider for your call costs.

In addition to Swisscom, Sunrise and TalkTalk can also bill your line rental directly.

INTERNATIONAL CALLS

The Swiss (or Swiss residents) make more international calls per capita than most other nations and all private telephones in Switzerland are on International Direct Dialling (IDD). Dial 1811 for the international operator to make non-IDD calls, person-to-person calls and international enquiries. Information regarding international calls, including a world time-zone map, can be found in your local telephone directory.

To make an international call, dial 00 followed by the country code, then the area code without the first zero and finally the subscriber's number. The area codes for major towns in most countries are listed in telephone directories. If you regularly make international calls, it's important to shop around and compare rates, as huge savings can be made by choosing the cheapest carrier (see **Charges** above).

For example, TalkTalk (🖳 www.talktalk.ch) has very competitive rates for international calls and has an additional advantage in that all customers receive a free SIM card for their mobile which allows them to make international calls for the same low rates as from their fixed line (e.g. CHF 0.05 or 0.06 per minute to most European countries). TalkTalk also allow customers to make free calls to other TalkTalk customers.

Other providers also have attractive prices, but you usually need separate contracts for fixed and mobile phones. Swisscom offers what are called half-price subscriptions, where you pay a monthly flat fee in order to make national and international calls at half price; however, these 'low' rates are still more than the full price some other providers charge.

Another way to save money on international calls is to buy prepaid-cards, which you can use from any touch-pad telephone. After dialing a free access number (indicated on the card) a multi-lingual operator asks you to enter the card number followed by the subscriber's phone number. Prior to the call the operator tells you how many minutes credit you have left and whether it's sufficient for your call. This 'pedestrian' method is useful when making calls from public telephones or to exotic destinations. There are a number of companies offering telephone cards including Econophone, Telecom FL and Teleline, which cost CHF 10, 20 or 30 from post offices, kiosks, petrol stations, newsagents and shops.

However, this is a lot less convenient than simply dialling someone's number, especially when you have the number stored in your phone, and due to the rounding up of rates and expired credit you may not make much of a saving compared with the cost of the cheapest fixed-line providers.

Bear in mind that there may be an extra charge of around CHF 0.50 for card calls made from public telephones and that telephone cards have an expiry date!

DIRECTORIES

Swiss telephone subscribers are listed in directories (*Telefonbuch*, *annuaire téléphonique*) divided into cantons (the smaller cantons share directories). If you don't have the latest local directory when you move into an apartment, you can obtain one free of charge from your local post office. Directories for cantons other than your canton of residence cost around CHF 10 each.

You can also access all phone books – *White* and *Yellow Pages* – online (see 🖳 www. directories.ch or http://tel.search.ch). When using directories.ch you search for someone by their last name. However, when searching via search. ch you can find a number by entering the street address (or just the street and all those with a phone in the street will be listed), a maiden name (if it was listed in the original registration) or even a first name – you can also limit the search by entering the canton or city (if known).

Information in telephone directories is divided into sections, as follows:

1   advertising and information about entries;

2   international connections;

3   short numbers;

4   pink pages – a list of all Swiss postcodes, including the codes by street for large towns and cities;

5   white pages – private subscriber listings by town in alphabetical order (businesses and services may be listed under their type of business or service and/or their name).

Private subscribers are usually listed under the husband's name (if applicable) in telephone directories and also include the wife's maiden name (in brackets) and may include the subscriber's profession. If you want to have more than one entry in your local telephone directory, e.g. when a husband and wife both retain their family names, or when two or more people share a telephone, there's a charge each time a new directory is published. Subscribers are listed

under their town or village and not alphabetically for the whole of a canton or city. Businesses aren't always listed under their name but under a group heading, for example a restaurant may be listed under restaurants and not under its name.

Calls to directory enquiries (☎ 1811) are valid for two queries and costs CHF 1.50 plus CHF 0.70 per minute for the first minute plus CHF 0.22 per minute from the second minute. New printed directories are published every two years, although not all at the same time, while new CD directories (Twixtel) are published twice a year. The latter also usually includes a train timetable, the most important Swiss laws and other information about Switzerland.

Yellow Pages are available for most areas and for the major areas are produced by Swisscom Directories AG (Die Gelben Seiten, ☎ 0848-868 086, 🖳 www.directories.ch). While your local Yellow Pages are free, directories for other regions are relatively expensive. Unlike Swisscom directories, subscribers in the Yellow Pages are listed under a business or service heading for the whole area covered by the directory. Yellow Pages – which are also available via the internet (🖳 www.gelbeseiten.ch) – aren't as widely used in Switzerland as they are in North America or the UK, where they're indispensable. Free local telephone directories containing only business numbers are produced by council boroughs (Bezirk, district).

Swisscom has pioneered a new electronic telephone directory (Teleguide) that enables users of payphones to obtain Swiss telephone numbers and addresses at the touch of a button. Teleguides are replacing paper telephone directories in public call boxes, where you can look up several addresses and numbers for a fee of CHF 0.50 and also send emails, faxes or SMS (text messages).

MOBILE PHONES

There are three mobile phone providers in Switzerland with their own network infrastructure: Orange (🖳 www.orange.ch), Sunrise (🖳 www.sunrise.ch) and Swisscom (🖳 www.swisscom.com). There are also a number of other providers who use one of these networks, including Aldi, Co-op, Migros, Red Bull, TalkTalk and Yallo. Rates vary considerably between providers, although Swisscom's charges are the highest, but it has the best network cover. To compare rates you need to check provider's websites for the latest rate schedules.

Mobile phones – which the Swiss call a 'Natel' (natel/portable) or a 'Handy' – can be bought in department stores and specialised phone shops. Phones linked to a provider are cheaper, but there's usually a contract of 12 to 24 months which can make the telephone quite expensive, particularly if you don't use it very often.

It has been calculated than Swiss mobile users waste over CHF 3bn a year because they're on the wrong tariff!

The 'rolling renewal' system is applied, which means that if you don't cancel your contract in writing (by registered letter) by the time limit stated in your contract (usually three months before the end) then it will automatically be renewed for another year. You also need to send a registered letter to cancel your contract if you're leaving the country. Read your contract carefully and note the terms and conditions for cancelling. The Comparis website (🖳 www.comparis.ch – see 'Tips and Information') contains sample mobile phone termination letters which can be printed.

If you carry a mobile phone mainly in order to receive calls, prepaid cards (pay-as-you-go) are a more flexible option; you can either buy new cards as required or top-up your account online with a credit card. If you're looking for a solution to only pay for your use per minute, combined with a monthly bill (rather than pay-as-you-go), then you may wish to consider TalkTalk, which allow you to combine your mobile and fixed-line bills (and calls to other TalkTalk customers are free).

Most mobile phone providers offer mobile internet packages. Plans range from a nominal CHF 10 monthly fee and CHF 3.50 (Orange and Sunrise) or CHF 4.50 (Swisscom) per day charges, to all-inclusive monthly plans from around CHF 99 (including unlimited surfing). It pays to shop around and compare the various options, including those where you simply pay low rates per MB downloaded. All plans/prices are for calls within Switzerland and if you use your mobile

abroad (for calls or accessing the internet) you'll be charged very (very) high rates.

PUBLIC TELEPHONES

Most public telephones (*öffentliche Sprechstelle, téléphone public*) or payphones have International Direct Dialling (IDD). International calls can also be made via the operator. Payphones in Switzerland are owned and operated by Swisscom and most accept pre-paid cards, called Taxcards. You can buy a Taxcard for CHF 5, 10 or 20 from post offices, Swisscom shops, railway station booking offices, petrol stations, campsites, newsagents, kiosks, hotels, government buildings and hospitals.

You need to insert the Taxcard in a slot in the payphone and the cost of calls and the remaining credit on the card is indicated on a digital display. A card can be changed during a call without interrupting it, simply by inserting a new card within 30 seconds. All cards have an expiry date printed on them. Taxcards are produced in a variety of designs and (as in many other countries) have become collectors' items.

Some payphones also accept Postcards, credit cards and coins.

MOVING OR LEAVING SWITZERLAND

When moving house or leaving Switzerland, you must notify Swisscom and other telephone companies (as applicable), preferably 30 days in advance. If you move within the same code area you can retain your number.

It's particularly important to notify Swisscom early if you're leaving Switzerland and need to get a deposit refunded.

EMERGENCY NUMBERS

The national emergency numbers (*Notfallnummern, numéros d'appel en cas d'urgence*) shown in the table below, are listed on page one of all telephone directories.

The above telephone numbers are manned or provide recorded information (in the local language – French, German or Italian) 24 hours a day and can be dialled from anywhere within Switzerland.

Fire Service

The fire service, besides extinguishing fires, attending traffic accidents and natural disasters, also deals with the victims of accidents such as drowning, asphyxiation (lack of oxygen), choking, electrocution, serious burns and hanging. They're certainly the best people to call when faced with a life or death situation.

Swiss Air Rescue Service

The Swiss air rescue service (known as REGA) has 13 bases from which a helicopter or an air ambulance jet can be dispatched. Everywhere in Switzerland (except the Valais) is within 15 minutes flying time. The service also covers the whole world using jet aircraft. The cost of the REGA service is covered by Swiss third party car insurance.

You can become a member of REGA for CHF 30 a year for a single person aged over 16, or

Emergency Numbers

Tel. Number	Service
117/112	**Police** (*Polizeinotruf, police secours*) 112 is the international emergency number
118/112	**Fire** (*Feuermeldestelle, feu centrale d'alarme*) 112 is the international emergency number
144	**Ambulance** (*Sanitätsnotruf, appel sanitaire d'urgence*)
1414	**Helicopter Rescue** (REGA – *Rettung mit Helikopter, sauvetage par hélicoptère*) – see below (CHF. 0.20 per call)
145	**Poison Emergency Service** (*Vergiftungsnotfall, intoxication en cas d'urgence*); CHF. 0.08/0.04 per minute
143	**Samaritans** (*Die dargebotene Hand, La main tendue*) – see below (CHF. 0.20 per call)
140	**Vehicle Breakdown** (*Strassenhilfe, secours routier*)

CHF 60 a year for a couple. The annual fee for families, including all children aged under 18, is CHF 40 (one-parent family) or CHF 70 (two parents).

Contact REGA for information (☎ 0844-834 844, 🖳 www.rega.ch). Some towns (e.g. Sion, Zermatt) also have a local helicopter rescue service.

Samaritans

The Samaritans (*Die dargebotene Hand, la main tendue* ☎ 143, 🖳 www.143.ch; CHF 0.20 per call) provide a confidential and anonymous counselling service in times of personal crisis and receive over 200,000 calls a year. If the duty counsellor doesn't speak English, he'll ask you to call at a time when an English-speaking counsellor is present.

TeleAlarm

Swisscom provides an emergency TeleAlarm (🖳 www.telealarm.ch, ☎ 032-327 25 40) call service (*Telefon-Notruf, téléphone-alarme*) for elderly or disabled people for either a monthly rental fee (including a base station and transmitter bracelet) or it can be purchased outright. In the event of an accident, subscribers can transmit an emergency pre-recorded call for help by simply pressing a button on the bracelet.

SERVICE NUMBERS

The following service numbers (*Dienstnummern, numéros de service*) are described in the blue section at the front of telephone directories and can be called from anywhere in Switzerland. Unless specified, recorded information is given in the local canton language or languages (French, German or Italian). If you dial a service number where no information is available, you're informed via a recorded message.

THE INTERNET

The Swiss are among the world's most avid internet users. According to the internet world stats website (🖳 www.internetworldstats.com), some 85 per cent of Swiss households had internet access in 2012. Broadband (via ADSL/DSL and cable) has become increasingly popular in recent years, with around a third of subscribers choosing this option. Mobile internet access is increasingly popular and is soon expected to surpass fixed web usage in Switzerland.

There are some 150 internet service providers (ISPs) to choose from in Switzerland, so getting online is easy. Although many people still have dial-up internet, most people who have the option

Service Numbers	
Number	**Service**
1811 or 1818	National and International enquiries (**1811**: CHF. 1.50 basic fee plus CHF. 0.70 for the first minute and CHF. 0.22 from the 61st second; **1818**: CHF. 1.60 basic fee plus CHF. 0.70 for the first minute and CHF. 0.19 from the 61st second.)
1812	Automated enquiries (CHF. 0.80 plus 0.10 per minute)
140	Roadside assistance (CHF. 0.20 per call)
1600	*Regional News and information about exhibitions and fairs (CHF. 0.50 plus 0.50 per minute)
161	*Speaking clock (CHF. 0.50 per call)
162	*Weather forecasts (CHF. 0.50 plus 0.50 per minute)
163	*Traffic reports (CHF. 0.50 plus 0.50 per minute)
164	*Sports news and lottery results (CHF. 0.50 plus 0.50 per minute)
175	Fault repair service (*Störungsdienst, Service des dérangements*)
187	*Avalanche bulletins (winter) and lake wind conditions (summer, CHF. 0.50 per call)
0900 77	Automatic wake-up service (CHF. 0.50 per call)
0800 801 141	Reverse charge calls
* Recorded information	

CHF 0.06

CHF 0.00

CHF 0.10

CHF 0.08

CHF 0.07

CHF 0.06

Talk**Talk**

www.talktalk.ch
Tel 0800 300 250

to choose a broadband connection (often via cable), which is not only faster but allows you to surf the net and make phone calls on the same line at the same time. Cablecom (🖥 www.cablecom.ch/en) provide one of the fastest broadband services (via fibre optic cables) and also offer cable TV and telephone services.

Broadband fees vary with the provider and the usage, but you can expect to pay around CHF 50 per month for unlimited access and download speeds of up to 100mpbs (which is 12.5mb per second). Such a subscription typically includes a number of email addresses. There may be other initial charges such as connection fees or modem/router costs – it pays to shop around. The minimum contract length is usually one year.

Popular providers include Bluewin (☎ 0844-844 884, 🖥 www.bluewin.ch), Econophone (☎ 0800-188 188, 🖥 www.econophone.ch), Green (☎ 056-460 23 23, 🖥 www.green.ch), Orange (☎ 0800-700 700, 🖥 www.orange.ch), Sunrise (☎ 0800-707 707, 🖥 www.sunrise.ch) and Tele2 (☎ 0800-242 424, 🖥 www.tele2.ch), the last three of which have English web pages.

Cable internet access accounts for around a third of broadband subscriptions. Prices vary, for example CHF 0.33 per MB or CHF 45 per month. Major providers include Cablecom (☎ 0800-660 800, 🖥 www.cablecom.ch), Datazug (☎ 041-748 49 59, 🖥 www.datazug.ch) and Quickline (☎ 0800-841 020, 🖥 www.quickline.com). For a map showing providers by canton, visit 🖥 www.cablemodem.ch and click on '*Anbieter-/Provider-Liste*' at the top of the page. Cable isn't available in rural areas.

It's also possible to access the internet via a mobile phone. Check with your mobile service provider for the latest information and rates (see **Mobile Phones** above).

There are internet cafés in the major cities and popular tourist resorts, although fees can be very high, e.g. CHF 3 for the first 10 minutes and CHF 0.30 for each additional minute. There are hundreds of internet 'hot spots' in the major cities (see 🖥 www.hotspot-locations.com, and search using the drop down boxes), including almost 500 public hotspots (includes internet cafés) and over 1,000 commercial hot spots (including many hotels). You can purchase a Swisscom PWLAN Value Card which provides access to public hot spots at airports, railway stations, hotels, etc., although it's an expensive option (e.g. CHF 30 or 50 for limited access).

Most Swiss websites have French, German and Italian versions (German is often the default) and many are also in English; look for the language option buttons, often located at the top of the

> Most Swiss websites have French, German and Italian versions (German is often the default) and many are also in English; look for the language option buttons, often located at the top of the screen.

Lake Brienz, Berne

8.
TELEVISION & RADIO

Television (TV) and radio services in Switzerland are operated by the Swiss Broadcasting Corporation (Schweizerische Radio und Fernsehgesellschaft, Société Suisse de Radiodiffusion et Télévision – SRG/SSR), which is a private non-profit company and a public service financed by advertising and licence fees

TELEVISION

The quality of Swiss TV leaves much to be desired, although it's no worse than the fare served up in most other European countries. The German-speaking Swiss reportedly watch less TV than almost anyone in Europe and other Swiss also watch much less TV than the European average. The choice of Swiss TV stations has increased in the last few years with the introduction of numerous local cable TV companies. Cable TV is available throughout the country and some 90 per cent of homes in Switzerland receive their TV via a communal aerial or cable. Due to the wide availability of cable TV, satellite TV (see below) isn't common in Switzerland, although it's popular with expatriates.

TV programmes are listed in daily and weekly newspapers and published in weekly TV magazines. Without cable TV (i.e. using a standard antenna) you'll only be able to receive the Swiss TV channels in the interior and up to 20 channels if you live in a border area.

Television Standards

Due to differences in transmission standards, foreign TVs and video recorders (i.e. equipment made for other markets) won't always function in Switzerland. Until 2006, Switzerland used the European PAL system but in 2006 it began introducing digital TV which was rolled out across the country by early 2008. Most digital TVs and DVDs should work in Switzerland, but equipment from the US won't due to the different system employed there.

If you have an old analogue TV (as many Swiss homes still do) it won't function in Switzerland (assuming it's compatible) without a set-top digibox to receive digital TV, an HDTV or a special digital-enabled TV such as a CI+ (common interface plus) TV. The latter incorporates a slot for a smartcard and allows users to subscribe to a pay TV (cable) service without requiring a set-top box.

The amount of advertising permitted on Swiss TV is strictly controlled by the Swiss Broadcasting Corporation (☎ 031-350 91 11, 🖥 www.srg.ch) and is 8 per cent of air time.

Television Stations

In most cities and many rural areas, the vast majority of buildings are wired for cable TV (see below), which enables households to receive up to 100 channels (average around 40) and some 30 radio stations. The TV stations available include the six Swiss stations (two French, two German, two Italian) plus Austrian, French, German and Italian stations, and a variety of cable and satellite TV stations. Without cable TV, only five or six stations (including the Swiss stations) can be received, depending on the area.

The SRG/SSR is responsible for producing and relaying programmes in the four Swiss national languages (Swiss TV programmes are listed on teletext). Other stations broadcast in English, French, German or Italian. Foreign programmes, including films, are usually dubbed in the language of the broadcasting channel, the main exception being the occasional old black and white film. However, some recent films have a dual soundtrack.

Cable Television

Cable TV (*Gemeinschaftsantenne*, *antenne collective*) is available in most areas of Switzerland, but is restricted to towns and buildings wired for cable. Over 90 per cent of Swiss households are connected to a communal antenna or a cable network, making Switzerland third in the world in cable TV provision (after Belgium and the Netherlands). There are around 250 cable TV providers in Switzerland – you can find your local provider by entering your address on the Swiss Cable website (🖳 www.swisscable. ch) – which offer around 100 stations.

Cable TV consists of cable relays of Swiss and foreign national TV stations, dedicated cable-only stations and satellite stations. English-language cable TV stations are widely available and may include CNN International, Eurosport, MTV Europe and NBC Superchannel.

You can choose between various programme packages which may include sports, films, music or foreign-language (e.g. English) channels. You must pay a monthly fee and you usually have a choice of packages to choose from. Companies also offer attractive combi-packages which include digital radio and TV, broadband internet and telephone. For example, Cablecom offers a fast fibre optic internet service, free fixed-line Swiss phone calls, and pause and rewind digital TV programmes for a monthly subscription of CHF 75.

Cablecom (🖳 www.cablecom.ch/en) offers a wide choice of digital TV packages, including a 'mini' subscription for CHF 4 per month (55 digital channels plus analogue channels), a 'classic' subscription from CHF 5 per month (115 digital channels), a 'comfort' package from CHF 12.50 per month offering 165 channels including several English-language channels. All packages include a digital set-top box and a one-off activation fee of CHF 49, and include a number of HD channels. The monthly fees shown are in addition to the standard cable TV charges. You can choose to rent or buy a set-top box, which costs around CHF 150.

Cablecom also offer a DigiCard (CHF 99), which is a small plug-in card with an integrated smartcard that's used to receive digital television via the Cablecom network. An additional receiver (set-top box) isn't required if you're using the DigiCard. You do, however, need a CI+ (common interface plus) compatible TV, where the card is simply inserted in the slot provided in the TV, enabling you to receive digital channels without a digibox, including HD channels. Without a CI+ TV you'll need a set-top digibox (decoder) with a smartcard (or DigiCard), which can be rented or purchased from digital TV providers.

Cable TV isn't always available in remote areas of Switzerland, in older buildings, and in small towns and villages. If you want to receive English-language cable TV, check that it's available (and which stations) before signing a lease. Cable TV providers charge an average of around CHF 23 per month, depending on your provider and the channels on offer (the cost is usually included in your apartment's monthly extra costs or billed quarterly or annually). If you don't own a TV, you may be able to get the cable TV company to seal the aerial outlet and thus avoid paying the monthly rental charge. This is easy enough if you live in a house, but may be impossible if you live in an apartment, where cable TV costs are shared and included in your apartment's extra costs.

Internet TV

Internet TV (also known as web TV and IPTV – Internet Protocol TV) allows you to watch TV via the internet on your computer monitor, with a modem and a special 'set-top box'. The most popular service (with over 100,000 subscribers) is Swisscom TV (☎ 0800-081 081, 🖳 www. swisscom.ch/en/residential/swisscom-tv.html), which features over 200 channels, some 20 of which are in English, 120 radio stations (including BBC radio), live sporting events (pay-per-view) and over 2,000 films on demand. Various subscriptions are available costing from CHF 14 to 31 per month (or CHF 89 with internet and fixed-line telephone), plus a one-time installation fee of CHF 99 (although you can install it yourself). There's a minimum contract period of 12 months. Other web TV providers include Zattoo (🖳 www. zattoo.com) with 18 English-language stations and Nello (🖳 www.nello.tv).

Slingbox (🖳 www.slingmedia.com) is a system which allows you to watch live television via the internet on your computer or mobile phone, so that you can enjoy your favourite programmes or sporting events wherever you are. See the website for information.

The disadvantages of web TV are that the picture and sound quality are often poor, changing channels is slow and you can only watch programmes on a computer screen or mobile phone. On the other hand there are low or non-existent fees (but you still need a TV licence – see below) and a relatively wide range of channels to choose from.

Satellite TV

There are a number of satellites positioned over Europe carrying hundreds of stations broadcasting in a variety of languages. Satellite TV has been widely available in Switzerland since the '80s, although most homes with satellite TV are owned by foreigners.

Astra

The Astra satellites offer a huge choice of English and foreign-language channels – most available from Sky (see below) – a total of over 500 with digital TV, all of which can be received throughout Switzerland with an 85cm dish. The signal for many channels is scrambled (the decoder is usually built into the receiver) and viewers must pay a monthly subscription to receive programmes. The best served by unscrambled (clear) channels are German-speakers. Further information can be found on Astra's website (🖳 www.astra.lu).

A bonus for Sky subscribers is the availability of radio stations, including all the national BBC stations (see **Radio** below).

Sky Television

In order to receive Sky television you need a Sky digital receiver (digibox) and a dish. There are two ways to obtain a receiver (digibox) and Sky 'smart' card. You can subscribe in the UK or Ireland (personally, if you have an address there, or via a friend) and take the Sky receiver and card to Switzerland. However, there may be restrictions as the digibox is supposed to be connected to a phone line and Sky can determine where the receiver is being used (and when it isn't connected to a phone line) and may terminate the service if it isn't being used in the UK or Ireland. Alternatively, you can obtain Sky channels in Switzerland from Teleclub (🖳 www.teleclub.ch) or Insat International (🖳 www.insatinternational. com), although you may be restricted in your choice of channels.

In the UK, a basic Sky subscription costs around £21 per month and give you access to around 100 channels, including BBC1, BBC2, ITV1, CH4 and CH5. Various other packages are available costing up to around £55 per month, for which you have access to all channels, including the Movie and Sports channels. For further information, see 🖳 www.sky.com.

Equipment

A satellite receiver should have a built-in Videocrypt decoder (and others as necessary) and be capable of receiving satellite stereo radio. A 60cm dish may be adequate in some areas of Switzerland, although an 85cm dish or a signal booster is better and necessary in many regions. A basic fixed satellite system (which will receive channels from one satellite only) costs around CHF 500 and a motorised dish (which will automatically adjust its orientation so that you can receive channels from other satellites) will set you back three or four times as much.

If you wish to receive satellite stations on two or more TVs, you can buy a satellite system with two or more receptors. To receive stations from two (or more) satellites simultaneously, you need a motorised dish or a dish with a double feed antenna (dual LNBs). There are many satellite sales and installation companies in Switzerland (see 🖳 www.angloinfo.com for contacts). Shop around and compare prices. Alternatively you can import your own satellite dish and receiver and install it yourself.

Location & Installation

To be able to receive channels from any satellite, there must be no obstacles between the satellite and your dish, i.e. no large obstacles such as trees, buildings or mountains must obstruct the signal, therefore check before renting an apartment or buying a home.

Before buying or erecting a satellite dish – or even before buying or renting a home – check whether it's possible to install one. If you're renting an apartment you'll need to obtain permission from your landlord and if a satellite dish is larger than 80cm you may need a building permit.

Dishes can usually be mounted in a variety of unobtrusive positions and can be painted or patterned to blend in with the background. Apartment blocks may be fitted with at least one communal satellite dish or have cable TV, and it may not be possible to install your own dish.

Programme Guides

Most satellite stations provide teletext and extensive programme information. Sky satellite programme listings are provided in a number of British publications such as *What*

Satellite and Digital TV (💻 www.futureplc. com), which is available on subscription, and from some newsagents in Switzerland. Satellite TV programmes are also listed in expatriate newspapers and magazines in Switzerland. If you're interested in receiving TV stations from further afield, you can obtain a copy of the *World Radio TV Handbook (WRTV)* by Nicholas Hardyman (Watson-Guptil Publications, 💻 www.wrth.com).

Television Licence

A TV licence (*Fernsehempfangskonzession, concession de réception de télévisuelle*) costs CHF 293.25 per year (CHF 73.30 per quarter) and is required by all TV owners. The combined cost of a TV and radio licence (see below) is CHF 462.40 per year (CHF 115.60 per quarter). Registration for both licences can be done together via Billag (' 0844-834 834, 💻 www.billag.ch).

The fee covers any number of TVs owned or rented by you, irrespective of where they are located, e.g. holiday homes, motor vehicles or boats. Registration must be made within 14 days of buying or importing a TV. You'll be fined if you have a TV and don't have a licence when an inspector calls. However, if your TV is used only for video/DVD playback or as a computer monitor, no licence fee is payable – but you mustn't be able to receive any TV broadcasts.

DVDs

English-language DVDs can be rented from around CHF 4 per day from DVD shops and postal DVD clubs throughout Switzerland (e.g. 💻 www.dvdrental.ch/en). Rental costs can often be reduced by paying a monthly membership fee or a lump sum in advance and postal charges may be waived on orders above CHF 20. Check the conditions before hiring, as some companies levy exorbitant 'fines' if you forget to return films on

time (possibly more than the value of the DVD). Many public libraries also offer a variety of DVDs for rent for a nominal fee, e.g. CHF 2 per week.

Since 2003, retailers in Switzerland have been forbidden by law to import DVDs (whether for sale or rent) of the latest first-run films that haven't yet been shown in Switzerland, unless they won't be shown in Swiss cinemas. This doesn't affect re-runs of older films and first runs of art or cult films in specialised cinemas or film clubs.

RADIO

The good news for radio fans is that radios have the same standards the world over, although bandwidths vary. FM (VHF) stereo stations flourish in Switzerland and Medium Wave (MW or AM) and Long Wave (LW) bands are also in wide use throughout Europe. A Short Wave (SW) radio is useful for receiving international stations such as the BBC World Service, Voice of America, Radio Canada and Radio Sweden. The BBC World Service and the Voice of America are also available via cable radio in many areas (see below).

If you have digital cable or satellite TV you'll also be able to receive digital radio stations. Portable digital radio receivers are available that provide good reception, particularly on short wave, and expensive 'professional' receivers are capable of receiving stations from almost anywhere.

If you're interested in receiving radio stations from further afield, you can obtain a copy of the *World Radio TV Handbook (WRTV)* by Nicholas Hardyman (Watson-Guptil Publications, 💻 www. wrth.com).

Swiss Radio

There are over 40 private local radio stations in Switzerland, some broadcasting in English, e.g. Radio 74 (88.8 MHz FM) – broadcasting from France in English – and WRS World Radio Switzerland (88.4 MHz FM) in Geneva. Advertising is banned on radio stations run by the SRG/SSR, but is permitted on local radio stations. Swiss Radio International (SRI) transmits programmes via short wave, cable and satellite in Arabic, English, French, German, Italian, Portuguese and Spanish. The English language programme (24-hours a day) can be heard via the Astra satellite.

For more information, contact SRI (☎ 031-350 92 22, 💻 www.swissinfo.org). Swiss Radio publishes *Radio Magazin*, available on subscription from Radio Magazin (' 043-300 52 00, 💻 www.radiomagazin.ch).

TV). Many cable networks provide the BBC World Service, BBC Foreign Language Service, Voice of America, Swiss Radio International (English service) and Sky Radio, in addition to a wide selection of FM stereo stations from Switzerland (national and local), Austria, France, Germany and Italy.

Radio Licence

A radio licence (*Radioempfangskonzession, concession de réception radio*), which costs CHF 169.15 per year (CHF 42.30 a quarter), is required by all radio owners in Switzerland (including car radios). Both radio and TV licence (see above) registration can be done together by contacting Billag (☎ 0844-834 834, 🖳 www.billag.ch). The radio licence fee is payable quarterly with your TV licence fee (if applicable). It covers any number of radios irrespective of where they're located, e.g. holiday homes, motor vehicles or boats (but not radios in the work-place which should be covered by an employer's radio licence). Registration must be made within 14 days of buying or importing a radio – failure to register can result in a fine.

BBC & Other Foreign Stations

The BBC World Service is broadcast on short wave on several frequencies simultaneously and you can usually receive a good signal on one of them. The signal strength varies depending on where you live in Switzerland, the time of day and year, the power and positioning of your receiver, and atmospheric conditions. All BBC radio stations, including the World Service, are also available via the Astra satellite (see **Satellite Radio** below) and BBC World Service is available via cable radio (see below). You can view detailed programme information online at (🖳 www.bbc. co.uk/worldservice).

Many other foreign stations publish programme listings and frequency charts for expatriates seeking news from home, including Radio Australia, Radio Canada, Denmark Radio, Radio Nederland, Radio Sweden International and the Voice of America.

Satellite Radio

If you have satellite TV you can also receive many radio stations via your satellite link. For example, BBC Radio 1, 2, 3, 4 and 5, BBC World Service, Sky Radio, Virgin 1215 and many foreign (i.e. non-English) stations are broadcast via the Astra satellites.

Cable Radio

If your apartment is wired for cable TV (see above), it will also be wired for cable radio, providing reception of around 30 stereo stations (including digital stations if you can have digital

9.
EDUCATION

Switzerland is renowned for the excellence and diversity of its private schools. Although not so well known abroad, Swiss state (i.e. publicly funded) schools also have a good reputation in academic circles. The Swiss have always been in the forefront of educational progress and have produced a number of world-renowned philosophers (e.g. Froebal, Pestalozzi, Piaget and Steiner) whose pedagogical theories and research remain a strong influence throughout the world. Even today, Swiss teaching methods are in advance of those of most other countries, many of which send delegations to Swiss schools.

In many cantons school begins at the age of four or five with compulsory kindergarten. Primary and secondary education is for a minimum of nine years (there's an optional tenth year in most cantons) until the age of 16 or 17. Around 20 per cent of students attend school for 12 years until the age of 18, when they sit the maturity (*Matura*, *maturité*) examination.

There are many things to take into account when choosing an appropriate school for your children in Switzerland, among the most important of which is the language of study. The only schools using English as the teaching language are international private schools. If your children attend any other school, they must study in a foreign language. For most children, studying in a foreign language isn't such a handicap as it may appear. The majority adapt quickly and soon become fluent in the local language, assisted by the extra language tuition provided for foreign children (if only it were so easy for adults). Naturally all children don't adapt equally well to a change of language and culture, particularly teenage children. Before making any major decisions about your children's future education, it's important to consider their individual ability, character and requirements.

For many children, the experience of going to school and living in a foreign country is a stimulating challenge that they relish, providing invaluable cultural and educational experiences. Your children will become 'world' citizens, less likely to be prejudiced against foreigners and foreign ideas, particularly if they attend an international school with pupils from many

countries. Swiss state schools also have pupils from a large number of countries, with an average of around 20 per cent being non-Swiss, although it can be much higher or lower in some communities.

In addition to a detailed look at the Swiss state school system and private schools, this chapter also contains information about children's holiday camps, apprenticeships, universities, further education and language schools.

STATE OR PRIVATE SCHOOL?

If you're fortunate enough to be among those who can afford to send your children to a private school, you may be surprised to learn that the vast majority of Swiss parents choose to send their children to a state school, even when the cost of private education isn't an important consideration. If you're able to choose between state and private education, the following checklist will help you decide:

◆ How long are you planning to stay in Switzerland? If you're uncertain, it's probably best to assume a long stay. Due to language and other integration problems, enrolling a child in a Swiss state school is advisable only if you're planning to stay for at least a few years, particularly for teenage children, and preferably longer.

◆ What is the standard of the state schools in the area where you plan to live? Bear in mind that the area where you choose to live may affect your choice of school(s). For example, if you choose state education, you may need to send your children to the state school nearest your home.

♦ Do you know where you're going after Switzerland? This may be an important consideration with regard to your children's language of tuition and system of education in Switzerland. How old are your children and what age will they be when you plan to leave Switzerland? What plans do you have for their education and in which country?

♦ What educational level are your children at now and how will they fit into a private school or the Swiss state school system? The younger they are, the easier it will be to place them in a suitable school.

♦ How do your children view the thought of studying in a foreign language? What language(s) is best from a long-term point of view? Is schooling available in Switzerland in your children's mother tongue?

♦ Will your children require your help with their studies and, more importantly, will you be able to help them, particularly with the language(s)?

♦ If necessary, is special or extra tutoring available in the local language or particular subjects?

♦ What are the school hours? What are the school holiday periods? How will the school holidays and hours affect your family's work and leisure activities?

♦ Is religion an important aspect in your choice of school? In Swiss state schools, religion is usually taught as a compulsory subject. Parents may, however, request permission for their children not to attend.

♦ Do you want your children to attend a single-sex school? Swiss state schools are usually coeducational (mixed).

♦ Should you send your children to a boarding school? If so, where?

♦ What are the secondary and further education prospects in Switzerland or another country? Are Swiss examinations or the examinations set by prospective Swiss schools recognised in your home country or the country where you plan to live after leaving Switzerland?

♦ How large are the classes? What is the pupil-teacher ratio?

Obtain the opinions and advice of others who have been faced with the same decisions and problems as you're facing, and collect as much information from as many different sources as possible before making a decision. Speak to teachers and the parents of children attending schools on your shortlist.

Many cantons have schools with facilities for physically and mentally disabled children. Switzerland doesn't, however, provide special teaching facilities for gifted children with exceptionally high IQs, although in some cases bright children are allowed to skip a grade.

STATE SCHOOLS

The term 'state' schools is a misnomer, as there are no state (federal) schools in Switzerland, education being the jealously guarded responsibility of the cantons. Nevertheless, state is used here in preference to 'public' (to prevent confusion with the British term 'public school', which refers to a private, fee-paying school!) to refer to non-fee-paying schools funded by the cantons from local taxes.

The state school (*öffentliche Schulen, écoles publiques*) system in Switzerland is complicated compared with many other developed countries and differs considerably from the school systems in, for example, the UK and the US, particularly regarding secondary and university education. In 2006, the Swiss voted to 'harmonise' the cantonal school system, in order to ease integration for children (and parents) when moving to another canton. The process started in 2009 with a six-year transition period and currently has 15 cantons participating.

It's usually necessary to send your children to a school in your canton of residence where you pay your taxes. Some cantons, however, have agreements allowing children resident in neighbouring cantons (and sometimes countries!) to attend their schools. Pupils usually go to a nearby primary school, although attending secondary school may entail travelling quite long distances.

State schooling is free for all foreign children of parents with Swiss annual or permanent residence permits (B or C) and who work in Switzerland, although some school books must be purchased.

Most foreign parents (plus the vast majority of Swiss parents) send their children to a Swiss state school for reasons that aren't entirely financial. Swiss state schools have an excellent academic record, aided by the small average class size (around 20 pupils), and are rated among the best in the world. In international tests, Swiss pupils regularly out-perform children in most other countries (particularly in maths and science, as

Swiss pupils don't usually use calculators until secondary school), and Swiss schools have far fewer low-achieving pupils. Attending a state school helps children to integrate into the local community and learn the local language.

Swiss state schools usually impose more discipline than many foreign children are used to, for example regular daily homework, which may initially cause some stress, and which increases with the age of the child. Generally, the younger children are when they arrive in Switzerland, the easier they'll cope. Conversely the older they are, the more problems they'll have adjusting, particularly as the school curriculum is more demanding (including a number of mandatory languages). Parents should try to empathise with their children's problems. If you aren't fluent in the local language, you'll already be aware of how frustrating it is being unable to express yourself adequately. Lack of language ability can easily lead to feelings of inferiority or inadequacy in children (and adults!). State schools may provide supervised homework or extra classes for children who require them.

In general, the Swiss state school system is more disciplined and less flexible than schooling in many countries, but the results are generally excellent, with every child being given the opportunity to study for a trade, diploma or a degree.

Having made the decision to send your child to a state school, you should persevere for at least a year to give it a fair trial. It may take a child this long to adapt to a new language, the change of environment and the different curriculum.

Language

In the French- and Italian-speaking regions of Switzerland, the teaching language is the same as the spoken language and therefore foreign children are able to improve their language ability through their constant exposure to it. In German-speaking Switzerland the position isn't so straightforward. In kindergarten and early primary school classes, teachers speak the local Swiss German dialect. In first grade at primary school they officially begin to teach academic subjects in High German (*Schriftdeutsch/Hochdeutsch, bon allemand*) because Swiss German isn't a written language. However, although text books are written in High German the teacher normally speaks Swiss German during oral instruction, although this isn't always the case.

In later years, generally all non-academic study is in Swiss German, while all academic subjects are taught in High German, particularly when text books are required. One of the problems for both Swiss and foreign children, is that because most lessons are conducted in Swiss German, there's little opportunity to practise High German. This has led to all subjects being (officially) taught in High German in secondary schools in some cantons.

The Swiss German dialect isn't formally taught in any schools (nobody would know where to start!). This makes school life more difficult for foreign children, particularly teenagers, although young children (e.g. 5 to 12 years) generally have few problems learning Swiss German. If you prefer your children to be educated in the French language and you live in a German-speaking canton, it may be possible to send your children to a school in a neighbouring French-speaking canton. You may, however, be required to live in the canton where your children go to school and may not be permitted to move cantons if you're a new arrival (Catch 22!).

Children who don't speak the local language, particularly children of secondary school age, are usually placed in a 'reception' or special class, depending on the degree of language assistance required. This allows them more time to concentrate on learning the language (with extra language tuition), as they'll usually have already covered the syllabus. They integrate into the normal stream only when they've learnt the language and can follow the lessons. When the next promotion stage is reached, they must have attained a satisfactory standard in the local language or the year must be repeated.

Until recently, all children had to learn a second national language from their fifth school year at the latest. The compulsory second language in schools in German-speaking Switzerland was French and in French-speaking Switzerland it was (and still is) High German. However, many Swiss German parents prefer English to be taught as a second language in place of French and this has already been adopted in some German-speaking

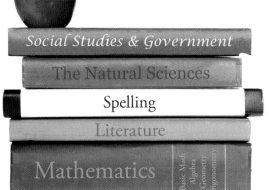

cantons, e.g. Zurich (much to the ire of the French Swiss). The German-speaking regions introduce English in the third grade and French in the fifth grade. The French-speaking regions introduce German in the fifth grade and English from the seventh grade at the latest.

English becomes compulsory only when a child is studying modern languages, for example in a high school (*Gymnasium/Kantonsschule*, *gymnase/école cantonale*). English Fun Language Clubs for children aged three to ten are popular; they also offer French, German and Spanish, but English is by far the most popular language.

For more information about Swiss languages and learning them, see **Languages** on page 29 and **Language Schools** on page 116.

Enrolment

When you arrive in Switzerland and register in your local community (*Gemeinde, commune*), you're informed about schooling and told when and where to apply for school entrance for your children. In city areas, you must apply to your area school commission (*Kreisschulpflege, commission scolaire du district*). School registration dates are announced in local newspapers. The start of the school year throughout Switzerland is between mid-August and mid-September. A detailed list showing school start (and holiday) dates for all cantons and communities is available at 🖥 www.edk.ch.

School Hours

Swiss school hours differ considerably from those in most other countries and often vary from school to school, as it's generally left to individual teachers to schedule their own classes. Children rarely spend all day at school and if you have children of different ages attending school (even the same school), they may be coming and going at different times. This is particularly true for younger children, where classes may be divided into sections with varied hours. City schools may offer before and after school supervision for pupils who need to arrive at school early or stay after school before they can go home or a parent arrives to collect them.

This is a difficult system for working parents, therefore many cantons have now introduced 'block times' (*Blockzeiten, horaires blocs*). At a school with block times, classes typically start at 8am and end at noon with a second session from 1.30 or 1.45 to 3.30pm. A one and a half lunch break is normal and most schools now provide hot lunches (the cost varies depending on the parents' income), although there's often limited space and there may be a waiting list. Children may also take a packed lunch to eat on the school premises, for which a room is provided.

It isn't uncommon for children to have a day off if their teacher's sick, as there are seldom substitute teachers to take over a class for one day. If a teacher is absent for longer than one day, a substitute teacher is usually arranged. Children receive a 'telephone alarm' list at the beginning of the school year and changes to school schedules are transmitted by telephone on the evening before a change of plan, e.g. the teacher is sick and not going to be teaching the following day. The teacher calls the first child on the list and each child then calls the next one on the list until the last one on the list calls the teacher. When the teacher receives a call from the last on the list, he knows the whole class has been informed (in some schools this system has now been replaced/supplemented by text messages). This of course poses complications for working parents, who are suddenly faced with a child staying home unexpectedly.

In secondary schools, hours are generally anywhere between 7 to 11am or noon and 1.30 or 2pm to 6pm. In a higher grade secondary school, e.g. a high school (*Gymnasium/Kantonsschule*, *gymnase/école cantonale*), the school day can last from 7.30am to 5pm (around 40 hours a week), which is a long day, particularly when travelling time is added.

The average travelling time to and from secondary school in German-speaking Switzerland is around 40 minutes, which together with the demanding school schedule is blamed for the high stress levels of some children. It isn't usual for parents to take their children to school in Switzerland; depending on the distance, children

walk, ride a bicycle or use public transport. Going to school on their own is considered an important part of becoming independent, and parents taking their children to school and picking them up by car is frowned upon in some areas. School buses are generally provided only for the disabled in the public sector, although some private schools provide buses.

> One or two afternoons a week (usually Wednesday or Thursday) are free, when working parents must make arrangements for young children to be cared for.

Provisions & Equipment

At kindergarten, children usually take a snack for both morning and afternoon breaks (hungry work being a kid). Teachers recommend fruit, vegetable or bread, rather than biscuits or cakes. On their birthdays, children are allowed a treat and it's customary to take a cake for the whole class. (This custom is continued throughout adult life in most of the country and you'll find that many adult Swiss provide cakes on their birthdays.)

Primary school children require a school bag or satchel (usually different for boys and girls, for reasons best known to the Swiss); a pencil case and pencils, etc.; slippers, gym shoes (plimsolls), shorts and a towel for games and exercise periods; and a sports bag for the above if the satchel is too small. (The school bag and pencil case are usually provided by a child's godparents, who play an important role in a Swiss child's life.)

Parents are required to supply all kinds of odds and ends for handicraft lessons, from toilet roll tubes to empty boxes. Keep a junk supply handy if you don't want to be caught short.

Children require good sturdy shoes or hiking boots (if they have them) for their annual school hike (*Schulreise, course d'école*). This entails children getting up in the middle of the night for a 10-30km hike (the distance depends on their age) around Switzerland to admire the cows, flowers and mountains.

Curriculum & Grading

Most state schools have little extracurricular activity; for example there are no school clubs or sports teams. If your children want to do team sports they must join a local club, which means that parents are required to ferry them back and forth for games and social events. In state schools, subsidised music lessons are given, although parents must usually provide the instruments. In some cases, instruments are loaned by the school for a period. (Mandatory music lessons will be introduced to the curriculum after a referendum in 2012.)

Two or three times a year, children receive a school report. Satisfactory progress is graded as 'definitive' and at the end of the school year the child goes up into the next class. If progress is unsatisfactory, a child's report is graded as 'provisional' – two 'provisional' reports means the child must automatically repeat the year. Foreign children who fail to reach a satisfactory standard in the local language must also repeat a year.

Children often repeat a year or even two (the maximum) and there's usually a fairly wide age range in the higher school classes. There's generally no stigma attached to this repetition of classes, though some children resent it. Children, like adults, learn at different speeds and the Swiss school system simply recognises this fact. If a child fails to maintain the required standard in a higher grade secondary school, e.g. a high school, he may be required to join another school with a less demanding curriculum.

Health Insurance

All children are required to belong to a health insurance scheme, which must be specified on the school application form. Some aspects of children's health are supervised or carried out by the school authorities. All Swiss state schools have an extensive programme of vaccinations (inoculations) against polio, diphtheria, tuberculosis, whooping cough, measles, German measles and mumps. If your child has already undergone a course of vaccinations before arrival in Switzerland, you should show the certificates to the school health authorities.

In all primary and some secondary schools, children receive a free annual dental inspection by a school-appointed dentist or your family dentist, and an estimate is provided for any dental treatment required. Some communities pay a percentage of bills for low-income families and your health insurance company may also pay a portion, but only if your family is insured for dental treatment.

Schools provide insurance against accidents at school and on journeys to and from school. For this reason, children are required to go by a direct or approved route to school, and if they're cycling, must use cycle paths to avoid invalidating their insurance policy. Outside these times children should be covered against accidents by your family health insurance policy.

Holidays

The typical state school holiday (*Schulferien, vacances scolaires*) periods are shown below.

The dates and length of holidays vary with each canton, but in general pupils have one to two weeks 'Sport' vacation between January and February, two weeks Spring vacation, five weeks Summer vacation (longer in the French and Italian-speaking cantons) and one or two weeks Autumn vacation, in addition to a Christmas break (usually two weeks) and other State holidays. For the holiday schedule in your canton or community, see 🖳 www.feiertagskalender.ch. The main school holidays are shown in the table below:

School Holidays	
Month	**Length of Holiday**
January to March	1 to 2 weeks
April	2 to 3 weeks
July/August	5 to 7 weeks
September/October	1 to 3 weeks
December/January	1 to 2 weeks

Schools are also closed on public holidays (see page 37), if these don't fall within school holiday periods. School holiday dates are published by schools and local communities well in advance, thus allowing you plenty of time to schedule family holidays during official school holidays.

Normally parents aren't permitted to withdraw a child from classes during the school term, except for visits to a doctor or dentist, when the teacher should be informed in advance (if possible). In primary school, a note to the teacher is sufficient, but in secondary school you must complete an official absence form, which must be signed by the teacher concerned and delivered to the school office. For reasons other than sickness, children are generally allowed only one half day off school each year. Anything longer isn't allowed without written permission, which is difficult to obtain in some areas.

If you're refused permission and insist on withdrawing your child from school, **you can be prosecuted and fined or even imprisoned on your return!** Unfortunately some school authorities don't make allowances for families who want to make, for example, a 'once in a lifetime' trip to visit relatives overseas and who are unable to go during official school holidays.

Kindergarten

One year's attendance at a kindergarten (*Kindergarten, école enfantine/jardin d'enfant*) is compulsory in most cantons. Each community is required to provide a kindergarten for six-year-olds and often takes four- and five-year-olds also, although places may be limited. Kindergarten lasts for two-and-a-half to three hours in the mornings, or two hours both mornings and afternoons. Classes are generally held five days a week, with some afternoons free, or a few mornings only.

Kindergarten is highly recommended, particularly if your children are going to continue with a state education. After one or two years in kindergarten they're integrated into the local community and will have learnt the local language (more or less) in preparation for primary school. Children are given road safety training by policemen and are provided with reflective clothing to wear to and from kindergarten. Pre-primary school children aren't allowed to ride their bicycles on public roads.

In major cities, private playgroups are available that accept children as young as three.

Primary School

In most cantons, children must be six years old before 30th April (or 30th June in some cantons) to start primary school (*Primarschule, école primaire*) the following year. To register your children for primary school, contact your local community in rural areas or your local school commission in cities. This may be unnecessary if your children have attended a local kindergarten. Coeducation (mixed classes) is normal and primary classes have an average of around 20 pupils, who are generally taught all subjects by one teacher.

Primary education lasts from four to six years, depending on the canton, until children are aged 11 to 13 (in most it's six). When primary school is for six years, classes are split into three grades or steps (*Stufe, degré*). The first two years are termed 'lower grade' (*Unterstufe, premier degré*), the next two years 'middle grade' (*Mittelstufe, deuxième degré*) and the final two years 'upper grade' (*Oberstufe, troisième degré*).

In some small communities, multi-age classes (i.e. grouping children of different ages in the same class) are commonplace. Sometimes, when there are relatively few pupils and resources are limited, one teacher takes all classes, from first grade to the last year of primary school.

In their first or second year of primary school, children receive bicycle road safety training from local policemen, who may also warn them about the risks of talking to strangers. Children must be seven years old and attending primary school before they're allowed on public roads (kindergarten doesn't count, even when a child is already seven). For many teenagers (minimum age 14) a moped is the vehicle of choice. These are permitted on pavements, which makes them a bit safer traffic-wise (though not for pedestrians), but mopeds can be difficult to steer (for kids) and pick up speed quickly, so caution is advised.

In the Swiss state school system, a child's marks in his last primary school year usually determine what sort of secondary school he goes to (see below). Children are normally assessed on the average results of tests set by their teacher throughout the year. The most important primary school subjects are the local language, mathematics and Swiss history and geography (*Heimatkunde, histoire et géographie régionales*). While it's important for children to do well in their last primary school year, a child's future education isn't fixed on leaving primary school.

Secondary School

Secondary school (*Sekundarschule, école secondaire*) education in Switzerland lasts for three to seven years, depending on the type of school and the canton. The Swiss secondary school system allows for promotion and demotion, both within a school and from school to school, up to the age of 15 or even later. If your children receive good marks in their last primary school year, they have a better chance of going to an advanced secondary school or high school (*Gymnasium/Kantonalschule, lycée/école cantonale*), possibly leading to a university or technical institute. If you think your child has been incorrectly graded, you can apply for him to take an entrance examination to a higher (or lower) school.

In some cantons, a so-called orientation cycle (*Orientierungsstufe/cycle d'orientation*) has been introduced, where pupils of varying ability share the same class, rather than being streamed into different classes. Some main subjects are, however, divided into courses of different grades. The kinds of secondary school provided vary from canton to canton; those listed below, based on the structure in Canton Zurich, serve as an example.

◆ **Secondary Modern School** (*Oberschule, école supérieure*): This type of school provides three years' general education in a practical curriculum that includes woodwork, metalwork and home economics, as preparation for an apprenticeship in the manual trades. Secondary modern schools are for less academically-gifted children, usually around 5 per cent of the total.

◆ **Technical School** (*Realschule, école technique*): Technical schools provide three years of more demanding academic education than secondary modern schools, but are also directed towards training in the manual trades. The second-largest number of children (around 35 per cent) attend a technical school.

◆ **Secondary School** (*Sekundarschule, école secondaire*): Secondary schools provide three or more years' education in languages, sciences, geography and history as a preparation for entrance to a higher school. Most children (around 50 per cent) go to a secondary school, many going on to apprenticeships. Some parents prefer to send their children to a secondary school, at least for a few years, rather than to a more demanding high school. Many will have an opportunity to attend a high school or vocational school later, when they may be better equipped to handle the curriculum.

◆ **Pre-high School** (*Progymnasium/ Untergymnasium/Bezirks-schule, prégymnasium/lycée inferieur*): Pre-high school, as the name implies, prepares children for high school in some cantons. Latin is usually compulsory and entrance requirements are based on grades and teacher recommendation, and many cantons set an entrance exam. The age-level compares to Junior High School in the US.

♦ **Commercial or Business School** (*Handelsmittelschule, école de commerce*): Provides three years' training (federally recognised) for a commercial diploma and a good basic grounding for a business career, but is also useful for a career in social work, nursing or as an interpreter;

♦ **Teacher Training School** (*Lehramtschule/ Unterseminar, école normale*): The course lasts four to five years and qualifies only primary school teachers. Entrance qualifications vary and training may include a two- to three-year practical period. Training for secondary school teaching (two to three years) and higher school teaching (four to five years) is undertaken at university.

♦ **Diploma Middle School** (*Diplommittelschule, école professionelle*): A three-year preparatory school for kindergarten teachers, nurses and medical technicians.

♦ **High School** (*Gymnasium/Kantonsschule, lycée/école cantonale*): High school education prepares students for a university or technical college education and lasts for six to seven years, when the 'maturity examination' is taken (see below). A written entrance examination in French, German and mathematics is necessary, and only the top students (around 10 per cent of the total) are admitted. Children are on probation for the first three to six months to see how they progress. A Swiss high school provides roughly the same standard of education as an English grammar or high school, but higher than that provided by an American high school or two-year college.

Vocational Schools

The following schools are attended after two or three years in secondary school (with the exception of High School) from the age of 15 or 16. All require students to pass an entrance examination.

Maturity Examination

Students at a high school study for the maturity (*Matura, maturité*) examination, usually consisting one of six syllabuses. If they pass the maturity examination, they obtain the maturity diploma (*Maturitätsdiplom, diplôme de maturité*). All students generally study French, German, mathematics, geography, history, biology, physics, chemistry and music or art. Other subjects depend on the syllabus chosen and are typically as shown in the table below.

All European universities and most American colleges recognise the Swiss maturity diploma as an entrance qualification, although foreign students must provide proof of their English language ability to study in the UK, US and other English-speaking countries.

Maturity Examination

Syllabus	Subjects
A	classical languages (Latin and Greek compulsory);
B	Latin plus English or Italian;
C	mathematics, sciences and descriptive geometry; English or Italian are compulsory;
D	modern languages; German, French and English are compulsory, plus Italian, Spanish or Russian;
E	economics, including law, science of industrial management and political economy and social sciences; English or Italian are compulsory;
M	music and art as a preparation for academies of music and the other arts.

The syllabus chosen will often determine the field of study at university.

PRIVATE SCHOOLS

Switzerland is famous for the quality and variety of its some 600 private day and boarding schools (*Privatschulen, écoles privées*). Schools cater for as few as 20 to as many as 2,000 pupils – a total of around 100,000, two-thirds of whom are Swiss. Fees vary considerably according to (among other things) the grade (primary school is cheaper than high school), quality, reputation and location of the school. Day school fees vary from around CHF 5,000 to over 30,000 per year (e.g. the International School of Basle charges 32,450 per year for the last two years of high school), while annual boarding school fees are anywhere between CHF 30,000 and 65,000.

If you send your child to a private school, your canton may contribute to the cost. For example, canton Basle Country (Baselland) pays CHF 2,500 biannually towards private education, provided a child's education isn't being paid for by a company (e.g. your employer) and the student was living in the canton on 15th May and 15th November of the school year (to qualify for biannual payments).

Fees aren't all-inclusive and extra obligatory charges are made, e.g. for clothing, health and accident insurance, text books and stationary. Some schools charge parents for every little thing. There may be additional optional charges, e.g. for outings, and you may have to provide items such as art supplies and sports equipment. (Some schools will even arrange to have your child met at Geneva or Zurich airport and be conducted by private plane and chauffeured limousine to school – at a price!) Most private schools have an entrance examination, e.g. in English and mathematics, plus an IQ test.

Private schools have a more relaxed, less rigid regime and curriculum than Swiss state schools and provide a more varied and international approach to sport, culture and art, and a wider choice of academic subjects. Their aim is the development of the child as an individual and the encouragement of his unique talents, rather than teaching on a 'production line' system. This is made possible by small classes which allow teachers to provide pupils with individually tailored lessons and tuition.

The results speak for themselves and many private secondary schools have a near 100 per cent university placement rate. Private school pupils are more likely to question rules and regulations (no wonder most Swiss prefer to send their children to state schools!), be open-minded, express themselves more spontaneously, and be more aware of world problems and politics.

You should make applications to private schools as far in advance as possible – you're usually required to send previous school reports, exam results and records. Before enrolling your child in a private school, make sure that you understand the withdrawal conditions in the school contract.

> ☑ **SURVIVAL TIP**
>
> Bear in mind that not all Swiss private schools live up to the reputed high standards and there are a number of schools that simply cash in on the good reputation of the best schools.

Always use caution when selecting a school and don't accept what's stated in the school brochure or prospectus at face value. The checklist below will help you choose an appropriate private school.

A free booklet entitled *Private Schools in Switzerland*, containing a complete list of private day and boarding schools in Switzerland, is available from the Swiss Federation of Private Schools (☎ 031-328 40 50, 🖳 www.swiss-schools.ch), which represents some 260 schools. For detailed research on private schools (in German only), including a copy of the Federation's annual booklet, *Privatschulen*, see 🖳 www.privatschulverzeichnis.com.

You may prefer to send your child to an international school (see below) or a private day school across the border, for example in France. Alternatively you can send a child to a boarding school in Switzerland or abroad, e.g. in the UK or the US.

International Schools

There are international primary and secondary day schools in or close to all major cities in Switzerland, where demand usually exceeds supply. One of the main advantages of an international school is that lessons are generally conducted in English, though there are also French-speaking international schools in Geneva. In recent years, private bilingual primary schools teaching in English/French or English/German have become more widespread and popular. Bi-lingual schools usually teach certain subjects in French/German and others in English. There are also private schools in Switzerland for children with special language requirements other than English, for example the Japanese School in Zurich.

International schools offer curricula designed for a wide variety of examinations including the Swiss maturity examination (see above), British A-Levels, the French *baccalauréat*, the German *Abitur* and the Italian *Maturita*. Many international schools offer curricula tailored to the American college entrance CEEB and British GCSE examinations, and may also offer the International Bacclaureate (*Bakkalaureat*, *baccalauréat*) school leaving certificate, an internationally recognised university entrance qualification. Note that some Swiss international schools have examinations that are recognised everywhere **except** in Switzerland, where they aren't accepted for entry to Swiss universities!

One negative aspect of international schools, apart from the high fees, is usually a high pupil turnover. This can have an adverse effect on some children, particularly when close friendships are severed. Some international schools have pupils from as many as 80 countries.

Choosing a Private School

The following checklist is designed to help you choose an appropriate and reputable private school in Switzerland:

◆ Does the school have a good reputation? How long has it been established? Does it belong to one of the Swiss private school associations (see above)?

◆ Does the school have a good academic record? For example, what percentage of pupils obtain good examination passes or go on to good universities? All the best schools will provide exam pass rate statistics.

◆ How large are the classes and what is the student/teacher ratio? Does the class size tally with the number of desks in the classrooms?

◆ What are the qualification requirements for teachers? What nationality are the majority of teachers? Ask for a list of teaching staff and their qualifications.

◆ What are the classrooms like? For example, their size, space, cleanliness, lighting, furniture and furnishings. Are there signs of creative teaching, e.g. wall charts, maps, posters and students' work on display?

◆ What is the teacher turnover? A high turnover is a bad sign and may suggest underpaid and poorly motivated teachers and poor working conditions.

◆ What extras must you pay?

◆ Which countries do most students come from?

◆ Is religion an important consideration in your choice of school?

◆ Are special English classes provided for children whose English (or other language) doesn't meet the required standard? Should you send your child to a bi-lingual school where instruction is in both the local language and English?

◆ If you're considering a boarding school, what standard and type of accommodation is provided?

◆ What is the quality and variety of food provided? What is the dining room like? Does the school have a dietician?

◆ What languages does the school teach as obligatory or optional subjects?

◆ What is the student turnover?

◆ What are the school terms and holiday periods? Private school holidays are usually much longer than state schools, e.g. four weeks at Easter and Christmas and ten weeks in the summer, and they often don't coincide with state school holiday periods.

◆ If you're considering a day school, what are the school hours?

◆ What are the withdrawal conditions, should you need or wish to remove your child? A term's notice is usual.

◆ What does the curriculum include? What examinations are set? Are examinations recognised both in Switzerland and internationally? Do they fit in with your long-term education plans? Ask to see a typical pupil timetable to check the ratio of academic/non-academic subjects. Check the number of free study periods and whether they're supervised.

◆ What sports instruction and facilities are provided? Where are the sports facilities located?

◆ What are the facilities for art and science subjects, for example arts and crafts, music, computer studies, biology, science, hobbies, drama, cookery and photography? Ask to see the classrooms, facilities, equipment and some of the students' projects.

◆ What sort of outings and holidays does the school organise and are they included in the fees?

◆ What medical facilities does the school provide, e.g. infirmary, resident doctor or

nurse? Is medical and accident insurance included in the fees?

♦ What sort of discipline and punishments are applied and for what offences?

♦ What reports are provided for parents and how often?

♦ Last but not least – unless someone else is paying – what are the fees?

Before making a final choice, it's important to visit the schools on your shortlist during term time and talk to teachers and students, and if possible, former students and their parents.

☑ SURVIVAL TIP

Where possible, check the answers to the above questions in person and don't rely on the school's prospectus to provide the information. If you're unhappy with the answers, look elsewhere.

Finally, having made your choice, keep a check on your child's progress and listen to his complaints. Compare notes with other parents. If something doesn't seem right, try to establish whether a complaint is founded or not and, if it is, take action to have the problem resolved. You or your employer is paying a lot of money for your child's education and you should demand value for money. See also **State or Private School?** on page 103.

HOLIDAY CAMPS

Holiday camps (*Ferienlager, camps de vacances*) for children are organised during school holidays throughout the year. These include both day and residential camps run by private and state schools, clubs and organisations (e.g. youth organisations, scouts and brownies), churches and private organisations. Activities include skiing, swimming and various other sports; excursions; arts and crafts; and academic subjects. Most camps are reasonably priced. 'Club Migros' (*Klubschule Migros, école club Migros*) has a summer and autumn holiday centre called Milandia (☎ 044-905 66 66, ⌨ www.milandia.ch).

Most cantons organise a variety of sports courses during summer holidays. Village Camps (☎ 022-990 94 00, ⌨ www.villagecamps.com) is one of the largest Swiss operators of summer and

winter camps (both in Switzerland and in other European countries) for boys and girls aged 8 to 18. Eurocamp Travel AG (☎ 052-560 70 00, ⌨ www.eurocamp.ch) operates family holiday camps throughout Europe. Another excellent year-round camp operator is My Swiss Camp (⌨ www.myswisscamp.com), which offers instruction in a wide range of sports and language lessons in English, French and German.

Ask your school or community office for information about holiday camps. A list of children's camps is available from the offices of Pro Juventute (see your telephone directory), which also operates holiday camps for the disabled.

APPRENTICESHIPS

Around 70 per cent of young people in Switzerland undertake an apprenticeship or vocational training. A Swiss apprenticeship (*Lehre, apprentissage*) is a combination of on-the-job training and further education, where one or two days a week are spent at a training college and the remainder in the workplace. The syllabus for both schoolwork and practical training is co-ordinated by the Federal Office for Education and Technology. There are plans to introduce a new scheme, where apprentices do a year of theoretical education in school followed by two years of practical work.

An apprenticeship lasts two to four years and can be in almost any vocation, for example waitressing, secretarial work, cooking, plumbing and chimney sweeping. The employer pays a small salary that increases with age and experience, and he may also pay for apprenticeship schooling and the cost of travel to and from school. An apprentice has five weeks' holiday a year. School careers' officers are available to advise parents and students on a choice of career.

The Swiss apprenticeship system is one of the best in the world. It isn't for failures or students who aren't sufficiently academically gifted to go to high school or university (many successful businessmen and politicians in Switzerland were apprentices). If desired, it's possible to go on to higher education later, for example at a college of technology or a university, after completion of, or even during an apprenticeship. Around 12 cantons pay a vocational training allowance of between CHF 150 and 450 per month for children who are in full-time education or training.

You may also be interested in the activities of Intermundo, the Swiss umbrella association for many international youth exchange organisations.

There are 14 member organisations, all of which are non-profit with no political or religious ties. Exchanges are organised worldwide to further cultural understanding, provide work and practical experience, and learn or improve a foreign language. Participants vary in age from 15 to over 30, depending on the particular exchange programme. Exchanges can last from one week to one year. For further information, contact Intermundo (☎ 031-326 29 20, 🖳 www.intermundo.ch).

Many books are published in Switzerland detailing career possibilities for school leavers. One such book is *Studieren und dann?*, *Carrefour Uni* (*Study and then?/University Crossroads*) published in both French and German by AGAB (Bleichemattstr. 15, CH-5000 Aarau, ☎ 062-823 57 30, 🖳 www.agab.ch). A useful website is 'Careers Advice' (🖳 www.berufsberatung.ch), although it isn't available in English.

HIGHER EDUCATION

Around 30 per cent of Swiss students attend one of Switzerland's higher educational establishments, slightly below average for OECD countries, which is partly explained through the system of education which doesn't require a university degree for certain vocations which in other countries require university studies, for example, nursing.

The country has ten universities (*Universität, université*), in Basle, Berne, Fribourg, Geneva, Lausanne, Lucerne, Neuchâtel, St Gallen, Ticino and Zurich, plus two Federal Institutes of Technology, in Lausanne (EPFL) and Zurich (ETHZ). In addition, there are a number of schools for applied sciences (business and technical) under the name of *Fachhochschule/haute école spécialisée*. These are open to students who may not have a maturity or similar qualification but have completed a three- or four-year apprenticeship and obtained a federal diploma.

Seven Swiss universities have were ranked in the world's top 200, as assessed by the British Times Higher Education rankings for 2012-13 (🖳 www.timeshighereducation.co.uk/world-university-rankings). Switzerland's top university, the Federal Institute of Technology in Zurich, climbed from 15th to 12th position – the highest outside Britain and the US – while the Federal Institute of Technology in Lausanne improved from 46th to 40th place (the only other non-British/US establishment in the top 40).

Swiss universities have adopted the international Bachelor and Master's Degree programmes, taking three years to obtain a Bachelor's degree and another one and a half to two years to complete a Masters. A PhD adds another two and a half to three years to a Masters, making a total of six to seven years.

All Swiss higher education facilities, including several technical colleges, are open to foreign students, who comprise around 20 per cent of the total intake. There are usually quotas for foreign students and the number of places available is strictly limited at some universities and for particular courses, e.g. medicine. Foreigners with a B permit (see page 48) are always subject to foreign student quotas and those with a C permit (see page 48) are accepted only if they've attended a Swiss state school for a number of years. The University of St Gallen is the only Swiss university which requires prospective students to sit an entrance exam, irrespective of whether they have a recognised diploma (foreign students are limited to 25 per cent of the total).

The maturity examination (see page 110) is the usual entrance requirement for Swiss nationals and foreigners who have studied in Switzerland. A Swiss university may accept three British A-Level passes but an American high school diploma isn't usually accepted; American students usually require a minimum of a BA, BBA or BSc degree. All foreign students require a thorough knowledge of the language of study (French or German), which is usually examined unless a certificate is provided.

Fees, which are between CHF

500 to 2,000 per year, are payable each term or semester and there are usually higher fees for foreign students, although students (or their parents) who have been residents and taxpayers for at least two years in the canton where the university is located, pay the Swiss rate. Scholarships and student low-interest loans may be available to foreigners after completion of four terms (semesters) and fees may be reduced after the tenth term. Cantons without their own universities must pay fees for students studying in another canton, but fees for foreign students are usually partly subsidised by the federal government.

Although fees have increased in recent years, it's mainly the high cost of living that makes studying in Switzerland expensive. For example, in Geneva the authorities recommend a minimum of around CHF 1,500 to 2,000 per month for accommodation and food, plus university and local taxes, and health insurance (compulsory for everyone living in Switzerland). Parents are legally obliged to support their children during their full-time education in Switzerland and not surprisingly, many students continue to live with their parents until they've finished their degree courses. For those who don't live at home, shared housing is common as dormitories are rare – for room-share ads, see 💻 www.wgzimmer.ch.

FURTHER EDUCATION

Switzerland has over 50 private colleges and university-level institutions, many affiliated to foreign (often American) universities. These include business and commercial colleges, hotel and tourism schools, and the world-famous Swiss finishing schools for young ladies. Fees at finishing (boarding) schools are around CHF 60,000-70,000 per year and students are usually aged from 16 to around 24. The traditional training in French cooking, domestic science, floral art, etiquette and savoir vivre is nowadays supplemented by courses in commerce, languages and catering.

Study in all further education establishments is in small groups and may be full or part time, including summer courses. Many schools offer an American Master of Business Administration (MBA) course in subjects such as banking, communications, economics, European languages, information systems, management, marketing, public relations, and social and political studies.

Switzerland is also renowned for its hotel and restaurant training schools (where classes are often taught in English), widely recognised as the best in the world. These include the world-famous Swiss Hotel School in Lausanne, where parents enrol their children 'at birth' to ensure a place. Tuition costs are high and study periods strictly organised. Most establishments have a good reputation, particularly in the business world.

The Federation of Swiss Private Schools (Verband Schweizerischer Privatschulen, Fédération Suisse des Écoles Privées) publishes a booklet entitled *Private Schools in Switzerland* containing the names of many further education establishments in Switzerland. It's available from Switzerland Tourism (💻 www.myswitzerland. com), Swiss embassies and consulates, and from the Verband Schweizerischer Privatschulen (see **Private Schools** on page 111).

See also **Day & Evening Classes** below and Intermundo under **Apprenticeships** above.

LANGUAGE SCHOOLS

If you don't speak the local language fluently, you may wish to take a language course. It's possible, even for the most non-linguistic person, to acquire a working knowledge of French, German or Italian. All that's required is a little help and some perseverance – or a lot of perseverance if you're surrounded by English-speaking colleagues and only have English-speaking friends! A big handicap for English-speakers in Switzerland is that there's often someone around who speaks English (even on top of a mountain), particularly when you want to practice the local language. Don't get caught in the trap of seeking refuge in the English language or allowing others to practice their English at your expense. You must persist in speaking the local language – give in too easily and you'll never learn.

Most foreigners in Switzerland find that their business and social enjoyment and success is directly related to the degree to which they master the local language(s).

There are language schools (*Sprachschule*, *école de langues*) in all cities and large towns. Most schools offer various classes depending on your language ability, how many hours you wish to study a week, how much money you want to spend, and how quickly you wish (or can reasonably expect) to learn. Some Swiss employers provide free in-house language classes or pay their employees' course fees (corporate courses for executives and managers are big business).

Courses generally fall into three categories. 'Extensive' courses involve between 4 and 15 hours training a week and 'intensive' courses from 15 to 30 hours. For those for whom money is no object (hopefully your employer), there are 'total immersion' (i.e. sink-or-swim) courses for two to six weeks, where you study from 8am to 5pm, five days a week. The cost for a Berlitz two-week total immersion course is around CHF 15,000! At the other end of the scale, free language courses are available in some cities, e.g. at the Worker's and Popular universities in Geneva.

Don't expect to become fluent in a short period unless you have a particular flair for languages or already have a good command of a language. Unless you need to learn a language quickly, it's best to arrange your lessons over a long period. However, don't commit yourself to a long course of study (particularly an expensive one) before ensuring that it's the right one. Most schools offer free tests to help you find your level and a free introductory lesson, and a choice between small groups or individual tuition.

Among the cheapest language schools is Migros Club School (🖳 www.klubschule.ch), a subsidiary of the Migros supermarket chain. Migros provides inexpensive evening courses at all levels, usually consisting of two, two-hour sessions per week. The People's High School (*Volkshochschule*, *université populaire* – 🖳 www. up-vhs.ch), Coop leisure centres (*Coop Freizeit Center*, *centre de loisirs Coop*) and various voluntary organisations (e.g. FAWCO – 🖳 www.

fawco.org – see page 55) also run inexpensive classes. Many language schools run inexpensive classes designed for au pairs.

You may prefer to have private lessons, which are a quicker but more expensive way of learning a language. The main advantage of private lessons is that you learn at your own speed and aren't held back by slow learners or left floundering in the wake of the class genius. You can advertise for a teacher in your local newspapers, on shopping centre bulletin boards or university notice boards, and through your or your spouse's employer. Your friends or colleagues may also be able to help you find a suitable private teacher or choose a language school.

Swiss universities hold summer language courses for perspective students and many holiday language courses are organised (summer and winter) throughout Switzerland for children and young adults aged up to 25. Switzerland Tourism publish a brochure entitled *Holidays and Language Courses* listing summer language courses in English, French, German, Italian, Romansch and Spanish. Eurocentres (☎ 044-485 50 40, 🖳 www.eurocenters.com), operated by a Swiss charitable foundation, offer reasonably-priced intensive language courses both in Switzerland and other countries, inclusive of accommodation with a local family. If you already speak the local language(s) but need conversational practice, you may wish to enrol in an art course at an institute or local club, for example pottery, painting or photography (see **Day & Evening Classes** below). For further information about languages in Switzerland, see **Languages** on page 29.

☑ SURVIVAL TIP

The quality of language teaching is extremely variable and many language schools hire 'teachers' without formal training.

Swiss German

It's rarely necessary for foreigners to master Swiss German (*Schwyzertüütsch*, *suisse allemand*), although you may find yourself excluded from everyday life in German-speaking Switzerland if you don't understand it. You'll find that speaking Swiss German opens doors, both in business and socially, and is particularly important if you plan to settle permanently in a German-speaking area of Switzerland or are thinking of applying for Swiss citizenship.

Opinion is divided over whether it's an advantage to speak High German before attempting to learn Swiss German. If your High German is poor, learning Swiss German won't help you speak, read or write High German and may even be a hindrance. There are a significant number of foreigners in Switzerland who can speak Swiss German reasonably fluently, but are unable to speak, read or write High German properly.

There are many language schools offering Swiss German classes, such as Migros Club School (*Klubschule Migros, école club Migros,* 🖳 www.klubschule.ch) and the People's High School (*Volkshochschule, université populaire*), both of which run Swiss German classes in many areas (see above and **Day & Evening Classes** below). For 'Züritüütsch' (Zurich Swiss-German) classes as well as audio courses (which you can order online), see 🖳 www.schweizer-deutsch.ch.

Various books are available for students of Swiss German, including *Schweizerdeutsch für alle* by Urs Dörig and *Wörterbuch Schweizerdeutsch-Deutsch* (Swiss-German to German dictionary) by Gerd Haffmans, *Hoi, your Swiss German survival guide* by Sergio J. Lievano and Nicole Egger (Bergli Books), and *Learn to Speak and Understand Swiss German* (Pimsleur Language Programs – audio book).

Adult further education programmes are published in many areas (which may be delivered free to local households) and include all courses organised by local training and education centres. Local newspapers also contain details of evening and day courses. Many communities publish an annual programme of events, including day and evening classes, and tourist offices may also provide information. Most Swiss universities also organise non-residential courses, particularly in summer.

DAY & EVENING CLASSES

Adult day and evening classes are offered by various organisations in cities and large towns. The largest is the Migros Club School (*Migros Klubschule,* école *club Migros,* 🖳 www.klubschule.ch), funded by the Migros supermarket and department store chain. It has ten regional co-operatives which operate over 50 centres in major cities and towns throughout Switzerland. Over 300 different subjects are taught, including foreign languages and local language courses for foreigners (around 50 per cent of total classes), handicrafts, hobbies and sports (around 40

per cent), and further education, e.g. computer studies (some 10 per cent). Migros schools publish regional programmes containing a list of local clubs (available free from Migros clubs and stores). Other companies and organisations that provide day and evening classes include Co-op Leisure Centres (*Coop-Freizeit-Center, centre de loisirs Coop*).

The Federation of American Women's Clubs Overseas (FAWCO) and other expatriate organisations also run day and evening classes in many subjects, and some organisations provide classes for children (e.g. English), particularly during school holidays.

There are around 100 adult or further education centres in Switzerland, called the 'People's High School' (*Volkshochschule, université populaire,* 🖳 www.up-vhs.ch), which hold classes in general education, geography, culture and languages. These schools offer mostly evening classes plus some Saturday classes, with many subjects taught by university and high school teachers (classes are often held in school classrooms or at the universities). Course fees are reasonable (schools are subsidised by the cantons and communities) courses include French and German classes for foreigners with the possibility of taking official Goethe Institut or Alliance Française tests.

Education Guide Switzerland

A new guide cataloging English-language academic opportunities throughout the whole of Switzerland. Each page describes a preschool, school, university, or academic program available in English. The catalog-style of Education Guide Switzerland allows easy access to fast facts on the outer margin of each page. It is especially interesting to be able to see the tuition fees per year at the same time as how many students, faculty members or nationalities are represented.

For more information or to buy a copy, see 🖳 www. knowitall.ch.

Glacier Express

10.
PUBLIC TRANSPORT

Public transport services (*öffentlicher Verkehr*, *transport public*) **in Switzerland are excellent and provide a frequent, convenient and inexpensive service to every corner of the country. The government firmly believes that the benefits of a first class public transport system far outweigh the cost, even if it means increased public subsidies (although costs are causing concern). All modes of public transport are highly efficient, completely integrated, clean and usually punctual to the minute (among the most reliable clocks in Switzerland are those at railway stations). With some 24,500km (over 15,000mi) of fixed transport lines (trains, trams, trolley-buses and cableways), Switzerland has the most dense public transport network in the world.**

It isn't essential to own a car in Switzerland, particularly if you live in or near a large town or city. For example, Zurich has one of the world's best public transport systems, which even includes the free loan of bicycles (bicycles, including electric bicycles, can also be rented in many other towns and cities) and when you need a car you can hire one by the hour (see **Car Sharing** on page 155). This is verified by the frequency of use of public transport by its citizens, which is double that in many other major European cities. However, if you live in a remote village or a town off the main train and bus routes, you'll find it more convenient or even essential to have your own transport.

On first acquaintance, Swiss public transport may seem expensive to some foreigners. However, if you take advantage of the often bewildering range of discounts and season tickets available, public transport provides excellent value for money and is often a bargain (particularly in relation to Swiss salaries).

In some cities free tickets are provided for visitors which allow you to travel to a city centre from an airport (e.g. Basle and Geneva), and a rail ticket or hotel booking in some cities includes 'free' travel on local public transport for a period, e.g. 60-80 minutes. In Geneva, anyone staying at a hotel, youth hostel or campsite is entitled to a free Geneva Transport Card, which permits the holder to use the entire city public transportation network (bus, train and boat) for the duration of their stay, including their departure day. If you're in Switzerland for less than four days, you can purchase day passes for most cities which provide unlimited travel on all regional transportation.

If you find all the different tickets for buses and trains bewildering, it's hardly surprising. The solution is simply to tell the ticket office clerk where you want to go, when and how often you want to travel, and (for train journeys) whether 1st or 2nd class. You can generally rely on him to provide you with the cheapest ticket available – unless it's his first day on the job, in which case he'll be just as confused as you are!

> With such an abundance of season and discounted tickets, the only thing you can be sure of is that if you aren't travelling free, you could be paying too much!

Even greater savings can be made with tickets combining travel on different public transport systems, e.g. railways, buses and trams. For example, there's a 'junior' card (*Junior-Karte*, *carte junior*), which is valid for one year and entitles children aged under 16 to travel free when accompanied by a parent. Other discounted tickets and passes are detailed in this chapter.

Any journey by rail, boat or PostBus may be broken without cost or formality, provided your ticket remains valid. It's advisable to notify the conductor when planning to do so, however, or he may retain or cancel your ticket.

TRAINS

The Swiss railway network is one of the most extensive in Europe, with around 5,000km (3,100mi) of track – most electrified – over 800 stations, some 300 tunnels (totalling 259km/160mi in length) and around 6,000 bridges (totalling 87km/54mi in length). It includes 2,000km (1,240mi) of private lines operated by some 50 'private' companies – they aren't strictly private as many are run by cantonal governments. The Swiss federal railway company is usually referred to by its initials, which vary according to the local language: SBB (*Schweizerische Bundesbahnen*) in German, used in this book to refer to Swiss federal railways, CFF (*Chemins de Fer Fédéraux*) in French and FFS (*Ferrovie Federali Svizzere*) in Italian – written as SBB-CFF-FFS on the side of Swiss trains.

Swiss trains run like clockwork and are seldom late, and when you need to make a connection the train is often waiting for you on the next platform.

The SBB, which celebrated its 160th anniversary in 2007, is renowned for its punctuality – although building or maintenance work and bad weather occasionally delay trains – comfort and speed (if you're sightseeing, take a slow train).

Despite frequent fare increases in recent years to try to reduce SBB's deficit, Swiss trains remain relatively inexpensive if you take advantage of offers, excursion fares, family reductions and holiday package deals (see **Discounted Tickets**

below). Over long distances trains are cheaper than buses. The Swiss are Europe's most frequent train travellers and average around 2,000km (ca. 1,250mi) per year, per head of population.

The New Rail Link through the Alps/NRLA (*Neue Eisenbahnalpentransversalen/NEAT*) project – usually referred to as the Alp Transit Project (💻 www.alptransit.ch) – is creating what will be the world's longest railway tunnel (57km/35mi) between Erstfeld (UR) and Biasca (TI), which is expected to be completed in 2017. It's one of the world's largest construction projects and includes the extension of two north-south railway lines through Switzerland and three new flat railway tunnels. The first north-south line, the Lötschberg base tunnel section (34.6km/21.5mi) in canton Berne, was completed in 2007 and allows passenger trains to reach speeds of up to 250kph/155mph, while the Wysshus underpass in Altdorf was opened to traffic on 28th September 2012.

Types of Trains

Swiss Trains are categorised as local trains (*Regionalzug, train régional*), fast trains (*Schnellzug, train direct*) and international trains. Fast trains include Intercity (IC), which serve the main Swiss cities; fast regional trains, called RegioExpress, operate in some areas, e.g. between St Gallen and Chur; and S-Bahn (the S is short for *schnell* or fast) suburban trains which operate in many regions, including Zurich. Eurocity (EC) trains provide services between major Swiss cities and over 200 European cities – most have sleeping cars and cars with seats which convert into berths (*couchettes*), e.g. CityNightLine trains. Most Swiss trains consist of first- and second-class carriages.

A supplement is payable by domestic passengers using EC trains, and bookings (costing CHF 5) are obligatory for international travel. Booking is optional on IC and many domestic fast trains, although it's recommended when travelling during public holiday periods or at weekends. Bookings can be made from 24 hours to two months in advance (up to three months for compartments in sleeping cars).

The SBB provides various kinds of carriages on IC trains, including a 'silent carriage' where mobile phones, noisy music (with or without headphones) and loud conversations are prohibited; 1st class business compartments (identified by a laptop pictogram) equipped with power sockets for laptops, mobile phones and PDAs; and a 'playroom car' for children, denoted by an illustration of a boy and a girl wearing sunglasses on the outside. Not all of these carriages are provided on all trains and it's also advisable to book.

Information regarding trains (and tickets) is available from information offices (denoted by a blue letter 'i' in a white circle on a blue background) at major stations or ticket offices at smaller stations.

> Information and seat reservations for Swiss rail services are also available by telephone (☎ 0900-300 300, CHF 1.19 per minute) or via the internet (🖳 www.sbb.ch).

General Information

Note the following regarding to Swiss rail services:

◆ All Swiss Intercity and long-distance trains provide a mobile drinks-and-snacks service, and most have a snack bar and/or restaurant car (some self-service). Restaurant cars are denoted by a crossed fork and knife on timetables.

◆ A person or guide dog accompanying a disabled or blind person travels free of charge but needs an SBB pass. The disabled or blind person must be a Swiss resident and have a medical certificate and an official identity card for disabled passengers issued by a cantonal authority.

◆ Dogs are permitted to travel in passenger carriages and require a second-class ticket (season tickets are also available), which is also valid in 1st class. Small dogs – up to 30cm (12in) at the shoulder – travel free when carried in baskets.

◆ The SBB runs a Junior-Club SBB (🖳 www. magicticket.ch) for children aged 6 to 16, which offers members reductions on excursions and a bi-annual magazine.

◆ Rail journeys can be combined with travel on local buses, PostBuses and lake ferries.

◆ A 'playroom car' for children, denoted by an illustration of a boy and a girl wearing sunglasses on the outside of the carriage, is provided on many routes. Look for the letters 'FA' alongside the time on SBB timetables. Playroom cars contain a central play area (free for families with children aged 2 to 12) equipped with a slide, swing, 'fairy-tale' telephones, books and games. They also have a nappy-changing room and folding seats to allow space for prams and push chairs.

SBB plans to begin fining passengers who occupy seats in full carriages with their jackets or bags – you have been warned!

Station Services

The following facilities can be found at Swiss railway stations:

◆ Many main railway stations offer a choice of restaurants and snack bars, generally providing good food at reasonable prices.

◆ Major stations have a 'RailCity' shopping centre with long opening hours, including Sundays and public holidays. Shops in the vicinity of most stations (within around 200m) tend to also have extended opening hours.

◆ Many large railway stations provide wash, shower and brush-up facilities (branded, sadly, 'McClean'), including hair-dryers (there's a fee). Some provide nappy (diaper) changing rooms.

◆ There are instant passport photograph machines at most stations.

◆ Park and ride car parks are provided at many railway stations, where you can park from around CHF 5 per day, depending on the station.

◆ Wheelchairs for disabled passengers are provided at many railway stations. Most trains have facilities for the storage of wheelchairs and new trains have carriages which accommodate wheelchairs. The SBB publishes a brochure entitled 'Passengers with a Disability' (available only in German). There's also a hotline for disabled travellers (☎ 0800-007 102).

◆ Main railway stations have banks with long opening hours and many smaller stations provide money changing facilities. At many stations you can buy and sell foreign currencies, buy Swiss franc travellers' cheques and cash travellers' cheques.

◆ Bicycles can be rented from many railway stations and transported on trains (see **Bicycle Rental & Transportation** below). Bicycle and moped parking, both covered and uncovered, is provided at most stations.

◆ You can pick up a rental car at some 75 major railway stations (see **Car Sharing** on page 155).

◆ Most SBB information leaflets are available at railway stations in French, German, and Italian (many are also in English).

Information regarding trains (and tickets) is available from information offices (denoted by a blue letter 'i' in a white circle on a blue background) at major stations or the ticket office at smaller stations. Finally, if you want to encourage someone to visit you, you can send them an SBB travel gift voucher.

Luggage

Three items of luggage can be carried on a train without charge – officially with a combined weight of no more than 30kg, although nobody checks or weighs them. However, the SBB has many ways of lightening your load (and taking a load off your mind) when travelling with luggage, including the following.

Unaccompanied Luggage

Provided you have a valid ticket for the same route, luggage can be sent unaccompanied for CHF 12 per item (CHF 10 for groups and card holders) and collected at your destination station. Depending on your destination, international luggage can be sent unaccompanied for CHF 33 (CHF 27 for groups) per piece, up to a maximum weight of 25kg. Skis, ski boots or snowboards can also be sent for CHF 12 for each item or a number of items together in a ski bag for CHF 12 (up to a maximum weight of 25kg). Luggage can be booked in at PostBus depots for delivery to a railway station or airport.

☑ SURVIVAL TIP

Luggage can also be sent unaccompanied to Switzerland from abroad with a customs declaration form. It's advisable to register your luggage early, at least the day before departure.

There may be a storage charge of around CHF 2 per day, per item, depending on the station. Insurance is available for luggage when travelling within Switzerland.

Bicycles

Bicycles can be sent between any two stations in Switzerland with a 1-day bike pass costing CHF 18 (CHF 12 with a half-fare travel card – see below), provided you have a valid ticket and load it yourself. You can also send a normal bike internationally, for which the price varies depending on the destination. For short trips, a bike ticket costs half the normal fare with a half-fare travel card. You can also purchase an annual bike pass.

Trolleys & Lockers

Many stations have luggage trolleys (at major stations you must pay a returnable deposit of CHF 2) and luggage lockers in several sizes (from around CHF 5 for a medium-size locker).

Tickets & Fares

Tickets (*Billette, billets*) can be purchased online, via mobile phones (increasingly popular) and from ticket offices or ticket machines at most stations. Most ticket offices are open from around 6am until 7.30pm (even later at major stations). You must buy a ticket before boarding a train (see also **Validating Tickets** below).

Single (*einfach, aller-simple*) and return (*Retour/hin und zurück, aller-retour*) tickets for Swiss destinations can be purchased from touch-screen ticket machines in most stations, which are easy to use and have instructions in several languages, including English (touch the button to select the desired language). If you wish to pay with cash, make sure that the machine you choose accepts notes and coins, as some accept only credit cards (machines are clearly marked). All coins except for 5 cents are accepted, as well as CHF 10, 20 and 50 notes, but change is returned only up to CHF 20 (and only in coins).

Other methods of payment include Euros, REKA cheques, Postcards, and credit and debit cards. It's recommended that you use the ticket counter for anything remotely complicated, which will prevent money being wasted on useless tickets, although you can return a ticket purchased in error and obtain a replacement or a refund.

Bookings (reservations) can be made (for CHF 5) on all IC, ICE, CIS, EC and TGV trains, and are sometimes obligatory. A second-class ticket can be upgraded to 1st class on payment of the fare difference.

Validating Tickets

If you have a General Season ticket, commuter ticket or a dated ticket issued from a ticket machine or the ticket office, you don't need to validate your ticket. If you have a multi-journey ticket or a day pass you must validate it in an orange ticket validating machine (*Entwerter, oblitérateur*) – provided on all platforms – by inserting the ticket in the slot.

All trains now require passengers to have a valid ticket before boarding and you can no longer buy a ticket from the conductor on a train. Failure to buy or validate a ticket can result in a minimum CHF 80 fine if you're discovered during a spot-check, in addition to which you must pay the correct fare.

Make sure that you don't accidentally travel in a first-class carriage with a second-class ticket, which also incurs a fine.

Discounted Tickets

Many season tickets (*Abonnement*) and other discounted tickets are available in Switzerland. These include tickets for families, the young (16-25), senior citizens, commuters and groups of ten or more, as well as 'ski-day', hiking and cycling tickets, and other holiday and excursion tickets. Information is available from information or ticket offices at railway stations (staff usually speak English). A brochure is also available from railway stations describing the various season and discounted tickets available.

Half-fare Travel Card

The best rail offer in Switzerland (the world?) is the half-fare travel card (*Halbtax-Abo, abonnement demi-tarif*), a joint venture of Swiss transport operators, costing CHF 165 for one year, CHF 300 for two years or CHF 400 for three years. A half-fare travel card for 16-year-olds (who must usually pay full price for tickets) is available for CHF 96. Over 2m *Halbtax* cards are sold annually and entitle holders to half-fare travel on all SBB trains, PostBuses, selected city buses and trams, and many ferries and cable cars – a total network of around 24,500km (over 15,000mi). Half-fare travel cards are available from all railway stations and many PostBus depots and travel agents, on production of a passport photo and the fee. You must sign your half-fare travel card below your photograph.

Holders of a half-fare travel card may purchase day cards which provide unlimited travel for a whole day on all SBB trains and PostBuses. Day cards cost CHF 68 each for 2nd class (CHF 112 1st class) or six day cards for the price of five (CHF 340 2nd class, CHF 560 1st class). Cards don't need to be used on consecutive days and can be used by anyone with a half-fare travel card.

A child's day card is also available for CHF 15 2nd class (CHF 30 1st class). As with any other ticket, day cards must be validated before use. Those aged under 25 can purchase a card called 'Track 7' (*Gleis 7/Voie 7*) for CHF 304 (CHF 129 for the Track 7 card and CHF 165 for a one year half-fare card) which provides half-fare travel before 7pm and free travel after 7pm. A monthly travel card is also available to half-fare travel card holders which converts your half-fare travel card into a general season ticket (see below) for one month.

Many Swiss cities and towns sell day cards at much reduced prices (between CHF 30 and 40) to residents. Only a limited number of cards are available per day, and weekend cards (Sat/Sun) are usually sold out quickly but can be reserved months in advance. Enquire about community day passes (*Gemeinde Tageskarte, cartes journaliéres CFF*) at your community offices or see 🖥 www.tageskarte-gemeinde.ch. Tickets can usually be reserved online and must be collected and paid for within seven days (they can also be reserved, paid for and collected in person, usually at a town hall or post office). Tickets are pre-dated and valid for use only on the date stamped on them and aren't refundable. You don't need a half-fare card to buy day cards, but you must be a community resident (proof is required).

More information can be obtained by telephoning the Half-Fare Travelcard Helpdesk (☎ 0848-33 55 77).

General Season Ticket

The general season ticket (*Generalabonnement – GA, abonnement général – AG*), which is purchased by over 300,000 people each year, provides unlimited travel on all SBB trains, PostBuses, and other buses and trams in some 35 cities and towns, plus many private railways and lake steamers. It also includes a 50 per cent reduction on other licensed coach operators, mountain railways and aerial cableways. A GA ticket can be extended during a holiday or other 'long' period spent abroad by depositing it at a railway station and collecting it on your return.

A general season ticket costs CHF 3,550 per year 2nd class (CHF 5,800 1st class) for those aged over 25; CHF 2,530 2nd class (CHF 4,310 1st class) for those aged between 16 and 25 (and higher education students); CHF 2,550 2nd class (CHF 4,200 1st class) for senior citizens; CHF 2,300 2nd class (CHF 3,760 1st class) for the disabled; and CHF 1,570 2nd class (2,630 1st class) for children aged under 16. Tickets aren't transferable (outside the listed users) and adults require a passport photo. There are a number of combinations for families – ask at ticket offices for information. Cards can be ordered online at ⌨ www.sbb.ch/en/travelcards-and-tickets/railpasses/the-general-abonnement/ga-for-individuals.html.

There's even a general season ticket for dogs, which costs CHF 760 (both 1st and 2nd class) – no picture required! Although annual season tickets may appear to be expensive, if you do a lot of travelling on public transport, they're a bargain. Transferable general season tickets cannot be extended during absences from Switzerland.

☑ SURVIVAL TIP

If you have a 15-year old child and purchase a child general season ticket one day before he or she turns 16, the child can travel for a year for CHF1,570 instead of the normal general season ticket price (CHF 2,530) for a 16-year-old (a saving of CHF 960).

Commuter Tickets

If you're a regular train commuter, you can buy a weekly, monthly or annual 'point-to-point' season ticket (*Streckenabonnement, abonnement de parcours*). An annual point-to-point season ticket costs around the same as nine monthly tickets. In some cantons, the rail network is divided into zones and season tickets are available for a number of zones or the whole network. A photograph is required for an annual season ticket. Multiple journey cards (usually valid for 6 or 12 journeys) can save you time and sometimes money. You can make further savings by combining bus (both PostBuses and local services) and rail journeys. Ask at any railway station.

Junior Card

A 'junior' card (*Junior-Karte, carte junior*) is valid for one year and entitles children aged up to 16 to travel free when accompanied by a parent. The parent must have a full-fare or half-fare ticket, but not a commuter ticket. The junior card can be used on all SBB trains, private railways, PostBuses and lake steamers. It can also be used in around 35 towns to purchase city bus and tram day-cards under the same conditions as for trains. Junior cards are available from railway stations (and PostBus depots) for CHF 30 for the first and second children and free for subsequent children. The card must be signed and dated by the holder.

Supersaver Tickets

One of the best bargains on Swiss railways is Supersaver single tickets, which provide large discounts on selected long-distance routes. Book early (up to 14 days before travel) as there are only a limited number of Supersaver tickets per train, and they are only on sale for a limited period (e.g. October to January). Tickets are valid for a specific journey and time and aren't refundable or transferable. For more information and to book tickets, see ⌨ http://sparbillette.sbb.ch.

Youth Fares

Youth fares are available for those aged 16 to 25 (30 for full-time students). Discounts are also available on some international routes.

BUSES & TRAMS

Two, separate bus services are provided throughout most of Switzerland; the PostBus service, and city and suburban bus networks. Together they cover most towns and villages in Switzerland. There's also an extensive tram or trolley bus network in all major cities. Like the SBB (Swiss railways), bus companies offer many discounted day, multi-ride and season tickets. There are also international bus services (e.g. Eurolines) to various countries.

Combined bus (PostBus and local buses) and train commuter tickets are available from railway stations, offering large savings compared with the cost of separate bus and train tickets.

PostBus

The PostBus service (*Postauto, Car Postal*), which celebrated its centenary in 2006, covers around 10,450km (6,530mi) of Switzerland's principal roads and provides regular services to over 1,600 localities on its 750+ routes. Many remote villages are served only by PostBuses, which carry over 120m passengers a year.

PostBuses are painted bright yellow and distinguished by a red stripe and an alp horn motif on their sides. They have a distinctive (real) horn to warn motorists of their approach on mountain roads.

The PostBus service is comfortable, punctual, inexpensive and safe, and employs one of the most modern fleets of buses in the world (safety features include two independent braking systems and a handbrake). PostBus drivers inspire confidence and are among the world's best professional drivers. It's probably the best national bus service provided anywhere in the world.

As its name implies, the main task of the PostBus service is to deliver and collect post. Around one-third of Swiss homes rely on the PostBus service for their post and newspapers, which is one reason why PostBuses have the right of way on all roads. Trailers are often attached to the rear of buses to carry parcels and luggage (in winter a ski trailer may be used).

Like trains, PostBuses also use the eye symbol (see page 122), although on a bus it signifies that a ticket validation machine (*Entwerter*, *oblitérateur*) is installed inside the bus for holders of multi-ride tickets. Passengers without tickets must board at the front of the bus and buy a ticket from the driver. When a bus stop is situated outside a post office or railway station, you should buy your ticket there to avoid delays on boarding a bus.

PostBuses don't automatically stop at all stops, and it's usually necessary to press the stop button to instruct the driver to stop when you want to get off. A stopping sign (*hält an*, *arrêt*) is illuminated at the front of the bus when it's about to stop. You must usually press another button to open the doors. If you're waiting at a 'request' stop, you'll need to flag the bus down (wave to the driver) to get the driver to stop.

For more information, see 🖳 www. postauto.ch/en.

General Information

The following general information applies to PostBus services:

♦ Passengers can take hand luggage (no weight limit), although a charge is made for unaccompanied baggage.

♦ Dogs are carried for half-fare (small dogs in baskets are carried free).

♦ Bicycles are transported for CHF 18 (CHF 12 with a half-fare travel card – see above) with a 1-day card, either

inside the bus or in a luggage compartment or trailer (booking is strongly recommended). On local buses the fare is half the normal fare with a half-fare travel card.

♦ Children aged under six travel free and children aged 6 to 16 pay half-fare.

♦ There's a 20 per cent reduction for groups of ten or more.

♦ Bookings are necessary on some long-distance routes.

♦ Journeys may be broken but tickets must be validated at the start of each journey.

♦ PostBuses operate weekly bus tours abroad, which include hotel accommodation, full board (all meals), excursions and entrance tickets.

♦ The half-fare travel card (see above) allows half-fare travel on all PostBuses and some local bus services.

City Buses & Trams

Most towns and cities in Switzerland are served by local bus services, and main cities also have tram or trolley bus services. Tickets for both single and multiple journeys must normally be purchased from ticket machines (located at most stops) before boarding. Tickets are also sold at ticket offices, newspaper kiosks and railway stations near bus and tram stops. Tickets can sometimes be purchased from the driver but a surcharge may be payable if there was a ticket machine (in operation) at the stop where boarding.

Berne old town

The procedure for buying a ticket from a machine is roughly the same throughout Switzerland and instructions on machines and in information leaflets are usually given in English. The stop where you're located may be marked by an arrow or a red spot on a route map, and zones are shown in different colours. Fare selection buttons are usually colour coded to match the different zones, although with some machines you press the button corresponding to the postcode of your destination or simply press the button for your destination. A single arrow denotes a single ticket and two arrows pointing in opposite directions denote a return ticket. Machines usually accept all coins from ten cents and some also accept notes but may not give change!

In some cities, e.g. Zurich, there are machines that sell tickets for all city transport, including local trains, trams, buses and boats. The procedure for buying tickets from these machines is virtually identical to buying rail tickets (see above). The main difference is that there are coloured buttons for the different zones. If you want a day pass, press the button marked with arrows in opposite directions. These machines don't accept banknotes, although some accept credit cards. If you're in doubt about how to use a ticket machine, ask someone to help you; kicking it won't help (but may make you feel better!). In some cities, e.g. Geneva, there are 'rechargeable' tickets, which you can recharge in machines at bus stops.

Tickets are usually valid for both buses and trams, if applicable, and journeys may combine the two modes of transport, provided you travel in one direction only. You can break your journey, but must complete the overall journey within the time limit shown on your ticket (e.g. one hour), depending on the number of zones selected. You must validate (time and date stamp) a multi-ride ticket in a machine (*Entwerter*, *oblitérateur*), either before boarding or on board a tram or bus (many trams and buses have a machine inside). If there's no validation machine at the stop where you're boarding or on board, you should pay the driver and keep your ticket for a future journey.

There are no conductors on buses or trams, but random checks are made by ticket inspectors. If you don't have a valid ticket, you must pay a fine (e.g. CHF 80 if paid on the spot) and possibly also the correct fare, depending on the inspector. If you refuse or are unable to pay the fine, you can be arrested (persistent offenders are put in the stocks!).

Journeys on most city bus and tram services can be combined with travel on PostBuses and SBB rail services, often with large savings.

General Information

The following general information applies to bus and tram travel:

◆ Trams and buses don't usually operate between around midnight and 5.30am, although major cities have a 'night bus' system for party-goers, shift workers and insomniacs.

◆ Children under six don't require a ticket when accompanied by an adult. Children aged 6 to 16 usually pay a reduced fare. You must generally pay half-fare for dogs and non-collapsible baby carriages; prams usually require an additional full fare.

◆ School bus and tram passes may be invalid after around 8pm and on Sundays and school holidays.

◆ A person or guide dog accompanying a disabled or blind person travels free of charge, but a pass is required. The disabled or blind person must be a Swiss resident with a medical certificate and an identity card for disabled passengers (issued by cantonal authorities).

◆ Groups of ten or more people usually qualify for a group discount.

◆ Ticket machines don't always give change, so check before inserting coins. If in doubt, insert the exact fare.

◆ On many buses and trams you must press a button to open the doors to get on or off (doors are closed by the driver). Trams halt at most stops, although the doors may not open unless

you press a button. On buses you must usually request the driver to stop by pressing a 'stop' button when you near your destination. When waiting at a 'request' bus stop, you may need to signal the driver to stop (hold out your arm or wave to him).

◆ Always check the line number and direction of a tram or bus before boarding. If in doubt ask someone.

Tickets

Multi-journey Tickets

A multi-journey ticket (*Mehrfahrtenkarte, carte multicourse*) provides six journeys for a 10 per cent reduction. Half-fare travel card holders and children under 16 receive a 50 per cent discount. Tickets are transferable and can be used by several people travelling together and are valid for three years. Tickets can be purchased at train stations and PostBus depots and via the internet (🖳 www.sbb.ch).

Point-to-point Season Tickets

A Point-to-point Season Ticket (*Streckenabonnement, abonnement de parcours*) is for commuters or anyone who regularly travels the same route (point-to-point). There's a choice of tickets, valid for a week, a month or a year. The price depends on the distance or the number of zones travelled.

There are adult and youth passes available. Passes aren't transferable, require a photograph and must be signed by the holder. They can be combined with services operated by other bus companies and are available from bus depots, train stations and online (🖳 www.sbb.ch).

Discounted Tickets

There are a variety of discounted city bus and tram tickets available in most regions, including the following:

◆ Single and multi-ride (e.g. 12 single trips) tickets for different zones, with a time limit to

reach your destination, e.g. 30 minutes to two hours, depending on the number of zones. You may change buses or trams but must travel in one direction only.

◆ Day cards offering unlimited travel within 24 hours on city trams, buses and suburban trains (plus boats and funiculars, if applicable) are available in 38 towns from around CHF 8 (the price depends on the number of zones). You must usually sign a day card and it isn't transferable. In some towns a multiple day pass is available, e.g. a six-day pass is available in Zurich, which must be validated before use each day.

◆ Tickets allowing unlimited travel on city buses and trams are provided for visitors to trade fairs and conventions, as well as guests at some hotels. Ask at the local public transport information office, tourist office or hotel desk.

◆ 'Green' season tickets (*Umweltschutzabonnement/Umweltpass, Abonnement onde verte*) are available in some regions, which allow unlimited travel on all local buses, trams and trains (excluding fast, Intercity and Eurocity trains).

◆ There are reduced price tickets for students under 30 (with a student identity card), pensioners and the disabled (buses designed for wheelchair users are provided in some cities).

◆ Monthly and annual season tickets are available for under 25s, pensioners, the disabled and other adults. A monthly pass is available in most cities, allowing unlimited travel on all city transport.

◆ Family and day tickets are available and the half-fare travel card (see above) is valid on most local bus services, where the same conditions apply as for trains and PostBuses.

FERRIES

Over 140 ferries and paddle steamers with accommodation for a total of some 60,000 passengers are in service from spring to autumn (April to October) on lakes and rivers throughout Switzerland. Regular car and passenger services operate year round on the main lakes, although services are reduced in winter and bad weather sometimes causes cancellations. In summer there are round trips including breakfast or lunch, as well as folklore and dinner and dance cruises. Reduced fares are usually offered for groups, school parties and holders of a Swiss Card (see below), while holders of an SBB general season ticket (see above) or Swiss Pass (see below) travel free.

The Swiss Boat Pass (CHF 50) provides a 50 per cent discount on all boat cruises and is valid for one year on 14 lakes served by the Swiss Shipping Company and its partners. The Swiss Family Boat Pass costs CHF 80 a year and gives parents a 50 per cent discount, while children under 16 travel free (🖳 www.vssu.ch). Ships can be chartered for private cruises on most lakes. Ferry passengers may break journeys without formality.

Car ferry services are provided on lakes Constance, Lucerne and Zurich. Passenger ships of the Köln-Düsseldorf (KD) German Rhine Line operate scheduled services between Basle and points in Germany, France and the Netherlands. Free or reduced price steamer services are available for Eurailpass and Eurail youthpass holders (see **Rail Passes** above).

CABLE CARS & MOUNTAIN RAILWAYS

There are over 700 cog and rack railways, funiculars and aerial cableways in Switzerland, extending to over 2,000km (some 1,250mi). Most operate throughout the year (bad weather excepted) and in winter an additional 1,700 ski-lifts (i.e. chair-lifts and T-bars) are in use.

Cable cars and mountain railways are generally expensive, particularly those that scale the heights, for example Jungfraujoch (3,454m/11,332ft) and the Klein Matterhorn in Zermatt (3,884m/12,743ft). It costs CHF 177.80 to travel from Interlaken to Jungfraujoch full fare, although there are many special offers (see 🖳 www.jungfraubahn.ch). Holders of a half-fare travel card (see above) or general season ticket can obtain reductions on many cable cars and mountain railways, so don't forget to ask before buying a ticket.

A cheaper, but nevertheless spectacular, option is the Vitznau-Rigi Bahn (the first mountain rack railway in Europe and only the second in the world) which takes you to the summit of Rigi Kulm (1,752m/5,748ft) from where there are panoramic views (see 🖳 www.rigi.ch/en/welcome.cfm).

If you plan to travel to the top of a mountain, take sunglasses and a warm pullover, and bear in mind that the view, which on a clear day can stretch for hundreds of kilometres, is often disappointing.

AIRLINE SERVICES

Switzerland is well served by airlines, both international and domestic, but no longer has its own international airline – Swiss was taken over by Lufthansa in 2005 (a blow to Swiss air transport and Swiss pride!), although it retains its Swiss identity (🖳 www.swiss.com). Swiss International Air Lines was named the Best Airline Western Europe at the 2011 World Airline Awards.

Although standard air fares to and from Switzerland aren't the most competitive in Europe, a range of reduced fares is available. The major Swiss airports are served from the UK by a number of low-cost carriers, including Easyjet (🖳 www.easyjet.com) and Flybe (🖳 www.flybe.com). Geneva is the main gateway for budget flights, while very few budget airlines fly to Zurich.

The introduction of 'no-frills' flights into the Swiss market has been revolutionary and has provided some welcome competition, forcing Swiss and other airlines to reduce their fares. Budget airline fares can be as little as £25 single (e.g. from London), although fares vary considerably depending on the time of day, day of the week and the season. Usually the further you book in advance, the lower the fare. However, bear in mind that budget airlines' advertised prices don't include more than one checked bag, credit card fees and whatever else they can charge extra for (seats, water, using the toilet, etc.).

If you're planning a trip abroad during the school holidays, book well in advance, particularly if you're going to a popular destination.

Airports

Most major international airlines provide scheduled services to and from Switzerland via one of the three 'Swiss' international gateway airports (*Flughafen, aéroport*) of Basle (EuroAirport), Geneva-Cointrin and Zurich-Kloten. Internationally, Zurich is the most important Swiss airport, although Geneva

– due largely to its proximity to France and French ski resorts – has by far the largest number of flights from the UK, with direct flights from around a dozen UK airports. Berne, the capital of Switzerland, doesn't have an 'official' international airport, although its airport (Bern-Belp) provides a few scheduled international flights and it's also served by domestic flights from the major Swiss airports.

Besides the three main airports, there are over 40 smaller regional airports and airfields in Switzerland, including Ambri (TI), Berne (BE), Bex (VD), Birrfeld (AG), Bressaucourt (JU), Buttwil (AG), Dübendorf (ZH), Emmen (LU), Engadin (GR), Grenchen (SO), Gruyere (FR), Langenthal (BE), Lausanne (VD), Lugano (TI), Motiers (NE), Schaenis (SG), Sion (VD), St Gallen-Altenrhein (SG), Triengen (LU) and Yverdon-les-Bains (VD). The regional airports of Berne, Sion and St Gallen-Altenrhein handle a few international flights, while others handle mainly private and chartered business flights.

You can check-in at the major Swiss airports using self check-in machines, which are also provided at airport railway stations, and there's usually a baggage-drop close to machines with no queues. This also applies to those who check in online.

The major airports provide bus and rail transport to the nearest city and beyond, and car hire is also available. All major airports have websites (see box), although information isn't always provided in English (see table below), and most provide useful tourist information, including accommodation options as well as airport information.

The following general information applies to the three major Swiss airports:

♦ Swiss airports have wheelchairs and ambulance staff to help disabled travellers, and airlines also publish brochures for disabled travellers.

♦ Long- and short-term parking is available at all major airports, including reserved parking for the disabled.

♦ Both Geneva and Zurich airports have shopping centres open from 8am to 8pm, seven days a week.

♦ A welcome surprise at Swiss airports (particularly Zurich) is an ample supply of luggage trolleys, which also allow you to take your baggage up and down escalators, although they may not be free, e.g. CHF 2 in Geneva.

♦ SBB provides a 'Fly Rail Baggage' service for travellers using Geneva and Zurich airports, whereby you can check-in your baggage (and receive your boarding pass, depending on the airline) at over 50 railway stations and on to your final destination. This also applies to passengers arriving at Geneva and Zurich airports, who can have their baggage forwarded to their destination Swiss rail station and don't need to collect it at the airport and go through customs.

TIMETABLES

Swiss timetables are truthful and accurate, meaning that a train or bus due at 8.17am will arrive at or very close to this time. (What else would you expect from the country that invented precision?) In mountainous areas, avalanches and landslides do, however, occasionally upset timetables.

Local bus and train timetables (often sponsored by Swiss banks) are posted in offices, factories and restaurants and available from post offices. All services run frequently, particularly during rush hours. Your local public transport company may have a website where you can print out a timetable.

At major airports and railway stations, arrivals (*Ankunft, arrivée*) and departures (*Abfahrt, départ*) are shown on electronic boards. Regional timetables (*Regionalfahrplan, horaire*

Flight Information

Airport	Telephone Number	Website
Basle-Mulhouse	061 325 31 11	www.euroairport.com
Berne	031 960 21 11	www.flughafenbern.ch
Geneva	022 717 71 11	www.gva.ch
Lugano	091 610 11 11	www.lugano-airport.ch
Zurich	0900 300 313	www.zurich-airport.com

régional) for both train and bus services are available free of charge from stations and bus depots. A separate timetable is published for trains with restaurant cars.

If you're a frequent traveller, the official timetable (*Offizielles Kursbuch, indicateur officiel*), published annually at the end of December, is a must. It costs CHF 16 from railway information or ticket offices (it's also available on CD-ROM for CHF 16) and includes the following three timetable books:

1. Swiss railways, cableways and ferries;
2. PostBuses;
3. International rail services.

Books 1 and 2 are published annually and the international rail services timetable is published biannually, summer and winter. The international timetable for the second half-year (winter) is sent free on application (a post-free postcard is included in the summer edition). The Swiss railway timetable includes the services of many privately-operated railways. All timetables contain information in English.

A timetable is also available via SMS (text), which is useful when you're en route. Simply send your departure destination station name to ☎ 222 (Orange/Swisscom Mobile) or ☎ 999 (Sunrise) and you'll receive a list of the next connections (CHF 0.60 per SMS).

☑ SURVIVAL TIP

Nowadays many people use the SBB timetable app to obtain train information (and buy tickets). See 🖥 www.sbb.ch/en/timetable/mobile-timetables/mobile-apps.html for information.

Rail information can be obtained from the SBB's Rail Service Number (☎ 0900-30 03 00, costing CHF 1.19 per minute) and from station information offices. An interactive timetable for Swiss trains, ships and post buses is also available via the internet (🖥 www.sbb.ch).

An excellent railway map of Switzerland, including 13 city plans, can be purchased at SBB stations. A variety of free local and regional maps is also published.

TAXIS

Swiss taxis are among the most expensive in the world, with a basic charge of CHF 6, plus CHF 3.80 for each kilometre (rates quoted are for Zurich), depending on the area and time of day. In Zurich there are no additional charges for baggage, while in Lucerne, for example, each piece of baggage costs CHF 1. In Basle and some other cities there are special reduced prices (10-30 per cent reduction) for woman travelling alone at night with a 'Lady Profitcard' (see 🖥 www.33ertaxi.ch).

In most major cities, including Basle, Berne, Geneva and Zurich, a service charge is included in the fare, although drivers may expect a tip. Waiting time is charged at around CHF 69 per hour. Due to an increase in violence, some towns and cities have lowered night taxi rates for women (see above).

Taxis cannot always be stopped in the street but can be hired from taxi ranks at railway stations, airports and hotels, or ordered by telephone. Taxis are usually plentiful – except when it's raining, you have lots of luggage or you're late for an appointment.

In winter, many taxis have ski racks, particularly in ski resorts. When travelling with skis or other large objects, mention it when booking by telephone. Wheelchair-accessible taxis are provided in major cities, most of which have a central telephone number, e.g. ☎ 141 in Geneva and Lausanne.

11.
MOTORING

The total Swiss road network covers some 71,300km (44,500mi) – around 1,800km (1,120mi) of which are motorways – all of which have excellent surfaces and are among the best in the world. Switzerland is constantly improving its road system and spends a higher percentage of its motoring tax revenues on its roads than most countries. Every second person in Switzerland owns a car, making it one of the most heavily motorised countries in the world. However, despite the heavy traffic, Switzerland has fewer fatal accidents (per vehicle) than most other European countries. Although the country has an excellent public transport system, many Swiss prefer to travel by car and vigorously protest against any plans to restrict their freedom.

Traffic density in the major Swiss cities is fast approaching the choking levels already experienced in many other European countries, although generally there are fewer traffic jams, and parking, although a problem, isn't impossible. During rush hours, from around 6.30 to 9am and 4 to 6.30pm Mondays to Fridays, the flow of traffic is naturally slower and any interruptions (roadworks, breakdowns and accidents) can cause huge traffic jams (*Stau, embouteillage*). City centres are to be avoided during rush hours, particularly Geneva and Zurich.

Motorway travel is generally fast (the speed limit on motorways is 120kph/75mph), although it's occasionally slowed to a crawl by road works and the favourite Swiss motor sport of shunting the car in front. Outside rush hours, motoring is usually trouble-free and driving on secondary roads in country areas is enjoyable. In winter, many mountain passes are closed due to heavy snowfall from between November and May, and vehicles using pass roads that remain open require snow chains (shown by a sign, which also indicates whether a pass is open or closed). Cars are banned in some mountain resorts.

Although Switzerland has some of the most stringent anti-pollution motoring laws in Europe, traffic pollution is a major concern, particularly in large cities. Nevertheless, it's generally lower than in most other western countries.

General road information is available from the telephone service number (' 163) and Meteoswiss (www.meteoswiss.admin.ch/web/en/services/road_conditions.html). Signs on motorways show the local radio frequency on which road and traffic bulletins are broadcast.

Emergency SOS telephones are located on mountain passes and motorways at 1.6km (1mi) intervals and every 150m in tunnels, where there are also fire extinguishers. Black arrows on white posts at the roadside show the direction of the nearest SOS telephone. The Swiss Bureau for the Prevention of Accidents (see www.suva.ch/english) publishes safety leaflets for motorists, motorcyclists, cyclists and pedestrians.

CAR IMPORTATION

If you plan to take a motor vehicle or motorcycle to Switzerland, either temporarily or permanently, you should be aware of the latest regulations. Check with the manufacturer's export department, the Swiss importers or the local canton vehicle licensing authority in Switzerland. If you're tempted to buy a tax-free car prior to coming to Switzerland, make sure that it conforms to Swiss regulations. Swiss residents can import one car a year for their personal use with minimum testing and modifications. Any car sold in the EU automatically conforms to Swiss standards and can be imported without modifications.

If you wish to import a car (even temporarily), inform the border customs staff on arrival in Switzerland. It's advisable to enter via a major

Geneva Motor Salon

frontier post (e.g. Basle or Geneva) as smaller frontier posts aren't equipped to deal with car importation without advance notice. Registration can, however, also be done at customs offices in major cities. You're required to complete a form and show your car documents. The amount of tax and import duty payable and when due, depends on how long you've owned the car. Before importing a car, check the documents required with your local Swiss embassy or consulate, or contact the Head Customs Office (*Eidgenössische Zollverwaltung/EZV, Direction des Douanes,* ☎ 031-322 65 11, 💻 www.zoll.admin.ch).

Cars Owned Less Than Six Months

If you've owned a car for less than six months, you must pay import duty and tax when importing it into Switzerland. You need to provide documentation confirming the value of the vehicle, the country of origin and an EUR1 certificate (if applicable). Clearance can either be done on entry into Switzerland at main border posts or inland in major cities, on authorisation from the border customs office. The customs post issues you with an authorisation (form 15.25) valid for two days, by which time the car must be presented at a customs depot in the interior.

Import duty is calculated on the weight and/ or engine size of a vehicle, therefore you should remove all luggage and non-standard spares before having it weighed; duty is calculated at CHF 15 per 100kg plus 4 per cent of its value (based on the cost of the vehicle – an invoice must be produced) and VAT at 8 per cent. In addition to import duty, you must also pay a 3 per cent statistical charge (expensive things statistics, especially considering they're usually wrong!).

Cars Owned Longer Than Six Months

If you've owned a car for at least six months and are importing it as part of your personal effects, it's exempt from customs duty and VAT for two years.

You're allowed to drive a car in Switzerland for a maximum of one year on foreign registration plates or until they expire if they're only temporary.

You're given a permit (*Bewilligung, permis*) that must be produced on demand if you're stopped by the police in Switzerland. The car must be for your personal use only and mustn't be lent, rented or sold to a third party in Switzerland for one year from the date of importation. Ensure that you're legally insured to drive in Switzerland during this period (see **Foreign Registered Vehicles** on page 144).

Around one month after importing a car, you'll receive a letter from your canton's motor registration office (*Strassenverkehrsamt, office de la circulation routière*), informing you that in one year's time your car will require an official serviceability test (*Fahrzeugkontrolle, contrôle des véhicules à moteur*). If your foreign registration plates are only temporary and aren't renewable, you must have your car tested in order to obtain Swiss registration plates (see **Serviceability Test** on page 138).

There's sometimes a delay in calling up cars for the serviceability test and you may be able to run your car on foreign plates for longer than one year. When your car is called up for the test, it may be expensive to comply with Swiss safety and pollution regulations, and may not be worth the expense – a local garage or motoring organisation can provide a estimate. If you have a right-hand drive car or an old car, it's usually advisable to buy a car in Switzerland before your first year is completed or when your car is called up for the test. The authorities may give you just a few weeks' notice of the test date and if you decide not to have your car tested you must inform them and export it before the test is due.

After your car passes the test it requires Swiss road tax, insurance and registration plates. However, you aren't required to pay import duty or tax yet. You can apply to your motor registration office for deferred duty plates, which are valid for one year and usually renewable for a further year. These plates are distinguished by a red stripe on the right-hand side and display the year and month of expiry in white. Swiss registration plates indicate the canton of residence of the owner (e.g. GE = Geneva, ZH = Zurich) and have both a Swiss flag emblem and the canton's flag on the rear number plate. After running a car on deferred duty plates for one or two years, you must have it weighed for duty payment. The amount payable also depends on the age and value of the car. You may change your car during the deferred-duty period, but proof of export of your old car must be provided.

Tax-free Importation

If your stay in Switzerland is only temporary and you're domiciled outside Switzerland (e.g. foreign students and businessmen), you may be eligible to buy a duty-free car in Switzerland and run it on tax-free 'Z' plates (*Zollschilder, plaques d'immatriculation douanières*) for a maximum of two years. You may need to provide documentary evidence of your status, as most Swiss residence permit holders are considered to be domiciled in Switzerland and aren't eligible. Like deferred duty plates, Z plates are initially issued for one year and can be renewed for a second year. They're available from your canton's motor registration office on presentation of a special certificate from a Swiss insurance company, which states that you have valid insurance and that your car has passed the official Swiss serviceability test (see below). Insurance may be more expensive with Z plates.

If you're planning to leave Switzerland and take up domicile abroad, you may be entitled to buy a duty-free car in Switzerland and run it on 'Z' plates for up to three months prior to your departure. An emigrating person who retains Swiss domicile may take delivery of a duty-free car ten days before departure, but may not re-import it into Switzerland without paying duty and tax.

BUYING A CAR

Cars are cheaper in Switzerland than in many other European countries and you can also obtain a discount of around 10 per cent off the list price of most new cars, even when leasing. If you aren't offered a discount, ask for one. Dealers usually have incentive campaigns throughout the year and it pays to consult importers' websites for the latest campaign – see ⌨ www.vsai.ch for links to all car importers in Switzerland.

In recent years, importers have moved away from discount wars and offer other incentives such as longer warranties, free servicing, etc. If you aren't able to negotiate a lower price, ask for something free, for example a set of winter tyres (in addition to the summer tyres on the car).

If you're buying a used car from a garage and aren't trading in another vehicle, try to negotiate a reduction, particularly when paying cash. In Switzerland the car is insured and not the driver, so if you test-drive a car it must be insured – you cannot drive it on your own insurance (see page 142). If a car has licence plates it should be insured, as you're unable to obtain them without insurance.

New Cars

Making comparisons between new car prices in different countries is often difficult, due to fluctuating exchange rates and the different levels of standard equipment. It's often cheaper to buy a new car from the factory of a European manufacturer or from an exporter in countries which levy high car taxes. This option is worth considering, particularly if you're planning to buy an expensive car. In some countries (e.g. the UK) a tax free car can be purchased up to six months prior to being exported. Personally importing a car from the US is usually much cheaper than buying the same car in Switzerland or elsewhere in Europe, although you must ensure that it conforms to Swiss specifications. Contact manufacturers and exporters directly for information.

When you buy a new car in Switzerland it usually means ordering a car and waiting for it to be delivered – it isn't like in some other countries where you go to a dealership and choose a car off the lot (although this is more common nowadays). When you order a new car you can obviously choose the options you want and the colour/upholstery, with delivery taking anywhere from six weeks to three months.

Used Cars

Used cars (*Occasionswagen, voiture d'occasion*) in Switzerland are usually good value for money, particularly those over five years old (most Swiss wouldn't be seen dead in an old car unless it's a classic), which are usually in good condition. Popular used-car websites include ⌨ www.autoscout24 and www.car4you.ch, while Comparis (⌨ www.comparis.ch) offers good advice about buying used cars and has a used car search facility.

If you intend to buy a used car in Switzerland, whether privately or from a garage, check the following:

◆ that the seller is the registered owner if buying from a private party;

◆ the next exhaust test (see below) date, shown on the exhaust test sticker displayed on the side window;

◆ that the handbook for the car, sound system and (if applicable) the satnav system are provided (or that you can obtain a copy);

◆ that it has passed the official serviceability test (see below);

◆ that it hasn't been involved in a major accident and suffered structural damage. A declaration that it's accident free (*Unfallfrei, sans accident/ non-accidenté*) should be obtained in writing;

◆ that the chassis number tallies with the car registration document (*Fahrzeugausweis, permis de circulation*);

◆ that the service coupons have been completed and stamped and that servicing has been carried out by an authorised dealer (if under warranty);

◆ that the price roughly corresponds to that shown in the Touring Club of Switzerland (TCS) monthly guide to used car prices or close to the price of similar cars advertised on the web (e.g. 🖳 www.autoscout24.ch) or see the Eurotaxglass website (🖳 www.eurotaxglass.ch), where you can select the make and model (and current prices) on the 'configurator'.

◆ that import tax and duty have been paid (if applicable);

◆ whether a written guarantee is provided.

When buying a car from a garage, some protection is afforded if it's a member of the Swiss Motor Trade Association (*Autogewerberverband Schweiz, Association Suisse des Automobilistes*, 🖳 www.agvs.ch). Most garages provide a warranty on used cars, e.g. three months or 4,000km (around 2,500mi).

Second-hand car prices in the more remote parts of Switzerland (e.g. Graubunden or Valais) are generally higher than in the major cities, e.g. Geneva and Zurich. If you live in a remote area, it's worthwhile comparing prices on the internet.

You can download a free sample vehicle sales agreement from 🖳 www.comparis.ch.

Leasing

If you don't want to buy a car, you can usually lease a new or used car from a main dealer. You're still eligible for a discount on most new cars, which should be offered automatically (if you aren't offered a discount, ask for one). Usually there are no leasing restrictions for foreigners with a B permit (see page 48), although you may not be eligible to lease a car during your first three months in Switzerland.

Bear in mind that the reason there are so many leasing companies is that it's a lucrative way to make money and is generally the most expensive way for an individual to own a car (unless the payments are tax deductible, which they usually aren't for individuals!).

On the other hand, interest paid on a car loan, e.g. from your employer or from a bank is tax-deductible, the terms are more transparent and it's usually a lot cheaper. Many leasing contracts have high exit costs, i.e. if you want to cancel the contract early you must pay a higher interest for the period that you've had the car, which can amount to several thousand francs.

Most car manufacturers/importers have their own leasing schemes. Shop around as leasing contracts and incentives vary from garage to garage. Leasing incentives are common nowadays and special and limited editions are attractive and usually include free optional equipment. Comparis (🖳 www.camparis.ch) provides an online independent leasing comparison.

SERVICEABILITY TEST

All cars are liable for a stringent official serviceability test (*Motorfahrzeug-kontrolle/MFK*,

contrôle des véhicules à moteur/expertisé). New cars are eligible for the test only after they're four years old. The next test is due when a car is seven years old and thereafter every two years. When a vehicle is ten years or older and is being sold, it must be tested if the last test was more than a year previously.

In practice, tests may be less frequent, as vehicles require testing only when the owner has been officially informed by a test centre. In some cantons there's a backlog of cars waiting for the test and there have been instances of cars not being called up for months after the due date. You can apply to have your car tested earlier than required, for example if you want to sell it. Many people won't buy a used car that hasn't had a test in the last year, even when it's offered at a bargain price (the Swiss are a suspicious lot!).

If you own an old or imported car which is called up for test, it may be advisable to get a garage to take it in for you or take a mechanic with you. Apart from the fact that their local language ability is probably better than yours, they're usually looked upon more favourably than the general public. If you have any questions regarding the test, it's advisable to discuss them with the testing station in advance. If you have a garage do a pre-test check on your car, don't ask them to repair it to test standard as this could result in unnecessary expense. Get them to take it for the test to find out what (if anything) needs fixing. Essential repairs recommended by a garage may not be the same as those officially required after the test.

You can have the Automobile Club of Switzerland (ACS) or the Touring Club of Switzerland (TCS – see page 156) check your car before taking it for the test (in some cantons the TCS is authorised to carry out official serviceability tests). This is sometimes advisable, particularly if you plan to register an imported car in Switzerland, as they'll tell you what modifications (if any) need to be made.

It can be expensive to get a car through the test. For example, a windscreen with a tiny stone chip may need replacing (although this may be covered by part or fully comprehensive insurance in Switzerland) and tyres must have at least 1.6mm of tread over their entire surface. The test is normally completed while you wait and takes around 30 minutes.

The test centre is usually located at your canton's motor registration office, the address of which is listed on both your driving licence and car registration document (*Fahrzeugausweis, permis de circulation*). Business hours vary but are usually around 7.30am to 4pm, Mondays to Fridays. The test costs anything from CHF 60 to 150 depending on the canton, while a full or minor retest (after a failure) is cheaper. When you apply for a test, you're sent a form which must be completed and returned with your car registration document.

If your car fails the serviceability test and you wish to have it repaired at a later date, you can have the registration document stamped 'invalid' and you won't be required to pay road tax or insurance from this date. When you wish to have the car tested again, you can obtain a 'day plate' from the police to take the vehicle to the test centre. If you miss an appointment you must pay the full charge and schedule a new appointment (which can be done online).

EXHAUST TEST

All Swiss registered cars with a catalytic converter require an exhaust emission test (*Abgastest, test anti-pollution*) every two years, while cars without one must be tested annually. The amount of carbon monoxide, carbon dioxide and hydrocarbons emitted by the exhaust mustn't exceed the manufacturer's limits. If they do, adjustments or repairs must be made to the engine, fuel system or exhaust, as necessary. Cars registered in Switzerland before 1st January 1971 are exempt, while older cars registered after this date must have the exhaust test.

> The exhaust emission test certificate (*Abgas-Wartungsdokument, fiche d'entretien du systeme antipollution*) must be kept in your car and be produced when asked for by the police.

A green and white sticker is fixed to the rear or a side window of your car, showing the year and month when the next test is due. The exhaust emission test costs between CHF 50 and CHF 150 and is usually reduced when combined with a service. If you're stopped by the police without a valid exhaust test certificate you can be fined up to CHF 200 (it varies depending on the period since the last test; one month overdue is CHF 40, 1-3 months overdue CHF 100, over three months overdue CHF 200). Vehicle anti-pollution controls in Switzerland are among the strictest in Europe and police have pollution meters to detect cars that exceed pollution levels.

CAR REGISTRATION

In Switzerland, a new or used car doesn't have registration plates (*Nummernschild, numéro d'immatriculation*) when purchased. Car registration plates are personal and when a car is sold they're returned to the issuing canton's motor registration office or transferred to the owner's new car. When you apply to register a car in Switzerland for the first time, you must apply to your canton's motor registration office for registration plates. If you're buying a new or used car from a garage, they will usually apply for the registration plates on your behalf and complete the formalities. When applying for Swiss registration plates for the first time, you must provide the following:

◆ your Swiss or foreign driving licence (before you've completed one year's residence in Switzerland you must obtain a Swiss driving licence);

◆ your foreigner's permit (*Ausländerausweis, livret pour étrangers*);

◆ a certificate of residence (*Wohnsitzbescheinigung, carte d'indigène/ attestation de domicile*), available for a fee of around CHF 10 to 20 from your community office;

◆ a certificate from an insurance company confirming that the car is insured for third party liability.

A new car must undergo an official test (*Vorführung, contrôle de mise en circulation*) at a canton's motor registration office to ensure that it meets Swiss specifications. The test fee (for a car purchased from a Swiss dealer) costs between CHF 50 and 150 and the cost of the car registration document (*Fahrzeugausweis, permis de circulation*) is around CHF 40 to 60, depending on the canton. The test is arranged by the garage.

When changing cantons or leaving Switzerland, registration plates must be returned to your canton's motor registration office (see **Chapter 20**) If you don't remember to clean them beforehand, don't worry, there's a registration plate wash basin at motor registration offices – no joke – and you need to make sure that they're spotless! Notify your canton's motor registration office within 14 days of a change of car or address, a change of canton or when leaving Switzerland. When you register a car or inform your canton's motor registration office of a change, they send you a bill (or a refund) for road tax and the car registration fee, as applicable.

If you're buying a new car and haven't

sold your old one, or you intend to run two or more cars but not simultaneously, you can obtain interchangeable registration number plates (*Wechselnummer, plaques interchangeables*) from your canton's motor registration office. These allow you to drive two or more cars on the same insurance and to swap one set of registration plates between them (see **Car Insurance** below). Note, however, that only the vehicle bearing the interchangeable registration plates can be parked or used on a public road.

SELLING A CAR

The main points to note when selling a car are:

◆ If you plan to buy another car, you must retain your registration plates and transfer them to your new car, provided you remain a resident of the same canton. Car registration includes road tax and you're billed for (or reimbursed) the difference when you register a new car. When leaving Switzerland or changing cantons you must return your licence plates to the issuing canton's motor registration office within 14 days. An application for new plates must be made in your new canton within 14 days of taking up residence.

◆ Inform your insurance company. Your insurance for a vehicle is cancelled automatically when your registration is cancelled or transferred. It's the responsibility of the new owner of a car to register his ownership with his canton's motor registration office. The seller or buyer is required to have a car's registration document cancelled at his canton's motor registration office. It isn't advisable to sell your car and give the registration document to the new owner before you've cancelled your registration – you cannot cancel your insurance until the registration in your name has been cancelled, and the new owner may delay doing this.

◆ If you're selling your car privately, insist on payment in cash (rather than a banker's draft, etc.), which is normal practice in Switzerland.

◆ Include in the receipt that you're selling the car in its present condition (as seen) without a guarantee (*ohne Garantie, sans garantie*), the price paid and the car's kilometre reading. The new owner may ask for a declaration in writing that the car is accident free (*unfallfrei, sans accident/non-accidenté*), which means major accidents causing structural damage and not slight knocks.

♦ The best place to advertise a car for sale is on the internet such as 🖥 www.autoscout24.ch, www.car4you.ch or http://auto.ricardo.ch, or an expat forum such as 🖥 www.xpatxchange. ch, www.englishforum.ch, www.knowitall.ch or www.glocals.ch.

DRIVING LICENCE

The minimum age for obtaining a driving licence in Switzerland is 18 for a motor car or a motorcycle over 125cc, 16 for a motorcycle of between 50 and 125cc and 14 for a moped (see page 149). Holders of a full foreign driving licence may drive in Switzerland for one year using a foreign or international driving licence. If you or any members of your family hold a foreign driving licence and intend to remain in Switzerland for longer than one year, you must apply for a Swiss driving licence (*Führerschein, permis de conduire*) during your first year in Switzerland.

> **☑ SURVIVAL TIP**
>
> If you don't apply for a Swiss driving licence during your first year in Switzerland, you aren't permitted to drive after this period until you've passed a Swiss driving test.

You can apply for a Swiss licence at any time after your arrival, provided you're living in permanent accommodation and not, for example, in a hotel. Most foreigners including EU, Australian and US nationals aren't required to take a practical or written driving test, and their driving licence is automatically exchanged for a Swiss one. However, some foreigners, including those from Turkey and some African, Asian, Central and South American countries, must pass a practical driving test. If you fail the practical driving test, you're required to take a full Swiss driving test, including a written examination. Some foreign licences, for example licences printed in Arabic or Chinese, must be translated into an official Swiss language or an international licence must be obtained.

If you're required to take a Swiss driving test, you should note that it's more comprehensive than many foreign tests and includes a written examination and the completion of a first-aid course. The written exam may be taken in English and other languages, although according to some the English is almost unintelligible and the local language version may be easier – provided of course you can understand it! You're permitted to make just five mistakes in 60 questions. It can take some months to obtain a Swiss driving licence if you fail the written test a few times, during which time you aren't permitted to drive in Switzerland.

To apply for a Swiss driving licence you need to:

♦ Obtain an application form from your canton's motor registration office.

♦ Arrange a sight test (around CHF 20) with your doctor or an approved optician (listed on the back of the application form). The optician will complete a section on the back of the form after the test is completed. The sight test is valid for six months. You require some form of official identification, e.g. a passport or identity card.

♦ Provide one to three colour passport photographs (approximately 35 by 45 mm and not older than 12 months), as requested by the cantonal authority. These can be obtained from photo booths at most railway stations.

♦ Complete the application form and take it to your canton's motor registration office (the address is listed on the back of the form) with the following:

  – your foreign driving licence and if applicable, an international driving licence;
  – your Swiss residence permit;

- the completed application form, including the sight test report;

- one to three passport photographs;

- a police certificate (*Strafregisterauszug, certificate de bonne conduite*), if applicable. This is required in some cantons and is available from your canton's foreigners' police (*Fremdenpolizei, police des étrangers*) for around CHF 20.

Your Swiss driving licence (similar to a credit card in size) is sent to you around one week later with a bill and is valid for life. The cost varies from around CHF 80 to 140, depending on your canton of residence. The driving licence doesn't show your address and therefore doesn't need to be re-issued every time you move home. If you move to a different canton you need to inform the canton's motoring authority in writing of your new address and the number of your driving licence.

International Driving Permit

An international driving permit (IDP) is required if you plan to drive in some countries. This may vary depending on which driving licence(s) you hold. Check with a Swiss motoring organisation (see page 156). An IDP is obtainable from the ACS or TCS and cantonal motor registration offices for CHF 30 to 50 and is valid for three years. You must provide your passport, a Swiss or foreign driving licence, a passport-size photograph and the fee. A translation of your Swiss or foreign driving licence is required for some countries and is obtainable from Swiss motoring organisations or a canton's motor registration offices for around CHF 30.

Holders of a car driving licence can ride a 'motorcycle' of up to 50cc in Switzerland without a special licence. For motorcycles over 50cc you must have a motorcycle licence.

CAR INSURANCE

The following categories of car insurance are available in Switzerland:

◆ **Third party** (*Haftpflicht, responsibilité civile*): Third party insurance includes passenger cover and is compulsory in all cantons.

◆ **Part comprehensive** (*Teilkasko, casco partielle*): Known in some countries as third party, fire and theft, part comprehensive includes cover against fire, natural hazards (e.g. rocks falling on your car), theft, broken glass (e.g. windscreen) and damage caused by a collision with animals (for example a collision with a deer is possible on some country roads,

which incidentally must be reported to the local police). You can usually choose to pay an excess (*Selbstbehalt, franchise*), for example the first CHF 500 to 2,000 of a claim, in order to reduce your premium. Part comprehensive insurance is compulsory in some cantons.

◆ **Full comprehensive** (*Vollkasko/ Kollisionskasko, casco intégral (complète)/ assurance tous risques*): This type of insurance covers all risks including self-inflicted damage to your own car. You can choose to pay an excess (*Selbstbehalt, franchise*) in order to reduce your premium. (It also covers high fliers against collisions with aircraft.) It's usually compulsory for leasing and credit purchase contracts.

If you take out third party insurance with a Swiss insurance company and wish to increase your cover to full comprehensive later, you aren't required to do this through your third party insurance company, but may shop around for the best deal. Separate passenger insurance is unnecessary as passengers are automatically covered by all Swiss motor insurance policies. However, extra passenger cover (*Insassen Versicherung, assurance passager/accidents des occupants*) is available for a small extra charge, providing higher financial cover for passengers and including the owner-driver, which third party doesn't. Swiss motor insurance always includes a green card (available free on request), which extends your insurance to most European countries.

The cost of motor insurance in Switzerland is high and varies considerably between insurance companies. Your foreign no-claims bonus is usually valid in Switzerland, but you must provide written evidence from your present or previous insurance company (not just an insurance renewal notice). The no-claims bonus in Switzerland is a maximum of 70 per cent and is more generous

than in many other countries. However, it may vary for third party and full comprehensive insurance and there isn't a no-claims discount on the part comprehensive part of your insurance.

Claims are calculated in 'steps' (*Bonusstufen/ étapes de bonification*) or percentages according to your number of years no claims. It's usually 10 per cent after one year (or 'step'), 20 per cent after two years (or two 'steps'), 25 per cent after three years, with an additional 5 per cent a year up to a maximum of 70 per cent after 12 years. After a claim you usually lose two steps (20 per cent) or two years' no-claims bonus. Accident prone drivers can, however, find themselves paying up to 170 per cent (the maximum) **above** the basic premium.

Inexperienced, young and drivers with a poor accident record, must usually pay an extra excess (*franchise*). Drivers under 25 must pay a 20 per cent loading or the first CHF 500 of a claim and inexperienced drivers (holders of a licence for less than two years) may also need to pay the first CHF 500 of a claim The extra premium for full comprehensive insurance for young or inexperienced drivers can be from CHF 300 to 3,000, depending on the car. Some insurance companies, for example AXA, offer a 15 per cent discount to young drivers if they allow the insurance company to install a 'crash recorder', an automobile 'black box', in the vehicle (see 🖥 www.crashrecorder.ch).

Your type of permit (see **Chapter 3**) and nationality may also influence the cost of car insurance; B and C permit holders usually pay the standard rate, but L permit holders and those on short-term contracts may need to pay up to double and in advance. Shop around for an insurance policy and ask companies whether they have higher premiums for foreigners, as not all do. If you'll be in Switzerland for only a short period, check whether you can take out a fixed period policy or terminate your insurance at short notice without penalty.

Most insurance companies try to tie you to a five or ten-year contract, which you cannot cancel unless your premium is increased (which happens frequently) or you change vehicles. You can, however, tell your insurance broker that you want a shorter term or request that the contract can be cancelled at the end of each year (usually with a notice period of three months). If you want to change companies, you must notify your insurance company in writing by registered letter (your new insurance company is usually happy to do this for you).

Some employers may have an arrangement with a car insurance company, whereby employees receive a discount. Ask your colleagues for their advice and shop around. Motor insurance premiums are valid for a full calendar year from January to December. If you take out a policy in mid-year, you may be billed to the end of the year only. Many companies send out bills in advance with 30 days to pay, so that payment is received before the start of the new insurance period.

If you own two or more cars, you need only insure the most expensive one, provided you (or your family members) intend to drive only one car at a time. If this is the case, contact your insurance company and ask them for am interchangeable registration number (*Wechselnummer, plaques interchangeables*) for the vehicles involved. There's an extra insurance charge of around CHF 100 a year. Registration plates can be fitted with a quick release mount, so that they can be easily swapped between cars. This also means that you pay road tax (see below) only on the most expensive car, as only one car can be on the road at a time. An interchangeable number cannot be swapped between a car and a motorcycle.

☑ **SURVIVAL TIP**

If you insure two cars in the same name, you can claim a no-claims bonus for one car only and you must pay the full premium for the other.

If you're going to be abroad for at least 30 days but less than one year, you can save a proportion of your car insurance and road tax. To qualify you must remove your car plates, return them with the registration document to your canton's motor registration office and inform your insurance company. Upon your return, notify your insurance agent, who will authorise you to reclaim your licence plates from your canton's motor registration office. A car mustn't be driven or parked on a public road without registration plates. Some people garage their cars for around three months during winter, preferring to use public transport when road conditions are bad. Due to the fees and effort involved, it isn't worthwhile taking a car off the road (and reclaiming insurance and road tax payments) for a period of less than three months.

For an extra premium of around CHF 100 per year, your insurance company will cover your legal costs (*Rechtsschutz, protection juridique*) arising from road accidents. A special federal insurance

(*Bundesversicherung, assurance fédérale*) scheme covers victims of hit-and-run accidents (see **Accidents** on page 151).

Foreign Registered Vehicles

It isn't mandatory for cars insured in an EU/EFTA country to have an international insurance green card (*Internationale Versicherungskarte für Motorfahrzeuge, carte internationale d'Assurance automobile/carte verte*) for Switzerland. Most insurance companies in Western Europe provide a 'free' green card, which extends your normal domestic insurance cover to other western European countries, although it doesn't always include Switzerland.

This doesn't include the UK, where you can usually obtain a green card for a maximum of three months and it's expensive. A green card must be signed to be valid and in some countries, e.g. the UK, all drivers must sign it, not just the car owner. Your insurance cover may be invalid if you drive in Switzerland with a foreign insurance policy stating that you're a resident of another country, when you're actually resident in Switzerland. Contact your insurance company to find out your legal position.

If you bring a foreign-registered car to Switzerland, you may need a new insurance policy, which can be either a special European insurance policy (expensive) or insurance with a Swiss company. Some Swiss insurance companies will insure a foreign registered car, but usually for a limited period, e.g. one year.

ROAD TAX

Road tax (*Verkehrssteuer, impôt sur la circulation*) rates in Switzerland vary considerably from canton to canton. It's calculated on the engine size (CC), power (DIN-PS) or the weight of your car, depending on your canton of residence. (Canton Ticino are the exception, where they charge a basic premium of around CHF 150 and add the DIN-PS figure, times the weight of the car, divided by 800 – creating these calculations keeps thousands of civil servants in work!). In 2010, some cantons (e.g. Geneva) introduced a bonus/penalty system based on the CO_2 (emission) value of a new car. If the CO_2 is over 220g/km you receive a 50 per cent surcharge and if it's below 120g/km you receive a 50 per cent discount.

In canton Zurich the road tax for popular engine sizes is shown in the table below.

When you register a car with your canton's motor registration office, the road tax bill is sent with your car registration document. A refund is possible if you leave Switzerland, change cantons

or take your car off the road for more than 30 days (see **Car Insurance** above). If you have two or more cars using the same registration number, you pay road tax only on the most expensive one, as only one vehicle can be used on a public road at a time (unless you drive one without plates!).

An additional motorway tax of CHF 40 applies to all vehicles up to 3.5 tonnes using Swiss motorways (see **Motorway Tax** on page 52).

Road Tax	
Engine Size	**Road Tax**
1,100cc	CHF. 232.50
1,200cc	CHF. 265
1,600cc	CHF. 330
1,800cc	CHF. 362.50
2,000cc	CHF. 395
3,000cc	CHF. 557.50

GENERAL ROAD RULES

The following general road rules may help you adjust to driving in Switzerland:

◆ The Swiss drive on the right-hand side of the road – it saves confusion if you do likewise.

◆ All motorists must carry a red breakdown triangle, which must be stowed inside the car within reach of the drivers seat, not in the boot (which may be damaged and jammed shut in an accident). If you have an accident or breakdown, the triangle must be placed at the edge of the road at least 50 metres behind the car on secondary roads and at least 150 metres on 'roads with fast traffic', e.g. motorways.

◆ Swiss traffic regulations state that you should carry first-aid equipment and some chalk (to mark the position of vehicles in case of an accident!). In many European countries it's mandatory to carry a fire extinguisher, a first-aid kit and a reflective security vest, which drivers in EU countries must don if they break down and get out of a vehicle. If you witness an accident, you must stop and render assistance and give evidence if required. Only give medical assistance when absolutely necessary and when qualified (see also **Accidents** below).

◆ In towns you may be faced with a bewildering array of signs, traffic lights and road markings. If in doubt about who has priority, always give way (yield) to trams, buses plus all traffic coming from your RIGHT. All drivers must give way to police cars, ambulances and fire engines in emergencies (with disco lights and wailing sounds) and trams and buses, e.g. leaving stops. On secondary roads without priority signs (a yellow diamond on a white background, used throughout most of Europe) you must give way to vehicles coming from your RIGHT. Failure to observe this rule is the cause of many accidents. The priority to the right rule usually also applies in car parks. If you're ever in doubt about who has the right of way, it's generally wise to give way. As the Swiss say 'fairness above all' (*Fairness vor allem, fair-play avant tout*) – particularly when confronted by a 28-tonne truck (might is right!).

♦ On roundabouts (traffic circles), vehicles on the roundabout have priority and not those entering it, who are faced with a give way sign. Traffic flows anti-clockwise around roundabouts and not clockwise as in the UK and other countries driving on the left.

♦ The wearing of seatbelts is compulsory and includes passengers in rear seats when seatbelts are fitted. In the event of an accident, a Swiss insurance company isn't obliged to pay the whole cost of damages when it 'appears' that those injured weren't using their seatbelts (benefits may be reduced by up to 50 per cent). Children under the age of 12 may ride in the front of a car, but only when it's impossible for them to ride in the back, e.g. it's already full of under 12-year-olds.

Children aged 12 and under who aren't 150cm (4ft 11in) tall must occupy a special child's seat (not a booster seat), under a law which came into effect on 1st April 2010. If a child is taller than 150 cm then he doesn't need to be in a special child seat. A child's car seat must be an ECE certified seat with the test number 03 or 04. If you're discovered with a child under 12 (or under 150cm – do the police carry tape measures?) who isn't occupying a child's seat, you'll be fined CHF 60. Statistics show that over 90 per cent of Swiss wear seatbelts, with the Swiss Germans more law-abiding than their compatriots in French- and Italian-speaking regions.

For information about car seats and the law, see the TCS website (🖳 www.tcs.ch – Kindersitze); the TCS also publish a 'Kinder im Auto' leaflet available in nine languages.

♦ Don't drive in bus, taxi or cycle lanes unless necessary to avoid a stationary vehicle or obstruction, and give priority to authorised users. Bus drivers get irate if you drive in their lanes, and you can be fined for doing so. Be sure to keep clear of tram lines and outside the restricted area shown by a line.

♦ Dipped (low beam) headlights must be used in tunnels, fog, snowstorms, heavy rain and when visibility is reduced to less than 200 metres. While it isn't mandatory to have your dipped headlamps on during daytime, the Swiss authorities advise you to for safety reasons. It's illegal to drive on parking (side) lights at any time, although many people do it.

Front fog or spot lights must be fitted in pairs at a regulation height and should be used only when visibility is less than 50 metres. Rear fog lamps are officially permitted on the offside only (to prevent following vehicles mistaking two fog lamps for brake lights) and although many cars have two, only the offside lamp should be fitted with a bulb. Unfortunately, many Swiss drivers don't know what fog lamps are for and use them when visibility is good (or forget to turn them off), but fail to use them in fog.

♦ Headlight flashing has a different meaning in different countries. In some countries it means 'after you' (generally also in Switzerland) and in others 'get out of my ******* way. (It may also mean 'I am driving a new car and haven't yet worked out what all the switches are for'.) A vehicle's hazard warning lights (both indicators simultaneously) may be used to warn other drivers of an obstruction, e.g. an accident or a traffic jam.

◆ The Swiss have a love of amber flashing lights, which are usually a warning to proceed with caution, for example for roadworks, non-functioning traffic lights and to indicate special speed restrictions, particularly on motorways. Many crossroads and junctions have flashing amber traffic lights outside rush hours. Flashing amber lights also operate in conjunction with normal traffic lights, as a warning to watch for cyclists and pedestrians when turning right at junctions.

◆ You may notice that many traffic lights have an uncanny habit of changing to green when you approach them, particularly during off-peak hours. This isn't magic or a result of your magnetic personality, but due to sensors installed in the road that change the lights to green when no other traffic has priority.

◆ When two vehicles meet on a narrow mountain road, the ascending vehicle has priority – the other must give way or reverse, as necessary. PostBuses always have right of way irrespective of direction and their drivers usually sound their horns to announce their approach to blind corners and narrow turns. When the road is too narrow to pass, PostBus drivers have the authority to give other road users instructions regarding reversing or pulling over to one side.

◆ On-the-spot fines can be imposed for traffic offences such as minor speeding; not being in possession of your car documents; not removing your ignition key when leaving a vehicle unattended; not using dipped (low beam) headlights at night, in tunnels or in poor visibility; and parking infringements. Non-resident foreigners must pay fines on the spot. Residents who are unable to pay on the spot are given a giro payment form, payable within ten days. A fine of over CHF 50 (for any offence) is recorded for posterity on your canton's register. It pays not to contest a fixed fine unless you have a cast-iron defence, because if you lose the case the fine will be increased.

◆ Many motorists seem to have an aversion to driving in the right-hand lane on a three-lane motorway, which in effect, reduces the motorway to two lanes. Motorists should signal before overtaking and when moving back into an inside lane after overtaking, e.g. on a motorway. If you drive a right-hand drive car, take extra care when overtaking – the most dangerous manoeuvre in motoring.

◆ There are regulations in some cantons and towns requiring motorists to switch off their engines when waiting at traffic lights or railway crossings, where there may be a sign instructing you to do so, e.g. 'For purer air – switch off engine' (*Für bessere Luft – Motor abstellen*) or 'Cut your motor' (*Coupez le Moteur*). You can be fined for not switching off your engine. When stopped in tunnels, e.g. due to a breakdown, accident or traffic jam, you must switch off your engine (carbon monoxide poisoning can drastically shorten your life expectancy).

☑ SURVIVAL TIP

If you have to flee a tunnel (for example because of a fire) you must leave the keys in the ignition, so that emergency crews can move your car if necessary.

◆ Approach a railway level crossing slowly and **STOP**:

– as soon as the barrier or half-barrier starts to fall;

– as soon as the red warning lights are on or are flashing;

– in any case when a train approaches.

◆ A heavy vehicle that's slowing traffic is required to stop at the '300 metre' sign before closed railway crossings to allow other vehicles to pass it.

◆ Be particularly wary of moped (*Motorfahrrad/ Mofa, vélomoteur*) riders and cyclists. It isn't always easy to see them, particularly when they're hidden by the blind spots of a car or are riding at night without lights. Many moped riders seem to have a death wish and tragically many (mostly teenagers) lose their lives annually in Switzerland (maybe 14 years of age is too young to let them loose on the roads?). They constantly pull out into traffic or turn without looking or signalling. When overtaking mopeds or cyclists, ALWAYS give them a wide. . . WIDE berth. If you knock them off their bikes, you may have difficulty convincing the police that it wasn't your fault.

◆ Drive slowly when passing a stationary tram or bus, particularly a school bus. Where passengers must cross a road to reach a pedestrian path, for example from a tram stop in the middle of the road, motorists must stop and give way.

◆ A 'CH' (from the Latin *Confoederatio Helvetica*) nationality plate (sticker) must be affixed to the rear of a Swiss-registered car when motoring abroad. Drivers of foreign-registered cars in Switzerland must have the appropriate nationality plate affixed to the rear of their car. You can be fined on the spot for not displaying it, although it isn't often enforced judging by the number of cars without them (maybe German and Italian-registered cars are exempt?). Cars must show only the correct nationality plate and not an assortment.

◆ If you need to wear glasses or contact lenses when motoring, it's noted on your Swiss driving licence and you must always wear them. You must also carry a spare pair of glasses or contact lenses when driving.

◆ A roof rack load may be a maximum of 50kg (110lb) for vehicles registered after January 1st 1980 and 10 per cent of a vehicle's unladen weight for vehicles registered before this date.

◆ Trailers registered in Switzerland may be up 2.1m (6.9ft) wide and 6m (19.7ft) long (tow-bar included). Trailers registered abroad may be up to 2.2m (7.2ft) wide and 7m (23ft) long, but they aren't permitted to use Swiss mountain passes. A special permit must be obtained at Swiss border posts. If a towing vehicle has insufficient power to pull a trailer or caravan up an incline in heavy traffic, a journey over mountain passes mustn't be attempted. When towing a caravan or trailer of up to 1,000kg (2,204lb) in weight, you're restricted to 80kph (50mph) on motorways and 60kph (37mph)

on all other roads, except where lower speed restrictions apply.

◆ It's illegal to use a mobile phone when driving in Switzerland (unless it's a hands-free phone), for which you can be fined CHF 100.

◆ A *Handbook of Swiss Traffic Regulations* is available for around CHF 12 from a canton's motor registration offices and customs offices. It's essential reading for all motorists and is available in various languages, including English.

SWISS DRIVERS

The most popular Swiss motor sport is a public-road variation of stock car racing, commonly referred to as 'tail-gating' or 'shunting'. The rules of tail-gating are relatively simple: drivers are required to get as close as possible to the car in front without making contact, e.g. smashing into its rear. Unfortunately (as with all motor 'sports') there's an element of risk involved, which in this case is exacerbated by the low level of skill of the average participant, many of whom have yet to master the art of stopping at 120kph (or often faster) within a few car lengths. This results in quite a few collisions, often in motorway tunnels and always during rush hours.

A tailgater usually sits a few metres (centimetres?) from your bumper and tries to push you along irrespective of traffic density, road and weather conditions, or the prevailing speed limit. There's no solution, short of moving out of his way, which is often impossible. Flashing your rear fog lamp or warning lights usually has no effect and braking can be disastrous – nothing deters the habitual tailgater.

Sudden stopping and braking are allowed only in an emergency and motorists have been successfully sued for damages by someone who has run into the back of them, because they stopped for no apparent reason. Always try to leave a large gap between your vehicle and the vehicle in front. This isn't just to allow you more time to stop, should the vehicles in front decide to come together, but also to give the inevitable tailgater behind you more time to stop. **The closer the car behind you, the further you should be from the vehicle in front.**

The majority of motorists in Switzerland (and many other countries) drive much too close to the vehicle in front and have little idea of stopping distances. The *Handbook of Swiss Traffic Regulations* (see above) states that the safe stopping distance (including thinking distance) is 45m (147ft) at 60kph (37mph), which increases to a massive 144m (472ft) at 120kph (74mph). These stopping distances are on dry roads with good visibility and are greatly increased on wet or icy roads. Although these distances may be generous, they aren't stupid. If further proof is needed of how dangerous and widespread tail-gating is, simply check the statistics on the number of 'concertina' (multiple car) accidents in Switzerland, particularly on motorways.

The Swiss have a few other motoring idiosyncrasies, one of which is an aversion to using their handbrakes, even when stopped on a hill (they would rather burn their clutch out). Don't get too close as they're likely to roll back into you (it's all part of the racing image, as a good getaway is all important). Other common habits are a tendency to drive in the middle of the road on country lanes and sudden braking when approaching a 50kph (31mph) or other speed restriction. In general, Swiss drivers are above average (average is bad) and no worse than most other European drivers. However, some foreigners consider Swiss drivers to be more aggressive and impolite than motorists in some other countries (e.g. the UK and the US). They are, for example, often reluctant to give way to a motorist waiting to pull out into traffic, and on motorways many drivers remain in the overtaking lane and cut across at the last moment when they want to take an exit. Swiss motorists are, however, usually law abiding (except with regard to speed limits), observe parking restrictions more than most other European motorists and are kind to animals.

Don't be too discouraged by the tailgaters and road hogs. Driving in Switzerland is often a pleasant experience, particularly when using country roads, which are relatively traffic-free outside rush hours. If you come from a country where traffic drives on the left, you should quickly get used to driving on the 'wrong' side of the road. Just take it easy at first, particularly in winter, and bear in mind that there may be other motorists around just as confused as you are.

WINTER DRIVING

Winter driving in Switzerland needn't be a survival course. Most motorists fit snow tyres (*Schneereifen/Winterreifen, pneus neige*), which although not compulsory help make winter driving safer. If you have an accident on snow in a vehicle that isn't fitted with snow tyres, you may be considered to be at fault if the other vehicles involved have snow tyres, irrespective of other circumstances. In some rural areas, roads aren't cleared of snow, in which case snow tyres may be a necessity. In towns, many roads are salted or gritted in winter, although some cantons have cut

down on the use of salt due to its corrosive and anti-environmental properties.

Most motorists change to snow (winter) tyres in winter, which are usually on steel wheels; shop around for the best buys, as prices vary considerably. It's necessary or even compulsory to fit snow chains (*Schneeketten, chaîne à neige*) on a vehicle's driving wheels in some areas, particularly on mountains roads and passes (see below). When chains are necessary, it's indicated by a road sign; ignore it at your peril. Buy good quality snow chains and practice putting them on and removing them before you get stuck in the snow – even getting the container undone can be a trial with cold numb fingers, let alone fitting them. Studded tyres (spikes) may be used on vehicles up to 3.5 tonnes from 1st November to 31st March. Vehicles with studs are restricted to 80kph (50mph) and aren't permitted to use motorways.

Winter driving courses are held in all areas of Switzerland, where motorists can learn how to drive on snow and ice (don't, however, expect to compete with Scandinavian rally drivers after a day's tuition). The cost is between CHF 300 and 500 and courses usually last a whole day (drivers aged between 18 and 29 usually receive a reduction of CHF 100 from Swiss motoring organisations). It isn't necessary to use your own car, as you can hire (rent) one from the centre (better than wrecking your own). If you use your own car, you can take out special insurance cover for around CHF 15 to 20 a day, which is usually included in the course fee. Contact your canton's motor registration office or Swiss motoring organisations for more information.

The Swiss Conference for Road Traffic Safety (*Schweiz. Konferenz für Sicherheit im Strassenverkehr, Conférence Suisse de sécurité dans le Trafic Routier*) subsidises advanced and special driving courses, e.g. anti-skid courses, for both motorists and motorcyclists throughout Switzerland.

☑ SURVIVAL TIP

Skis carried on ski roof racks should have their curved front ends facing towards the rear of the car.

Take it easy in winter. In poor road conditions you'll notice that most Swiss slow down considerably and even the habitual tailgaters leave a larger gap than usual between them and the car in front. Even a light snowfall can be treacherous, particularly on an icy road. When road conditions are bad, allow two to three times longer than usual to reach your destination. Many rural roads are lined with two-metre high poles, which mark the edges of the road when there's heavy snow.

Mountain Passes

Snow chains must be fitted to all vehicles crossing mountain passes in winter (even in summer, freak snow storms can make roads treacherous). Always check in advance whether a pass is open, especially if using a pass means making a detour. A sign on the approach road indicates whether a pass is open (*offen, ouvert*) or closed (*geschlossen, fermé*) and whether chains are necessary.

The following mountain passes are open year round, although opening times may be reduced in winter (e.g. from 7am to 6 or 9pm): Bernina, Brünig, Flüela, Forclaz, Julier, Maloja, Mosses, Ofen (Il Fuorn), Pillon and Simplon. The following passes are open for part of the year: Oberalp, San Bernadino, Susten, Umbrail, St Gotthard and Splügen open from May to November; Furka, Great St Bernhard, Grimsel and Klausen open from May to October; Albula opens from June to November and Lukmanier from April to December.

The Great St Bernard, St Gotthard and San Bernadino passes have alternative road tunnels open all year round. There's a toll of CHF 29.20 (one way – return within 30 days CHF 46.70) for cars to use the Great St Bernard road tunnel between Bourg St Pierre and Aosta (Etroubles) in Italy.

An quicker alternative to using the passes are the many 'Autoverlad' (💻 www.bls.ch/e/autoverlad/autoverlad.php) car trains, e.g. Kandersteg-Goppenstein and Kandersteg-Iselle (Italy), which run every 30 minutes from around 6am to 11 or 12pm.

MOTORCYCLES

Switzerland is a great country for bike enthusiasts and its clean mountain air, excellent roads, beautiful scenery and generally good weather (from spring to autumn) make it a Mecca for bikers.

Mopeds

The following rules apply to riders of mopeds (*Motorfahrrad/Mofa, vélomoteur*) up to 50cc:

◆ riders must be aged at least 14;

◆ permission must be obtained from a parent if a rider is aged under 18;

◆ you must have an eye test and pass a written road rules test;

◆ a licence plate (*Kontrollschild, plaque*) must be obtained and/or a *vignette* from your community, which includes road tax and third party insurance. The cost varies (e.g. from CHF 50 to 70 a year) depending on your canton of residence and is renewable annually by 31st May. Insurance is also available from Swiss motoring organisations.

◆ a lock must be fitted which blocks a wheel or the steering, or a cable or chain lock must be used;

◆ a crash helmet must be worn.

An application for a licence must be made to your canton's motor registration office with the following:

◆ your Swiss residence permit;

◆ two photographs;

◆ a completed application form, available from your community.

The maximum permitted speed for mopeds is 30kph (19mph). Motorists with a car licence (Swiss or foreign) may ride a moped without passing a test or obtaining a special licence. Theft insurance can be taken out separately and breakdown assistance is available from Swiss motoring organisations (see page 156) from around CHF 65 a year. Swiss motoring organisations also run motorcycle instruction courses.

Many moped riders are killed each year in Switzerland, mostly teenagers. If you have a child with a moped, it's important to impress upon him the need to take care (particularly in winter) and not take unnecessary risks, e.g. always observe traffic signals, signal before making a manoeuvre and **WEAR A CRASH HELMET** (some riders don't bother, although it's against the law). Car drivers often cannot see or avoid moped riders, particularly when they're riding at night without lights or when they shoot out of a side street without looking.

⚠ Caution

Mopeds in the wrong hands can and do KILL!

Motorcycles 50 to 125cc

The following rules are applicable to riders of motorcycles (*Motorrad*, *moto*) between 50 and 125cc:

♦ you must be aged at least 16 to ride a 50cc motorcycle and 18 to ride a 125cc bike;

♦ you must attend eight hours of traffic theory and pass a practical test;

♦ a crash helmet must be worn;

♦ dipped (low beam) headlights must be used at all times;

♦ you must have valid third party insurance;

♦ you must carry your insurance certificate and driving licence.

The same application form is used to apply for a motorcycle licence as for a car driving licence and includes an eye test. After you pass the written road rules test, a provisional licence is issued for three months. This can be extended for a further two months, after which a practical test must be taken.

If you already have a car licence, you don't need to take a road rules or practical test, but you must still take a traffic theory course.

Motorcycles Over 125cc

The following rules are applicable to riders of standard motorcycles (*Motorrad*, *moto*) over 125cc:

♦ you must be aged at least 25 or have held a motorcycle licence (for a motorcycle between 50 and 125cc) for at least two years;

♦ you must attend 12 hours of traffic theory (6 hours if you've already passed the test for

motorcycles up to 125cc) and pass a practical test;

♦ a crash helmet must be worn;

♦ dipped (low beam) headlights must be used at all times;

♦ you must have valid third party insurance;

♦ you must carry your insurance certificate and driving licence.

For all licences you must have had an eye test, attended a first aid course and passed a road rules test before you can apply for a provisional driving licence. Note that most DMVs don't carry out motorcycle driving tests between November and February for safety reasons.

CAR DOCUMENTS

The following documents must be carried when driving:

♦ driving licence (Swiss if held);

♦ vehicle registration document;

♦ exhaust test certificate (Swiss-registered cars only);

♦ your insurance certificate and green card (international motor insurance certificate) if applicable. Motorists must also carry their insurance certificate or green card when driving outside Switzerland.

It's also advisable to have a European accident report form (*Europäisches Unfallprotokoll, rapport européen des accidents routiers*), although it isn't compulsory, which is usually provided by insurance companies.

ACCIDENTS

If you're involved in an car accident (*Verkehrsunfall/Autounfall, accident d'auto*) in Switzerland, the procedure is as follows:

1 Stop immediately. Place a warning triangle at the edge of the road at least 50 metres behind your car on secondary roads or 150 metres on fast roads, e.g. motorways. If possible, a triangle should be placed in both directions. If necessary, for example when the road is partly or totally blocked, switch on your car's hazard warning lights and dipped (low beam) headlights and direct traffic around the hazard. In bad visibility, at night or in a blind spot, try to warn oncoming traffic of the danger, e.g. with a torch or by waving a warning triangle. Motorists who witness an accident are required by law to stop and render assistance.

2 If anyone is injured you should immediately call a doctor or ambulance (dial ☎ 144 in most areas), the fire brigade (dial ☎ 118) if someone is trapped or oil or chemicals have been spilled, and the police (dial ☎ 117). If someone has been injured more than superficially the police MUST be summoned. Don't move an injured person unless absolutely necessary to save him from further injury and don't leave him alone except to call for an ambulance. Cover him with a blanket or coat to keep him warm. The REGA helicopter service (see page 91) is available for the evacuation of seriously injured people (' 1414 in an emergency).

3 If there are no injuries and damage to vehicles or property isn't serious, it's unnecessary to call the police to the accident scene, which may result in someone being fined for a driving offence. If you and any other driver(s) involved aren't willing to let your insurance companies deal

with the matter, then you're at liberty to call the police. For anything other than a minor accident it's advisable to call the police, as it will be too late to try to sort out who was at fault afterwards. It's advisable to report any minor accident to the police within 24 hours to avoid any repercussions later. If another motorist reports an incident (such as fender bender) and you don't, you could find yourself in trouble and can even end up losing your licence for a period.

4 If the other driver has obviously been drinking or appears incapable of driving, call the police. In all cases you mustn't say anything that could be interpreted as an admission of guilt (even if you're as guilty as hell!). Apparently admitting responsibility for an accident, either verbally or in writing, can release your insurance company from responsibility under your policy. You must say nothing or only that your insurance company will deal with any claims, and let the police and insurance companies decide who was at fault.

5 If either you or the other driver(s) involved decide to call the police, don't move your vehicle or allow other vehicles to be moved. If it's necessary to move vehicles to clear the road, mark their positions with chalk (have you ever tried writing on snow or ice with chalk?). Alternatively take photographs of the accident scene if a camera (or mobile phone camera) is available or make a drawing showing the positions of all vehicles involved before moving them (there's a space for this on the insurance accident report form).

6 Check whether there are any witnesses to the accident and take their names and addresses, particularly noting those who support your version of what happened. Note the registration numbers of all vehicles involved and their drivers' names, addresses and insurance details. Give any other drivers involved your name, address and insurance details, if requested.

7 If you're detained by the police, you have no right to contact anyone or to have legal representation. If you're travelling with a passenger, ask him to contact anyone necessary as soon as you realise that you're going to be detained. Don't sign a statement, particularly one written in a

foreign language, unless you're CERTAIN you understand and agree with every word.

8 If you've caused material damage, you must inform the owner of the damaged property as soon as possible. If you cannot reach him, contact the nearest police station (this also applies to damage caused to other vehicles or property when parking).

9 Complete the accident report form (*Europäisches Unfallprotokoll, rapport européen des accidents routiers*) provided by your insurance company as soon as possible after the accident and send it to your insurance company, even if you weren't at fault. **Don't forget to sign it.** If you have an accident, obtain another accident form as soon as possible (accidents usually happen in threes!).

Useful Telephone Numbers

Number	Service
117	Police (emergencies only)
118	Fire (emergencies only)
144	Ambulance (emergencies only)
1414	Rega Helicopter Rescue
140	Vehicle Breakdown (CHF 0.20 per call)
163	Road Reports (recorded information)

The above telephone numbers can be dialed from anywhere within Switzerland and are manned or provide recorded information (in the local language: French, German or Italian) 24 hours a day. See also **Emergency Numbers** on page 91.

Hit-and-run Accidents

If you're the victim of a hit-and-run accident, report it to the local cantonal police immediately, preferably before driving your car away (if possible). They will inspect your car and take photographs and paint samples. This isn't just to help them catch the culprit, but to enable you to make a claim on a special federal insurance (*Bundesversicherung, assurance fédérale*) covering hit-and-run accidents. You or your insurance company must pay the first CHF 1,000 of a claim and the federal insurance pays the rest.

DRINKING, DRUGS & DRIVING

As you're no doubt aware, driving, drugs and drinking don't mix – an estimated 20 per cent of Swiss road deaths are a result of drunken driving. In Switzerland, you're no longer considered fit to drive when your blood alcohol concentration exceeds 50mg of alcohol per 100ml of blood, although if you cause an accident you can still be fined if you've been drinking, even when below the legal limit. The law regarding drunken driving is strict. If convicted you'll lose your licence for a period (drivers who register above 0.8g/l automatically lose their licence for at least three months), receive a heavy fine (several thousand Swiss francs) and may even be imprisoned. To ensure that they have the same impact on everybody, fines are usually calculated as a percentage of the offender's salary. Anything more than one beer or a glass of wine may be too much for some people. Random breath tests can be carried out by the police at any time.

Also driving under the influence of illegal drugs is strictly forbidden and the police can conduct tests if they have any suspicions. If you test positive for illegal drugs, a blood sample is taken and analysed, and if it's still positive you'll lose your driving licence for at least three months.

If you have an accident while under the influence of alcohol or drugs it can be very expensive. Your car, accident and health insurance may all be nullified, which means that you must pay your own (and any third party's) car repairs, medical expenses and other damages.

Anyone who holds a driving licence and travels in a car with a drunken or drugged driver is held equally responsible under Swiss law.

CAR THEFT

Car theft is relatively rare in Switzerland, so rare in fact that there are officially no cars stolen at all in some years! However, you shouldn't take any unnecessary risks and should always lock your car and stow any valuables in the boot or out of sight, particularly when parking overnight in a public place.

Outside Switzerland car theft is rife. When visiting some of Switzerland's neighbouring countries (particularly Italy) you would be well advised to have foolproof theft insurance and have your car fitted with every anti-theft device on the market. This is particularly important if you own a car that's particularly desirable to car thieves.

PETROL

In October 2012 unleaded (*Bleifrei, sans plomb*) BF95 petrol cost around CHF 1.72-1.88 a litre, 'super plus' unleaded (BF98) CHF 1.79-1.92 and diesel CHF 1.81-1.95 a litre. Prices vary considerably depending on where you buy it – check Tanktip (🖥 http://tanktipp.ch) for the lowest prices in your area or canton. In common with most other countries, prices have risen considerably in the last few years (but are still lower than summer 2008, when they were around CHF 2 per liter).

Leaded petrol is no longer available but large petrol stations sell an additive that allows unleaded fuel to be used in older cars. Unleaded petrol is 95 (BF95) octane and super plus unleaded 98 (BF98) octane. The price of petrol generally varies by around CHF 0.10 to 0.20 per litre, with motorway petrol stations the most expensive and supermarkets the cheapest. The cost of petrol in Switzerland is generally lower than in neighboring countries.

Most large petrol stations are open from around 6am until 10pm or midnight. When paying at self-service petrol stations, either tell the cashier your pump number or hand him the receipt issued by the pump (if applicable). In Switzerland you aren't required to pay before filling your tank. Outside normal business hours, many petrol stations have automatic pumps accepting CHF 10 and 20 notes. Petrol pumps may also accept credit cards and cards issued by petrol companies.

Not all petrol stations accept credit cards and some may just accept certain kinds, which may not include Mastercard or Visa.

You're permitted to carry spare petrol in plastic cans in Switzerland, up to a maximum quantity of 25 litres. Many countries have restrictions on how much petrol you're allowed to carry in your car (other than in the petrol tank) and some ban plastic petrol cans. For more information, check with a motoring organisation (see page 156).

GARAGES

Garages in Switzerland are generally open from 7am to 6pm and most close for lunch between noon and 1.30pm. Servicing and repairs are expensive (particularly in major towns), but the quality of work is generally of a high standard. You may find that smaller garages (not unqualified back street places, but reputable garages who guarantee their work) are cheaper than main dealers. If you require a major repair job or service and are able to drive your car, it may pay you to have it done outside Switzerland. Similarly, if you require new tyres or a new exhaust, they may be cheaper in one of Switzerland's neighbouring countries.

Most garages, including all main dealers, provide a replacement car (*Ersatzwagen, véhicule de remplacement*) for around CHF 50 a day, while your car is being serviced. Some garages supply a free car when you have a service done and charge only for petrol. If you're a member of a Swiss motoring organisation such as the TCS, you can have your car tested for around CHF 60 and receive an accurate estimate of any necessary repairs.

SPEED LIMITS

The following speed limits apply throughout Switzerland:

Speed Limits	
Motorways	120kph (75mph)
Dual-carriageways	100kph (62mph)
Country Roads	80kph (50mph)
Towns	50 or 60kph (31 or 37mph) – 50kph if not sign-posted
Residential Roads	30kph (18mph) or as sign-posted; sometimes 30 or 40kph is indicated for sharp bends.

Some cantons have introduced controversial temporary speed limits (coupled with intensified speed checks) of 100kph (62mph) for cars and 70kph for trucks and cars towing caravans on certain stretches of motorways in July and August, in an attempt to reduce 'summer smog'. If a reduced speed limit is in effect it's indicted on overhead signs (it applies only on motorways). In many cities, e.g. Zurich and Basle, 'blue' zones have been established where speed limits have been reduced to 30kph (20mph). Roads in blue zones are liberally dotted with 'sleeping policemen' (speed bumps) and other obstacles to slow traffic.

When towing a caravan or trailer, you're restricted to 80kph (50mph) on motorways and 60kph (37mph) on all other roads. Mobile radar traps and laser detectors (more accurate than radar) are regularly set-up around the country, in addition to permanent photographic radar traps. If you're caught speeding, the police may send you a souvenir picture of your car number plate, with the fine (*Busse/Strafe, amende*). Cameras are also positioned at major intersections to photograph the registration numbers of cars that drive through red lights. Fines for many motoring offences have been sharply increased in recent years.

Swiss law requires motorists to adapt their speed to the weather, visibility and road conditions. In particular, you must be able to come

to a full stop within the distance you can see. This means that you can be fined for speeding, for example at night or in bad weather, even if you were driving within the actual speed limit.

Speeding fines depend on the speed above the legal speed limit, and for serious offences, the offender's number of previous motoring convictions. For marginal speeding of 1-5kph above the limit, the fine is CHF 40, except on motorways where it's CHF 20. Fines for driving more than 5kph above the speed limit depend on where the offence was committed, e.g. town centre, town suburb or country road/motorway. Fines for 6 to 10kph above the limit are from CHF 60 to 120; for 11 to 15kph above the limit CHF 120 to 250; for 16 to 20kph above the limit CHF 180 to 240; and for 21 to 25kph above the limit CHF 260 (on a motorway). If you're caught doing over 15kph above the speed limit in a town centre, over 20kph in a suburb or on a country road or over 25kph on a motorway, you must appear in court and will be heavily fined (e.g. CHF 500 to 1,000) and could also lose your licence for a period.

If you were driving at over 21kph above the limit in a town centre, 26kph in the suburbs or on a country road, or 31kph on a motorway, your licence will be suspended for a period.

If you're stopped by the police for marginal speeding (where a fixed penalty applies), fines can be paid on the spot or by giro payment within ten days; they must be paid on the spot if you're a foreign visitor, although if you're unable to pay they won't usually impound your car. Fitting and using radar warning devices is illegal in Switzerland and in most other European countries. You're forbidden to drive on motorways in the fast lane unless you're overtaking, and where sign-posted, below a **minimum** speed limit (you can be fined for doing so). Switzerland doesn't have a licence points system where driving licences are 'endorsed' (stamped) when you commit an offence, but nevertheless an accumulation of offences (not just for speeding) can result in a driving ban.

Many Swiss motorists have a complete disregard for speed limits, particularly during rush hours on motorways. The police could have a field day any time they wanted, although police cars are rarely seen on motorways except when attending accidents (although they also use unmarked cars). Motorists tend to drive faster in southern Switzerland and are generally less disciplined than motorists in the north (it must be something to do with the proximity to France and Italy, where everyone's a budding racing driver).

ROAD MAPS

Road maps (*Strassenkarte, carte routière*) are available from various sources:

♦ Good free maps of Switzerland are available from city tourist information offices, car hire (rental) offices and many Swiss banks. Switzerland Tourism offices sell a good map of Switzerland.

♦ A detailed Swiss road map book entitled *Auto Schweiz* (*Suisse*) is published by Kümmerly + Frey, containing 35 town plans (it's also available without the town plans).

♦ The ACS and TCS Swiss motoring organisations produce many Swiss road maps.

♦ Free local town maps are available from many tourist information offices. More detailed maps are available from bookshops, news agencies, kiosks and railway station booking offices. Local village maps can usually be obtained from community offices.

Unfortunately Switzerland doesn't have any large-scale maps for rural areas containing a comprehensive street index, but internet maps (such as 🖳 www.multimap.com) and GPS devices are good alternatives.

CAR HIRE

Major international car hire (rental) companies (e.g. Avis, Budget, Europcar and Hertz) are represented in most Swiss cities and at international airports (where offices are usually open from early morning to late evening). Cars can also be hired from local garages and car hire offices in most towns; look under *Autovermietungen/Mietwagen, location de voitures* in the telephone directory or on the internet.

Car hire is generally very expensive in Switzerland and around double the cost in some other European countries and up to three times the rate in the US.

Hire costs vary considerably between companies, particularly over longer periods (weekly and monthly rates are lower). Hiring a car from an airport is the most expensive, as are one-way hires. Older cars can be hired from many garages at lower rates than those charged by the multinational companies. In winter, hire cars are fitted with winter tyres and usually supplied with snow chains and ski racks at no extra charge. Hire cars can also be ordered with a luggage rack and child seats (for an extra charge).

In addition to standard saloon cars, you can hire a 4WD car, estate (station wagon), minibus, luxury car, armoured limousine or a convertible, often with a choice of manual or automatic gearbox. Minibuses accessible to wheelchairs can also be hired, e.g. from Hertz. In some cities, e.g. Geneva, electric cars with a limited range can be hired from Avis, Hertz and Sixt-Alsa. Vans and pick-ups are available from the major hire companies by the hour, half-day or day, or from smaller local companies, which are cheaper than the multinationals. When you have your car serviced or repaired, most garages will hire you a car for a nominal sum or even lend you one free of charge.

To hire a car in Switzerland you require a valid Swiss, European or international driving licence, which must have been held for a minimum of one year. The minimum age of a driver must usually be 20 or 21 and can be as high as 25 for some categories of cars. It's usually necessary to have a credit card to hire a car in Switzerland. Don't be late returning a car as it can be expensive. Swiss car hire companies may restrict or prohibit travel to other countries.

One way to reduce the cost of car hire in Switzerland is to hire a car through the US office of an international car hire company and pay by credit card. This is a legitimate practice and can save you up to 50 per cent on local rates. The US freephone (800) numbers of hire companies, such as Alamo, Avis, Budget and Hertz can be obtained from international directory enquiries or via the internet, and must be prefixed by the international access number.

Car Sharing

One way to save money on motoring in Switzerland is to use car sharing, such as the service offered by Mobility CarSharing (🖳 http://mobility.ch), which allows you to enjoy the benefits of car use without the costs and hassles of ownership – and it's good for the environment as there are fewer cars on the road. **Note that Mobility CarSharing is designed to combine travel by public transport with car sharing.**

The term car-sharing, as used here, doesn't mean riding as a passenger in someone else's car or sharing your car with others. It's actually a form of car rental (hire), but unlike traditional car rental, you can 'rent' a car for as short a period as you wish and aren't required to return the car to where you got it from.

Combining Mobility CarSharing with public transport is estimated to save at least 50 per cent on your annual transport costs, when the full costs of car ownership are taken into account, such as depreciation, maintenance, repairs, insurance, etc. Hourly rates (between 7am and 11pm) range from CHF 2.80 to 4.40 per hour or CHF 0.54 to 0.98 per km for the first 100km (above 100km the rate is lower). The rate depends on the vehicle category: there's a choice of ten different categories ranging from a two-seater to a transporter.

Mobility has some 2,600 vehicles at over 1,340 'stations' in 480 towns or city suburbs throughout Switzerland. First-time customers (see subscriptions below) can make a 'Click & Drive' reservation and pay for the rental car by credit card; you then pick up the Mobility-Card and the key to the vehicle at any one of 75 major SBB railway stations. Once you have used Click & Drive, you retain the Mobility-Card and can simply log onto the Mobility website to make further bookings.

Regular customers can take out a subscription (there are different subscriptions for private and business customers) costing CHF 70 (CHF 40 with a Migros Cumulus card) for a trial subscription of four months. An annual subscription costs CHF 290, or CHF 190 with a general season ticket or a half-fare travel card (see **Discounted Tickets** on page 125). Alternatively, you can become a member of the Mobility Cooperative (CHF 1,000 refundable share certificate plus CHF 250 membership fee), for which you pay no annual fee and also benefit from a member's special rate.

Vehicles can be booked round-the-clock online and by phone, and you're charged an hourly and a kilometre rate. Booking online is quick and convenient and allows you to make a single or a series of reservations, enter feedback, change or renew your subscription, pay invoices, create statistics and much more.

MOTORING ORGANISATIONS

There are three Swiss motoring organisations:

◆ **Automobile Club of Switzerland/ACS** (*Automobil Club der Schweiz, Automobile Club Suisse*, ☎ 031-328 31 11, 🖥 www.acs.ch);

◆ **Touring Club of Switzerland/TCS** (*Touring Club der Schweiz, Touring Club de Suisse*, ☎ 0844-888 111, 🖥 www.tcs.ch);

◆ **Transport Club of Switzerland/VCS** (*Verkehrs-Club der Schweiz, Association*

Suisse des Transports, ☎ 0848-611 611, 🖥 www.verkehrsclub.ch).

The above organisations have offices in all major cities and large towns. There are few essential differences between the services provided by the two largest Swiss motoring organisations, the ACS and TCS, although charges vary slightly. The services provided by the VCS are more limited. The annual membership fee for the TCS varies depending on your canton and is from CHF 85 plus CHF 75 for European coverage for one person (VCS adult membership is CHF 65). All organisations have reduced fees for spouses, families and juniors, and company membership is also possible.

The ACS and the TCS (and, to a lesser extent, the VCS) provide a wide range of services, which may include official control and pre-control car serviceability tests; estimation of repair costs; verification of repairs and bills; guarantee claims; holiday luggage and travel insurance; car, motorcycle and cycle insurance; travel bureau and ticket office services; hotel bookings; valuations of used cars; legal and technical advice; advice on buying cars; running cost estimates (per km); tyres and car accessories; customs' documents; information about road conditions; tourist information; road maps and tourist guides; free national and cantonal magazines; international driving licences; and translations of Swiss driving licences.

☑ **SURVIVAL TIP**

Members of Swiss motoring organisations who break down anywhere in Switzerland can call service telephone number ☎ 140 (24-hour service, CHF. 0.20 per call) for free help; non-members can also obtain assistance, but it can be expensive.

Emergency SOS roadside telephones (painted orange) are provided throughout Switzerland on motorways, mountain passes and in tunnels. Black arrows on white posts at the side of motorways show the direction of the nearest telephone (situated every 1.6km/1mi). Keep your membership card in your car and quote your number when calling for help. In Switzerland, membership includes the breakdown patrol service, towing to a garage or transportation of your car to your home garage. When necessary the cost of a taxi to the nearest bus or rail station, a taxi home or a hotel room (so make sure that you have family cover if you're a couple, even if you aren't married) is paid for. Swiss motoring organisations have reciprocal arrangements with motoring organisations in most other European countries and internationally.

All Swiss motoring organisations provide a comprehensive international travel insurance policy, called a 'protection letter' (*Schutzbrief, livret*), which covers most travel accident possibilities. If you have a car accident or a breakdown abroad, the 'protection letter' insurance pays for hotel and medical costs, car hire and essential repairs, or shipment of your car back to Switzerland. This insurance is valid irrespective of the mode of transport used and can be taken out with the TCS for Europe (including Russia) and the Mediterranean countries, or the whole world. VCS offers world and Europe/Mediterranean cover, which includes Turkey and some ex-USSR states, while ACS offer worldwide cover only. Travel insurance costs from around CHF 80 to 150 a year, depending on the motoring organisation and whether you have European or worldwide cover.

'Protection letters' also cover car hire (vouchers for Avis or Hertz), repairs, emergency medical attention, legal aid, technical survey and police fines (resulting from an accident). The 'protection letter', which must be signed, and your identity card (*Ausweiskarte, carte d'authentification*) should be kept in a safe place. The TCS protection letter also covers holiday or travel cancellation fees or fees incurred by curtailment of a holiday when caused by an emergency. The insurance provided by the protection letter is cheaper than most holiday travel insurance – you don't need to travel by car – but you should ensure that it includes all your travel insurance requirements.

Legal expenses insurance (*Rechtsschutz, protection juridique)*, covering legal costs in the event of an accident, is also available from Swiss motoring organisations, but is usually cheaper from Swiss motor insurance companies, who offer both motorised and non-motorised cover.

The ACS or TCS can also help you when you're locked out of your car.

PARKING

Parking in Swiss towns can be a problem, particularly on-street parking. In most towns there are many public and multi-storey car parks, indicated by the sign of a white 'P' on a blue background. In cities there are also hundreds of parking meters, but they usually seem to be constantly occupied, particularly on Saturdays.

In some cities there are signs that direct you to a car park with 'free' places. Parking in towns costs CHF 2 to 3 per hour. Parking in a centrally located city car park costs at least CHF 2 an hour and 24 hours can cost CHF 40 or more.

Cheaper parking is often available not far from city centres and some city shopping centres allow a period of free parking, e.g. up to three hours. You may prefer to drive to a convenient railway station or a park and ride (P+R/Parking Relais) area, where bus or train connections are available to city centres. A 'P+R' parking ticket may also include the cost of the bus or tram journey to and from the local town centre. P+R parking at railway stations costs from CHF 2 to 15 per day (average CHF 4) and monthly rates are available for commuters (typically a 50 per cent reduction).

If you park in a multi-storey car park, make a note of the level and space number where you park, as it can take a long time to find your car if you have no idea where to start looking! Tear-off slips showing the parking level (*Geschoss/Stockwerk, étage*) are sometimes provided at lifts in multi-storey car parks. On entering most car parks you take a ticket from an automatic dispenser and must pay before collecting your car, either at a cash desk (*Kasse/Caisse*) or via a machine, which may accept both coins, notes and credit cards. You cannot pay at the exit. After paying you usually have around 15 minutes to exit, where you insert your ticket in the slot of the exit machine (in the direction shown by the arrow on the ticket).

In some ski resorts, parking in a multi-storey car park is free for skiers or anyone using the ski lifts. You must stamp your car park ticket in a machine, usually at the station above the car park level, in order to exit from the car park without paying.

Swiss companies don't usually provide employees with free parking facilities in large cities and towns. Outside main towns, free parking is usually available at or near offices or factories. Disabled motorists are provided with free or reserved parking spaces in most towns, shopping centres and at airports, but must display an official disabled motorist badge inside their windscreen (some city car parks also have spaces reserved for women near the exit). Regular drivers for the disabled can also obtain special parking permits in some cities. Apart from off-street parking, e.g. multi-storey car parks, the following kinds of on-street parking are provided in most towns:

♦ **parking meters**, where the maximum permitted parking period varies from 15 minutes to ten hours. Meter-feeding is illegal and you must vacate a parking space when the meter time expires. Meters usually accept a combination of 50¢ or one franc coins. The costs varies, e.g. CHF 1-2 per hour in a city centre and CHF 0.50-1 outside the central area. Most meters are in use from 7am to 7pm, Mondays to Fridays and from 7am to 4pm on Saturdays (check the meter to be sure) and some are free during lunch periods, e.g. noon to 2pm. Meters at railway stations may be in use 24 hours a day.

♦ **blue zones** (*Blaue Zone, zone bleue*), indicated by blue road markings, require a parking disc (*Parkscheibe, disque de stationnement*) to be displayed behind your car windscreen. EU-compatible

parking discs are available free from Swiss motoring organisations, police stations, banks, hotels, insurance offices, kiosks and tourist offices. Motor accessory shops and garages also sell them for a few francs. The parking disc must be set to the next half or full hour and then allows one hour's parking from that time. For example, if you arrive at 9.50am you set your parking disc on 10am and can leave the car in the parking space until 11am. If you arrive at 10.05 am you set the car to 10.30 am, you're permitted to use the parking space until 11.30am. Free parking is also permitted from 6pm until 9am the next day. In some towns it's possible for residents to purchase a permanent pass from the local traffic office or some police stations, valid for extended parking in a blue zone, for example in Geneva (*carte macarone*, CHF 180 per year) or Zurich (*Anwohnerparkkarte*, CHF 240 per year).

♦ **white zones**, indicated by white road markings and a sign, permit free unlimited parking.

♦ **pay and display** parking areas, where you must buy a parking ticket (showing the parking expiry time) from a ticket machine and display it behind your car windscreen. These areas include both on and off-street parking areas and may include park and ride (P+R) car parks, e.g. at railway stations. There may be a maximum parking period of around two hours in town centres.

The attitude towards illegal parking is much stricter in Switzerland than in most other European countries, although the Swiss still seem to park randomly in cities. You're forbidden to park on footpaths (even with one or two wheels) anywhere in Switzerland, unless sign-posted and marked otherwise (in some towns parking spaces include part of the footpath, shown by a line).

You can be fined for parking illegally in a private parking area. Parking illegally in reserved car parking spaces can result in a heavy fine, e.g. CHF 100 (private parking spaces may be reserved by local residents and aren't used only during business hours). Private parking spaces are sacred in Switzerland and very expensive.

For minor parking offences in some car parks, e.g. exceeding the permitted parking time by up to half an hour, you may be fined CHF 10, which must be inserted in the envelope provided and deposited in a special box at the exit. Official parking fines are high, e.g. CHF 40 for exceeding the allowed/paid time by up to two hours, CHF 60 from two to four hours and CHF 100 for four to ten hours.

autociel.ch

buy and sell your cars in another way

» We provide you with new and used cars (any brand) at best prices! We work without stock and without fees in order to serve you best!

» We import your car/motorcycle/caravan

» We rent you a car when you arrive (about half the price of the rental companies)

» We help you find the right insurance and car finance

» We deliver your new car <<key in hand>> at your home or office

» We can help you resell your car at the best possible price

» Other services on demand

autociel.ch

Route de la Conversion 261
CH-1093 La Conversion

For Expatriates

In some towns you can even be fined for parking facing the wrong way, i.e. you must be able to pull out directly into the flow of traffic on the same side of the road as you're parked. If you receive a parking ticket, it's usually thoughtfully accompanied by a giro payment form (*Einzahlungsschein, bulletin de versement*) and is payable within ten days. You're sent a reminder letter if you don't pay a fine on time and it may be increased as a consequence.

> Be careful where you park your car in the mountains, particularly during spring when the snow is melting and the weather is wet and/or stormy. It isn't unknown for falling rocks (even small ones) to make large dents in cars.

PEDESTRIAN ROAD RULES

The following road rules apply to pedestrians in Switzerland:

◆ Motorists must stop for a pedestrian waiting at a pedestrian crossing if the pedestrian shows by any action his intention to cross the road. However, you should still take extra care when using pedestrian crossings in Switzerland as Swiss motorists aren't fond of stopping. If you come from a country where motorists routinely approach pedestrian crossings with caution and stop when pedestrians are waiting, take extra care (some 20 per cent of Swiss road fatalities are pedestrians).

◆ Pedestrians are forbidden to cross a road within 50 metres of a pedestrian crossing, bridge or subway (pedestrian underpass).

◆ Teach your children the green cross code: look left, look right, look left again, before crossing the road (remember that traffic drives on the RIGHT side of the road). In school, children are taught to stop, look, listen and walk.

◆ Pedestrians must wait for a green light before crossing the road at a pedestrian crossing with pedestrian lights, irrespective of whether there's any traffic. You can be fined for jay walking, i.e. crossing the road where it's prohibited or against a red pedestrian light.

◆ Pedestrians must use footpaths where provided or may use a bicycle path when there's no footpath. Where there's no footpath or bicycle path, you must walk on the left side of the road facing oncoming traffic.

MOTORING ABROAD

When motoring abroad NEVER assume that the rules, regulations and driving habits are the same as in Switzerland. Always take your Swiss (or foreign) driving licence, car registration and insurance documents (e.g. green card), and bear in mind that such things as breakdown insurance, essential spares, and security for your car and belongings.

Check that your car complies with local laws and that you have the necessary equipment, such as a warning triangle(s), first-aid kit, reflective vest and fire extinguisher. If in doubt, check the latest laws and regulations with a Swiss motoring organisation. See also the Tispol website (🖳 www.tispol.org > Country Driving Guides), where you can obtain a guide to driving in most European countries.

The most dangerous European countries for motorists vary depending on which newspapers, magazines or websites you read and whose statistics they use. However, it's undeniable that the likelihood of having an accident is much higher in some countries. Driving in some European cities is totally chaotic, a bit like fairground bumper cars without the fun, and nerve-wracking at the best of times. It's no way to spend a relaxing holiday. If in doubt about your ability to cope with the stress or the risks involved, you would be wiser to fly or take a train.

Geneva International Motor Show

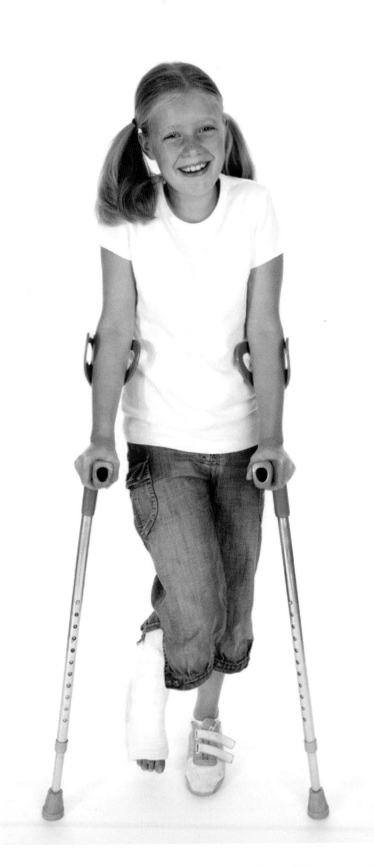

12.
HEALTH

Switzerland spends around 11 per cent of its GDP, some CHF 55,000bn a year, on health, which is one of the highest percentages in the OECD. Although Swiss health insurance is expensive (only North Americans spend more on health care) and becoming dearer every year, the country's health services are excellent and among the best in the world. Switzerland has a wealth of modern hospitals, highly-trained doctors (the highest ratio of doctors to patients in the world) and experienced nurses, and employs the latest equipment and medical techniques. There are generally no waiting lists for operations or hospital beds and the standard of treatment is second to none. If you must get sick, you could hardly choose a better place – provided of course that you're insured or can afford to pay the bills!

Two yardsticks used to measure the quality of healthcare worldwide are the infant mortality rate and life expectancy; Switzerland has one of the lowest infant mortality rates in the world (around four deaths in the first year for every thousand live births) and its life expectancy of 85 for women and 80 for men is one of the highest in the world.

Nevertheless, the famous Swiss air isn't always as fresh as the guidebooks would have you believe. Despite strenuous efforts to reduce pollution, impure air and high ozone levels in summer in the major cities are causing health problems (mainly respiratory ailments and allergies), particularly among children. However, compared with what passes for fresh air in most countries, Swiss city air is pure oxygen. Pollution is also caused by smokers, as Switzerland rates highly in the world smoking league (per head of population) and has a relatively high proportion of young women smokers. The main causes of death are cardiovascular disease (around 37 per cent) and cancer (some 26 per cent).

The Swiss are prominent in the lucrative 'immortality' business, which includes plastic surgery, rejuvenation and regeneration clinics, spa treatment centres and therapies by the dozen. Cellular rejuvenation (a snip at around US$10,000) is especially popular, where patients are injected with live sheep cells – Switzerland abounds with geriatrics prancing around like spring lambs. Complementary medicine is also popular (particularly homeopathy) and is usually paid for by Swiss health insurance.

Hay fever sufferers can obtain the daily pollen count (*Pollenbericht, pollen bulletin/indice de pollen*) from March to July from daily newspapers and at 🖥 www.meteoswiss.ch (under Health).

Switzerland has courted controversy in recent years with its assisted suicide law and is one of the few countries in the world where it's legal (see 🖥 www.dignitas.ch).

Pre-Departure Health Check

If you're planning to take up residence in Switzerland, even for just part of the year, it's wise to have a health check before your arrival, particularly if you have a record of poor health or are elderly. If you're already taking regular medication, you should ask your doctor for the generic name as the brand names of medicines vary from country to country. If you wish to match medication prescribed abroad, you'll need a current prescription with the medication's trade name, the manufacturer's name, the chemical name and the dosage. Most medicines have an equivalent in other countries, although particular brands may be difficult or impossible to obtain in Switzerland.

It's possible to have medication sent from abroad, when no duty or value added tax is usually payable. If you're visiting a holiday home in Switzerland for a short period, you should take sufficient medication to cover your stay. In an emergency, a local doctor will write a prescription that can be filled at a local pharmacy, or a hospital may refill a prescription from its own pharmacy. It's also wise to take some of your favourite non-prescription medicines (e.g. aspirins, cold and flu remedies, lotions, etc.) with you, as they may be difficult or impossible to obtain in Switzerland, or be much more expensive. If applicable, you should also take spare spectacles, contact lenses, dentures and a hearing aid, which will probably be more expensive to replace in Switzerland.

EMERGENCIES

Emergency medical services in Switzerland are among the best in the world. Keep a record of the telephone numbers of your doctor and local emergency hospital and other emergency telephone numbers (see page 91) near your telephone. Emergency first-aid information is available at the back of telephone directories in French, German and Italian. If you're unsure who to call, dial the police on 117, who will tell you who to contact or will contact the appropriate service for you. The action to take in a medical 'emergency' (Notfall, urgence) depends on the degree of urgency and may include one of the following:

◆ Call ☎ 144 for an ambulance. Most ambulances are equipped with cardiac equipment, and 'cardiomobiles' are provided for emergency heart cases. Details of the Swiss air rescue service (REGA) can be found on page 91.

◆ If you are able to do so, you can go to the emergency treatment centre (Notfalldienst, service d'urgence) of a hospital or to an emergency clinic (Pikett-Dienst, permanence) for minor casualties in French-speaking Switzerland. You may need to show proof of health insurance. Non-Swiss residents without insurance and no means to pay may be turned away, although this is unlikely and certainly won't happen in a life or death situation.

◆ Call your family or personal doctor. Outside surgery hours an answering machine gives you the telephone number of the doctor on call.

In major cities, a telephone number is provided where a doctor is available to advise you on medical and psychiatric emergencies, listed in local newspapers, or call the operator on ☎ 1811 and ask for the emergency medical service (Ärztlicher Notfalldienst/Zentrale Örtliche Notfalldienst, médecin de service/médecin de jour). The operator keeps a list of doctors,

dentists, pharmacies and veterinarians who are on call 24 hours a day. Doctors and dentists are categorised by speciality, location and the languages spoken.

ACCIDENTS

If you have an accident resulting in an injury, either to yourself or to a third party, inform the following, as necessary:

◆ your family doctor or another doctor (if treatment is necessary);

◆ the police (contacting the police within 24 hours may be compulsory for insurance purposes);

◆ your accident insurance company (who will send you a form to complete);

◆ your employer.

If you have an accident at work, report it to your manager as soon as possible. If you work more than eight hours per week and have an accident outside work, you should inform your employer, as he must provide you with accident insurance (see page 178).

An accident report form must be completed for all accidents where medical treatment is necessary, and which result in a claim on your accident insurance. As a general rule, Swiss accident or health insurance policies pay for medical treatment only when the patient remains in Switzerland. Journeys abroad while undergoing a course of treatment as the result of an accident may require the consent of your insurance company.

> The length of time during which you remain on full pay after an accident usually depends on your length of service (see Salary Insurance on page 38).

For information about how to prevent and avoid accidents (e.g. road, sport, household, garden and leisure), contact the Swiss Bureau for the Prevention of Accidents (Schweiz. Beratungsstelle für Unfallverhütung, Bureau suisse de prévention des accidents, ☎ 031-390 22 22, 🖥 www.bfu.ch). The bureau publishes numerous free leaflets and a magazine, available on subscription.

DOCTORS

There are excellent doctors (Arzt, médecin) throughout Switzerland, many of whom speak reasonable or good English. Many embassies in Switzerland maintain a list of English-speaking doctors (or doctors speaking their national language) in their area and your employer or colleagues may be able to recommend someone. Doctors are listed in telephone directories under *Ärzte*, *médecin* and their speciality. General practitioners (GPs) or family doctors are listed under *Allgemeine Medizin or médecin général*. A list of doctors can also be found on ⌨ www.doktor. ch (in German only). Most doctors list both their surgery and home telephone numbers. A zero with a diagonal line through it (Ø) alongside a telephone number signifies a 24-hour answering service. Many major cities operate an emergency medical service (*Ärztlicher Notfalldienst*, *médecin de service*), where a list of doctors is kept, categorised by speciality, location and languages spoken.

If you're working or studying in Switzerland it's mandatory to have health insurance (see page 181), which may determine or restrict your choice of doctor. Otherwise, you can usually go to any doctor anywhere, although each canton has different rules and procedures. An appointment must usually be made before visiting a doctor (except in 'emergencies').

Most surgeries are closed one day or afternoon a week and many doctors hold Saturday morning surgeries. Be prepared to wait anything up to an hour past your appointment time (the only time your doctor will be punctual is when you're late!). Doctors in Switzerland make house calls only *in extremis*.

Many doctors' surgeries in Switzerland are equipped to do simple tests (e.g. blood and urine), take X-rays and carry out most out-patient treatment performed in a clinic or small hospital. This is particularly true in villages and remote areas, where the nearest clinic or hospital may be some distance away. Your doctor is able to give advice or provide information on all aspects of health or medical care, including blood donations, home medical equipment and counselling. There are also specialist doctors in many fields of medicine which in many other countries are treated or dealt with by a general practitioner (GP), including children's illnesses, internal disorders and maternity-related problems.

It isn't always necessary to be referred to a specialist by your family doctor and you may be free to make an appointment directly with, for example, an eye specialist, gynaecologist or orthopaedic surgeon. If in doubt, ask your health insurance company for advice (see also **Health Insurance** on page 181). Note, however, that there may be a long waiting list for an appointment with a specialist if you aren't an urgent case, and your GP may be able to secure an earlier appointment.

If you visit your doctor for treatment of an injury as the result of an accident, e.g. skiing, you must inform your accident insurance company within a few days. If you work over eight hours a week, treatment is free, as you're covered by compulsory accident insurance (see page 38).

When you receive a bill from your doctor, you should pay it within the period specified (usually 30 days) or send it to your health fund. A health fund (see page 181) usually reimburses up to 90 per cent of the cost. If you send your health fund your bank account details (bank name, branch and account number), they'll pay refunds directly into your account and advise you when payment has been made. You should scrutinise all bills carefully, as it isn't unknown for doctors to overcharge.

Keep all receipts for health treatment. If your family's total health bills (including dental bills) that aren't covered by health insurance amount to 5 per cent or more of your annual income, you can offset the cost against your income tax bill.

MEDICINES

Medicines prescribed by a doctor are either given to you in your doctor's surgery or obtained from a chemist (*Apotheke*, *pharmacie*), denoted by the sign of a green cross on a white background. In recent years, an increasing number of doctors have been stocking prescription medicines, which has led to pharmacies complaining that doctors are taking away their business (they are trying to get legislation passed to forbid this practice).

In most cities, several chemists' are open until late evening (e.g. 10pm) and some provide a 24-hour service on certain days or even seven days a week. Ask the telephone operator (' 1811) for the address. At least one 'duty' chemist (pharmacy) is open outside normal opening hours in all areas (a

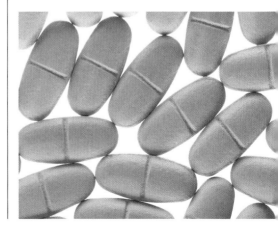

list is published in local newspapers and posted on chemists' doors) for the emergency dispensing of drugs and medicines. A list of all 'duty' chemists is also available on the internet (⌨ www.sos-apotheke.ch).

Switzerland has some of the highest prices in Europe for prescribed medicines, some 50 per cent higher than the EU average. As with various other items, many medicines are sold cheaper in Switzerland's neighbouring countries, particularly France and Italy.

☑ SURVIVAL TIP

There's a surcharge, e.g. CHF 30 in Lucerne, on medicines purchased outside normal business hours.

If there isn't a chemist in the village where your doctor practises, he'll usually provide medicines from his own supplies. If he doesn't have them in stock he'll write a prescription. Some medicines, e.g. herbal and homeopathic medicines, aren't recognised by a health fund and you must pay the full cost for them. Usually your doctor will tell you when this is the case and he may offer to prescribe an alternative.

Medicines are prescribed in the following four ways:

♦ once only when the prescription is filled;

♦ one repeat dose without the need for a second prescription;

♦ repeat doses as often as necessary within a three-month period;

♦ repeat doses for up to a year (e.g. for birth control pills).

Chemists are permitted to charge a fee for providing advice (irrespective of whether they actually proffer any advice or simply hand you the medication) and another fee for keeping your details on their computer. (These fees were introduced to compensate chemists for a reduction of margins on medication and are covered by health insurance.)

Most health insurance companies issue an insurance card that you show to the chemist with the prescription from your doctor. The chemist takes your insurance number and details and invoices the health insurance company directly, who will send you an invoice for the annual excess and/or the 10 per cent you must pay

yourself. Some health insurance companies – usually those with the lowest premiums – don't automatically pay chemists but require you to pay for medication and send the invoice to them for a refund.

If you have a long-term prescription, it's cheaper and more convenient to have your medication delivered to your home. Zur Rose Versandapotheke AG (☎ 0848 842 842, ⌨ www.zur-rose.ch) is a company that provides this service in conjunction with health insurance companies.

Non-prescription medicines can be purchased from a chemist or a drug store (*Drogerie, droguerie*) and are expensive. A drug store also stocks cosmetics, toiletries, cleaning supplies and a few unexpected items, such as alcohol (official recognition of its medicinal qualities perhaps?). A health food shop (*Reformhaus, magasin de produits diététiques*) sells health foods, diet foods and eternal-life-virility-youth pills and elixirs, for which the Swiss are famous.

HOSPITALS & CLINICS

Most Swiss towns have a hospital (*Krankenhaus/Spital*, *hôpital*) or clinic indicated by a sign showing a white 'H' on a blue background. Hospitals are listed in telephone directories under *Spitäler*, *hôpitaux*. Depending on the canton and region of Switzerland, hospitals may be designated as cantonal, 'zonal', regional or specialised, or be a private clinic-hospital. A university/teaching hospital is the largest and best equipped, with the most experienced staff. However, unless you're a private patient, you often cannot choose your hospital and your medical insurance and place of residence are usually the deciding factors.

Clinics are usually private and treatment there isn't generally covered by medical or accident insurance unless specifically stated in your policy. In French-speaking Switzerland there are emergency clinics (*Pikett-Dienst, permanence*) providing 24-hour treatment for minor accidents and 'emergencies' (there are also 24-hour emergency dental clinics).

Except for emergency treatment, you may be admitted to a hospital or clinic only after consultation with a doctor. Normally you're admitted to a hospital in your own canton (or zone in a city), unless specialist surgery or treatment is necessary that's unavailable there. Children are usually treated in a special children's ward, well stocked with games, toys, books and other children. Children who require

long-term hospitalisation may, depending on their health, be given school lessons in hospital.

Your choice of hospital and type of accommodation also depend on your level of health insurance cover (see page 181). Many doctors treat patients only at certain hospitals and you may have to choose between having your usual doctor or specialist attend you, or treatment in a particular hospital. Patients with standard cover are accommodated in a general ward (two to four beds), those with half-private cover in a two-bed ward and those with private cover in a private room. Patients without private or half-private insurance are usually unable to choose their own doctor. Note that nurses may not speak English, particularly in French- and Italian-speaking areas.

If you're a non-resident and aren't a member of a health fund or don't have Swiss medical insurance, hospitals usually require a deposit on your admittance (they aren't taking any chances on your survival!). This may range from CHF 2,000 to 10,000, depending on whether you're resident in the canton where the hospital is located, elsewhere in Switzerland, or abroad. The actual cost of treatment is calculated later and you receive a rebate or a bill for the difference (usually they overestimate the cost). In some private clinics, foreign patients must make a deposit of up to CHF 50,000 on admission and Swiss residents may be required to present a guarantee up to a certain amount issued by their insurance company (many clinics refuse American 'medical tourists' for fear of law suits).

Hospital visiting times vary depending on whether you're in a private, half-private or general ward (no prize for guessing which patients have the longest visiting hours) and are shown in telephone directories. In private clinics there may be no restrictions on visiting.

A publication entitled *Private Hospitals Switzerland* (there are over 100) and a brochure giving details of convalescence homes and hotels is available from Switzerland Tourism (see page 211). Information is also available from Private Hospitals Switzerland (Privatkliniken Schweiz, Cliniques Privées Suisses, ☎ 031-380 85 98, 🖥 www.privatehospitals.ch).

CHILDBIRTH

Childbirth in Switzerland usually takes place in a hospital, where a stay of three to five days is usual, or ten days for a caesarean. The father is usually encouraged to attend the birth, unless difficulties are expected or he looks as if he's about to faint. You can also have a baby at home. Ask your family doctor or obstetrician for information and advice.

Maternity costs (in a general ward) are fully covered by basic Swiss health insurance (see **Health Insurance** on page 181) and some private clinics are covered by health fund insurance (private hospital cover); ask for a list of charges in advance. You can choose a gynaecologist in advance (if you don't, one is assigned at the hospital) and you can usually request an English-speaking midwife. For childbirth, a hospital usually requires a voucher from your health insurance company.

Foreigners giving birth in a Swiss hospital must bring the following papers with them on admittance:

♦ passport;

♦ Swiss residence permit;

♦ *marriage licence or divorce papers;

♦ *birth certificates of both parents.

* These may not be necessary, but check in advance.

When a Swiss national gives birth in a Swiss hospital, she must provide a name or names for both sexes in advance, from an approved list of names. Although the approved list of names may not apply to foreigners, you may need to show that the name you choose is normal in your country (how do you do that?). See also **Births & Deaths** below.

If a couple aren't married, the mother chooses the name and when married the mother and father choose the name together. Swiss hospitals have an online 'baby gallery' with vital statistics and a picture of the new-born (within hours of birth!). The birth must be registered with your community, which is done by the hospital (if applicable). A child born in Switzerland doesn't receive Swiss citizenship unless at least one parent is Swiss.

You must notify your health insurance company of your new arrival, as babies must be insured within three months of their birth (it should be done in advance from the expected month of birth, but if you give birth prematurely, don't forget to inform your health insurance company.) If you're on maternity leave, notify your employer of the birth and check that child allowance is paid with your salary.

Most communities provide a free post-natal nursing service (*Säuglingsschwester*, nurse). The nurse visits you at home, usually once only, and you may take your child to the nurse's clinic for regular check-ups during the following year. The nurse is an excellent source of information on all baby health matters but may not speak English. She'll provide a certificate if you breastfeed your child, for which many communities pay an allowance. Switzerland has a comprehensive vaccination programme for babies and children of all ages.

Your local community may present you with a toy for your child, and around ten cantons pay a birth allowance, e.g. CHF 600 to 1,500. Expect to be inundated with advertisements for everything from baby food and toys to banks offering to make a donation of CHF 20 to 50 if you open a savings account for your child. Baby changing facilities are provided in some public toilets and most department stores.

Useful publications for new mothers and parents in Switzerland include *Mothering Matters*, a bi-monthly newsletter (💻 www.mmjournal.com), and *The New Stork Times*, a magazine published ten times a year (💻 www.thestork.ch).

DENTISTS

There are excellent dentists (*Zahnarzt*, *dentiste*) throughout Switzerland, many of whom speak reasonable or good English. Many embassies keep a list of English-speaking dentists (or dentists speaking their national language) in their area, and your employer or colleagues may also be able to recommend someone. Dentists are listed in telephone directories under *Zahnärzte*, *dentistes*. A zero with a diagonal line through it (Ø) alongside a telephone number indicates a 24-hour answering service. Some dentists hold Saturday morning surgeries.

Most major cities have a dental emergency telephone number, where a list of dentists is kept, categorised by speciality, location and the languages spoken. (Many family dentists in Switzerland are qualified to perform specialist treatment, e.g. periodontal work, which is carried out by a specialist in many countries.) In some areas, e.g. Geneva, there are 24-hour emergency dental clinics. Call the telephone operator on ☎ 1811 for information.

Switzerland's annual consumption of over 12kg (26lb) of chocolate per head annually is the world's highest and ensures that dentists (and Swiss chocolate manufacturers) remain financially healthy – especially as dental treatment is expensive, e.g. over CHF 5,000 to straighten a child's teeth isn't unusual. Fees are calculated according to a points system and you're entitled to an itemised bill.

If you or your children require expensive cosmetic dental treatment, e.g. crowns, bridges, braces and false teeth, it's usually cheaper to have treatment outside Switzerland (see below). Alternatively, ask your dentist if he can reduce the cost by reducing the work involved. This may

be possible, as Swiss dentists usually strive for perfection, e.g. when straightening a child's teeth. In primary and (sometimes) secondary school, children receive a free annual dental inspection from a school-appointed dentist. An estimate is provided for any dental treatment required and communities may pay a percentage of bills for low-income families. Your health insurance company may also pay a percentage if your child is insured for dental treatment (see page 185).

Dental treatment is cheaper in all of Switzerland's neighbouring countries and may be even lower in your home country (Swiss newspapers contain ads for dental treatment 'holidays' in the Czech Republic, Hungary and Poland). This option, although less convenient, may be worth considering if you're faced with expensive treatment (see also **Dental Insurance** on page ?185), but check the cost carefully (both in Switzerland and abroad). **Also bear in mind that there have been reports of inferior work in some Eastern European countries.** You should, in any case, always obtain a detailed written estimate before committing yourself to an expensive course of treatment.

OPTICIANS

The optician or optometrist (*Optiker, opticien*) business is competitive in Switzerland. Prices for spectacles and contact lenses aren't fixed, as they are for many other professional services, therefore it's wise to compare costs before committing yourself to a large bill. Prescription spectacles and contact lenses may be partly covered by your health insurance. The prices charged for most services, e.g. spectacles, lenses, and hard and soft contact lenses, vary considerably and are usually higher than in most other European countries. Disposable and extended-wear soft contact lenses are also widely available.

You may go to an oculist or eye specialist (*Augenarzt, occuliste*) for an eye test, who can make a more thorough test of your eyesight than an optician, and is able to test for certain diseases which can be diagnosed from eye abnormalities, for example diabetes and certain types of cancer. The cost is covered by most medical insurance.

HOME CARE SERVICES

Most communities operate a home nursing service for house-bound invalids, the cost (e.g. CHF 30-50 per hour when prescribed by a doctor and covered by health insurance) of which depends on the patient's or family's income. You can join a housekeeping and nursing service association (*Haus- und Krankenpflegeverein, société des aides familiales et des soins à domicile*) such as Spitex (☎ 031-381 22 81, 🖥 www.spitex.ch), which reduces the cost of home nursing and household help such as meals-on-wheels. Free services such as blood pressure checks may be provided for members.

Many communities provide families with a cleaning and general household service (including cooking) when the main carer (mother or father) is ill. The service is cheaper if you're a member of a housekeeping and nursing service association. Most health insurance companies offer an optional premium to cover the cost of home help when a carer is ill for more than a few days (the cost of a stand-in mother/housekeeper is tax deductible). For information, ask your family doctor.

Pro Senectute provides help for the elderly, including social and community work and homecare, e.g. home help, cleaning services, mobile mending and laundry, meals-on-wheels, pedicure, transport and home visits. The charge for services varies with the canton and is usually the actual cost incurred (those on low incomes may be partly or fully reimbursed). Foreigners are treated the same as Swiss, except that they must have five years' continuous residence in Switzerland to qualify for financial support. For information, contact Sozialberatung Pro Senectute (☎ 044-283 89 89, 🖥 www.pro-senectute.ch).

SPAS

There are some 20 spas or thermal baths (*Bad/Kurort, station thermale*) in Switzerland, which, although called *Bad* in German, are good for you and provide therapeutic and medicinal benefits. Spa treatment is recommended for a number of illnesses, including the alleviation of arthritic and rheumatic pains. The cost may be covered by your health fund when treatment is prescribed by a doctor. Most spas can be visited on an 'outpatient' basis, with day tickets usually having a time limit of around two hours. The usual maximum immersion time is 20 to 30 minutes, followed by a rest period (reclining chairs are provided) of around the same duration.

Switzerland Tourism provides information about spas (🖥 www.myswitzerland.com – always up-to-date/wellness) and publishes a brochure titled *Wellness Hotels*

COUNSELLING & SOCIAL SERVICES

All cantons in Switzerland provide counselling (*Beratung, conseil*) and assistance for certain health and social problems. These include drug addiction, alcoholism (Alcoholics Anonymous), compulsive gambling, attempted suicide and psychiatric problems, youth-related problems, battered children and women, marriage problems and rape. Many cantons have a telephone number where children can obtain confidential help, e.g. in cases of physical or sexual abuse. Counsellors provide advice and help for sufferers of various diseases (e.g. multiple sclerosis and muscular dystrophy) and the disabled (e.g. the blind and deaf). They also help critically and terminally ill patients and their families to come to terms with their situation. The Samaritans (*Die dargebotene Hand, la main tendue*) also provide a free telephone counselling service in times of personal crisis (☎ 143).

In times of need there's usually someone to turn to and all services are confidential. In major towns, counselling is usually available for foreigners in their own language – if you need help someone speaking your language will be found. Many cantons publish a handbook of counselling centres. Contact your canton's health service (*Kantonsärztlicher Dienst des Gesundheitsdepartment, service médical cantonal*) or ask your family doctor for advice. The website 🖥 www.infoset.ch provides information (in German and French) about addiction therapy in Switzerland.

In an attempt to combat one of the highest per capita rates of drug addiction in Europe, some cantons treat drug addiction as a social rather than a criminal problem and provide medical support, social workers, methadone treatment, and free or inexpensive food and drink, syringes and accommodation. Free drugs are provided for registered addicts in some cities (e.g. Basle and Zurich) in a controlled programme to help them kick their habit. In a move to combat AIDS (see below), local authorities in some Swiss cities also provide free needles and a 'fixing' room for drug addicts' use, with a nurse on hand.

Children with learning disabilities in Zurich can obtain help from Foundations for Learning (🖥 www.foundationsforlearning.ch), a non-profit organisation established by expats, offering therapies and consultations in English. They provide support for families including classes for both children and parents, as well as common-interest workshops such as 'Third Culture Kids'.

AIDS & HIV

Switzerland has one of the highest per capita levels of AIDS cases in Europe, particularly among people aged 35 to 54. As part of the Swiss campaign against AIDS (it's naïve slogan is 'Love Life, Stop AIDS'), many supermarkets and department stores (e.g. Coop and Migros) stock condoms (*Präservative, préservatifs*) in their cosmetics sections. Condom dispensing machines have been installed in some schools and in many public toilets, and there's a national telephone helpline (☎ 044-477 11 11) and website (🖥 www. aids.ch).

All cases of AIDS and HIV-positive blood tests in Switzerland must be reported to the federal authorities, although patients' names remain confidential.

BIRTHS & DEATHS

Births and deaths in Switzerland must be reported to your local registrar's office (*Zivilstandamt, bureau de l'état civil*). In the case of a birth, registration is carried out by the hospital where the child is born. However, if you have a child at home or in a different community from where you live, you must do the registration yourself within three days. (If a child is born en route to the hospital, there will be an exciting legal wrangle to decide its community of birth!) Ask the registrar's office for information. A Swiss birth certificate (*Geburtsschein, acte de naissance*) is issued automatically.

In the event of the death of a Swiss resident, all interested parties must be notified. A doctor will provide a certificate specifying the cause of death – you should make around ten copies as they're required by banks, insurance companies and various other institutions. A death certificate is required before probate can be granted for a will.

A body can be buried (very expensive) or cremated in Switzerland or the body or ashes can be sent to another country. Most bodies are cremated and the ashes stored in urns in a shared burial chamber (crypt).

Burial land in Switzerland is recycled after 25 years, when graves are excavated and the land reused for further burials.

Births and deaths of foreigners in Switzerland should be reported to their local consulate or embassy, for example to obtain a national birth certificate, passport and social security number for a child.

Lion memorial, Luzern

13.

INSURANCE

Switzerland isn't exactly a nation of gamblers, a fact reflected by how much the average Swiss household spends on insurance (*Versicherung, assurance*), including pensions, which at an average of around 20 per cent of their monthly income (including car insurance) is one of the highest in the world. The Swiss don't care to take any chances, particularly when they can insure against them – they spend some CHF 30bn a year on life insurance premiums alone!

The Swiss government and Swiss law provide for various obligatory federal and employer insurance schemes – the government spends around 30 per cent of its budget on social security and other insurance schemes. These include the following, for which premiums are obligatory for all employees in Switzerland and automatically deducted from your gross monthly salary by your employer:

◆ **Old age & survivors' insurance** (*Eidgenössische Alters- und Hinterlassen versicherung/AHV, Assurance-Vieillesse et Survivants fédérale/AVS*) and **Disability Insurance** (*Invalidenversicherung/IV, Assurance Invalidité/AI*), referred to by their English acronyms OASI and DI respectively. The contribution for all employees is 5.15 per cent of their gross monthly salary.

◆ **Company pension** (*Berufliche Vorsorge/BVG, prévoyance professionnelle/LPP*): Contributions vary from around 5.5 to 11 per cent of your gross monthly salary, depending on your age and your employer's pension fund.

◆ **Accident insurance** (*Unfallversicherung, assurance accidents*): Occupational accident insurance is non-contributory (paid for by your employer). Private accident insurance contributions vary with your employer from nothing (non-contributory) to a maximum of around 2 per cent of your gross monthly salary.

◆ **Salary insurance** (*Salärversicherung/ Lohnversicherung, assurance salaire*): Contributions vary from zero to around 2 per cent of your gross monthly salary.

◆ **Unemployment insurance** (*Arbeitslosenversicherung, assurance*

chômage): Contributions for all employees is 1.1 per cent of your gross monthly salary up to a salary of CHF 10,500 per month (CHF 126,000 per annum).

Other obligatory insurance (payable separately) includes:

◆ **Maternity insurance** (*Mutterschaftsversicherung, assurance maternité*): Employed and self-employed women receive 80 per cent of their salary (up to CHF 196 per day) for 14 weeks after giving birth.

◆ **Health insurance** (*Krankenversicherung, assurance maladie*): Compulsory for everyone except foreign diplomats and employees of international organisations.

◆ **Third party insurance** (*Haftpflichtversicherung, assurance responsibilité civile*): Obligatory for motor vehicles (see page 142), motorcycles, bicycles and some sports;

◆ **House contents insurance** (*Hausratsversicherung, assurance ménage*): Obligatory in most cantons.

Other insurance may also be obligatory depending on your age, canton of residence or employer. The most common types of optional insurance available in Switzerland include:

◆ public liability insurance;

◆ comprehensive car insurance (see page 142) – third party motor insurance is obligatory;

- ◆ breakdown insurance for cars, motorcycles, mopeds and bicycles;

- ◆ dental insurance;

- ◆ life & annuity insurance;

- ◆ private pension;

- ◆ personal effects insurance;

- ◆ travel insurance.

Details of most the above types of insurance are included in this chapter.

☑ **SURVIVAL TIP**

In all matters regarding insurance you're responsible for ensuring that you and your family are legally insured in Switzerland.

If you wish to make a claim against an insurance policy or a third party is claiming against you, you would be wise to report the matter to the police within 24 hours, which may be a legal requirement in some cases, e.g. if you set fire to a rented apartment. Swiss law may be different from that in your home country or your previous country of residence and may also vary from canton to canton. It's wise to follow the example of the Swiss and make sure that you're covered against most disasters. Regrettably, however, you cannot insure yourself against being uninsured or sue your insurance agent for giving you bad advice!

INSURANCE COMPANIES

Insurance is one of Switzerland's major businesses and there are numerous insurance companies to choose from, many of which provide a range of insurance services, while others specialise in certain fields only. The major insurance companies (such as Winterthur and Zurich) have offices or agents throughout Switzerland, including most small towns. Telephone insurance companies (such as Züritel, 🖥 www.zurichconnect.ch) have been introduced in recent years and usually offer lower premiums than traditional agents. All Swiss insurance companies provide a free analysis of your family's insurance needs and your Swiss bank may also provide independent advice (although they usually have an arrangement with an insurance company). Obtain a few quotations before signing

a contract and ask the advice of your colleagues and friends (but don't believe everything they tell you!).

In most cities you can find English-speaking independent financial advisers or insurance brokers who can advise you about insurance. Before choosing an adviser, ask whether he has experience dealing with expatriates, as your needs may be different from those of a Swiss family that never leaves the country. A good financial adviser or broker will also assist you when you need to make a claim.

You can compare the cost of insurance policies online via Comparis (🖥 http://en.comparis.ch/versicherung.aspx).

INSURANCE CONTRACTS

Read all insurance contracts before signing them. If you cannot obtain an English translation and you don't understand everything, ask a friend or colleague to translate a contract or take legal advice. Most insurance companies have English-speaking representatives and some provide information in English and an English translation of policies.

Most insurance policies run for a calendar year (1st January to 31st December). If you take out, change or cancel a policy during the year, you're billed or reimbursed the balance to the end of the year. All insurance premiums should be paid punctually, as late payment may affect your benefits or a claim.

While most policies have what looks like a fixed term, e.g. three years, they're still renewed automatically for another year if you don't give notice three months before the end of the term.

SOCIAL SECURITY SYSTEM

Switzerland has a three-part social security system for all employees, called the 'three-pillar' system (*Drei-Säulen-Konzept, système des trois piliers*). It consists of:

1. Compulsory federal old age and survivors' insurance and disability insurance, which is the Swiss federal social security pension scheme;

2. Compulsory private company pension funds for employees;

3. Voluntary tax-deductible private pension savings and life insurance.

The aim of the federal social security system is to guarantee employees at least a subsistence income on retirement or in the case of disability. To receive a full state pension you must contribute for the maximum number of years, which is 44. A full state pension and a company pension (see below) bring your pension to around 60 per cent of your final salary.

Old Age & Survivors' Insurance

The federal old age and survivors' insurance (OASI) and disability insurance (DI) comprise the Swiss federal social security pension scheme (*Staatliche Vorsorge, prévoyance sociale*). It's the first part of the three-part social security system and termed 'pillar one'. OASI and DI include the following:

◆ a retirement pension for a single person or a couple;

◆ a supplementary pension for a younger wife;

◆ a child's pension for the child of the beneficiary of a retirement pension;

◆ a widow's pension or gratuity (a widower can only claim a pension if he has children under 18);

◆ an orphan's single pension (one parent deceased) or double pension (both parents deceased);

◆ long-term treatment and all associated costs for the disabled;

◆ an invalidity pension for a disabled person;

◆ a disability allowance for those requiring full-time personal supervision (to qualify for a disability pension, contributions must have been paid for at least one year);

◆ appliances for a disabled person.

Contributions

All employees in Switzerland contribute to OASI/DI from 1st January of the year following their 17th birthday (earning a minimum annual salary of CHF 20,880 in 2012) until the official age of retirement (64 for women and 65 for men) or until their actual age of retirement if later. Non-employed people contribute from 1st January of the year following their 20th birthday. This includes 'leisured foreigners' (those who don't need to work) who are assessed on their assets, i.e. capital, investment income or pension, and income from annuities. If your spouse works and you don't, you're automatically included in his/her contributions. Contributions and qualifying years are also allocated to your pension for the time spent looking after children aged under 16.

If you retire before the official retirement age, you must continue to make OASI contributions until the official retirement age. If you earn above a certain sum after the official age of retirement, you must also continue to pay OASI, although this won't increase your pension above the maximum amount when you finally retire. When in receipt of an old-age pension, you're permitted to earn CHF 16,800 per annum (CHF 1,400 per month) before your liable for OASI/DI contributions.

Employees pay OASI/DI at 5.15 per cent of their monthly gross income and employers pay the same amount. The total of 10.3 per cent includes 8.4 per cent for OASI (old age and survivors' insurance), 1.4 per cent for DI (disability insurance) and 0.5 per cent for *APG/EO* (salary compensation insurance for the loss of earnings incurred during military service or women's military corps, Red Cross and civil defence service). If you're self-employed your contributions depend on your income, but are generally 7.8 per cent, although a falling scale allows a reduction to 4.2 per cent if you earn less than CHF 55,700 per annum.

The maximum contribution (2012) was CHF 23,750 for a single person or double this for a couple (CHF 47,500). The minimum annual contribution is CHF 475, payable by unemployed persons over 20 or those who aren't gainfully employed. When your salary includes income 'in kind', for example board and lodging or a car, the value is added to your salary and OASI/DI is payable on the total sum.

Everyone who pays OASI/DI receives an insurance certificate (*Versicherungsausweis/AHV-IV, certificat d'assurance/AVS-AI*), which contains your personal insurance number and the number of the OASI/DI compensation office (*Ausgleichskasse, caisse de compensation*) that has opened an account in your name. Addresses are listed on the last two pages in telephone directories. Make a note of this number and keep both it and the certificate in a safe place. If you change jobs, you must give your insurance certificate to your new employer so that he can register you with the local OASI/DI compensation office.

Benefits

The pension you receive on retirement depends on your average annual contributions and the number of years you've contributed. The minimum annual full pension in 2012 ranged from a minimum of CHF 1,160 per month (CHF 13,920 per annum) to a maximum of CHF 2,320 per month (CHF 27,840 per annum). The total old-age pension paid to a married couple or both members of a civil partnership may not exceed 150 per cent of the total maximum old-age pension, i.e. CHF 3,480 per month (CHF 41,760 per annum). A married couple's combined pension is divided into two equal portions and paid separately to each individual.

A full pension is paid only when you've contributed for at least 44 years. If you decide to draw your pension one or two years before the reaching the statutory retirement age (64 or 65), there's a 6.8 per cent reduction in your pension for each year of early retirement. On the other hand, if you delay drawing your pension for between one and five years (the maximum), you'll receive a higher pension depending on how long you have delayed it, as shown in the table below:

Pension Deferment	
No. of Years	Increase (%)
1	5.2
2	10.8
3	17.1
4	24.0
5	31.5

Pensions are adjusted, usually every two years, in line with the wage and price index. Complementary benefits are payable to foreigners with low incomes who have lived continuously in Switzerland for at least 15 years. Foreigners qualify for a reduced pension after contributions have been paid for one year.

Bilateral Agreements

Switzerland has bilateral agreements with over 25 countries including all western European countries, Chile, Israel, the Philippines, Canada and the USA, whereby your Swiss state pension contributions are transferred to your home country's pension scheme. Citizens of countries without a bilateral agreement receive a pension if they live in Switzerland but if they leave Switzerland permanently (including their spouse and children) they must apply for the return of their pension payments without interest. The form *Claim for refund of OASI Contributions* can be found on the AHV website (🖳 www.ahv.ch). You must contribute for at least one year to be eligible for a refund.

Contributions to OASI/DI are transferable to foreign national insurance schemes and aren't refundable if your country of domicile has a bilateral agreement with Switzerland. In the latter case, they count towards your pension entitlement in your home country.

If a bilateral agreement isn't applicable and you aren't entitled to a pension under Swiss law, your OASI/DI contributions are refunded when you leave Switzerland, provided you complete the necessary paper work and give the Central Compensation Office (Zentrale Ausgleichsstelle/Centrale de compensation, ☎ 022-795 91 11 🖳 www.avs-ai-international.ch) your address abroad.

If you live in Switzerland for a short period only, you may be exempt from paying OASI/DI, particularly if your country of origin has a bilateral agreement with Switzerland regarding pension contributions. To qualify you must usually be transferred to Switzerland by your employer for a maximum of 24 months and must remain covered by your home country's social security system. Non-working spouses and employees of international organisations (e.g. the United Nations) and diplomatic missions are exempt from paying OASI/DI.

General Information

As in most developed countries, Switzerland has too few employed people to pay the pensions of the increasing number of retirees. The over 65 population is expected to double in the next 50 years to around 40 per cent of the population, which will cause social costs to explode. The Swiss government is studying ways to avoid this

and one of the proposals is to increase the official retirement age.

For further information about OASI/DI, contact the Federal Office for Social Insurance (Bundesamt für Sozialversicherungen/Office Fédéral des Assurances Sociales, ☏ 031-322 90 11, 🖥 www.ahv.admin.ch) or the Central Compensation Office (Zentrale Ausgleichsstelle/Centrale de compensation, ☏ 022-795 91 11 🖥 www.avs-ai-international.ch).

Company Pension

A company pension fund (*Berufliche Vorsorge/BVG, prévoyance professionelle/LPP*) is a compulsory contributory pension scheme for employees. It's the second part of the Swiss social security system and is termed 'pillar two'. All employees earning over CHF 24,360 a year and over 17 years of age must be members of a company pension fund, which may be run by the company, a professional association or an insurance company. The maximum insured salary in 2012 was CHF 83,520. From this sum CHF 24,360 is deducted and the remainder (CHF 59,160) is the insured sum.

The self-employed aren't required to belong to a company pension fund and can choose to pay higher tax-deductible private pension contributions to compensate for the lack of a company pension (see **Private Pension** below).

Contributions

From 1st January after your 17th birthday (if employed, or from the 1st January after your 20th birthday if you're unemployed) until the age of 24, contributions are lower as only accident, death and disability are covered. From 1st January of the year following your 24th birthday, contributions are increased to include retirement benefits. Total contributions to a company pension fund increase from around 7 to 18 per cent, depending on your salary, age, sex and your particular fund, approximately as shown below:

Age	Contribution (%)
25 to 34	7
35 to 44	10
45 to 54	15
55 to 65	18

Contributions are increased by between 3 to 4 per cent for additional premiums for risk insurance, special measures and a security fund. Of the total pension fund premium of 10 to 22 per cent, your employer pays at least 50 per cent, meaning that the amount you pay varies from around 5 to 11 per cent of your gross salary.

If you join a company after the age of 24, you may have the option of paying a lump sum into the pension fund or paying higher monthly contributions in order to qualify for a higher pension.

If you change your employer, the accrued amount you've paid (plus interest) is credited to your new employer's pension scheme **plus** the employer's contributions (with interest).

Benefits

The benefits paid on retirement depend upon your accrued fund assets. The fund provides retirement, survivor's and disability pensions. A widow's pension is 60 per cent of the disability or retirement pension, and an orphan's and children's pension is 20 per cent.

In a move designed to encourage home ownership, employees may withdraw money from their company pension fund to buy a home in Switzerland, pay off an existing mortgage, or pay for renovations or alterations. The money must be used for their primary residence. Until the age of 50 the total accrued sum can be withdrawn, after which you can withdraw the total sum that was accrued when you reached the age of 50 or half the total sum currently accrued, whichever is higher. You can repay money to your pension fund at any time in order to restore your pension. If you sell your primary residence and don't buy another, you must re-pay any money withdrawn.

A cash payment of the accrued capital is possible only under the following circumstances:

♦ when you leave Switzerland for good. However, there's a bilateral agreement between Switzerland and the EU which restricts how much EU citizens can withdraw in cash from their pension fund when moving to another EU country. In the case of EU citizens leaving Switzerland, the equivalent of the compulsory minimum pension capital must remain in a vested benefits account in Switzerland up to the Swiss age of retirement. Any capital exceeding the compulsory minimum sum can be withdrawn.

♦ when you become self-employed; your local OASI/DI office must provide proof so that your pension fund recognises you as self-employed;

♦ when the total sum accrued is less than one year's pension payments.

Pensions are indexed to the cost of living. Your company pension fund rules are detailed in your employment terms (see **Chapter 2**) or in a separate document, and you receive regular pension fund statements from your employer or fund.

For more information, contact the federal department for social security (Bundesamt für Sozialversicherung, Office fédéral des assurances sociales/Fondation institution supplétive LPP, ☎ 031-322 90 11, 💻 www.bsv.admin.ch).

> The Swiss government has proposed reducing payouts to pensioners (by reducing the annuity-conversion rate set by the government at age 64 or 65) in order to make its compulsory private saving system more affordable. However, one proposal was rejected in a referendum in 2011.

Private Pension

The federal and company pension schemes (see above) are equal to a maximum of 60 per cent of earnings (for those who have worked in Switzerland their whole working life). To supplement these and bring your pension closer to your final salary, you can contribute to a private pension fund (*Alterssparheft*, *caisse privée de prévoyance-vieillesse*) and receive tax relief on your contributions (up to a limited amount). This is the third part of the Swiss social security system, called 'pillar three' (*Selbstvorsorge*, *épargne personelle*).

If you're a member of a company pension fund, you may pay up to 8 per cent of the maximum average 'pensionable' salary, which is CHF 6,739 a year (2013), tax-free into a private pension fund or a special bank account. If you aren't a member of a company pension fund, you may save up to 20 per cent of your annual income tax-free or a maximum of CHF 33,696 per year.

You can receive the benefits of a private pension scheme up to five years before the Swiss retirement age (65 for men and 64 for women), although you must pay a reduced rate of tax on a portion of the amount. A private pension can also be redeemed in the following circumstances:

♦ if you become an invalid;

♦ if you leave Switzerland permanently;

♦ if you become self-employed (after being an employee);

♦ if you join another pension scheme;

♦ if you purchase a (first) residence or repay a mortgage.

The interest paid by banks on private pension savings in Switzerland is around 1 to 1.5 per cent. There are no bank charges or bank taxes. You may find it worthwhile to compare the interest on a private pension fund in Switzerland with that paid in other countries. However, you should take care which currency you choose, as your savings could be considerably reduced if the currency is devalued (and you may have to pay tax on the interest).

You can compare who offers the best interest rates and the difference between individual providers via Comparis (💻 http://en.comparis.ch/banken/vorsorge/3a-2013.aspx).

ACCIDENT INSURANCE

There are two categories of mandatory accident insurance (*Unfallversicherung*, *assurance accidents*) for employees in Switzerland:

♦ **Occupational accident insurance** (*Betriebsunfallversicherung*, *assurance accidents professionels*): Compulsory for employees and paid by employers, it covers accidents or illness at work and accidents that occur when travelling to and from work, or when travelling on company business. One of the best known accident insurance

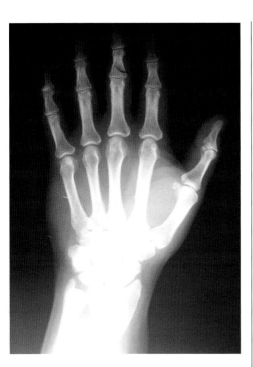

companies is SUVA/CNA (*Schweizerische Unfallversicherungsanstalt/SUVA, Caisse nationale suisse d'assurance en cas d'accidents/CNA*, 🖥 www.suva.ch).

♦ **Non-occupational accident insurance** (*Nichtbetriebsunfallversicherung, assurance accidents non-professionels*): This is compulsory for all employees who work over eight hours per week and all part-time employees who make OASI/DI contributions. An employer may pay the whole cost of non-occupational accident insurance or pass part or all of the cost on to employees. The portion payable by the employee is a maximum of around 2 per cent of his gross monthly salary up to a maximum salary of CHF 126,000 per year/CHF 10,550 per month (2012). Where applicable, your contribution is deducted from your salary at source.

If you work less than eight hours a week, you usually have only occupational accident insurance (but you're covered for other accidents by your health insurance) unless you make OASI/DI contributions. Accident insurance paid by employers only includes employees and not their family members. The self-employed must inform their health insurance providers that they are self-employed and will need to take out supplementary insurance to cover accidents.

You must ensure that your family is covered by private accident insurance, which can be combined with health insurance, otherwise you must pay the full cost of any treatment yourself.

Accident insurance allows for a total disability pension of 80 per cent of your annual salary and, in the event of death, a survivor's pension of up to 70 per cent of your annual salary. If you engage in dangerous or high-risk pursuits, you should check whether your accident insurance has any exclusion clauses. Skiing and most sports accidents are, however, fully covered by non-occupational accident insurance.

You must usually make a claim on your accident insurance within three months of an accident. If you fail to meet this deadline, you must either pay the bill yourself or make a claim on your health insurance.

When medical treatment is necessary abroad as the result of an accident, you're refunded a maximum of double the costs that would have been incurred in Switzerland.

SALARY INSURANCE

Many companies provide salary (or salary continuation) insurance (*Salärausfallversicherung/ Salärlosenversicherung, assurance salaire*), which provides sick pay (*Taggeld, indemnité journalière*) in the event of illness or an accident, although it may cover you for a limited period only (usually 720 days). Employees usually pay part of the premium, e.g. 50 per cent of contributions, although some employers pay the whole premium and others pass the whole cost on to employees. The percentage payable by the employee is a maximum of around 2 per cent of his gross monthly salary, usually up to a maximum limit. Salary insurance also applies to part-time employees who have been employed for three months or longer.

Your salary is usually paid in full during the first month of an illness or accident. After the first month, you're normally paid 90-100 per cent of your salary for up to two years, though the amount may be 80 per cent for single employees and 85 per cent for married employees with no children.

If the company has no insurance, the period for which you're entitled to sick pay depends on your length of service and may be calculated as a percentage of your hourly rate. The minimum period is usually three weeks in your first year of service.

UNEMPLOYMENT INSURANCE

Unemployment insurance (*Arbeitslosenversicherung/ALV, assurance chômage*) is compulsory for all employees. The employee's contribution, deducted at source from his gross monthly salary, is 1.1 per cent up to a salary of CHF 126,000 per year (CHF 10,500 per month). The employer's contribution is also 1.1 per cent, making a total contribution of 2.2 per cent. Contributions for gross salary between CHF 126,000 and 315,000 is 0.5 per cent (employment insurance isn't payable above CHF 315,000) for both the employer and employee. Unemployment insurance is often included with OASI/DI on your salary statement.

Unemployment benefits are paid when you're on short time or when an employer is unable to pay your wages, e.g. he has gone bankrupt, in addition to when you're unemployed. Part-time employees are also entitled to unemployment benefits when they're wholly or partly unemployed. Benefits provide for retraining, further education and other schemes for the unemployed. To qualify for unemployment benefits, you must have worked and contributed in Switzerland for at least 12 months during the previous two years. You must register within a few days of losing your job or of your employer being unable to pay you.

The amount paid depends on your previous salary and marital status, and may also depend on whether you were made redundant or were fired or resigned voluntarily (not advisable if you wish to receive unemployment benefits!). Benefits usually represent around 70 per cent of the insured salary and is paid as a daily allowance, although it can rise to 80 per cent for those with dependent children aged under 25 and the disabled.

Lower benefits are paid if you resign from your job, unless you can prove that your working conditions were intolerable (which is extremely difficult). Additional payments are made to cover children's allowances and educational costs, as prescribed by Swiss law. The length of time you receive unemployment benefits depends on your length of prior employment.

When you're unemployed you must report monthly to your local employment office (*Arbeitsamt*, *office du travail*). The payment of benefits is contingent on you seeking employment, with the help of the employment office and your community, although you may restrict your job hunting to the area where you live and the field or profession in which you're qualified. You should apply in writing for around ten suitable jobs each month and the authorities may ask to see your letters and any replies.

You're obliged to accept any reasonable job offered you by the employment office (if you're a brain surgeon you won't be offered a job as a waiter or waitress!). If you're offered a job with a lower salary than the amount you receive in unemployment benefits, you must accept it, although you're compensated by the employment office for one year.

Benefits are paid only while you live in Switzerland, except for benefit for non-payment of your salary by an employer, e.g. when he has gone bankrupt, which is paid even if you've already left Switzerland. If you leave Switzerland before the benefit period has ended, no further monthly payments or lump sum payments are made. If your residence permit expires before the benefit period has elapsed, it's extended on application. Employees of foreign embassies, missions and international organisations who don't pay OASI/DI or unemployment insurance, aren't eligible for unemployment benefits. Additional information can be obtained from your local employment office.

If you're unemployed and no longer entitled to unemployment benefits, your residence permit may be cancelled. When your entitlement to federal unemployment benefits has expired, you're dependent on supplemental cantonal programmes, which vary with the canton. Under federal law those earning below a certain amount per year are eligible for social security/welfare (such as rent or health insurance assistance), and cantons and communities also provide financial assistance to families whose income falls below a minimum figure ('existence minimum') of CHF 24,650 a year for a couple and two children under the age of six. Misuse of the welfare system in recent years has led to much stricter controls.

Employers in Switzerland aren't required to make redundancy payments. Irrespective of how long you've been employed, you're entitled only to the notice period stated in your employment contract or conditions, usually one month, or payment in lieu of notice. Note, however, that under Swiss law the notice period is one month during the first year, two months during the second to ninth years, and three months from the tenth year of service. Executive positions may provide for a cash payment (a 'golden handshake') if you're sacked or made redundant.

HEALTH INSURANCE

It's particularly important to ensure that your family has comprehensive health insurance in Switzerland, whether you're visiting or living or working there permanently. If your current health insurance won't cover you in Switzerland, you should take out a travel or holiday insurance policy.

Basic health insurance (*Krankenversicherung, assurance maladie*) is compulsory for everyone living in Switzerland for three months or more (and their dependants), with the exception of international civil servants, foreign diplomats and employees of international organisations (and their families). They can, however, apply to join the Swiss health insurance system within six months of taking up residence in the country. Foreigners must obtain health insurance within three months of their arrival in Switzerland and babies must be insured within three months of their birth. Employees are usually insured from their first day of work in Switzerland.

Some large companies have their own health insurance schemes which offer advantageous conditions and reduced premiums for employees and their families. If you're a member of a health insurance scheme sponsored by your employer or a professional association, premiums may be deducted at source from your salary. Private health insurance premiums may be paid annually, quarterly or monthly by standing order from a bank account. Your employer may pay all or part of the cost of your health insurance, although this isn't usual.

Types of Health Insurance

Health insurance in Switzerland can be taken out with a health fund (*Krankenkasse, caisse maladie*) or a private health insurance company (*Krankenversicherung, assurance maladie*), similar to BUPA in the UK and BlueCross/BlueShield in the US. Health funds try to exert some control over doctors' and hospital fees, and are the cheapest form of health insurance in Switzerland. The premiums of those with low incomes are subsidised by cantons, although you must make an application.

All insurance companies must offer identical basic cover as prescribed by law, which includes treatment by doctors, chiropractors, midwives and certain other practitioners (e.g. nurses and physiotherapists) when treatment is approved by a doctor; medication and laboratory tests; dental treatment as the result of an accident or illness; hospitalisation in a general ward; and emergency treatment abroad. Existing conditions cannot be excluded from the basic cover, including pregnancy, although supplementary insurance can be refused.

Hospital treatment in a general ward is usually restricted by health funds to hospitals in your canton of residence, although you can choose to pay extra to be treated in a public hospital outside your canton of residence and for a half-private (two-bed) or private room. A health fund pays for treatment in a private clinic only when similar treatment isn't available locally in a general hospital.

A private health insurance scheme usually includes half-private or private hospital cover as standard, and may include medical services and medicines that aren't covered by a health fund. You can sign up for basic health insurance with one insurance company and have additional coverage (e.g. half-private or private) with another.

Premiums

Premiums have been increasing in leaps and bounds in recent years, particularly private and half-private hospital cover (which can double your premium), and premiums vary depending on your canton and whether you live in a city (where premiums are higher). Premiums for private and half-private cover can be reduced by payment of an excess or deductible (*selbstbehalt, franchise*). The minimum compulsory excess is CHF 300 per year for adults (zero for children), although you can choose to pay up to CHF 2,500 (the maximum). Patients must pay 10 per cent of all non-hospital costs (treatment, medicines, etc.) above the excess.

Standard cover (e.g. a general hospital ward) from a health fund usually costs between CHF 230 and 500 per month for an adult, depending on the insurer, where you live, your age, which deductible you choose, and whether or not you (or your spouse or partner) are covered for accidents by an employer (employees who work more than eight hours a week are insured by their employer against occupational and non-occupational accidents).

Health insurance companies offer various plans, designed to save you (and the insurance company) money. One plan (which saves you 10 to 15 per cent) limits your free choice of doctors (you choose from a list) and requires you to consult your GP before, for example, consulting a specialist. Another, called 'Telmed' or 'Premed24', requires you to call a hotline before making an appointment with a doctor. This is useful, as hotline staff can advise on medical issues and may even save you a trip to the doctor – if necessary they'll authorise a doctor's visit and also save you around 8 per cent. Hotlines are staffed by registered nurses, and doctors are available for consultation when necessary. However, plans will only save you money if you follow the rules. If, for example, you visit a doctor without obtaining authorisation on the 'Telmed' plan, you'll be charged more – unless it's an emergency.

Standard health cover is valid worldwide and pays a maximum of twice what the same treatment would cost in Switzerland, which could be a problem in the US (and some other countries), where it's advisable to take out supplementary cover or travel health insurance. However, under bilateral treaties between Switzerland and the EU, Swiss and EU citizens travelling to an EU country receive only the cover that's compulsory in that country, which may be different from Switzerland. It's therefore advisable to have additional travel insurance, which can be obtained from many Swiss insurers for an annual premium of around CHF 150-200 for a family.

The Federal Office of Public Health (FOPH) offers a premium comparison service via its website (🖳 www.priminfo.ch) as does Comparis (🖳 http://en.comparis.ch/krankenkassen/default. aspx), which also gives you the option of an insurance offer via its website. Shop around and compare quotes from a number of sources.

If you live and/or work in Switzerland, you may also wish to consider becoming a member of the Swiss air rescue service (known as REGA, 🖳 www.rega.ch – see page 91), whose services may not be fully covered by your health or accident insurance.

General Information

The following general points apply to most health insurance policies in Switzerland:

◆ You must enrol your spouse and children as members, as they aren't automatically covered by your (i.e. an employee's) membership.

◆ Private medical and extra dental cover (and other optional benefits) may become effective only after a qualifying period of around three months. This may be waived if you can prove membership of another insurance scheme (Swiss or foreign) with the same or a higher level of cover.

◆ Your doctor usually sends you a bill for each illness within a three-month period. If you're forced to visit different doctors (e.g. when your

doctor is sick or doing military service) for the same illness, the bills should be sent to your health fund together. If you change doctors of your own accord during a course of treatment, you must pay twice.

◆ If you wish to see a complementary medical practitioner, you must usually be referred by your doctor, unless you're a private patient and pay the bill yourself. Your health fund may pay all or part of the cost of acupuncture treatment, an osteopath or chiropractor, massage (not the sort provided in 'massage' parlours), spa treatment, chiropodist or witch doctor. Standard cover also includes Chinese medicine, homeopathy, anthroposophic medicine and neural therapy. Check with your health fund what percentage of the bill (if any) they'll pay, before committing yourself to a course of treatment and a large bill.

All doctor fees are bound by the suggested TARMED prices (TARMED is an abbreviation of 'tariff' or fee and 'med' or medical). Hospitals and doctors generally have different rates, as follows (lowest rate first):

– patients with health insurance cover within the canton;

– patients with health insurance cover in another canton;

– private patients who don't belong to a Swiss health fund or a Swiss health insurance scheme.

◆ All bills, particularly those received for treatment outside Switzerland, must include **precise** details of treatment and prescriptions received. Terms such as 'consultation' or 'dental treatment' are insufficient. It's helpful if bills are written in a language intelligible to your health fund, for example English, French, German or Italian.

There are no restrictions on changing insurance companies other than the details in your contract. Policies can be terminated on 30th June if a registered letter is sent no later than March 31st and the insurance is standard (basic) and the deductible not more than CHF 300. All other insurance policies can be terminated only on the 31st December in writing by registered post by 30th November at the latest. If the premiums are increased you can cancel according to the term in your contract, e.g. one month's notice or at the end of the year. The termination rules vary depending on the insurance company – for more information and a sample termination letter, see 🖥 www.comparis.ch.

☑ SURVIVAL TIP

If you're planning to change your health insurance company, ensure that no important benefits are lost. If you change your health insurance company, it's advisable to inform your old company if you have any outstanding bills for which they're liable.

If you're leaving Switzerland, you must cancel your insurance in writing and give at least one month's notice. When leaving Switzerland, you should ensure that you have continuous medical insurance. Note, however, that if you're elderly or have a poor health record, you may find it difficult or impossible to obtain health insurance in some countries at an affordable price.

Checklist

When comparing costs and the level of cover provided by different health insurance schemes, the following points should be considered:

◆ Are discounts available for families?

◆ Are saving schemes available?

◆ Is private, half-private and general hospital cover available (as applicable)? Are private and half-private rooms available in local hospitals? What are the costs? Is there a limit on the time you can spend in hospital? What are the restrictions regarding hospitalisation in a canton other than your canton of residence?

◆ Is dental cover available? What exactly does it include? Can it be extended to include extra treatment? Dental insurance usually contains numerous limitations and doesn't cover cosmetic treatment.

◆ Are accidents, e.g. sports injuries, automatically covered, and can they be excluded should you wish? It may be to your advantage to exclude them, as employees in Switzerland are automatically covered by their employer's obligatory accident insurance and car accidents are usually covered by Swiss motor insurance.

◆ Are high-risk sports included, e.g. paragliding or rock climbing?

◆ What emergency ambulance or other transport fees are covered?

◆ What is the qualification period for benefits and services?

◆ What level of cover is provided in the rest of Europe and/or the rest of the world? What are the limitations?

◆ Are all medicines covered for 90 per cent of their cost or are there restrictions?

◆ Does the insurance company issue an insurance card that enables chemists to bill the company directly?

◆ Are convalescent homes or spa treatments covered when prescribed by a doctor?

◆ What are the restrictions on complementary medicine, e.g. chiropractic, osteopathy, naturopathy, massage and acupuncture? Are they covered? Must a doctor make a referral?

◆ Are extra costs likely and, if so, what for?

◆ Are spectacles or contact lenses covered and, if so, how much can be claimed and how frequently? Some Swiss health funds allow you to claim for a new pair of spectacles every two or three years.

◆ Is the provision and repair of artificial limbs and other essential health aids covered?

Those with accident insurance can reduce their premiums by up to 10 per cent by omitting accident insurance from a health insurance policy, although as a general rule health insurance includes cover for accidents.

International Health Policies

If you're living or working in Switzerland for less than three months (e.g. on a contract basis) and aren't covered by Swiss compulsory health insurance, you'll need an international health insurance policy. These usually offer members a choice of premiums: to cover average health costs or to provide cover in countries with high medical costs, which includes Switzerland. Besides the usual doctors' and hospital fees, claims can generally be made for body scans, convalescence, home nursing, outpatient treatment, health checks and surgical appliances. With an international health insurance policy, you may be able to renew your cover annually, irrespective of your age, which could be important. If you already have private health insurance, you may be able to extend it to cover your family in Switzerland.

HOUSEHOLD INSURANCE

In most cantons it's mandatory to take out household insurance (*Hausratsversicherung/ Haushaltversicherung, assurance ménage*) covering your belongings against hazards such as fire, flood, gas explosion and theft. Rental contracts usually require renters to have house contents and liability insurance, but even when it isn't mandatory, both are highly recommended. Most people take out household insurance together with private liability insurance (*Privathaftpflichtversicherung, assurance responsibilité civile*) – see below. Together these cost around CHF 300-350 a year for a couple with

a two-bedroom apartment and no children. House contents insurance is inexpensive, at around CHF 200 per year for cover totalling some CHF 75,000, plus an extra CHF 20 for each additional CHF 10,000 of cover.

Most house contents insurance policies cover the cost of replacing items at their replacement cost ('new for old') and not their second-hand value, including bicycles, skis and snowboards (depending on your insurer). House contents insurance doesn't include accidental damage caused by you or members of your family to your belongings. It may also exclude accidental damage to fixtures or fittings (e.g. baths, wash basins, electrical fittings and apparatus), which can be covered by a private liability insurance policy (see below). A supplement may be payable to cover special window glass, which is expensive to replace.

Most policies include cover for personal items when used outside the home, such as bicycles, laptops, cameras and mobile phones, up to a certain value.

Take care that you don't under-insure your house contents and that you periodically reassess their value and adjust your insurance premium accordingly. Alternatively, you can arrange to have your insurance cover automatically increased annually by a fixed percentage or amount by your insurance company. If you make a claim and the assessor discovers that you're under-insured, the amount due will be reduced by the percentage by which you're under-insured. For example, if you're insured for CHF 50,000 and you're found to be under-insured by 20 per cent, your claim totalling CHF 5,000 will be reduced to CHF 4,000. You should keep a record and receipts for all major possessions.

Insurance companies will provide you with a free estimate based on the number of rooms in your home, the number of occupants and whether you have expensive possessions or worthless junk (like struggling authors!). Don't forget to mention any particularly valuable items, e.g. the family jewels or a priceless antiques collection. House contents insurance can be combined with private liability insurance (see below).

PRIVATE LIABILITY INSURANCE

It's customary in Switzerland to have private liability insurance (*Privathaftpflichtversicherung, assurance responsibilité civile*), for both tenants and owners. Cover should include material damage, health treatment and compensation, including salary loss, and a pension for the bereaved or compensation for a disability. To take an everyday example, if your soap slips out of your hand and flies out of the window while you're taking a shower, and your neighbour slips on it and breaks his neck, he (or his widow) will sue you for millions of francs (joke! – see box). With liability insurance, you can shower in blissful security (but watch that soap!).

The American habit of suing people for $millions at the drop of a hat is fortunately almost unheard of in Switzerland, although for peace of mind (and your wallet) it's advisable to have liability insurance.

If you flood or set fire to your rented apartment, your landlord will claim against your liability insurance (if you don't have insurance, the authorities will lock you up and throw away the key). The cost is around CHF 100-125 per year for cover of CHF 5m, which is the recommended amount. For some claims or policies, you may be required to pay an excess, e.g. the first CHF 100 to 200 of a claim.

Private liability insurance is usually combined with house contents insurance (see above) – which may provide a discount – and covers all members of a family, including damage or accidents caused by your children and pets (for example if your dog or child bites someone). However, where damage is due to severe negligence, benefits may be reduced. Check whether it covers you against accidental damage to your apartment's fixtures and fittings. Some sports accidents aren't covered by private liability insurance; for example, if you accidentally strike your opponent with your squash racket, he cannot claim against your liability insurance to have his teeth fixed (but he can claim against his accident insurance).

You may require additional liability insurance if you keep wild animals, work from home, provide services or are self-employed, or participate in certain sports or pursuits such as horse riding. An insurance company or broker should discuss all the options with you before you take out a policy.

DENTAL INSURANCE

Basic dental insurance (*Zahnarztversicherung, assurance dentaire*) can be taken out as a supplement to Swiss health insurance. Health funds and health insurance companies offer dental cover or extra dental cover for an additional premium, although there are many limitations and cosmetic treatment is excluded. It's unusual to have full dental insurance in Switzerland as the cost is prohibitive. A dental inspection may be required before you're accepted as a reasonable risk. Dental treatment can be very expensive in

Switzerland (you don't always receive gold fillings, but you do pay your bills in gold!) and you should obtain an estimate before committing yourself to a large bill.

There are usually no restrictions on where (either in Switzerland or abroad) you obtain dental treatment, although you must provide your health insurance company with a detailed itemised bill. The amount payable by your health insurance for most treatment is fixed and depends on your level of dental insurance; a list of the amounts refunded is available from health insurance companies.

You can use a health insurance form to pay your dental bill, although most people pay their dental bills directly (after pawning the family jewels and taking out a second mortgage) and then send the bill to their health insurance company for a refund.

See also **Dentists** on page 168.

LIFE & ANNUITY INSURANCE

Swiss 'life' policies are usually for life insurance and not, for example, as in the UK, for assurance. Assurance is a policy which covers an eventuality which is certain to occur sooner or later, e.g. your death, unless the Swiss invent an immortality drug; thus a life assurance policy is valid until you die. An insurance policy covers a risk that may happen but isn't a certainty, for example an accident (unless you're **very** accident prone).

Some Swiss companies provide free life insurance (*Lebensversicherung, assurance vie*) as an employment benefit, although it may be accident life insurance only. You can take out a life insurance or endowment policy with numerous Swiss and foreign insurance companies.

In Switzerland, a life insurance policy is generally valid until you're 70 years old, depending on the company. If you die before you're 70 they pay up, but if you live longer than 70 years they pay nothing. Health insurance companies work closely with the medical profession to ensure that you don't die before you're 70, and even sponsor fitness courses to keep people fit and healthy so they live to a ripe old age (and they rake in the profits).

☑ SURVIVAL TIP

A life insurance policy is useful as security for a bank loan and can be limited to cover the period of the loan (some lenders insist upon it).

PERSONAL EFFECTS INSURANCE

You can take out personal effects insurance (*Diebstahlversicherung*, *assurance vol*) to cover your belongings when travelling or when you're away from your normal home (this is usually added to your house contents insurance). The cost is around CHF 80 a year for cover of CHF 2,000. Some companies may require you to pay the first 10 per cent or CHF 200 of a claim.

HOLIDAY & TRAVEL INSURANCE

Holiday and travel insurance (*Reiseversicherung*, *assurance voyage*) are recommended for anyone who doesn't wish to risk having their holiday or travel ruined by financial problems or to arrive home broke. As you probably know, anything can and often does go wrong with a holiday, sometimes before you even get started (particularly when you don't have insurance!). The following information applies equally to residents and non-residents, whether you're travelling to, from or within Switzerland. Nobody should visit Switzerland without travel and health insurance.

Travel insurance is available from many sources, including travel agents, insurance companies and brokers, banks, motoring organisations and transport companies (airline, rail and bus). You can also buy 24-hour accident and flight insurance at major airports, although it's expensive and doesn't offer the best cover. A peculiarly Swiss product is the protection letter (*Schutzbrief*, *livret*), a comprehensive travel insurance policy, available from Swiss motoring organisations (see page 156). It covers most travel and holiday emergencies and is valid irrespective of the mode of transport used, and can be for Europe, worldwide, Switzerland and Europe, or Switzerland and worldwide.

Short-term holiday and travel insurance policies may include cover for holiday cancellation or interruption; missed flights and departure delay at both the start and end of a holiday (a common occurrence); delayed, lost or damaged baggage; lost belongings and money; medical expenses and accidents (including evacuation home); personal liability and legal expenses; and default or bankruptcy, e.g. a tour operator or airline going bust. Travel insurance usually excludes 'high-risk' sports (see below).

If you belong to a Swiss health fund or health insurance scheme, you're usually covered for health treatment worldwide for up to twice the cost of similar treatment in Switzerland, and if you work in Switzerland you'll also be covered for accidents. Note, however, that this may not include helicopter evacuation by REGA (💻 www. rega.ch), the Swiss air rescue service (see page 91), although this is covered by Swiss third party car insurance and accident insurance (which all Swiss employees have).

Always check any exclusion clauses in contracts by obtaining a copy of the full policy document, as all the relevant information won't be included in an insurance leaflet. High risk sports and pursuits should be specifically covered and listed in a policy (there's usually an additional premium). Special winter sports policies are available and more expensive than normal holiday insurance (high-risk sports are excluded from most standard policies). Third party liability cover should be CHF 5m in North America and CHF 2.5m in the rest of the world. However, this doesn't usually cover you when you're driving a car or other mechanically-propelled vehicle.

Montreux, Vaud

14.
FINANCE

Switzerland is one of the world's wealthiest countries with one of the highest gross domestic products (GDP) per head at around US$79,810 (2011, source: *The Economist* magazine), and the Swiss are also among the world's richest people in terms of average personal wealth. Swiss banks and financial institutions are renowned for their efficiency and security (although even they got embroiled in the sub-prime lending scandal). Zurich is one of the world's major financial centres – generally recognised as the world's fourth most important financial centre after New York, London and Tokyo – and Switzerland is the world capital of private banking. The biggest problem facing the economy is the Swiss franc's safe-haven status, which has driven up the currency's value and eroded the country's export competitiveness and threatened deflation.

Financially, Switzerland is the safest country in the world and it has traditionally been a favourite bolt-hole for 'hot' money. The world-famous (infamous) secrecy surrounding Swiss numbered bank accounts extends to most customer accounts, and heavy fines and even imprisonment can result for anyone who breaches this confidentiality. The Swiss have, however, succumbed to international pressure in recent years and introduced tougher rules to combat money laundering and tax evasion. In 2009, Credit Suisse was fined US$539m for breaking US sanctions on Iran and UBS was fined US$780m and compelled to reveal the names of thousands of American clients using Swiss banks to avoid US taxation. (Not surprisingly, most Swiss banks will no longer open accounts for non-resident US citizens.)

One of the surprising things about the Swiss is that they don't usually pay bills with cheques (no longer used) or credit cards and use cash more than anywhere else in the developed world. When you arrive in Switzerland to take up residence or employment, ensure that you have sufficient cash, travellers' cheques, credit cards, luncheon vouchers, gold and diamonds to last at least until your first pay day, which may be a month or two after your arrival. During this period you'll also find a credit card useful.

This chapter contains information about the cost of living, currency, banking and taxation. See **Chapter 13** for information about company and private pensions, and life and annuity insurance.

If you plan to live in Switzerland, whether temporarily or permanently, you must ensure that your income is (and will remain) sufficient to live on, bearing in mind currency devaluations, rises in the cost of living, and unforeseen expenses such as medical bills or anything else that may drastically reduce your income (such as stock market crashes). You can obtain an assessment of your tax liability from a cantonal tax office.

COST OF LIVING

No doubt you would like to know how far your Swiss francs are likely to stretch and how much money (if any) you'll have left after paying your bills. First the good news. As you're probably aware, Switzerland has one of the world's highest standards of living and its per capita income and purchasing power is among the highest in the world. The country also has relatively low taxes and an historically low inflation rate, which was -0.4 per cent in September 2012. On the other hand, it's estimated that many thousands of people live below the poverty line – reckoned to be an income less than around 50 per cent of the national median income.

The bad news is that Switzerland has one of the highest costs of living in the world, particularly the cities of Geneva and Zurich, which are among the most expensive in the world. Residents of Geneva and Zurich tend to pay around 20 per cent more on average for products, services and accommodation than residents in other Western

European cities. The International Geneva Welcome Centre estimates that a family of four living in Geneva needs a monthly net income of at least CHF 7,000 just to maintain a modest standard of living.

The average price of many goods and services in Switzerland is up to 40 per cent higher than in EU countries and up to 60 per cent higher than in the US. According to the European Statistical Department, rental costs in Switzerland (including heating and electricity) are around 70 per cent higher than the EU average, food 50 per cent more expensive and meat almost 100 per cent dearer (now you know why Swiss salaries are so high!). However, prices of many goods and services (e.g. most retail goods, government-fixed prices such as hospital, postal and railway charges, insurance premiums and credit costs) are monitored and controlled by the office of the Price Controller to prevent unjustifiable price increases.

In the Mercer 2012 Cost of Living Survey (🖳 www.mercer.com/costofliving) of 214 cities worldwide, Geneva was in 5th position (the same as 2011), Zurich in 6th (7th in 2011) and Berne in 14th (16th in 2011). Tokyo, Luanda (Angola), Osaka and Moscow had the dubious honour of filling the top four places. Selected other rankings were: Singapore (equal 6 with Zurich), Hong Kong (9), Sydney (11), Melbourne (15), Shanghai (16), London (25), New York (33 – the only US city in the top 50), Paris (37), Rome (42), Auckland (56), Amsterdam (57), Toronto (61), Vancouver (63), Los Angeles (68), Brussels (71), Dublin (72), Wellington (74), San Francisco (90), Washington DC (107), Miami and Chicago (110), Birmingham, UK (133), Aberdeen (144), Glasgow (161) and Belfast (165).

> The fundamental flaw with most cost of living surveys is that they convert local prices into $US, which means that any changes are caused as much (or more) by currency fluctuations as they are by price inflation. Therefore in the last few years, Switzerland and Japan, with their hard currencies, have become more expensive in dollar terms, while the UK (e.g. London) with its weaker pound, and the Eurozone have become cheaper.

Food and especially meat is so much more expensive than in most EU countries and North America (Switzerland's food prices are exceeded worldwide only by Japan's), therefore your food bill will almost certainly be higher; the actual difference will depend on what you eat, where you lived before coming to Switzerland and whether you refrain from buying imported food. Around CHF 1,000 should feed two adults for a month in most areas, excluding frequent dining out, fillet steak, caviar and alcohol (living in Switzerland provides an excellent incentive to cut down on all those expensive, rich foods!).

Your cost of living in Switzerland will depend very much on where and how you live. The inhabitants of canton Appenzell-Innerrhoden enjoy the highest levels of disposable income after tax and fixed costs such as housing, followed by those of Obwalden, Glarus, Thurgau and Appenzell-Ausserrhoden. Geneva residents are the worst off, followed by Basle City, Vaud, Basle Country and Zurich.

It's also possible to compare the cost of living between various cities, using websites such as the Economist Intelligence Unit (🖳 http://eiu.enumerate.com/asp/wcol_wcolhome.asp), for which a fee is payable. There are also websites that give you an idea of daily living costs in Switzerland, such as 🖳 www.numbeo.com/cost-of-living. However, information should be taken with a pinch of salt as it may not be up to date, and price comparisons with other countries are often wildly inaccurate (and often include irrelevant items which distort the results).

The Union Bank of Switzerland (🖳 www.ubs.com/global/en/wealth_management/wealth_management_research/prices_earnings.html) publishes *Prices and Earnings* every three years (latest edition 2012), covering 72 cities in 58 countries, comparing the purchasing power and containing interesting analyses and evaluations of changes in exchange rates and inflation. According to UBS, the high purchasing power in Switzerland more than offsets the high cost of living.

Despite the high cost of food and housing, the cost of living in Switzerland needn't be astronomical. If you shop wisely, compare prices and services before buying, and don't live too extravagantly, you may be pleasantly surprised at how little you can live on. In high rent areas (such as Geneva), you can save money by renting an apartment in an unfashionable suburb or a rural area – or even in a neighbouring country – and commuting further to work.

You can also save on motoring, as petrol (gas) in Switzerland is cheaper than in neighbouring countries. The price of cars is around average for Europe but running a car (including depreciation) is relatively expensive; according to the Swiss Touring Club it costs around CHF 11,000 a year to drive a medium-sized car 15,000km. Leasing a car may save you money, as will running a diesel car. Even better, if you live in a city – where public transport is excellent and good value for money (especially with an annual pass or half-fare card – see **Chapter 10**) – you may not need a car at all! (You can hire a car by the hour when required – see **Car Sharing** on page 155.)

If you live near a border you can also make savings on food and many other goods by doing you weekly shopping and buying 'big ticket' items abroad. You can also save money by comparing prices using a comparison website such as Comparis (🖳 http://en.comparis.ch), where you can compare the cost of housing (to rent and buy), mortgages, insurance, cars (purchase and lease), telephones (mobile and fixed), the internet and consumer electronics.

SWISS CURRENCY

The unit of Swiss currency is the Swiss franc (*Frank, franc*), one of the strongest and most stable currencies in the world, with a central bank interest rate of just 0.25 per cent (since 12th March 2009). The Swiss franc is divided into 100 cents (*Rappen, centime*) and Swiss coins are minted in values of 5, 10, 20 and 50 cents and 1, 2 and 5 francs. Banknotes are printed in denominations of 10, 20, 50, 100, 200 and 1,000 francs (small change in Switzerland!). High-tech banknotes with a wide range of security features have been introduced in recent years and are allegedly 'virtually impossible' to counterfeit. The new notes contain five visible safety features, plus a second level detectable by special equipment and a third level known only to the central bank.

The Swiss franc is usually written CHF (the official international abbreviation), as used in this book. When writing figures in Switzerland, a quotation mark (') is used to separate units of millions, thousands and hundreds, and a comma (,) to denote cents, e.g. 1'500'485,34 is one million, five hundred thousand, four hundred and eighty five francs and 34 cents – a nice healthy bank balance! Values below one franc are written as a percentage of a franc rather than in cents, e.g. 0,34 is thirty four cents. In this book figures are written in the standard English format, with a comma separating millions, thousands and hundreds and point instead of a comma before cents, e.g. CHF 1,500,485.34.

In the last few years the Swiss franc has been a major beneficiary of the worldwide economic meltdown – being traditionally seen as a refuge in times of turmoil – during which it has gained in value against most major currencies. According to the Economists' 'Big Mac' index (🖳 www.economist.com/node/21542808), the Swiss franc was 62 per cent over-valued in January 2012.

IMPORTING & EXPORTING MONEY

Switzerland has no currency restrictions – you may bring in or take out as much money as you wish, in any currency (Euros are accepted by many businesses). The major Swiss banks will change practically all foreign banknotes without batting an eyelid and may even exchange coins, although at a lower rate than banknotes. Banks give a higher exchange rate for travellers' cheques than for banknotes. The most popular foreign currencies can be changed to Swiss francs via machines at airports and major railway stations. The big banks (UBS and Crédit Suisse) charge a fee of CHF 5 for cash currency exchanges if you don't have an account with them, while the Coop Bank, Migros Bank and many cantonal banks don't charge fees and often offer better exchange rates. Many Swiss hotels and shops accept and change foreign currency, but usually at a less favourable exchange rate than banks.

The Swiss franc exchange rate (*Wechselkurs, taux de change*) for most European and major international currencies is listed in banks and daily newspapers or can be found on online currency websites such as 🖳 www.xe.com. Most Swiss banks sell palladium, platinum, gold and silver (bars and coins), which are a good investment – particularly when the world's stock markets are in a panic. Swiss gold coins are a favourite gift from Swiss godparents to their godchildren, although

the 'standard' gift is a gold bracelet with the name of the child engraved on it.

Many railway stations provide a money-changing service, which is particularly handy for 'spur of the moment' trips abroad (although nowadays all you need is to keep a few hundred euros handy). Major SBB stations have change bureaux (with extended opening hours) where you can buy or sell foreign currencies at favourable rates, buy and cash travellers' cheques, and obtain a cash advance on credit cards. In over 300 smaller stations, you can buy currency and travellers' cheques in the most popular foreign currencies. Railway station offices are open during normal railway booking office hours from around 6am until 7.30pm, including weekends, and even later at major stations.

The SBB and Swiss Post are also representatives of Western Union and will send or receive (by telegraphic transfer) cash in as little as ten minutes, although fees are **very** high. When sending money abroad, you may receive a better exchange rate from a post office than a bank.

BANKS

If there's one place in Switzerland where you can be sure of a warm welcome, it's a Swiss bank (unless you plan to rob it!). It will probably come as no surprise that there are lots of banks in Switzerland, although many have closed in recent years or been swallowed up by the major banks. Switzerland is one of the most 'over-banked' countries in the world and in addition to the two major banks (UBS, Switzerland's largest bank, and Crédit Suisse), which have branches in most towns, there are many smaller regional, cantonal, loan and savings banks, plus private (mainly portfolio management) and foreign banks.

If you do a lot of travelling abroad, you may find that the comprehensive range of services provided by the major Swiss banks is more suited to your needs than those of smaller banks. The major banks are also more likely to have staff who speak English and other foreign languages, and they can provide statements and other documentation in English and other non-Swiss languages. Major Swiss banks offer 24-hour banking via ATMs and the internet, although this applies to most banks nowadays. In a small country town or village, there's usually a branch of one of the local banks (e.g. Raiffeisenbank, Banque Raiffeisen) and a post office, but not a branch of a major bank. Local banks usually provide a more personal service, may offer cheaper loans and mortgages than the major banks, and (in most cantons) provide a guarantee for deposits. Many Swiss prefer using local cantonal banks.

General Information

The following points apply to most Swiss banks:

♦ All bills can be paid through your bank. Simply send the payment forms to your bank with a completed payment advice form (provided by banks on request) or drop them in your bank's post box, and your bank will make a payment order (*Zahlungsauftrag, ordre de paiement*). This method of payment is free and has the advantage that your payments (or the total payment) are recorded on your monthly bank statement. Alternatively you can pay your bills at a post office (see page 85) or online.

♦ Internet banking is provided by most Swiss banks and is usually free.

♦ Buying stocks and bonds in Switzerland is normally done through a bank and not through a stockbroker. Most banks post the latest major Swiss share prices in all branches and some have computer enquiry systems where information is displayed on a screen. Swissquote (⌨ www.swissquote.ch) is the leader in online trading in Switzerland.

♦ You can open a foreign currency account with any Swiss bank. However, if you receive a transfer from abroad, make sure that it's deposited in the correct account – it could be deposited in a foreign currency account, even if you don't have one!

♦ All correspondence from the major Swiss banks can be requested in English and certain other non-Swiss languages, in addition to French, German and Italian.

Note that banks charge postage for each item sent to you, which depends on whether you choose 'A' or 'B' class post.

♦ Many banks offer extra interest to students or youths aged, for example, from 16 to 20. This costs the banks very little as most students are broke, but all banks know that you need to 'get 'em while they're young', as few people change banks, which is why banks offer to open a savings account for your new baby with a free deposit of CHF 25 or 50!

♦ An account holder can create a joint account by giving his spouse (or mistress) signatory authority. A joint account can be for two or more people. You can specify whether cheques and withdrawal slips need to be signed by any joint account holder or require all account holders' signatures.

◆ At the end of the year (or more frequently, depending on your bank) you'll receive a statement listing all bank charges, interest paid or earned and taxes, e.g. federal withholding tax (see page 204), deducted during the previous year. If you're a Swiss taxpayer, you should keep this in a safe place, as when you complete your income tax return you can reclaim the withholding tax and any interest paid is tax deductible.

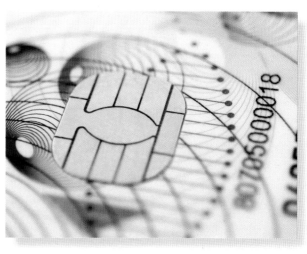

◆ The charge for standing orders from a salary account is around CHF 15-20 a year. Standing orders are paid automatically, provided there are sufficient funds in your account to cover them. If you have insufficient funds in your account, your bank may not pay your standing order payments (*Dauerauftrag*, *ordre permanent*) and may not inform you of this.

◆ If an American citizen wishes to hold US securities in a Swiss account, he must sign a declaration stating that either the Swiss bank is allowed to inform the IRS about the account or that on the sale of the securities a withholding tax of 31 per cent of the profits or capital gains will be levied. All other account holders must sign a statement to the effect that they **aren't** American citizens and have no tax liabilities in the US.

◆ All major Swiss banks produce numerous free brochures and booklets (many in English) describing their services and containing interesting and useful information. The major banks also publish newsletters in English and other languages, which are sent free to customers.

Opening Hours

Normal bank opening hours are from 8 or 8.30am to 4.30 or 4.45pm Mondays to Fridays, with continuous service during the lunch period in cities and large towns. Most banks are open late, e.g. until 5.30 or 6.30pm, on one day a week, depending on the bank and its location. In cities, a few banks have extended opening hours during the week and are open on Saturdays from around 9am to 4pm. In large shopping centres (*Einkaufszentrum*, *centre commercial*) most banks are open until 5pm on Saturdays and major banks are also open on Saturdays in many tourist areas.

There are no general opening hours for 'village' banks, which may be closed on Monday mornings and Wednesday afternoons and open on Saturday mornings. They usually close for lunch, which may extend from 11.45am until 2pm, but often remain open until 5.30pm, Mondays to Fridays. Banks at Swiss airports and major railway stations are open from around 6.30 or 7am until 6.30pm (10.30pm at major airports).

In major cities there are 24-hour automated banking centres, where you can purchase foreign currencies, change foreign currency into Swiss francs, buy travellers' cheques and gold, change Swiss banknotes and coins, and rent safety deposit boxes. You can also obtain 24-hour telephone customer advice, stock market and general banking information via computer terminals. These services are provided in addition to the usual automatic banking facilities, such as cash withdrawals, deposits and checking account balances.

Opening a Bank Account

One of your first acts in Switzerland should be to open a bank account. Simply go to the bank of your choice and tell them you're living or working in Switzerland and wish to open a private (*Privatkonto*, *compte personnel*) or current account (*kontkorrent*, *compte currante*). Some companies have an arrangement with a particular bank, which may offer lower bank charges for employees. Current accounts in Swiss francs and foreign currencies are available to all residents.

Banks offer a range of other accounts, including a variety of savings accounts providing higher interest rates than a salary or current account. Migros bank (🖥 www.migrosbank.ch), owned by Switzerland's largest supermarket chain, usually pays higher interest than most other banks.

After opening an account, if you'll be working in Switzerland don't forget to give the account details to your employer (or you won't be paid). Your salary is normally paid by your employer directly into your bank account. Your monthly salary statement is sent to your home address or given to you at work. You may need to wait one or two months for your first pay cheque, although this is unusual; check with your employer. If necessary, you may be given an advance on your salary.

Bank statements are usually issued monthly (optionally daily, weekly or quarterly); interest is paid on deposits and an overdraft facility is usually available. With a salary account, as well as a monthly or quarterly statement, you receive confirmation of payment of standing orders and cheques (debit advice), and a credit advice for deposits other than your salary. Bank charges are levied annually, plus postal and other charges. Note that if you ask your bank to retain your post for collection, fees can be astronomical. You don't receive a cheque book with any account, but an account 'debit' card containing your encoded account information.

There are considerable differences in bank fees, for example UBS and Crédit Suisse are the most expensive for accounts with relatively small balances, although if your balance averages over CHF 10,000, fees are reduced. Some banks charge fees only if you don't maintain a minimum balance. If you have less than CHF 10,000 in your UBS account, you pay CHF 0.30 for payments to another Swiss bank and CHF 5 for payments to banks outside Switzerland. Smaller banks, such as cantonal banks, Migros and Co-op bank, usually have lower fees.

If you pay a cheque drawn on a non-Swiss bank into a Swiss bank account, it may take weeks to be cleared and can be very expensive.

Paying Bills

In contrast with many other countries, cheques drawn on bank accounts aren't the most important everyday means of payment in Switzerland; in fact cheques are no longer issued by Swiss banks. Most people pay their bills via the post office giro service (see page 85), online (via e-banking) or via machines in bank branches which look like ATMs (ask for a demo). It costs around CHF 0.30 to pay a bill via a machine compared with around CHF 30 if it's done manually over the counter!

An orange or red giro payment form (*Einzahlungsschein, bulletin de versement*) is usually included with every bill you receive by mail. The payment date (*Fällig am . . ./Zahlbar bis . . ., payable le . . ./échéance . . .*) is usually stated on the bill accompanying the giro payment form, or the number of days within which you must pay the bill. Payment is usually due immediately or within 10, 30 or 60 days. Some creditors offer a discount for prompt payment of bills or payment in cash. If it's a regular bill (e.g. rent or utility) you can give your bank a permanent bank payment (standing) order.

When writing figures in Switzerland (or anywhere within continental Europe) the number seven should be crossed to avoid confusion with the number one, which is written with a tail and looks like an uncrossed seven to many foreigners. The date is written in the standard European style, for example 10th May 2013 is written 10/5/13 and not as in the US (5/10/13).

Payment forms produced by a computer include all the necessary details including your name and address, the payee's name and account number, and the amount due. If it's a non-computerised form you'll need to enter these details. If you're paying in person at a post office, post office payment forms must be completed in blue or black ink and in BLOCK CAPITALS. If you make a mistake you must complete a new form as you aren't permitted to make corrections. If you're paying via your bank (e-banking/bank business machines or a permanent payment order) then it doesn't matter if you make a mistake as you can correct it.

The left hand stub of the payment form is your receipt and is stamped by the post office clerk and returned to you when you pay bills at a post office.

Value	
9,179.53	
11,426.60	
9,611.01	
7,189.65	
6,550.22	

Cash & Debit Cards

Most banks offer customers a combined cash and debit card called a Maestro card, which costs CHF 20-40 per annum and can be used to withdraw cash from ATMs or pay in shops. There's no charge for withdrawals in Switzerland but a fee of 1 per cent of the amount withdrawn or a minimum of CHF 1.50 per transaction abroad. A Maestro card has a PIN number and can be used throughout the world. Maestro cards can also be used to make deposits (*Anzahlung, acompte*) or payments via machines, check account balances, order forms, and print a mini-statement and balance. They can also be used in foreign currency machines. Account cards are issued free to salary and current account holders.

LOANS & OVERDRAFTS

Interest rates for borrowers are low in Switzerland, but so is the interest paid on deposits. Some banks won't give foreigners with a B permit an unsecured loan (*Darlehen, emprunt/prêt*) during their first year in Switzerland and you're generally unable to obtain any loan or an overdraft (*Kontoüberziehung, dépassement de crédit*) until you've been in Switzerland at least three months.

The net interest margin charged by most Swiss banks is among the lowest in the world, although you should still shop around for the best deal. Interest rates vary considerably with the bank, the loan amount and the period of the loan. Don't neglect smaller banks, as it isn't always necessary to have an account with a bank in order to obtain a loan. Some insurance companies also provide loans. If you have collateral, e.g. Swiss property or insurance, or have someone who will stand as a guarantor for a loan, you may be eligible for a loan at the (lower) mortgage interest rate, although some banks require you to take out a life insurance policy for the duration of a loan.

It's usually easier to obtain an overdraft than a loan, particularly during your first year in Switzerland, although credit may be limited, e.g. to CHF 10,000. The overdraft interest rate is usually a few percentage points higher than the mortgage rate, but much lower than the rate for a standard loan. Some banks allow salary or personal account holders an automatic overdraft equal to one month's net salary without making any special arrangements, for which the current overdraft rate applies. A bank may insure an overdraft free of charge against you being unable to repay it. If you have a hire purchase (credit) agreement, e.g. for a car, a bank won't usually give you a loan or overdraft, but they may offer to pay off the outstanding debt with a loan.

Borrowing from private loan companies that advertise in some newspapers and magazines is expensive, as interest rates are high. Use them only as a last resort when all other means have been exhausted.

☑ **SURVIVAL TIP**

Loan companies may require you (as a foreigner) to find a homeowner or Swiss citizen to act as a guarantor, in which case you're advised to borrow from a bank.

CREDIT CARDS

Most large Swiss businesses accept credit cards, although they don't always advertise the fact. Credit cards aren't so readily accepted by small businesses, for whom the commission charge can be prohibitive. (The Swiss generally mistrust plastic money and prefer payment in cash, gold or diamonds!) You can apply for certain credit cards, such as a MasterCard or Visa, through your bank. Gold and platinum cards (with a higher spending limit and greater pose value) are available, but require a higher annual fee plus an 'entrance' fee, although the annual fee may be reduced by 50 per cent if you spend, for example, CHF 7,500 during a year and may be waived altogether if you spend say CHF 15,000 per year.

Some credit cards provide free travel and accidental life insurance when travel costs are paid for with the card. Before obtaining a card, compare the costs and benefits provided, particularly the interest rates charged. Special edition cards are issued periodically with colourful designs by Swiss artists, for which there's an extra fee.

Both Migros and Co-op (the largest grocery store chains in Switzerland) operate banks and both launched free MasterCard credit cards a few years ago. Prior to launching their own credit cards, it wasn't possible to pay for groceries at either of these stores with a credit card. Now you can pay for groceries with a Maestro, credit or PostFinance card and, of course, cash.

Major department stores issue their own credit or 'account' cards, e.g. Globus, Jelmoli and Manor. Some store cards allow credit, whereby the account balance may be repaid over a period of time, although interest rates are usually very high.

Many foreigners can obtain an international credit card in a country other than Switzerland (or can retain existing foreign credit cards) and be billed in the currency of that country. You may, however, find it more convenient and cheaper to be billed in Swiss francs than in a foreign currency, where you must wait for the bill from outside Switzerland, and payments can vary depending on the exchange rate.

If you lose a bank or credit card, report it immediately to the issuing office, when your liability is usually limited to CHF 100.

Even if you don't like credit cards and shun any form of credit, they do have their uses, such as no deposits on car hire, no prepaying hotel bills, safety and security, and above all, convenience.

INCOME TAX

Switzerland has no uniform system of taxation, with income tax (*Einkommenssteuer, impôt sur le revenu*) being levied by the federal government (direct federal tax), cantons and communities. The Confederation and the 26 sovereign cantons all have their own laws for the collection of taxes, as do the 2,750 municipalities. This means that taxes can vary considerably from canton to canton and to a lesser extent from community to community, and you can reduce your tax bill by comparing the rates in a number of cantons and communities.

The rate of income tax levied in Switzerland varies between around 20 and 40 per cent (the total tax burden is around 30 per cent of GDP), which is good news for many foreigners, particularly those from most other European countries, although (overall) Swiss taxes are higher than the US.

In general, Swiss income tax rates are progressive and different rates usually apply to single and married taxpayers, as the income of a husband and wife is aggregated. Cantons (including municipalities) play by far the most significant role in the tax system, collecting some 70 per cent of all tax revenues, while the federal government levies the rest. For the most part, spending decisions are made at the level at which taxes are levied and there's no disconnect between tax sovereignty and the spending authority.

Cantonal tax rates vary considerably. Usually, the tariff mentioned in the cantonal tax act results only in so-called 'basic rates', which are subject to cantonal and municipal multipliers. Church taxes are levied in the same way.

The canton of Obwalden introduced a regressive system of income tax in 2006, whereby the more you earned the less income tax you paid! However, this was declared unconstitutional and was replaced by a flat rate for individual taxpayers.

There are many websites that provide Swiss tax information, as well as tax comparisons between cantons or towns within a canton. The Federal Department of Finance (💻 www.estv. admin.ch) has an online tax calculator for each canton, while Comparis (💻 www.comparis. ch) provides cantonal and community tax comparisons and even has a facility to calculate the tax levied on foreigners who pay direct income tax (*Quellensteuer/impôt à la source*).

Liability

An individual is resident in Switzerland if the centre of his vital interests is there (and in the applicable canton/municipality respectively), which includes key factors such as where a person has a permanent home, where his family lives, and where his most important personal and economic contacts are. If you're domiciled or resident in Switzerland, you're liable for income tax on your worldwide income, subject to unilateral exceptions (e.g. foreign real estate) and tax treaty provisions (see below). You're considered resident in Switzerland if any of the following apply:

◆ you work in Switzerland for a minimum of 30 days or have a Swiss work permit;

◆ you carry on a business in Switzerland;

◆ you live in Switzerland for over 180 days a year, although if you remain in the same abode for 90 days a year you're considered to be a resident for tax purposes.

With the exception of the 'fiscal deal' method of taxation, Switzerland doesn't discriminate between Swiss residents and foreign employees of 'offshore' operations for the purposes of personal income tax. In any case, the Swiss authorities consider the various kinds of tax-privileged company as legitimate tax planning structures, which are available to both Swiss nationals and foreigners alike, and not as 'offshore' operations in the traditional sense of the word.

Double Taxation Treaties

Switzerland has double taxation agreements with around 70 countries, some of which cover only tax on income while others also cover net-worth (wealth) tax. Despite the name, double-taxation treaties are to prevent your paying double taxes, and **not** to ensure that you pay twice! Under double taxation treaties, certain categories of people are exempt from paying Swiss tax. If part of your income is taxed abroad in a country with a double taxation treaty with Switzerland, you won't

have to pay Swiss tax on that income. Tax treaties don't affect the fiscal privileges of members of diplomatic missions or consular posts provided by the general rules of international law or special agreements.

The treaties apply to persons (an individual or a legal entity) who are residents of one or both of the contracting states. In general, residents of Switzerland taxed under the lump-sum tax system also fall into the personal scope of application of Swiss treaties, as they are considered to be residents. There's an exception in the treaties with some countries, e.g. Austria, Belgium, Canada, Germany, Italy, Norway and the USA. Under these treaties, Swiss residents subject to tax under the lump-sum system are only considered as residents when all their income from source in these contracting states is subject to ordinary taxation in Switzerland (the so-called modified lump-sum system). In addition, under the treaty with France, French nationals resident in Switzerland who are taxed only on the basis of the rental value of their home residence, aren't treated as Swiss residents by France.

The conventions with Austria, France, Germany and Italy provide special rules with respect to border commuters, i.e. persons who reside in these countries and commute daily to their workplaces in Switzerland, who are taxed in their country of residence.

Citizens of most countries (the US is the main exception) are exempt from paying taxes in their home country when they spend a minimum period abroad, e.g. one year. It's your responsibility to familiarise yourself with the latest tax procedures in your home country or country of domicile. If you're in doubt about your tax liability in your home country, contact your country's embassy or consulate in Switzerland.

For further information about Swiss taxes, contact the Swiss Federal Tax Office (💻 www.estv.admin.ch).

Taxable Income

Swiss tax laws apply a rather broad concept of income which includes salaries and wages, and any other income derived for any activity performed in an employed or self-employed occupation. This includes secondary income derived from special services; commissions, allowances; seniority and anniversary gifts; gratuities; bonuses; tips and other wage- or salary-related remuneration; and benefits. Income from employment includes both the public and private sectors; associated supplementary income; benefits in kind; and employees' share option schemes. It also includes income from movable and immovable property, retirement income, compensations, etc. All types of income are pooled and taxed together, with the exception of capital gains on immovable property.

The income of spouses who are legally married, and living together as husband and wife, is combined. Alimony payments are deductible for the payer and taxable for the recipient. The rental value of owner-occupied dwellings is also added to your taxable income. The income of minor children is added to the income of the person who exercises parental control over them, except when a child obtains income from gainful employment, when it's taxed separately.

Recurring and non-recurring income of any kind is deemed income for tax purposes, including capital gains (see below), although capital gains made by residents on immoveable property in Switzerland are generally tax-exempt. Federal and cantonal tax regulations may differ in their treatment of exemptions, allowances and personal deductions; however, most cantons apply the same general principles in determining gross income. The concept of taxable income is broad and includes the following categories of income:

♦ earned income, i.e. income derived from any lucrative activity, including employment (salaries), professional and business income;

♦ investment income;

♦ compensatory income such as social security payments;

♦ income from other sources (sundry income).

Income from the above categories is usually combined and taxed at one rate, although annuities, pensions and other retirement income usually benefit from more favourable tax treatment. Income from real estate comprises the deemed rental value of a principal (owner-occupied) home owned by a taxpayer.

Certain kinds of income aren't subject to income tax, including inheritance, bequests, gifts or matrimonial property allocations; proceeds from capital insurance; subsidies paid from private or public sources; compensation for mental or physical pain suffered; and supplementary payments from retirement, survivors and disability insurance. Maintenance payments and other support finance to family members are tax-free (e.g. payments from the assets of a foundation), but alimonies are taxable. Most cantons also impose inheritance and gift taxes (see below).

Tax Breakdown

Swiss income tax consists of the following taxes:

♦ **Federal tax** (*Direkte Bundessteuer, impôt fédéral direct*) is levied at rates between 0.77 and 13.2 per cent, depending on your income, and comprises around 20 per cent of your total tax bill. It's assessed differently from cantonal and community taxes and entered on a separate tax form, sent with your community and cantonal tax forms. The deductions allowed against federal tax, based on your net annual salary, aren't the same as those for cantonal and community taxes.

♦ **Cantonal & community taxes** (*Staatssteuer/ Kantonssteuer, impôt cantonale* and *Gemeindesteuer, impôt communal*) comprise by far the major part of your total tax bill. Generally, the more wealthy the community, the lower its tax rate. You can compare the tax rate levied by cantons and communities on the Federal Department of Finance website (🖳 www.estv.admin.ch) and via Comparis (🖳 http://en.comparis.ch).

♦ **Fire service tax** (*Feuerwehrsteuer, taxe d'exemption au service de feu*) is paid by all community residents who aren't active members of the local fire service. It may be calculated as a percentage of your basic tax value (see **Tax Calculation** opposite) or may be a fixed sum (e.g. CHF 100 per year), depending on your canton. If you join the local fire department or you're aged over 44, you're exempt from paying fire service tax.

♦ **Church tax** (*Kirchensteuer, impôt écclésiastique*) is imposed in accordance with community income tax and is calculated as a percentage of your basic tax value. It's payable by all those who pay direct tax, but can be reclaimed by those who aren't registered as members of an official Swiss religion, i.e. the Reformed Church, the Roman Catholic Church and the Old Catholic (Protestant) Church. The amount payable varies from community to community depending on your canton and church, and may be up to 20 per cent of your basic tax value (or over CHF 1,000 a year for those earning CHF 100,000 per annum). For more information, see page 54.

Federal Tax

Federal income tax is payable on incomes above CHF 17,800 for a single person and CHF 30,800 for a married couple, and is capped at 11.5 per cent (under the Swiss constitution) when income exceeds CHF 755,300 for singles and CHF 895,900 for married couples. The rates apply to married couples living together and also to widowed, separated, divorced or single persons living with minor children or who are studying full-time. An unmarried couple living together are taxed as single taxpayers. The tables below show the rates for 2012 for singles and married couples:

Swiss Federal Tax 2012 - Single Taxpayers

Taxable Income (CHF)	Tax	%
0 to 17,700	0	0
17,800-31,600	0.77	25.41
31,700-41,400	0.88	132,53
41,500-55,200	2.64	220.54
55,300-72,500	2.97	585.17
72,600-78,100	5.94	1,101.94
78,200-103,600	6.60	1,435.20
103,700-134,600	8.8	3,120.40
134,700-176,000	11.00	5,850.60
176,100-755,200	13.20	10,406.80
From 755,300	11.50	86,859.50

Swiss Federal Tax 2012 - Married Taxpayers

Taxable Income (CHF)	Tax %	Tax on Base
0 to 30,799	0	0
30,800-50,900	1	25
51,000-58,400	2	228
58,500-75,300	3	379
75,400-90,300	4	887
90,400-103,400	5	1,488
103,500-114,700	6	2,144
114,800-124,200	7	2,823
124,300-131,700	8	3,489
131,800-137,300	9	4,090
137,400-141,200	10	4,595
141,300-143,100	11	4,986
143,200-145,000	12	5,196
145,100-895,800	13	5,425
From 895,900	11.5	103,028.50

Cantonal & Community Tax

The cantons not only set their own tax rates and tax brackets, but also have their own filing requirements, deduction provisions, and frameworks of rules to set and change tax laws. At the local level the 2,750 municipalities (*Gemeinde, commune*) also enjoy various degrees of sovereignty, depending on their respective canton's constitution. Canton and community taxes together comprise around 80 per cent of your income tax liability.

Tax rates are progressive – the more you earn the more tax you pay – apart from canton Obwalden which has a flat rate of tax of 1.8 per cent (the lowest in Switzerland). How progressive the system is also depends on the canton and varies according to whether you're married and how many children you have, as well as your community and religion. Married couples and their children under 18 are assessed jointly, while a divorced or legally separated person is assessed separately.

Tax rates vary considerably between cantons and communities, with the income tax burden varying by a multiple of five between the lowest- and highest-taxed cantons. For example, a couple with no children living in Zug and paying withholding tax on an income of CHF 120,000 would pay just 4.35 per cent cantonal income tax, while the same family in Basle (city) would pay 13.14 per cent (see table below). Other cantons fall somewhere between these extremes, with the lowest taxed cantons including Zug, Schwyz, Zurich, Valais, Ticino and Uri, and the highest Geneva, Basle-City, Neuchâtel, Jura, Vaud and St Gallen.

Note also that taxes can also vary considerably between communities, with the difference in some cantons, e.g. Schwyz, being as high as 100 per cent! However, this is an extreme example, although the difference between municipal tax in most cantons can still be, a not insignificant, 10-40 per cent. Generally, the lower the average tax rate in a canton, the larger the difference between communities.

The withholding tax (2012, source: Comparis) examples for the cantons shown in the table Overleaf are for a married couple (one earner), paying no church tax (see page 54) and with no children.

In recent years, many cantons have competed to offer lower taxes to incoming companies and wealthy individuals. As a result, the cantonal tax system has come under attack from the European Commission, which argues that the Swiss tax regime which allows cantonal

Cantonal Withholding Tax 2012			
Canton	Gross Annual Income		
	CHF 60,000	CHF 120,000	CHF 180,000
Basle-City	CHF 2,334	CHF 15,768	CHF 31,392
Berne	CHF 4,110	CHF 15,336	CHF 31,518
Fribourg	CHF 3,882	CHF 14,916	CHF 30,492
Geneva	CHF 618	CHF 13,068	CHF 30,780
Ticino	CHF 2,160	CHF 12,840	CHF 28,080
Vaud	CHF 3,612	CHF 15,128	CHF 32,544
Zug	CHF 930	CHF 5,220	CHF 13,554
Zurich	CHF 2,064	CHF 9,672	CHF 22,518
Ticino	CHF 1,357	CHF 10,912	CHF 44,283
Zug	CHF 1,207	CHF 7,210	CHF 29,263
Zurich	CHF 2,396	CHF 10,702	CHF 39,536

governments to set their own tax rates to attract companies and individuals, breaches the 1972 trade agreement between Switzerland and the EU by distorting trade and competition.

You can do a comparison of withholding tax in different cantons and communities via the Comparis website (🖥 http://en.comparis.ch/steuern/quellensteuerrechner/default.aspx).

Withholding & Direct Income Tax

All foreigners are subject to direct income tax (*Quellensteuer/impôt à la source*), unlike the Swiss and permanent residents (those holding a C Permit), who pay their tax in arrears under a system of self-declaration.

When a foreigner obtains a C permit (see **Chapter 3**) after five or ten years, he automatically ceases to pay direct income tax and must complete an annual income tax return and pay tax annually.

Withholding income tax is deducted from salaries each month by employers and generally settles your income tax liability, which may result in foreigners paying a higher tax rate than the Swiss. There are the following exceptions:

♦ anyone married to a Swiss citizen;

♦ those who own property in Switzerland;

♦ those who work in Switzerland but live in a neighbouring country (e.g. Austria, France, Germany or Switzerland), who pay the bulk

of their income and other taxes in the country where they're resident. However, they may still pay some income tax in Switzerland.

If you pay direct tax, you should be aware of anything that entitles you to a refund such as mortgage interest. You should write to your canton's tax authorities requesting a reduction of your tax liability if you have interest expenses such as credit cards, car loans, mortgages or child support payments, whether in Switzerland or another country (a letter documenting the expenses and requesting a refund will suffice). Most cantons require the letter to be received by 31st March of the year following the tax year for which you're claiming.

Some cantons don't require foreigners to pay direct income tax when their gross income is above a certain amount, e.g. CHF 120,000 per year, or when their cantons of residence and employment are different. However, foreigners without a C permit must pay direct income tax in most cantons irrespective of their income level, but those earning above CHF 120,000 per year can apply for an ordinary assessment and any tax withheld is credited against their final tax liability.

You're always subject to tax in your canton of residence and not your canton of employment if they're different; this is a constant source of conflict between some cantons, e.g. Geneva and Vaud, as thousands of residents of Vaud work in Geneva but pay no taxes there. The income of non-resident (Swiss or foreign) employees who are employed only for a short period in Switzerland or who are cross-border commuters, are subject to direct income tax. The Swiss income of non-resident entertainers (such as actors, musicians and public performers), athletes and lecturers, is also taxed at source.

Some cantons offer tax breaks (concessions) to expatriates such as tax deductions for relocation costs, travel costs (to your home country and back), schooling for children and even housing costs in Switzerland. There are conditions such as the length of stay and the position held and few expatriates qualify, but it may be worth checking with your canton's tax office.

Foreigners paying direct income tax aren't required to file a tax return, although it's advisable (and may be necessary) if your gross earnings exceed CHF 120,000 per year and/or you have considerable assets (such as property and investments), either in Switzerland or abroad.

In addition to Swiss taxes, you may be liable for taxes in your home country. Citizens of most countries are exempt from paying taxes in their home country when they spend a minimum period abroad, e.g. one year, although US nationals remain subject to US income tax while living abroad (lucky people!).

It's your responsibility to familiarise yourself with the tax laws in your home country or country of domicile (as well as Switzerland). If you're in doubt about your tax liability in your home country, contact your country's nearest embassy or consulate in Switzerland. US citizens can obtain a copy of the *Tax Guide for US Citizens and Resident Aliens* from American Consulates or from the IRS website (🖳 www.irs.gov/publications/p54/index.html).

Tax Deductions

In general, all expenses related to taxable income are deductible, including employment expenses. The following list is a rough guide to the deductions you can make from your gross salary when calculating your taxable income; note that deductions are different for federal and cantonal/community taxes.

◆ obligatory insurance contributions such as federal old age and survivor's insurance, disability insurance, accident insurance, health insurance, unemployment insurance and contributions to a company pension fund. Most obligatory insurance contributions are deducted from your gross salary by your employer.

◆ premiums for optional insurance such as life insurance, a private pension, accident insurance and sickness insurance, up to a maximum amount;

◆ business and travel expenses, e.g. car expenses (including travel from your home to your place of work); entertainment (if not paid or reimbursed by your employer; essential tools and special clothing; and board and lodging;

◆ interest on mortgages, loans and overdrafts;

◆ medical expenses for your family that aren't reimbursed by an insurance policy and which total 5 per cent or more of your annual income (in some cantons all medical expenses are deductible);

◆ alimony payments;

◆ study costs (employment-related training, education and books) if they aren't reimbursed by your employer;

◆ donations to recognised charities up to a maximum amount.

Standard allowances are permitted for many items, without proof of expenditure, above which claims must be verified by invoices, etc. Personal allowances vary according to your circumstances, e.g. single, married, divorced or widowed, and the number of children or dependants that you have. Allowances vary from canton to canton.

Self-employed taxpayers can also carry-forward losses (in general for seven years), but there's no 'carry-back' to previous tax years in Switzerland.

Tax Calculation

Your cantonal/community income tax assessment is based on a 'basic tax value' (*ordentliche Steuer/einfache Steuer, impôt de base*), calculated from your taxable income after all deductions have been made. The basic tax value is derived from tables produced by cantons and is different for single and married couples. A simple example of a tax calculation for federal and cantonal/community taxes is shown below:

Net annual salary	CHF 100,000
Deductions	(CHF 12,000)
Taxable income	CHF 88,000
Basic tax value	CHF 6,000
Tax Calculation:	
Canton tax (120% of basic tax value)	CHF 7,200
*Community tax rate (120% of basic tax value)	CHF 7,200
Parish church tax (20% of basic tax value)	CHF 1,200
Community fire tax	CHF 100
Total Canton/Community Tax	CHF 15,700

Income Tax Return

If you don't pay direct income tax you must complete an income tax return annually. Note that in some cantons, foreigners with a B permit paying direct income tax and earning above a certain amount, e.g. CHF 120,000 a year, must complete a tax return. The forms are sent to you by your community tax office, e.g. in January, and must usually be completed and returned by 31st March. If necessary, you can ask for a delay in completing the return, which should be a formality as it takes months to process them all.

It's advisable to contact a tax accountant (*Steuerberater, conseil fiscal/fiduciaire*), your local tax office (*Steueramt, service des contributions*) or your bank for help in completing your tax return. Apart from language problems and the tax knowledge necessary, a pile of forms must be completed. For most people it simply isn't worth the effort doing it themselves, particularly as a tax accountant may charge 'only' a few hundred francs to complete a simple return. If you need information regarding your tax return or with correspondence from your local tax office, it's best to visit them in person rather than telephone and to take someone with you if you don't speak the local language fluently.

Taxable income includes your total income from all sources and all net assets worldwide, excluding property. If part of your income is taxed abroad in a country with a double-taxation treaty with Switzerland, you won't have to pay Swiss tax on it. However, your Swiss tax rate (basic tax value) may be assessed on your total worldwide income, including the portion on which you've already paid tax.

Income derived from property outside Switzerland is exempt from Swiss tax, but may be taxed abroad. For information, contact the Swiss Federal Tax Office (☎ 031-322 71 06, 🖥 www.estv.admin.ch).

If you pay direct income tax and think you've paid too much, you can request a tax review (by completing an income tax return). Note, however, that there's the possibility that instead of giving you a rebate, the tax authorities may 'invite' you to pay additional tax!

Anyone can lodge an appeal against their tax assessment. If your tax status changes in the first year after completing a tax return, e.g. due to the birth of a child, marriage or a large change in your income, you can ask to have an intermediate assessment instead of waiting until the end of the tax period. If your spouse starts working, an intermediate assessment is obligatory. Tax for a period of less than one year is assessed on a pro rata basis.

All Swiss taxes must be paid when changing cantons or before leaving Switzerland.

Tax Bill

Income tax for Swiss nationals, foreigners with a C permit and others who aren't eligible to pay direct income tax is paid annually. Most cantons have now switched to a system whereby tax is based on the income of the preceding year and an assessment is made annually. If you have no income record in Switzerland, you receive a provisional assessment until a full tax year has passed, when the difference between what you've paid and your actual tax bill is payable (or, if you've paid too much, refunded).

Your tax bill (*Steuerrechnung, prélèvement fiscale*) usually comes in two parts: one for federal tax and one for cantonal and community taxes.

Federal Tax Bill

Federal tax bills are payable annually by 1st March. If you don't pay your bill by the due date, you can be charged interest on any outstanding sum. In practice it may be possible to pay your tax bill, or part of it, a month or two late without paying interest (but don't count on it). If you aren't going to be able to pay your tax bill on time, it's advisable to inform your community tax office (so they won't think that you've absconded).

Canton & Community Tax Bill

You usually receive your cantonal and community tax bill for the current year a few weeks after filing your tax return, although the date tax is due may be different for federal, cantonal and community taxes. In some cantons, tax is due before the end of the current tax year and it's up to you to estimate the amount in order to pay it on time. When you pay late, interest is charged. If you pay a bill early, the tax office pays you interest, which is usually higher than if you'd left the money in a savings account (and the interest isn't taxable!). Payment slips for advance payments are available from tax offices.

If you prefer to pay your tax bill monthly or quarterly, inform your tax office and they will send you the appropriate payment advices. If you receive a late assessment and bill for tax, you may be given an extra month or two to pay it, in which case your tax bill may consist of various parts, payable at different times.

Lump-sum Taxation

Retired or non-employed foreign (i.e. non-employed in Switzerland) residents may be able to choose to be taxed on a lump-sum basis (*Pauschalbesteuerung*, *forfait fiscal*) or 'fiscal deal', whereby tax assessment (at both the federal and cantonal/municipal levels) is made according to your 'lifestyle'. Tax isn't based on your actual income but on your rental payments (or the rental value of your home), and bears no relation to your real income, assets or wealth, which you aren't even asked to declare.

The fiscal deal is often criticised as a privilege for wealthy foreigners seeking to avoid taxation in their own countries – which, of course, it is! However, the number of people who benefit from it is relatively small at around 0.3 per cent of the foreign population or fewer than 5,500 people.

In recent years a number of cantons have voted to abolish tax breaks for wealthy foreigners, including Basel (2012) and Zurich (2009). However, some cantons have voted to retain it, including Glarus, Lucerne and St Gallen. In 2012, two-thirds of voters in Berne (which includes the billionaire stronghold of Gstaad) opposed scrapping the tax breaks, although the minimum tax payable was raised to CHF 400,000.

The lump-sum method is restricted to foreign residents who haven't been engaged in any substantial economic activity in Switzerland for the last ten years; they must be retired and undertake no professional activity or employment in Switzerland, but can 'oversee' their investments. To qualify you must officially spend a minimum of 180 days a year in Switzerland. Note that certain Swiss tax treaties only apply if the income derived from a partner state is subject to ordinary Swiss income tax. If treaty protection is important in such a case, the taxpayer may opt for a modified lump-sum taxation which includes such income.

The overall tax rate depends on your town and canton of residence; there are huge variations between cantons and sometimes towns. Most cantons have an unofficial minimum for the level of taxable income before they will grant a residence permit, although if you're flexible regarding the choice of canton the sum can be reasonable. It's highest in the cantons of Geneva and Vaud, where assessment is based on five times the annual (theoretical) rental of your accommodation (including a garage) or between 3 and 7 per cent of a property's value. You can usually obtain a ruling before moving to Switzerland, so that you'll know exactly how much tax you'll have to pay before deciding on the move.

The rates of tax payable under the lump sum scheme are the same as would apply normally, but the advantage is – of course – the fictitiously low proportion of your income on which you're assessed. You aren't required to declare your actual income or assets. Assuming your circumstances don't change, such as moving to a larger, more expensive home, you pay the same amount of tax each year (indexed for inflation). You can choose to give up your lump-sum taxation at any time and revert to the regular tax system.

To give an example of how the fiscal deal works, if you're planning to rent a home for CHF 4,000 per month, the annual rent would be 12 x 4,000 = CHF 48,000. let's assume that your taxable income is calculated at five times the annual rent, i.e. 5 x 48,000 = CHF 240,000. You annual tax bill would therefore be approximately 30 per cent of CHF 240,000, which is CHF 72,000. If you buy a home in Switzerland for CHF 3m, the rental value is calculated using a variable capitalisation rate (which decrease as the home increases in value) which is subject to negotiation. Assuming that the rate is say 2.5 per cent, this makes the annual rental value 3m x 2.5 per cent = CHF 75,000. Your taxable income would be five times the imputed annual rent, i.e. 5 x 75,000 = CHF 375,000, on which your annual tax bill would be approximately 30 per cent (CHF 112,500).

A comparison of regular income tax and lump-sum taxation is shown in the table above (for a person living in a CHF 3m home in Switzerland with other assets totalling CHF 17m).

There are many companies in Switzerland that specialise in helping wealthy foreigners to become Swiss residents and pay tax under the fiscal deal system. They will calculate the tax payable in different cantons, and, when you have decided where you want to live, negotiate your taxable income with the authorities and help you obtain residence permits.

FEDERAL WITHHOLDING TAX

A federal withholding tax (*Verrechnungssteuer, impôt anticipé*) of 35 per cent – the highest in the world – is deducted directly from investment income, which includes interest on all bank balances in Switzerland. The banks thus act as fiscal agents for the federal government, deducting withholding tax and paying it to the tax authorities, which is a powerful tool for fighting domestic tax evasion (note that in Switzerland, tax evasion is a civil and not a criminal offence). The tax is automatically deducted by banks from

Example of Lump-sum Taxation

Item	Sum (CHF)
Pension income	200,000
Dividend & interest income	500,000
Swiss real estate income	50,000
Total Income:	**750,000**
Ordinary Taxation:	
Swiss Income Tax (30%)	225,000
New Wealth Tax (on CHF. 20mn At 0.75%)	150,000
Total Swiss Taxes	**375,000**
Lump-sum Taxation:	
Expenses income	250,000
Lump-sum Tax (ca. 30%)	**75,000**
Saving	**300,000**

* Effective tax rate on actual income = 10%

the interest on deposits, but is reclaimable by individuals who pay Swiss income tax, provided they declare their assets. You may, however, be liable for wealth tax on your assets (see below).

If you pay direct income tax, federal withholding tax can be reclaimed for the preceding three years via a form available from your community office. If you declare and pay tax annually, a claim should be made on your income tax return. You can choose to have federal withholding tax repaid in cash or into a bank account or deducted from your next tax bill, when you'll be paid interest on the amount due.

WEALTH TAX

A wealth or net-worth tax (*Vermögenssteuer, impôt sur la fortune*) is levied on assets by all cantons and municipalities, but not at the federal level. Assets are valued at market value and those up to a certain threshold (from around CHF 50,000 to 200,000 depending on the canton) are tax-exempt. Assets include property, including your owner-occupied home, although you can deduct the amount of your mortgage, which is usually higher than the tax value.

The taxable value of your home is based on the value entered in the land register, known as the fiscal value, which is usually some 60 per cent of its actual market value (it cannot exceed the market value of a property). Check your tax assessment carefully – it's usually only adjusted after major structural changes or renovations have been made – as it has a major influence on the level of rental income value. If you think your property is over-valued, you can have it valued independently.

The net-worth tax base includes almost every type of asset held by individuals, including immoveable property, intangible personal property, securities, the cash redemption value of life insurance policies, investments in proprietorships or partnerships, and other beneficial interests. Wealth tax is also calculated on assets that don't yield an income.

Beneficial, not legal, ownership is used for the allocation of assets liable to wealth tax, which means that property under usufruct (i.e. from which you benefit – such as a field you farm or a home you use – but don't legally own) or under a fiduciary relationship is included in the tax base of the beneficiary. Usufruct of moveable and immoveable property is taxed at the end of the usufruct. Certain assets (personal and household effects, etc.) are exempt from taxation.

Resident Swiss taxpayers, who have an unlimited tax obligation, pay the cantonal wealth tax on all their assets, except immovable property in (and assets attributable to) a canton other than the one where they're resident or property in another country. If you own assets in several cantons, the assets located in a particular canton, less a proportional part of your liabilities, are subject to taxation by that canton. Generally intangible property is considered to be located at the residence of the taxpayer. Taxpayers with a limited Swiss tax obligation pay tax on immoveable property within the canton where it's situated and on assets belonging to a permanent home within that canton.

Personal debts, mortgages, bank loans and overdrafts are deductible from the taxable base, as well as certain personal deductions and allowances, depending on the canton. A 'fixed' deduction of between CHF 5,000 and 10,000 may also be allowed. The wealth tax rate is progressive in most cantons and varies from 0.18 (Nidwalden) to 1 per cent (Geneva) of the net value for assets valued at up to CHF 250,000. For taxable wealth of CHF 1m, the tax rate varies from 0.172 percent (Nidwalden) to 0.697 percent (canton of Fribourg). Where applicable, wealth tax is paid with your cantonal and community taxes.

CAPITAL GAINS TAX

There's no federal capital gains tax (CGT) in Switzerland on property or at any level for moveable assets such as shares, securities, art works, etc., unless they were business transactions. However, there's a cantonal real estate gains tax (*Grundstückgewinnsteuer; impôt sur les gains immobiliers*) in all cantons, applicable to both residents and non-residents.

If an owner-occupied principal home is sold and the revenue from the sale is used within an limited period (e.g. one to five years, depending on the canton) to buy or build a replacement property for immediate occupation (known as a replacement acquisition), capital gains tax is deferred. However, if you only reinvest a portion of the gain, the portion that isn't reinvested is taxed, but provided you live in the replacement home the tax remains deferred and the retention period for both properties is calculated as an aggregate total. Depending on the canton, the deferred real property gains tax is reduced or eliminated altogether, e.g. after 20 years in the canton of Zurich, when you sell the replacement property. However, if you move into rented property or move abroad, the deferred tax becomes due.

Real estate transfers based on gifts, inheritances, legacy, separation or divorce settlements, and changes of ownership due to a compulsory sale or forced execution, are usually exempt from CGT. Any tax due is usually taxed separately and isn't based on income or assets. It's calculated on the difference between the cost of property and the sale price, less purchase and sale fees and the cost of any improvements (remodelling), i.e. the cost of value-adding enhancements. If the sale's proceeds are greater than the total investment cost, the different is subject to CGT.

The rules regarding capital gains tax on property vary from canton to canton, including

the way in which it's calculated, the deductions and the tax rates. However, in all cantons the tax payable depends on the length of ownership; the longer you have owned a property the lower the amount of tax payable. Some cantons calculate the tax due using full years, while other calculate it in months, therefore it's worth timing a sale with this in mind. CGT is banded and decreases each year of ownership according to the canton, e.g. from 30 per cent in year one, 9 per cent after ten years, down to 1 per cent after 25 years. For information about local rates, contact your local cantonal tax authority.

INHERITANCE & GIFT TAX

There are no federal estate, inheritance (*Erbanfallsteuer, taxe successorale*) or gift taxes in Switzerland, but these taxes are levied by most cantons – the exceptions being Lucerne, which has no gift tax, and Schwyz which levies neither. In the cantons of Grisons and Solothurn, a tax on the estate (*Nachlasssteuer, taxe sur l'héritage*) is levied in addition or instead of the inheritance tax. In addition to inheritance tax, some cantons (e.g. Neuchâtel and Solothurn) also levy death duties on the non-apportioned property of the deceased. The canton of Graubünden levies only

a death duty, although communes may also levy inheritance tax.

Communities are also entitled to levy inheritance and gift taxes in a few cantons, e.g. Lucerne, although in most cases the communities share in the revenue from the cantonal tax. Note that even if you have no tax to pay in Switzerland, if you're a non-resident you may have to pay inheritance tax in your home country (Switzerland has double taxation treaties, which apply to inheritance tax with some countries, including the UK and the US).

The canton that has the right to levy inheritance and gift tax is the canton in which the beneficiary was last domiciled, with the exception of immoveable property (real estate) which is taxed where it's situated. Taxes on donations of moveable property are levied by the canton in which the donor had his domicile at the time of the donation. With inheritance, the market value of the estate at the time of the testator's death serves as the basis for assessment, while with donations (gifts), the tax due is based on the market value at the time of the transfer.

Tax rates vary from canton to canton – and are usually the same for inheritance and gift taxes – and are low compared with those in many other western European countries. However, rates vary considerably depending on the relationship of the beneficiary to the deceased or donor and the value of the bequest or gift. Generally, relatives (particularly the spouse and children) of the deceased pay lower rates of inheritance tax than non-related beneficiaries. For example, in many cantons the spouse and children of a deceased resident taxpayer are exempt from inheritance tax, and in some cantons, for example Basle-City and Berne, only unrelated beneficiaries are taxed. In eight cantons, estates and gifts to direct ascendants, i.e. parents, are also tax-exempt.

The most important variation between the cantons is the treatment of descendants and the applicable tax rates. Only eight cantons tax inheritances or gifts transferred to direct descendants (children): Appenzell-Innerrhoden, Berne, Lucerne (no gift tax and no inheritance tax at the cantonal level, although it's applies in around three-quarters of communities), Grisons, Jura, Neuchâtel, Solothurn and Vaud. Jura also taxes inheritances between spouses.

Where applicable, interspousal gifts and an inheritance by a surviving spouse are frequently exempt or taxed at very low rates, e.g. up to 6 per cent, whereas gifts and inheritances to unrelated persons attract rates ranging from 20 to 40 per cent. The taxable base is usually the market value of assets, with special provisions for securities and real property. After determining the applicable rate based on the value of the bequest or gift, the amount is subject to a multiplier according to the relationship between the donor and the recipient (see below).

Upon the death of a Swiss resident, an inventory is taken of the estate which serves as the basis for the inheritance tax assessment. The assessment of gift tax is based on a tax return, which must usually be filed by the donor.

Given the complexity of inheritance tax rules and the wide differences between rates in different cantons, you're advised to take advice from a tax professional, preferably one with knowledge of the inheritance tax laws of all the cantons and countries involved.

Inheritance & Gift Tax Example: Zurich

Inheritance and gifts left to spouses and direct descendants are exempt in the canton of Zurich, where the following allowances are also granted:

♦ CHF 200,000 for parents;

♦ CHF 15,000 for fiancés, siblings, grandparents, stepchildren, godchildren, foster children and home helps employed for at least ten years;

♦ CHF 50,000 for the partner of the deceased or the donor if a couple have lived together for at least five years in the same household and none of the above deductions apply;

♦ CHF 30,000 for dependent persons with a permanent or partial occupational disability.

Zurich Inheritance & Gift Tax Rates	
Tax Base (CHF)	Tax Rate
Up to 30,000	2%
20,001-90,000	3%
90,001-180,000	4%
180,001-360,000	5%
360,001-840,000	6%
840,001-1.5mn	7%

If the taxable inheritance exceeds CHF 1.5m, a flat rate of 6 per cent applies to the whole amount. A multiplier, which varies according to the relationship of the deceased and the beneficiary, is then applied to the calculated tax, as shown in the table below:

Inheritance & Gift Tax Multiplier	
Relationship	Multiplier
Parents	1
Grandparent, stepchildren	2
Siblings	3
Step-parents	4
Uncles, aunts and descendants of siblings	5
Others	6

For example, a brother is left CHF 300,000 by his sister, which is taxed at 5 per cent = CHF 15,000. This is then subject to a multiplier of three (siblings) = 15,000 x 3 = CHF 45,000, making the effective tax rate 15 per cent.

WILLS

It's an unfortunate fact of life that you're unable to take all those lovely Swiss francs with you when you make your final bow. All adults should therefore make a will (*Testament/testament*), irrespective of how large or small their assets. In general, all valid wills made in accordance with the law of the place of execution are recognised in Switzerland, both under the Hague convention, to which Switzerland is a signatory, and under the Swiss Private International Law Act 1987. Experts advise that you make a Swiss will for property situated in Switzerland, which can be registered with a local notary, and a separate will for each other country where you own property.

If you live in Switzerland and wish your will to be interpreted under Swiss law, you can state this and that you've abandoned your previous domicile. If you don't want your estate to be subject to Swiss law, you're usually eligible to state in your will that it's to be interpreted under the law of another country. This depends on your and your spouse's nationality and your ties with that country. A foreigner who also holds Swiss nationality **must** make his will under Swiss law if he's resident in Switzerland. If your estate comes under Swiss law, your dependants may be subject to Swiss inheritance laws.

Swiss law is restrictive regarding the distribution of property and the identity of heirs, and the estate is divided according to the number of children, who may receive the lion's share of the spoils. You may not be too concerned about this, but your other dependants might be!

In order to avoid being subject to Swiss inheritance tax (see above) and inheritance laws, you must establish your domicile in another country. Note, however, that foreigners living in Switzerland with a C permit are usually considered under Swiss federal and private international law to be domiciled in Switzerland. Take advice from an expert before establishing or changing your domicile to Switzerland or any other country.

Making a will in Switzerland is simple: it must be hand-written, state your full name, and be dated and signed. No witnesses are required. However, to ensure that the contents of your will comply with Swiss law, it's advisable to obtain legal advice.

Keep a copy of your will(s) in a safe place and another copy with your solicitor or the executor of your estate. Don't leave your will in a safe deposit box, which in the event of your death will be sealed for a period under Swiss law. You should store information regarding bank accounts and insurance policies with your will(s) – but don't forget to tell someone where they are!

If you die while working in Switzerland and have more than five years' service, your salary is usually paid for an extra month or two (maybe the Swiss – who all go to heaven – have access to ATMs there?).

VALUE ADDED TAX

Goods and services in Switzerland are subject to value added tax (*Mehrwertsteuer/MWSt, taxe sur la valeur ajoutée/TVA*) at rates of 2.5 to 8 per cent – the lowest in Europe (the average in EU countries is over 15 per cent). Certain products and services are exempt from VAT, including real estate sales and rentals, postal services, healthcare, social security/services, educational services, sport and cultural activities, insurance, current-account (money and capital market) transactions and exports.

VAT applies to other goods and services at the rates shown in the table below.

Most prices in Switzerland are quoted inclusive of VAT. Companies and sole traders (the self-employed) must register and add VAT to their bills when their annual turnover exceeds CHF 75,000. Smaller companies with an annual turnover of up to CHF 250,000 are exempt if their tax burden is less than CHF 4,000. Companies subject to VAT can deduct VAT paid at earlier stages in the economic process. To reduce the administrative burden, companies with a turnover not exceeding CHF 3m and an annual tax liability of less than CHF 60,000 can settle on the basis of fixed rates, known as the net-tax rate.

VAT Rates	
Rate	**Applicability**
2.4% (reduced)	food and drinks (excluding alcoholic drinks and cooked meals); meat; cereals; plants, seeds and flowers; some basic farming supplies; mains water; medicines; books, newspapers, magazines and other printed matter
3.6% (hotel rate)	hotel and other accommodation;
7.6% (standard rate)	all goods and services not listed above.

Spring carnival in Biel/Bienne

15.
LEISURE

North of Italy among the Alps, is Switzerland; it's a small state with no language of its own, producing little but goats and some timber; but possessing considerable wealth because of the large numbers of visitors who arrive every year for climbing or sightseeing.

(How Switzerland was described in a 1928 travel guide)

Not surprisingly a few things have changed since 1928 (see box), for example, there are fewer goats and trees. However, Switzerland still has immense wealth and catering for visitors has developed into a very profitable tourist industry. Tourism is Switzerland's third-largest industry, employing over 300,000 people directly or indirectly and earning more than CHF 20bn annually. Many people in mountain areas rely on tourism for a livelihood. However, in recent years the industry has suffered due to the high value of the Swiss franc, which has deterred many American and European visitors, although it has attracted increasing numbers of visitors from 'emerging' markets, such as the Middle and Far East.

Leisure activities and entertainment in Switzerland are of the high standard and diversity you would expect from a country that celebrated 220 years of tourism in 2007 (and the country's 700th anniversary in 1991) and is credited with having invented tourism. It offers a huge variety of entertainment, sports (see **Chapter 16**) and pastimes, and is blessed with a wealth of natural beauty hardly matched anywhere in the world in such a small area. The majority of tourists come to Switzerland to participate in outdoor sports, e.g. skiing and hiking, and not, for example, to savour the night life (which although lively enough for most people, may disappoint the international jet set). If you want to avoid road traffic and its ever-attendant pollution, you need to visit one of Switzerland's delightful car-free Alpine resorts: Bettmeralp, Braunwald, Mürren, Riederalp, Rigi-Kaltbad, Saas-Fee, Stoss, Wengen and Zermatt.

Switzerland is a small country and no matter where you live you can regard the whole country as your playground. Due to excellent road and rail connections, a huge area is accessible for day excursions and anywhere in Switzerland (and many neighbouring countries) is within easy reach for a weekend trip. The maximum distance from east to west is only 348km (216mi) and from north to south it's just 220km (137mi).

Information regarding local events and entertainment is available from tourist offices and local newspapers. In most cities there are magazines or newspapers devoted to entertainment and free weekly or monthly programmes are also published by tourist offices in all major cities and tourist centres. Many city newspapers publish free weekly magazines or supplements containing a comprehensive programme of local events and entertainment. Other useful sources of information include the monthly English-language magazine, *Swiss News* (💻 www.swissnews.ch). The latest entertainment information can also be obtained from Switzerland Tourism (see below) and dozens of websites, such as 💻 www.swissholidayco.com and www.stc.co.uk.

General tourist information is available in many excellent Swiss guide books, including the Dorling Kindersley *Eyewitbess Travel Guide Switzerland*, *Lonely Planet Switzerland* and the *Rough Guide to Switzerland* (see **Appendix B** for a list).

TOURIST OFFICES

There are tourist offices in all Swiss cities and tourist areas, where English-speaking staff can provide you with a wealth of information and also find you a hotel room. They're open daily, including Saturdays and Sundays, in most major cities and tourist centres. Telephone the tourist office or consult a guide book to check their business hours. In major towns, reduced opening hours are in operation during winter, while in smaller towns and resorts tourist offices close for lunch and may open during the winter **or** summer season only. Services provided by tourist offices include local information, hotel reservations, local and city tours, excursions, congresses, car hire (rental), guides and hostesses, and public transport information. In some towns, walking audio tours (with free maps) are available for a small fee.

Switzerland Tourism (ST, *Schweiz Tourismus, Suisse Tourisme*) is a mine of information and in addition to promoting tourism aims to 'further the understanding of Switzerland's special political, cultural and economic characteristics', in close co-operation with regional tourist promotion boards. Switzerland Tourism has offices in many countries including Australia, Austria, Belgium, Brazil, Canada, China, Czech Republic, Denmark, Dubai, Egypt, France, Germany, Hong Kong, India, Israel, Italy, Japan, South Korea, Malaysia, the Netherlands, Norway, Poland, Russia, Singapore, Spain, Sweden, Taiwan, Thailand, the UK and the USA.

ST produces over 100 publications (one in over 30 languages) totalling around 4m copies and distributes many more. It's continually revising, updating and replacing its publications, and therefore some of the brochures mentioned in this book may no longer be available.

Whatever you would like to know, ST will provide information directly or give you the name of a company or organisation that can help you. They answer telephone enquiries and send information by post, including an annual booklet entitled *Events in Switzerland*, listing music, theatre and film, folklore, public festivals, sports events, exhibitions, fairs, markets and congresses.

Switzerland Tourism is Switzerland's ambassador of tourism and in contrast to the sometimes cool reception from aloof Swiss embassies, they're a paragon of co-operation and friendliness. For further information, contact Switzerland Tourism (☎ 0800-100 200 30, 🖥 www.myswitzerland.com).

HOTELS

All Swiss hotels are comfortable, clean and efficient. The standard of hotel accommodation and service is excellent; whether it's a luxury 5-star hotel or a humble *pension*, it's almost impossible to find a bad hotel in Switzerland (the Dolder Grand in Zurich is a previous winner of the accolade 'world's best hotel', bestowed by readers of *Conde Nast Traveler*). Most

people should be able to find something to suit their budget and taste among the 6,000 hotels and boarding houses in Switzerland, offering a total of over 250,000 beds.

Not surprisingly, Swiss hotels and hotel training schools provide the best training ground for hotel staff in the world. Swiss hotels can, however, be very expensive (the Royal Suite in the Hotel President Wilson in Geneva costs over CHF 20,000 a night!), particularly in major cities, and are the most expensive in Europe (averaging over CHF 200 per night), although reasonably-priced rooms are also available. Though it has some of the world's best hotels, Switzerland also has the world's first 0-star (*null stern*) hotel, housed in a subterranean fallout shelter (🖥 www.null-stern-hotel.ch).

Hotel rates vary considerably depending on the standard, location, season and the amenities provided. The table below can be used as a rough guide.

The prices quoted above are per person, per night, sharing a double room with bath (prices are usually quoted per person and not per room in Switzerland). There's usually no charge for children up to six years old when sharing their parents' room and reductions for older children

Class	Rating	Price Range
Simple	1 star	CHF 60 to 120
Comfortable	2 star	CHF 90 to 150
Middle	3 star	CHF 150 to 220
First	4 star	CHF 190 to 350
Luxury	5 star	CHF 250 to 750+

Brienz, Berne

are usually provided, e.g. 50 per cent for those aged 6 to 12 and 30 per cent for those aged 13 to 16. Continental breakfast is often included in the cost and a British or American style cooked breakfast, sometimes buffet style (self-service), is provided in many 1st class hotels, although it may be an extra. Many hotels with restaurants offer half-board (breakfast and dinner) or full-board (breakfast, lunch and dinner) at reasonable rates. A hotel garni (similar to a hostal) provides bed and breakfast and beverages, but no meals.

Inexpensive accommodation, e.g. small one-star hotels and pensions, is usually difficult to find in the major cities, although in small towns and rural areas it isn't necessary to pay a fortune. A guide to over 200 'simple & cosy' hotels is available from Swiss Budget Hotels (☎ 0848-805 508, 🖥 www.rooms.ch), where accommodation varies from dormitory beds at CHF 30 per night up to the most expensive rooms at around CHF 150 per person, per night. They produce a booklet (available from their website) listing inexpensive hotels, inns and pensions for an average of around CHF 60 per night (including breakfast but without a bath or shower). See also **Youth Hostels** below.

The *Swiss Hotel Guide* (*Schweizer Hotelführer, Guide Suisse des Hôtels*) is published annually by the Swiss Hotel Association (SHA), and is available free from them (see below) and Switzerland Tourism offices. It contains the addresses, telephone numbers, opening dates, room rates and amenities of over 2,500 hotels, guesthouses and pensions, including hotels with special facilities for the disabled. It also lists restaurants, spas and climatic resorts. The SHA also publishes brochures for senior citizens, a list of hotels with special facilities for families, and information about country inns. For more information contact Hotelleriesuisse (☎ 031-370 41 11, 🖥 www. swisshotels.ch).

Many hotels in Switzerland have special rates for senior citizens and children. Holidays tailored specially for pensioners (a fast-growing sector) are organised by various travel companies, e.g. 'Best Agers 50 plus' holidays with 🖥 www.travel. ch. Information about hotels with special facilities for the disabled is available from Procap (Reisen für Menschen mit Handicap, ☎ 062-206 88 88, 🖥 www. procap.ch). Procap also produce holiday catalogues and city guides for the disabled for 26 Swiss towns and cities.

In most Swiss cities and resorts, the local tourist office will find you a hotel room for a small fee. They may also provide brochures and information regarding youth accommodation, hotels catering especially for children, and hotels with swimming pools and sports facilities. Residential hotels and one-room hotel apartments are available for longer stays. In mountain resorts, many hotels close for the summer months or close between the end of the summer season and the start of the winter season, e.g. October to November. If you want a room in a top class hotel during an international convention or fair or in a city or popular resort (particularly during school holidays), you should book well in advance.

In addition to hotels, bed and breakfast (*Zimmer zu vermieten, chambre à louer*) accommodation is available throughout Switzerland, particularly in small towns and villages in tourist areas. Local tourist offices may maintain a list of rooms to let in private homes.

☑ SURVIVAL TIP

An excellent resource for inexpensive accommodation is *Bed and Breakfast Switzerland* published by Nicole Neyroud (☎ 041-79 364 58 91, 🖥 www.bnb.ch).

Families with small children may be interested in 'sleep in the straw' holidays offered by some 200 farms (🖥 www.schlaf-im-stroh.ch). Rates for a 'bed' in a barn are CHF 20-30 per night for adults and CHF 10-20 for children aged up to 15. In addition, some farms offer camping, rooms and dinner for an extra fee. Guests can ride horses on some farms, most of which have a variety of animals. The Association of Swiss Holiday Farms offers bed and breakfast and/or apartments on farms, and accept children during school holidays without their parents (🖥 www.agrotourismus.ch).

SELF-CATERING ACCOMMODATION

You can find self-catering accommodation, e.g. apartments and chalets, in all holiday areas in Switzerland. Chalets and apartments can be rented through agencies or direct from owners. An apartment is generally cheaper than a hotel room, you have more privacy and freedom, and are able to prepare your own meals. Standards, while generally high, vary considerably, and paying a high price doesn't always guarantee a good location or a well-furnished apartment (most look wonderful in brochures).

Most holiday apartments are, however, comfortable and all are spotlessly clean. Apartments are generally well-equipped with bed linen, towels, cooking utensils, crockery and cutlery, although there may be an extra charge for bed linen (or you can bring your own). Some basic food stuffs (e.g. salt and sugar) and essentials such as toilet paper and soap may be provided, but don't count on it. Most people take essential foods and supplies with them, and buy fresh food on arrival. Shops in holiday areas may be open for a period on Sundays, particularly in ski resorts during the winter season.

You're normally required to do your own daily cleaning, as apartments aren't serviced unless part of a large private chalet or a hotel apartment complex, when chambermaids are provided. Don't, however, overdo the cleaning as you must pay for an apartment to be cleaned on your departure. Apartments are normally let on a weekly basis from Saturday to Saturday and you're required to vacate it by around noon on your last day, when a veritable army of cleaning ladies march in.

Apartments are best rented from owners and not through local tourist offices. Look up the village or canton that you're interested in on the internet (using a search engine such as Google) and enter *Unterkunft/Hébergement* to find a list of vacation rentals (*Ferienwohnung/ Appartements de vacances*). Many resort towns offer packages (*Pauschale*), which aren't only limited to accommodation but usually include discounted ski passes.

If you stay in an apartment you'll be charged a resort tax (*Kurtaxe/taxe de sejour*) of a few francs per person/per day. Most ski resorts provide free public transport and ski bus shuttles for guests (to keep people who don't know how to drive on ice and snow off the streets!).

The location is of particular importance if you're going to be skiing, as you'll need to know how far an apartment is from the nearest ski lift or ski bus shuttle stop; generally the nearer apartments are to ski lifts, the more expensive they are. Other aspects that influence the rental cost are the size, amenities, general quality and the season. Budget for at least CHF 300 to 400 per person, per week, for an apartment sleeping four in high season (less during the low season).

If you obtain a list of apartments from the tourist office or download it from the internet, you need to contact the owners or agents directly to find out the availability and further details, and to make a booking. Many resorts have integrated their vacation rental database into tourist office websites, and you can check the availability of accommodation online and make bookings. Many vacation home owners list their accommodation at 🖳 www.immoscout24.ch (Immobilien suchen/ Mieten/Ferien).

Book well in advance for public and school holiday periods, e.g. three to six months in winter. You may need to pay a deposit or the full cost in advance. Check whether there are any extras for

cleaning or breakages (sometimes included in the rent).

If you're looking for a rental with many beds (e.g. for a family reunion or a number of families) then 🖳 www.groups.ch may be able to help.

In summer you can usually find an apartment on the spot without any trouble, as most resorts cater mainly for winter sports fans (the exception is Ticino, where summer is the high season). Chalets and apartments can also be rented from many agents in Switzerland, such as Interhome-Schweiz (☎ 0800-84 88 88, 🖳 www.interhome.ch).

CARAVANNING & CAMPING

Switzerland has around 400 camping and caravan (trailer) sites, graded from one to five stars depending on their amenities, location and other factors. Many are open year round. The cost varies and starts around CHF 25 per night for a family of four with a tent and around double for a trailer. Electricity isn't included in the fees (around CHF 5 per day) and dogs are also charged extra (around CHF 5 per day). Resort tax isn't included in fees. Campers must have an international camping carnet, available from Swiss camping associations (see below). Permission is required to park or camp on private property or anywhere outside official camping sites. Caravans can be hired in most areas of Switzerland.

For detailed information about campsites, contact the Swiss Camping and Caravanning Federation (Schweizerischer Camping und Caravanning Verband, Fédération Suisse de Camping et de Caravanning, ☎ 062-777 40 08, 🖳 www.sccv.ch), who publish handbooks, available from bookshops throughout Switzerland, listing all Swiss campsites and their facilities. See also 🖳 www.camping.ch and www.camping-switzerland.ch.

The Touring Club of Switzerland (TCS – 🖳 www.tcs.ch) publish the *TCS Camping Guide*, available from TCS offices and bookshops. In addition to listing campsites in Switzerland, it also lists sites in France, Italy and Spain, including a section on naturist camp sites for those wishing to save on laundry bills. A list of campsites is also available from Switzerland Tourism offices.

YOUTH HOSTELS

If you're travelling on a tight budget, one way to stretch your precious financial resources is to stay in youth hostels, of which there are around 60 in Switzerland. Youth hostel accommodation is open to all, although children must be accompanied by an adult. All youth hostels provide separate dormitories for men and women and hot showers, and some provide cooking facilities, a laundry and an inexpensive restaurant. The cost of accommodation at most youth hostels ranges from around CHF 25 to over CHF 50 per night (average CHF 30 to 40) and includes a cotton sleeping bag or bed linen.

You don't need to be a member of the Swiss Youth Hostels (SYH) to stay in one, although membership offers reduced prices and an international membership card. Membership costs CHF 22 for those aged under 18 and CHF 33 for those aged over 18. Family membership is also available for CHF 44 (parents and children aged up to 18) and group leaders' membership for groups of ten or more (CHF 55). Youth hostels require guests to remain quiet until 7am and they don't allow alcohol on the premises. Smoking is restricted to designated rooms only.

☑ SURVIVAL TIP

To avoid disappointment you're advised to book at least five days in advance and in February, July, August and holiday periods, pre-booking is usually essential.

For more information, contact Swiss Youth Hostels/SYH (Schweizer Jugendherbergen, Auberges de Jeunesse Suisses, ☎ 044-360 14 14, 🖳 www.youthhostels.ch). The SYH publish a free 'Know How' map showing hostel locations and listing their facilities and a free booklet entitled *Downtown Switzerland*. Youth hostel information is also available from ST, who publish a free Swiss Hostel Guide.

STA Travel (☎ 058-450 40 40, 🖳 www. statravel.ch), provides information for travellers aged 16 to 35 and has offices in all major Swiss cities and towns. For private hostels, contact Swiss Backpackers (☎ 033-823 46 46, 🖳 www. swissbackpackers.ch), who offer dormitory lodging as well as double rooms and cater for both individuals and families.

MUSEUMS & ART GALLERIES

Switzerland has almost 1,000 museums, art galleries, gardens and zoos; Basle and Zurich zoos are world-famous and offer family and individual annual season tickets for regular visitors. Art treasures are housed in two National Museums in Zurich and at the Château de Prangins (near Nyon, Vaud), and in historical museums in Basle, Berne, Geneva and Zurich. Most museums are closed on Mondays and public holidays, which is standard practice in continental Europe. Admission is usually free on Sundays (first Sunday of the month in Geneva). Many museums close during lunch periods and opening times vary considerably, so check in advance. Some exhibitions make reductions for foreigners on production of a passport.

Lists of museums, zoological gardens and botanical gardens are available from Switzerland Tourism and 🖳 www.museums. ch. Museum lovers may also be interested in the *Swiss Museum Guide*, available from Swiss bookshops. All tourist information offices provide information about local attractions. An annual (CHF 155 adult, CHF 277 family) Swiss Museums Passport (🖳 www.museumspass. ch) is available from tourist information offices and is valid at over 470 museums throughout the country. The Michelin *Green Guide to Switzerland* includes a list of the major museums, sights, tourist attractions and summer cable-cars and chair-lifts, including costs and opening times.

If you're traveling on a Swiss Pass (🖳 www. swiss-pass.ch), you benefit from a free Swiss Museums Passport (see above).

CINEMAS

Over 300 cinemas (*Kino, cinéma*) throughout Switzerland show English-language films in the original language with German and French subtitles. Cinema listings in German-language newspapers show the original soundtrack language (first upper-case letter) and the subtitle languages (lower-case letters). For example, E/d/f denotes a film with an English original soundtrack with German (*Deutsch*) and French (*français*) subtitles, F/d denotes French soundtrack with German subtitles. In the French-speaking region of Switzerland, films are usually shown in French without subtitles and not in the original language. In French-speaking areas, '*v.o.*' denotes *version originale* (original language version). Programmes are shown on street posters in major cities.

Age restrictions vary from six years for Walt Disney type films to 9, 12 and 16 years for other films. In some cantons, cinemas must advertise the suitable age limit, but don't always enforce it when children are accompanied by an adult. Otherwise, for children accompanied by adults, the age restriction may be two years below the suitable age limit, e.g. in Basle if the general unaccompanied age limit is 12, then a child accompanied by an adult must be aged at least ten to see the movie. It isn't unusual for children (or adults) who look younger than their years to be asked for proof of their age, e.g. a school identity card.

Most cinemas accept telephone reservations and provide season tickets. You can also purchase 'Movie Cards' or other membership-type cards for most cinemas, which allow you to purchase subsidised tickets, make advance bookings online and other benefits. Ask at your favourite theatre for information. Film festivals are held in major cities, when cinemas may show films non-stop (24 hours a day) for a number of days and offer reduced admission prices. There are private film clubs in the main cities showing old classics.

For cinema programmes in the major cities, see 🖳 www.cineman.ch, which also offers 'Cinema Vouchers' valid for performances in all Swiss cinemas, although the savings are minimal (if any).

THEATRE, OPERA & BALLET

Switzerland has many excellent theatres (around 150) and thriving opera houses, including many small theatres and troupes, with performances in French, German, Italian and other languages. In major cities, amateur English-language theatre companies periodically stage plays, and incidentally, are always on the lookout for new talent. English and American repertory companies occasionally tour Switzerland (programmes are available from tourist information offices). Tickets for ballet and opera are in high demand, so you should apply well in advance (tickets can be purchased by subscription). Switzerland Tourism lists concerts, opera and theatre events on their website (🖳 www.myswitzerland.com).

Switzerland has a surprising number of travelling circuses, including the world-famous Circus Knie (the Swiss National Circus), which tours from March to November. Circus Knie spends the winter in Rapperswil, where they also run a children's zoo (Knies Kinderzoo, 🖳 www.knie.ch).

CONCERTS

Classical concerts, music festivals and solo concerts by international musicians and performers are staged regularly throughout Switzerland. Many Swiss international music festivals, from orchestral, choral and opera to jazz and rock, are world renowned. Season tickets are usually available for a whole season of classical performances or a selection of performances may be chosen from a prepared list. Although they aren't in the top tier, Basle, Geneva and Zurich all have excellent orchestras. Free organ and choral concerts are performed in churches throughout the year and free outdoor concerts are staged in summer. Look for announcements in local newspapers or ask at your local tourist office.

'Goodnews' (🖳 www.goodnews.ch) is a company that organises 80-100 concerts and events in Switzerland each year, presenting top international bands. A list of coming events and tickets are available on their website.

Country music has a strong following in Switzerland, as does country dancing such as line and square dancing. For country-western music and events, see Country Music (🖳 www.country-music.ch). There are several 'trucker' or country western festivals staged in Switzerland, the most popular of which is the trucker and country festival in Interlaken in summer (see 🖳 www.trucker-festival.ch).

The easiest place to purchase tickets for concerts and other events is from TicketCorner (☏ 0900-800 800, CHF 1.19 per minute 8am to 10pm, 🖳 www.ticketcorner.com). Tickets are also available at some department stores, music shops, and bookshops, notably Manor and Jelmoli department stores. Ticket prices in Switzerland are generally high and can be astronomical for 'superstars'.

For the musically talented there are musical (classical and brass bands) and choral societies in most towns and villages, and national orchestras for the really gifted (around 35 large professional orchestras). Those who cannot sing or play a musical instrument can join a yodelling group! A list of all major concerts and music festivals in Switzerland is provided in the Switzerland Tourism brochure, *Events in Switzerland*.

SOCIAL CLUBS

There are many social clubs and organisations in Switzerland, catering for both foreigners and Swiss. These include Ambassador clubs, American Women's and Men's Clubs, Anglo-Swiss clubs, Business Clubs, International Men's and Women's clubs, Kiwani Clubs, Lion and Lioness Clubs, and Rotary Clubs. Expatriates from many countries have their own clubs in major cities (ask at your local embassy or consulate in Switzerland). Many social clubs organise activities and pastimes such as chess, whist, art, music, sports activities and outings (such as theatre and cinema visits).

If you wish to integrate into your local community or Swiss society in general, one of the best ways is to join a local Swiss club. Most communities publish a calendar of local sports and social events.

DISCOTHEQUES & NIGHT-CLUBS

There are discotheques and night-clubs in all major Swiss towns and cities, although they're generally expensive. The entrance fee for discos, irrespective of whether they have a drinks licence, is usually between CHF 10 and 30 (it sometimes includes a 'free' drink). When available, drinks are expensive. Some discos offer free entrance to women until 10 or 11pm.

Although most Swiss aren't night owls, there are jazz and night clubs, bars, cabarets and discotheques open until between 2am and 6am in the major cities. Many clubs are private and don't admit casual visitors unless accompanied by a member. At weekends in the major cities, it isn't uncommon to have 'after-hours parties' lasting until noon the following day. The Swiss also organise rave-type parties that are held throughout the year, with house/techno and other youth-orientated music.

CASINOS

You could previously only play Boule, a sort of simplified roulette, in the 13 'B licence' Swiss casinos in Bad Ragaz, Crans, Courrendlin, Davos, Fribourg, Interlaken, Locarno, Mendrisio, Meyrin by Geneva, Pfäffikon, Schaffhausen, St Moritz and Zermatt. However, in a historic vote in 1993 the Swiss voted to remove the long-standing ban on 'real' casinos to aid the declining tourist industry and bolster government coffers. After much debate (and 12 years), seven 'A licences' (GrandCasino) were allocated (in 2005) to Baden, Basle EuroAirport, Berne, Lucerne, Lugano, Montreux and St Gallen.

'A licence' casinos can offer unlimited betting with no jackpot limit, while gamblers at 'B licence' casinos are allowed to bet a maximum of just CHF 5, with a jackpot of just CHF 5,000. The new GrandCasinos (along with the smaller, B licence ones) rake in over CHF 750m a year, with CHF 370m going to social security and a further CHF 50m to the cantons. Before the introduction of the GrandCasinos, all the big Swiss gambling money flowed over the border into the strategically placed casinos surrounding Switzerland, which reap 25 times the revenue of the Swiss 'B License' casinos.

BARS & CAFES

Bars and cafés abound throughout Switzerland, which, like most European countries, has sensible licensing laws. Most bars and local restaurants (i.e. bars providing food) are open from morning to midnight, including Sundays. Hot food, snacks and excellent coffee are usually available. There are also many English and Irish-style pubs where you can buy English, Irish and other foreign beers. Local Swiss beers and wines are generally good and imported beverages are widely available (local **hell** beer won't kill you, it just means light beer). Spirits and cocktails are outrageously expensive, particularly in hotels. Good local mineral waters are available everywhere.

☑ **SURVIVAL TIP**

Bear in mind that some tea-rooms and cafés don't sell alcohol. In bars, a choice of non-alcoholic drinks should be available at prices below the cheapest alcoholic drink, although this isn't always the case (non-alcoholic wines and beers are also usually available).

In Swiss bars you don't pay for each drink as it's served, except in crowded tourist haunts or a pub with English bar service. You usually receive a total bill at the end of the evening (the system is designed to help you drive home, as the size of the bill has an immediate sobering effect). While on the subject of drinking and driving, the law is very strict and penalties severe – if you have more than one or two small drinks you would be well advised to hitch a ride with a sober friend or use public transport. The legal age for drinking beer and wine in public places in Switzerland is 16, and 18 for spirits and alcopops.

A popular card game named Jass, remotely similar to bridge and requiring a special deck of cards, can be played in most bars and local restaurants. Most local bars have a family or regulars' table (*Stammtisch, table des habitués*), reserved for regular customers. It's usually denoted by a huge '*Stammtisch*' ashtray and you may be asked to move if you sit there. Like restaurants, most bars and cafés close on one or two days a week (*Ruhetag, jour de repos*), usually posted on the door.

Most cafés, bars and local restaurants provide free local newspapers and magazines, a common practice in continental Europe.

RESTAURANTS

There are some 30,000 restaurants in Switzerland, approximately one for every 250 inhabitants (and one on top of every mountain). Restaurants in Switzerland invariably provide good food and service, although there's little original Swiss cooking on offer apart from fondue, raclette and rösti, and most serve international cuisine. Like most continental Europeans, the

Swiss take their food seriously and the main meal of the day is usually eaten at midday (lunchtime). Unlike in some countries, it isn't usually necessary to have a meal in a Swiss restaurant and you can order a snack or a drink only. Note, however, that at lunchtime a white table cloth on a table means it's for diners only, although most establishments have a few tables without table cloths which are available for those who want just a drink.

All restaurants are obliged by law to display their menu and prices outside. A good meal for two with a modest bottle of wine costs around CHF 60 to 90 in an average restaurant (about the same price as in most northern European countries). Of course you can easily pay CHF 100 a head or more if you want the best and the cost of wine can be astronomical. In many expensive restaurants, nouvelle cuisine is fashionable, consisting of tiny portions artfully arranged on large plates – if you're starving, eat at a local bar. All restaurants offer a variety of house wines (*Offener Wein, vin ouvert*), which can be ordered by the deci-litre (but it's still expensive). Swiss restaurants and hotel bills include a 15 per cent service charge designed to cut out tipping. However, it's common to leave a small tip (which is appreciated) but if you don't the waiter won't abuse you or spill soup over you on your return (unlike, for example, in New York!).

Most restaurants offer a daily menu (*Tagesmenu, menu du jour*) at lunchtime, usually from noon to 2pm. It includes a choice of meals with soup or salad (and sometimes a dessert) and costs around CHF 15-20. Dinner in a local restaurant or bar is usually served from 7 to 10pm. Many restaurants offer half-portions for children or have a children's menu. Mövenpick restaurants are particularly good for children and offer a choice of menus, and McDonalds has branches in most major cities and large towns (you can also hire restaurants for children's parties). Many department stores have good value restaurants. If you like a glass of wine or a beer with your meal, avoid alcohol free (*Alkoholfrei, sans alcool*) restaurants (e.g. Migros), tea-rooms and cafés.

Foreign restaurants aren't as common in Switzerland as in many other European countries and can be expensive. Most foreign cuisine is, however, available in the major cities. It's advisable to make a reservation for the more expensive or more popular restaurants, particularly during lunchtimes, on Friday and Saturday evenings, and at anytime for parties of four or more people.

In most bars and local restaurants you're given cash register receipts for each item ordered, which are added when you request your bill.

Sliced bread may be provided free with a meal but bread rolls usually cost extra. If your waiter or waitress is going off duty, don't be surprised if you're asked to pay half-way through your meal.

Most restaurants close on one or two days a week (*Ruhetag, jour de repos*), which is usually posted on restaurant doors. Many bars and restaurants have a private room that can be used (usually free) for a club meeting or social function, provided you buy coffee or other drinks. The continental game of skittles (*Kegelbahn, jeu de quilles*) can be played in some bars and restaurants.

Among the best Swiss restaurant guides are the Michelin *Schweiz Red Guide* and the *Gault-Millau Guide Schweiz* (see also 🖥 www.swissholidayco.com/page/gault_millau). You can also find a Swiss restaurant via many websites, including 🖥 www.foodguide.ch and www.restaurant-guide.com/europe+switzerland.htm.

Since 1st May 2010, smoking has been banned in all restaurants and bars in Switzerland unless they have a separate enclosed 'smoking' room or are smaller than 80m² (when they can choose to be a 'smoking' establishment).

LIBRARIES

Most public libraries in cities and large towns have books in English, French, German and Italian.

Opening times vary but are usually around 9am to 6.30pm, Mondays to Fridays and 9am to noon or 4pm on Saturdays. Smaller libraries may open on only one or two days a week and opening hours may be reduced during the summer holiday period.

Most large towns and cities have a central library (*Zentralbibliothek, bibliothèque centrale*) with a large selection of English-language books, and most universities also have libraries open to the public. Library membership usually costs from CHF 10-30 per annum, although some libraries offer free membership. In addition, it's common to pay a fee for each item borrowed, e.g. CHF 1 per book (four weeks) and CHF 4 per DVD (two weeks).

Private libraries are fairly common in major cities, some of which have a large collection of English-language books, magazines and newspapers. The American library in Geneva is the second-largest English reading library on the continent, with around 20,000 titles. It's usually necessary to pay an annual membership fee to join a private library. The Federation of American Women's Clubs Overseas (see page 55) run English-language libraries in most major cities, which are open to non-members for a small subscription fee. For a list of all libraries in Switzerland (with internet links), see 🖥 www.bibliothek.ch.

16.
SPORTS

Among the most popular sports in Switzerland are skiing and other winter sports, hiking, cycling, mountaineering, tennis, squash and swimming; most water (sailing, windsurfing, water-skiing) and aerial sports (paragliding, hang-gliding, ballooning, flying) also have many devotees. Participation in some sports is expensive, although costs can be reduced through the purchase of season tickets, annual membership or by joining a club. Switzerland Tourism (ST) can provide information about practically any sport and the appropriate contact name and address. Various publications are available from tourist offices promoting special sports events and listing local sports venues.

Sports results are announced on the telephone service number ☎ 164 (CHF 0.50 basic fee plus 0.50 per minute) and on the Swiss news website 🖵 www.swissinfo.ch/eng/sport/index. html?cid=63854, while information about local sports' clubs is available in English via the Vive le Sport website (🖵 www.vive-le-sport.ch/e).

Leaflets containing information about how to prevent and avoid sports accidents and injuries, e.g. cycling, hiking, skiing, football and watersports, are available from the Swiss Bureau for the Prevention of Accidents.

AERIAL SPORTS

The Alps are ideal for aerial sports (particularly gliding, hang-gliding, paragliding and hot-air ballooning), due to the updrafts and the low density of air traffic (apart from all the gliders, hang-gliders and balloons). Hang-gliding has become increasingly popular in Switzerland and together with Paragliding (*Gleitschirm, parapente*), which entails jumping off steep mountain slopes with a parachute, there are over 20,000 registered 'pilots' in Switzerland and around 60 schools (the sport even has its own magazine, *Swiss Glider*).

Before you can go solo, you must pass a theory test, make either 30 flights in three different areas (hang-gliders) or 50 flights in five different areas (paragliders) and pass a flight test to obtain a licence. Participants must also have third party liability insurance for CHF 1m. Motorised hang-gliding and paragliding is forbidden in Switzerland. For more information, contact the Swiss Hang-gliding and Paragliding Association (Schweiz. Hängegleiter-Verband, Association Suisse de Vol Libre, ☎ 01-387 46 80, 🖵 www.shv-fsvl.ch/en). See also 🖵 www.flyland.ch, a website dedicated to paragliders.

Ballooning has a small but dedicated band of followers, although participation is generally limited to the wealthy due to the high cost of balloons. A flight in a balloon is a marvelous experience, particularly over the Alps. There is, however, no guarantee of distance or duration, and trips are dependent on wind conditions and the skill of your pilot. A list of ballooning clubs is available from Switzerland Tourism.

Light aircraft and gliders (sailplanes) can be rented with or without an instructor from most small airfields in Switzerland (provided you have a pilot's licence!). There are around 60 gliding clubs in Switzerland. Freefall parachuting (sky-diving) flights can be made from most private airfields; however, it's expensive and costs can run to over CHF 7,500 for training and equipment. Information regarding free-fall parachuting, para-gliding, gliding and flying is available from Switzerland Tourism and the Aero-Club of Switzerland (Aero-Club der Schweiz, Aéro Club de Suisse, ☎ 041-375 01 01, 🖵 www. aeroclub.ch). A special weather report for aerial sports is provided by 🖵 www.meteoschweiz.ch (see Services/Aviation).

Before taking up the above sports, you're advised to make sure that you have adequate health, accident and life insurance (see **Chapter 13**) and that your affairs are in order!

CYCLING

Cycling is popular in Switzerland, not only as a means of transport or a serious sport, but also as a relaxing pastime for the whole family. The weather from spring through to autumn is usually fine for cycling, mainly dry and warm and generally not too hot. There are over 6,000km (3,700mi) of marked bicycle paths in country areas. These include the 'Cycling in Switzerland network' officially opened in 1998, consisting of nine national cycle routes covering a total of over 3,300km (2,050mi) of paths; maps are available from Switzerland Tourism and railway stations, or visit 💻 www.cycling-in-switzerland.ch.

Serious cyclists abound in Switzerland, where cycle racing has a huge following and races are organised at every level. The *Tour de Suisse* is Switzerland's premier race, held in June over a 1,600km (1,000mi) route and one of Europe's major events. For information, contact the Swiss Cycling Federation (Schweiz. Radfahrer-Bund, Fédération Cycliste Suisse, ☎ 031-359 72 33, 💻 www.cycling.ch). Information about cycling can also be obtained from 💻 www.kettenrad.ch and www.tourenguide.ch.

For the recreational cyclist, a standard bicycle (*Fahrrad, vélo/bicyclette*) can be purchased for around CHF 750-1,000 (cheaper bikes are also available); shop around for the best buy (a professional racing bicycle can cost many thousands of francs). If you're feeling particularly energetic you can buy a 21-speed mountain bike and go cycling in the Alps (many resorts have special mountain bike trails). Mountain bikes are currently all the rage and cost from around CHF 1,000 for a good basic bike and many thousands for a top quality machine.

Apart from cycling to work, which many people do from spring to autumn, cycling is an excellent way to explore the countryside at your leisure and get some fresh air and exercise at the same time. Special cycling maps (*Velokarte, itinéraire pour cyclistes*) are produced by the Traffic Association of Switzerland (scale 1:50) and are available from bookshops everywhere. A *Bicycling in Switzerland* booklet is available from Switzerland Tourism, plus many regional cycling guides containing recommended one-day trips.

Mountain bikes are banned on many hiking paths due to the dangers and inconvenience to hikers, and cross-country 'off-piste' cycling is also prohibited in some areas to protect the flora and fauna. However, downhill cycling is a popular summer sport in ski resorts, where you can usually transport your bike on ski lifts.

Bicycle breakdown assistance and theft insurance is available from Swiss motoring organisations. Wearing a helmet is strongly advised, although (surprisingly) not compulsory; there have been discussions about changing the law to make it compulsory – at least for children – but it remains optional. Bear in mind that there are over 3m cyclists in Switzerland who are involved in around 30,000 accidents each year, some 1,500 of which result in severe head injuries.

> You no longer require a bicycle licence in Switzerland as the registration scheme was abolished from 1st January 2012. The licence included third party insurance against damage caused by cyclists, which is now covered by optional personal liability insurance – make sure you have it if you don't want to be sued!

An increasingly popular bicycling event which takes place throughout the summer in various regions is the 'slow-up' event, during which some 30km (19mi) of roads and even sections of motorways are closed to traffic so that people on bicycles, walking or skating can have the roads to themselves. It's like a big festival – food and refreshments are available – and ideal for the whole family. More information can be found at 💻 www.slowup.ch.

Important Notes

◆ All cyclists should be familiar with the road rules for cyclists contained in the *Handbook of Swiss Traffic Regulations*, available from cantonal motor registration offices.

◆ Take particular care on busy roads and don't allow your children onto public roads until they're experienced riders. Children aren't permitted to cycle on a public road until they're aged seven and attending primary school; kindergarten doesn't count, even when a child is already seven.

◆ If you cycle in cities you should wear reflective clothing, a light crash helmet (particularly for children) and a smog mask. Head injuries are the main cause of death in bicycle accidents, most of which don't involve accidents with vehicles, but are a result of colliding with fixed objects or falls. Always buy a quality helmet that has been subjected to rigorous testing and approved by a safety organisation.

◆ When rising at night, it's advisable to have flashing rear and front lamps, which make

cycles much more visible to motorists.

♦ Children up to the age of seven can be carried on the back of an adult's bicycle in a specially designed chair. Riders carrying children must be aged over 16.

♦ Bicycles must be fitted with an anti-theft device blocking a wheel or the steering. A basic locking device is already fitted to bicycles purchased in Switzerland (but not mountain bikes) and you can buy a more secure steel cable or chain with a lock from bicycle accessory shops and supermarkets, e.g. Migros. Note, however, that no devices are foolproof and some people take a wheel with them when leaving their bike unattended!

♦ Where special cycle tracks or lanes are provided, they must be used. Unfortunately there aren't many off-road cycle lanes in cities and towns, and you often take your life into your hands when venturing onto main roads, particularly during rush hours.

♦ You aren't permitted to ride on footpaths/ sidewalks (even for children) unless sign-posted otherwise or two abreast on roads. Being pulled along by a moped (*Motorfahrrad/ Mofa*, *vélomoteur*) is illegal and dangerous, and riding with your hands off the handlebars or feet off the pedals is also prohibited.

♦ If you import a bicycle, it must conform to Swiss safety standards. These include front and rear reflectors, front and rear lamps, pedal reflectors, bell, front and rear brakes, and good tyres. Off-road bikes, e.g. some racing

and mountain bikes, cannot be used on public roads (unless road legal), except when riding to and from race venues.

♦ Take drinks, first-aid kit, tool kit and a puncture repair outfit when on a long cycling trip.

♦ Take care not to get your wheels stuck in tram or railway lines.

♦ You can usually take your bicycle on trains, buses, trams but require a valid bicycle ticket (*Velobillette*).

Bicycle Hire & Transportation

A huge range of bicycles can be rented, including a country bike, mountain bike, children's bike or an electric (E-Bike) bike, from over 100 Swiss railway stations and returned to any other participating station (see 🖥 www.rentabike.ch) Bookings should be made by 6pm the previous day or a week in advance for groups. Fees start from around CHF 33 per day for an adult country bike (half price for a child aged under 16) and CHF 50 for an E-Bike (adults only) – there's a CHF 5 reduction if you have a half fare travel card.

A country bike can be fitted with a free child's seat, but you need to book, and helmets are included in the bike rentals. Bicycles can be left at any participating station for a fee, which is waived if you hire a bike for more than one day. Further information is provided in a brochure available from railway stations, which includes suggested routes. Bicycles can be hired from cycle shops in many towns, and mountain bikes are available to rent in some resorts for around CHF 50 per day.

You can transport your bicycle between any two stations for around CHF 16 per day, except for certain Eurocity and S-Bahn trains during peak periods. You must load and unload it yourself and have a valid ticket for the same destination (Intercity and fast trains excluded). Bicycles sent by train in Switzerland can be insured for CHF 5 per CHF 500 value. Using the train allows you to cycle one way and return by train (or vice versa). Swiss federal railways offer many special cycling tours and trips, and 'rail bicycle' brochures are available from railway stations. The SBB also publish a book entitled *40 Bicycle Tours* (with the train).

In some cities (e.g. Basel, Berne, Zug and Zurich) you can use a bicycle for free. In Berne (🖥 www.bernrollt.ch) and Zurich (🖥 www.zuerich. com/en/visitor/experience/nature/zueri-rollt. html), for example, you need to show personal identification and pay a security deposit of CHF 20 (in Berne the first four hours are free and additional hours cost CHF 1 per hour). These schemes may be restricted to spring and summer.

FISHING

Fishing facilities in Switzerland are superb. There are a huge variety of well-stocked waters totalling some 133,000 hectares (330,000 acres or 1,350 mi²) of lakes and 32,000km (20,000mi) of running water; enough to keep even the keenest of anglers busy for a few weeks! Lakes and mountain streams are stocked annually with trout, grayling and pike (there are over 50 native fish species in Switzerland).

You must buy a fishing permit for rivers and some lakes. which are usually available for a day, week or month from the local tourist office or the area council office (*Bezirksamt, administration de district*). You can obtain an annual permit for your own canton and monthly permits for other cantons. Fishing licences for non-residents of a canton can be expensive, although there are some unrestricted waters that don't require a permit. Contact the local area council office or local tourist office for information.

For more information, contact the Swiss Angling Association (Schweiz. Fischerei-Verband, Association Suisse des Pêcheurs, 🖥 www.sfv-fsp.ch).

> ## ☑ SURVIVAL TIP
>
> The fishing season and rules and regulations regarding the permitted size of fish which can be taken vary from canton to canton, so check before planning a trip.

GOLF

There are some 80 golf courses (9 and 18 holes) in Switzerland, plus mini-golf courses. Migros launched their 'Golf for all' golf courses (🖥 www.golfparks.ch) in the late '90s in an effort to make golfing in Switzerland a sport for all and not just the privileged. However, apart from the Migros 'Golf for all' courses (which are relatively inexpensive), golf is still an elitist and expensive sport in Switzerland, and it's almost impossible to join a city club without excellent contacts and a low handicap (the waiting list for membership of some clubs is longer than the average expatriate's stay in Switzerland!).

The average joining fee for an 18-hole club is CHF 20,000 to 25,000 and annual fees are an additional CHF 2,500-5,000 a year. Members of foreign and other Swiss golf clubs can usually play at Swiss clubs from Mondays to Fridays on production of a membership or handicap card.

Green fees are from around CHF 100 in urban areas and from CHF 75 to over CHF 100 in rural areas. Your best bet may be to play at a mountain resort course, where you can play golf in beautiful scenery (at around 1,500m/5,000ft) without being a member.

Many cities and resorts have indoor practice centres, where you can have a video analysis of your swing. Switzerland also has one of the world's largest indoor golf clubs (1,500m²/16,146ft²) at Zumikon, Zurich. For more information about golf in Switzerland, contact the Swiss Golf Association (Schweiz. Golfverband, Association Suisse de Golf, ☎ 021-785 70 00, 🖥 www.asg.ch).

An excellent *Official Guide to Golf Courses in Switzerland* is available from Switzerland Tourism. Many hotels offer special golf packages; for information, contact the Swiss Golf Hotels Group (☎ 081-300 44 22, 🖥 www.swissgolfhotels.ch).

Crazy golf (golf obstacle course) is played in many areas. It's taken seriously and competitions (even Swiss championships) are organised.

HIKING

Switzerland is a hiker's paradise with more than 31,000km (over 19,000mi) of marked main routes, including ten national hiking routes each covering a distance of 200 to 400km (around 125 to 250mi), and some 400 secondary routes. The country boasts a grand total of over 62,000km (38,750mi) of hiking trails in some of the most beautiful scenery in the world. This is an impressive figure when one considers that there are 'only' 71,300km (44,300mi) of main roads in Switzerland.

The Swiss are keen hikers, and infants to pensioners can be seen everywhere in their hiking gear. Although the main hiking season is from around May to September, hiking in Switzerland isn't just a summer sport. Most winter sports resorts keep several trails open for walkers throughout the winter – a total of some 4,600km (1,800mi). It's fun walking in the snow and the weather can be quite hot in the mountains in winter (you'll also be hot after walking for a few kilometres).

Many local communities and walking clubs organise walks (*Volksmarsch, marche populaire*). There's a small fee and a medal for any survivors (you'll have earned it by the time you reach the top of the Matterhorn!). A complete programme of hikes organised by local walking clubs is available from the Federation of Swiss Hiking Trails (Schweizer Wanderwege, Fédération Suisse de Tourisme Pédestre, ☎ 031-370 10 20, 🖥 www.swisshiking.ch), who publish a bimonthly magazine (*Wander-Revue*, *Revue Sentiers*) for hikers, available in French and German editions.

Membership of a cantonal branch of the Federation of Swiss Hiking Trails costs from around CHF 20 to 50 a year, depending on your canton of residence. Guided hiking tours are organised in many resorts and the Swiss Alpine Club (SAC) organises excursions for experienced hikers (see **Mountaineering & Caving** below). Contact Switzerland Tourism and local tourist offices for information. Orienteering is also a popular sport in Switzerland.

Many mountain resorts have a tourist information telephone number and/or website where the latest information is recorded about local weather conditions, cable-cars and other mountain transport services, and the condition of hiking paths. Telephone numbers are listed in telephone directories. The weather forecast is also available on service telephone number ☎ 162 (CHF 0.50 basic fee plus 0.50 per minute) and at 🖥 www.meteoschweiz.ch. See also **Climate** on page 256.

An abundance of wild mountain flowers are in bloom in the Alps from around May to August, July usually being the best month. Many mountain areas have alpine gardens and guide books to local flora and fauna can be purchased from tourist offices.

⚠ Caution

Many alpine plants are protected and you're forbidden to pick or uproot them (offenders can be fined).

Signs

Hiking paths (*Wanderweg, chemin pédestre*) are indicated by yellow metal signs showing the altitude and destination and often the approximate time required to reach it. Times are based on a walking speed of 4.2km (2.6mi) an hour on well surfaced flat land, which is generous enough for anyone but a tortoise – provided, of course, that you don't get lost. They sometimes also indicate the distance to the destination. Mountain paths (*Bergweg, sentier de montagne*) are marked by yellow signs with a red and white tip or arrow point. Where there are no signposts, routes are marked with yellow arrows or diamond-shaped signs on trees, rocks, posts and buildings (part of the challenge is trying to find the path). Signs may also be in cantonal colours. Some areas have hiking paths for those confined to wheelchairs. Always stick to marked paths, particularly in difficult terrain.

To commemorate Switzerland's 700th anniversary in 1991, the Swiss created the 'Swiss Path' (*Weg der Schweiz, la voie Suisse*) around lake Uri (part of the lake of Lucerne) at a cost of CHF 12m. Each canton was responsible for a stretch of the 35km (22mi) trail, which takes around 12 hours to negotiate (it's a two-day hike). A Swiss Path train pass can be purchased from anywhere in Switzerland and a plan of the walk is available in English for around CHF 5.

Books & Maps

You should plan a walk using a good map, for example Swiss ordnance survey maps (*Landeskarte der Schweiz, carte nationale de la Suisse*). These excellent maps are produced in both 1:25 and 1:50 sizes and sold at stationers, railway stations, and shops in walking and climbing areas. Special hiking maps (*Wanderwegkarte, carte des chemins pédestres*) can also be purchased from Swiss bookshops.

A good general book on hiking is *Walking Switzerland: The Swiss Way* by Marcia & Philip Lieberman (Cordee). It includes all the necessary advice required (unless you plan an assault on the north face of the Eiger) and includes a selection of walks. For a list of Swiss hiking books, see the Slow Travel Switzerland website (🖥 www.slowtrav.com/switzerland/planning/books.htm). See also **Further Reading** (Appendix B).

Free hiking brochures are produced by various organisations, including the post office, Swiss motoring organisations and Swiss banks. Local hiking maps are available in all areas from shops and tourist and community offices. Plans showing local hiking paths are also displayed at many railway stations. Many areas have a **hiking pass**, available from most railway stations and tourist offices, with suggested walking tours.

There are also a number of websites for hikers including Wanderland (🖳 www.wanderland.ch) where you'll find suggested hikes, organised hikes with accommodation, and lists of hiking books and maps, and Wandersite (🖳 www.wandersite.ch/def_english.html). The website of the Federation of Swiss Hiking (🖳 www.swisshiking.ch) also contains a lot of useful information, but only in French and German.

Emergencies

If someone is seriously injured, don't move him unless it's absolutely necessary to protect him from further injury. Keep him warm and seek help as soon as possible. The alpine SOS consists of a series of six signals evenly spaced over one minute (one every ten seconds) and then a repetition of six more after a minute's pause. The signals may consist of either six blasts on a whistle, six loud shouts, six flashes of a torch or six swings of an article of clothing (attached to a stick if possible) swung in a semi-circle from the ground. The reply to an emergency signal is three repeats of the visual or acoustic signal a minute, at one-minute intervals.

Standing upright with both arms stretched above your head signals a request for a rescue helicopter. Holding one arm up with the other arm held down at your side indicates that a rescue helicopter isn't required. The Swiss REGA helicopter service (see page 91) is the ambulance of the Alps and all SAC huts have radio telephones that can be used to summon a helicopter. If you need to call REGA (☎ 1414) for a rescue helicopter, you should provide the following information:

◆ your name, the location of the telephone and the telephone number;

◆ what has happened where;

◆ number of patients and their approximate injuries;

◆ location – give exact details, e.g. map co-ordinates;

◆ town, name and birth date of the injured person (it isn't essential to revive an unconscious patient and ask him);

◆ weather conditions and landing possibilities in the accident area;

◆ any helicopter obstructions in the accident area, e.g. pylons, cables and power lines.

Some resorts, e.g. Sion and Zermatt, provide a local helicopter rescue service. If you're going hiking with visitors to Switzerland, you should ensure that they have adequate accident insurance (see page 178), including helicopter rescue.

The cost of a rescue party or helicopter and medical treatment can be very expensive. However, if you work in Switzerland, you're covered for accidents by your compulsory employee, non-occupational, accident insurance.

General Information

The following notes may help you survive a stroll in the mountains:

◆ If you're going to take up hiking seriously, a good pair of walking shoes or boots is mandatory (available from most Swiss shoe and sports shops). Always wear proper walking shoes or boots where the terrain is rough. Modern walking boots are light and comfortable and are widely available from shoe and sports shops. Wearing two pairs of socks can help prevent blisters. It's advisable to break in a new pair of boots on some gentle hikes before setting out on a marathon hike around Switzerland.

◆ Don't over-exert yourself, particularly at high altitudes where the air is thinner. Mountain sickness usually occurs above 4,000m/13,000ft, but can also happen at lower altitudes. A few words of warning for those who aren't particularly fit; take it easy and set a slow pace. It's easy to over-exert yourself and underestimate the duration or degree of difficulty of a hike. Start slowly and build up to those weekend marathons. If you're unfit, use chair-lifts and cable-cars to get to high altitudes.

◆ **Don't attempt a major hike alone as it's too dangerous.** Notify someone about your route, destination and estimated time of return, and give them a mobile phone number on which you can be contacted or call for help if necessary (but bear in mind that reception is impossible in some areas!). Check the conditions along your route and the times of any public transport connections (set out early to avoid missing the last cable-car or bus). Take into account the time required for both ascents and descents. If you're unable to return by the time expected, let somebody know – if the rescue service is summoned in error you may have to pay. If you realise that you're unable to reach your destination, for example due to tiredness or bad weather, turn back in good time or take a shorter route. If you're caught in a heavy storm, descend as quickly as possible or seek refuge, e.g. in an SAC hut.

◆ Check the weather forecast, usually available from the local tourist office or 🖥 www.meteoschweiz.ch. Generally the higher the altitude, the more unpredictable the weather, even for Swiss meteorologists.

◆ Hiking, even in lowland areas, can be dangerous, so don't take any unnecessary risks. There are enough natural hazards including bad weather, rock-falls, avalanches, rough terrain, snow and ice, and wet grass, without adding to them.

◆ Don't walk on closed tracks at any time (they're sign-posted). This is particularly important in the spring when there may be the danger of avalanches or rockfalls. Tracks are sometimes closed due to forestry work or army exercises. If you're in doubt about a particular route, ask in advance at the local tourist office.

⚠ **Caution**

If the Swiss signpost anything as dangerous (*Gefahr/Lebensgefahr, danger*) – you can bet it is!

◆ Wear loose fitting clothes and not, for example, tight jeans, which can become uncomfortable when you get warmed up. Shorts (short trousers – not underpants!) are excellent in hot weather. Lightweight cotton trousers are comfortable unless it's cold. You can wear your shorts underneath your trousers and remove your trousers when you've warmed up.

◆ Take a warm pullover, gloves (in winter) and a raincoat or large umbrella (an excellent plastic raincoat is sold at main post offices). Mountain weather can change suddenly and even in summer it's sometimes cold at high altitudes. A first-aid kit (for cuts and grazes), compass, identification, maps, small torch/flashlight, a

Swiss army knife and a mobile phone may also come in handy. A pair of binoculars are handy for spotting wildlife (or hikers having fun in the bushes). Take a rucksack to carry all your survival rations. A 35 to 40-litre capacity rucksack is best for day trips or a 65-litre capacity for longer hikes.

◆ Take sun protection, for example a hat, sunglasses, and sun and barrier cream, as you'll burn more easily at high altitude due to the thinner air. Use a total sunblock cream on your lips, nose and eyelids, and take a scarf or handkerchief to protect your neck from the sun. You may also need to protect yourself against ticks and mosquitoes in some areas. Take a water bottle. This is much appreciated when you discover that the mountain restaurant that was just around the corner is still miles away because you took a wrong turn (there's a restaurant on top of every mountain in Switzerland).

◆ Beware of wild animals that appear ill or unnaturally friendly as they may have rabies (see **Pets** on page 263). There a few poisonous snakes in Switzerland, although you're unlikely to encounter one and the last death from a snakebite was in 1961.

◆ If you're gathering mushrooms, always present them to your local official 'mushroom inspector' (most communities have one), for checking, as some species are deadly poisonous (a number of people die each year from eating poisonous mushrooms or toadstools). There's usually a limit to the amount of mushrooms which can be picked per person per day, e.g. 1 to 3kg (2.2 to 6.6lb).

◆ Don't take young children on difficult hikes unless you enjoy carrying them. Impress upon children the importance of not wandering off on their own. If you lose anyone, particularly children, seek help as soon as possible and before nightfall. It's advisable to equip children with a loud whistle, some warm clothing and a mobile phone, in case they get lost.

Country Code

Hikers are asked to observe the Swiss Nature Society's green rules:

- Take care not to damage trees, flowers and bushes.

- Leave animals in peace (dogs mustn't be allowed to disturb farm animals).

- Be careful with fire and never start a fire in a forbidden area.

- Watch where you walk and keep to the paths.

- Don't litter the countryside.

- Close all gates after use.

- Think of others.

MOUNTAINEERING & CAVING

Those who find hiking a bit tame may prefer to try mountaineering, rock-climbing or caving (subterranean mountaineering), all of which are extremely popular in Switzerland. Switzerland has over 100 peaks of around 4,000m/13,000ft, which provide even the experts with plenty of challenges (usually consisting of trying to climb them all in one day!). If you're an inexperienced climber, you would be well advised to join an alpine club before heading for the mountains. Contact the Swiss Alpine Club (Schweizer Alpen-Club, Club Alpin Suisse/SAC, ☎ 031-370 18 18, 💻 www.sac-cas. ch) for information. The SAC maintain over 150 climber's mountain huts throughout Switzerland, listed on their website (see 'Hut information'). Members of the SAC get up to 50 per cent discount on hut stays.

Unless you're an experienced climber, you'll need to hire a registered guide, particularly when climbing glaciers (don't, however, follow your guide too closely – if he falls down a crevice it isn't necessary to go with him). There are mountaineering schools (around 30 in total) in all the main climbing areas of Switzerland. Contact the Swiss Federation of Mountain Sport Schools (Verband Bergsportschulen Schweiz, Ecole Suisse d'Alpinisme, ☎ 079-335 10 91, 💻 www. bergsportschulen.ch) for information. Guides are available at all mountaineering schools and in many smaller resorts. If you find a guide other than through a recognised school or club, ensure that he's qualified and registered.

A good map is important – Swiss ordnance survey maps (*Landeskarte der Schweiz, carte nationale de la Suisse*) are the best and available in both 1:25 and 1:50 sizes from stationery stores, railway stations and shops in climbing areas.

Scores of climbers are killed each year in Switzerland, many of whom are inexperienced and reckless. Many more owe their survival to rescuers who risk their lives to rescue them. Before taking up mountaineering, it's advisable to visit the alpine museum and graveyard in Zermatt (interesting, even if you aren't planning to take up residence). Over 500 climbers have died attempting to climb (or descend) the Matterhorn. If this doesn't succeed in bringing you to your senses, all that remains is to wish you the best of luck.

 Caution

It's extremely foolish – not to mention highly dangerous – to venture into the mountains without an experienced guide, proper preparation, excellent physical condition, sufficient training, the appropriate equipment and accident insurance.

Mountain walking shouldn't be confused with hiking as it's generally done at much higher altitudes and in more difficult terrain. It can be dangerous for the inexperienced and should be approached with much the same degree of caution and preparation as mountaineering. A free brochure entitled *Safer Mountain Walking* (*Bergwandern-Mit Sicherheit mehr Spass, la sécurité lors des radonnées en montagne*) containing advice about how to avoid accidents, fitness tips and safety rules, is available from the Schweizerische Beratungsstelle für Unfall-verhütung (☎ 031-390 22 22, 💻 www.bfu.ch). REGA, the Swiss helicopter rescue service (see page 91), has the job of rescuing climbers who get stuck on mountains and also provides safety guidelines for mountaineers.

RACKET SPORTS

There are excellent facilities in Switzerland for most racket sports, particularly tennis and squash. There are two main kinds of racket clubs: sports centres open to anyone and private clubs. Sports centres require no membership or membership fees and anyone can book a court. Private clubs usually have high membership fees running into thousands of francs a year, although court fees are low or non-existent. Some private clubs are fairly exclusive and it's difficult to join unless you're introduced by a member and/or are wealthy.

Tennis is the most popular racket sport in Switzerland and there's an abundance of covered and outdoor tennis centres. Tennis centres have coaches available for both private and group lessons. Many communities also have outdoor courts, often floodlit, for which fixed weekly bookings need to be made for the whole summer season.

Clubs catering exclusively for squash are rare, although many tennis centres have a number of squash courts, a total of over 600 in some 175 centres throughout Switzerland. The standard of squash isn't high due to the general lack of top coaching and top competition, although it's continually improving. Rackets and balls can be hired from most squash clubs for squash or racketball (the American version of squash).

Some tennis centres also provide badminton courts, which, due to their rarity, are fairly solidly booked on most weekday evenings (they're usually easier to book at weekends). Most badminton centres have clubs entitling members to play free of charge or on reserved courts at fixed times. Typical courts costs for tennis are around CHF 20-50 per hour in summer (outdoor courts) and CHF 30-60 in winter (indoor courts). Badminton and squash courts are slightly cheaper at CHF 20-40 per hour (or 45 minutes for squash). Costs are usually cheaper before 5pm and at weekends. Costs can be further reduced by paying for a fixed number of periods (e.g. 5 or 10) or reserving a court for a fixed time each week throughout the season. Note that you must usually cancel a booked court 24 hours in advance, otherwise you'll be charged for it if it isn't re-booked.

Many clubs provide 'free' saunas and whirl-pools, and solariums are often available for a small extra cost. Racket clubs sometimes have a resident masseur. Most public racket clubs have a restaurant (possibly alcohol-free) or snack bar and some have swimming pools. A free list and map of local tennis and squash centres is available from many clubs. Some hotels have their own tennis and squash courts and organise coaching holidays throughout the year. Information is available from racket clubs, travel agents and resorts.

Most racket centres run fee-paying clubs allowing members to play free of charge or at a reduced cost at certain times, and take part in club competitions. League and knockout competitions are organised, both within clubs and nationally, through affiliation to Swiss sports' federations. In order to play in inter-club competitions, competitors must be registered with the national federation for their sport (fees include accident insurance). There's a full programme of local and national league competitions for all racket sports.

To find the racket clubs in your area, enquire at your local community or tourist office, or contact the Swiss national associations listed below.

Roger Federer

Swiss National Associations		
Sport	Tel. Number	Internet
Badminton	031 359 72 55	www.swiss-badminton.ch
Squash	043 377 70 03	www.squash.ch
Tennis	032 344 07 07	www.mytennis.ch
Table Tennis	031 359 73 90	www.swisstabletennis.ch

Table tennis is a sport that's rarely played socially in Switzerland. Normally you must be a member of a club, although you can play casually at hotels, swimming pools and youth clubs. Membership of a table tennis club is usually divided into 'active' (those representing the club in leagues and competitions) and 'passive' members (those playing socially only). Costs vary but it's an inexpensive sport with little equipment necessary. Typical annual club fees are from CHF 100 to 150 for active membership.

RUNNING

Competitive running has a strong following in Switzerland and leisure jogging is one of the most popular sports. For serious competitive runners, a free annual booklet is produced by the Swiss Light Athletics Federation (Schweiz. Leichtathletik-verband, Fédération Suisse d'Athlétisme, ☎ 031-359 73 00, 🖳 www.swiss-athletics.ch). It contains a complete list of running events throughout Switzerland and is available from sports shops or the above address.

For those who jog to keep fit, Switzerland is a paradise with an abundance of well-marked jogging trails and even joint-friendly *Finnenbahn* tracks. These are usually situated in forests near towns and cities, between 500 and 750 meters long and made of sawdust, so that you can even run barefoot. Some *Finnenbahns* are floodlit for night use (until 9pm in winter and 10pm in summer), for example in Zurich, where there are five.

For those who like to combine running and exercises, there are around 500 courses (*Vita-Parcours*) throughout Switzerland sponsored by the Zurich Life Insurance Company. They consist of a route of 3 to 4km (2 to 2.5mi), with an exercise stop every few hundred metres to keep you in good shape (or kill you if you're in poor shape). See the Stiftung Vita Pacours website (🖳 www.vitaparcours.ch) for a complete list of courses.

Many communities organise local runs (*Volkslauf, course populaire*) of around 10km (6mi), where all competitors receive a commemorative 'medal' for finishing the course. Contact your local tourist office or community office for details of local races.

SKIING & SNOWBOARDING

A book about living in Switzerland would hardly be complete without a 'few' words about skiing. Skiing is Switzerland's national sport and some 40 per cent of the population ski or snowboard regularly, including many foreigners, plus another 2m visitors. Wherever you live you won't be far from the ski slopes, although in some areas the nearest facilities may be in a neighbouring country. Switzerland has around 200 ski resorts, most of which are located in attractive mountain villages. However, although it has largely resisted the temptation to construct purpose-built resorts in virgin areas, Switzerland has, like other countries, damaged its mountain environment by over development (the Alps are the world's most environmentally-threatened mountain range).

There are two main types of skiing in Switzerland: alpine or downhill (*Alpin*) and cross-country (*Langlauf/Ski-Wandern, ski de fond/ski nordique*). Many downhill skiers look down on cross-country skiing as boring and lacking in excitement. This may be because it's too much like hard work to most of them, although it would be fair to say that if it's excitement and exhilaration that you're after, downhill skiing is hard to beat.

Although originally thought of as a sport for those who are too clumsy to master the art of skiing, snowboarding is extremely popular, especially with teenagers. While snowboarders can generally use the same pistes as skiers, many winter sport resorts have special snowboarding schools and half-pipes (barrel-runs).

The ski season in Switzerland lasts from December to April in most resorts and from November to May in resorts at around 2,000-3,000m (6,500-10,000ft), although it's possible to ski year round on mountains with glaciers.

Alpine Skiing

Alpine or downhill skiing as well as snowboarding are expensive sports, particularly for families. The cost of equipping a family of four is around CHF 4,000 for equipment and clothing (about CHF 1,000 each). If you're a beginner, it's advisable to hire snowboarding or ski equipment (e.g. skis/board, poles, boots) or buy second-hand equipment until you're addicted, which, if it doesn't frighten you to death, can happen on your first day on the slopes. However, bear in mind that many a would-be skier has invested a lot of money in new

equipment, only to find they don't like skiing. Most sports shops have pre-season and end of season sales of equipment.

Ski-lift passes can cost over CHF 100 per day for an adult in a top Swiss resort and skiing in some resorts, particularly at weekends (Sundays are worst), entails a lot of time-consuming and 'expensive' queuing. In many resorts you can buy a limited area ski-lift pass or a half-day pass, e.g. from noon, which is cheaper than buying a day pass for a whole area (you often need to be an Olympian to ski a large area in one day). You can buy a ski-lift pass in most resorts for almost any number of days or for the whole season. Generally, the longer the period covered by a pass, the cheaper the daily cost. In bad weather conditions, which is quite often, many runs are closed and there's usually no compensating reduction or refund in the price of ski-lift passes.

It's advisable to leave the top resorts to the experts and frequent some of the smaller, cheaper areas, until you're sufficiently skilled and fit enough to take full advantage of the more difficult runs. That isn't to say that the bigger, more expensive resorts, don't provide good value for money. A top resort may offer up to ten times the number of lifts and prepared runs (*pistes*) than a small resort, while charging 'only' an extra 50 to 100 per cent for a ski-lift pass.

A day's skiing for a family of four, including the cost of travel, ski-lift passes and food and drinks, costs around CHF 300-400 in an average resort, but can be much higher. However, many small and medium-size resorts – listed on the Switzerland Tourism website (🖥 www.myswitzerland.com – family-friendly ski passes) – offer family ski lift packages enabling children to ski free, with the total cost for two parents and two to three children not exceeding CHF 150 (often lower and may also include lunch). Sometimes there are restrictions or limitations, e.g. only available on Saturdays, but generally there are no restrictions.

In many areas, local bus companies organise day trips to ski resorts (usually on Sundays) and make stops in local towns to pick up skiers. They're reasonably priced and include a ski-lift pass. Swiss railways also offer special day-trip excursions which include a ski-lift pass (*Snow'n'Rail*). All large and many smaller resorts provide baby-sitting services or a ski nursery school, although most ski schools won't accept children below the age of three. Contact Switzerland Tourism for information (see page 211) or resort tourist offices directly (most have websites).

Accommodation in ski resorts is more expensive during holiday periods (Christmas, New Year and Easter), when the pistes are crowded. During public and school holiday periods the crowds of schoolchildren may drive you crazy, both on and off-piste, particularly when queuing for ski-lifts (Swiss children aren't taught to queue and are born queue jumpers). Some resorts provide floodlit pistes in the evenings, but make sure that you check what time the lights go out or you could find yourself skiing in the dark!

It's unlikely, but not impossible, to have your ski equipment stolen in Switzerland, although it's common in some of Switzerland's neighbouring countries. The price of new skis purchased in Switzerland often includes a year's insurance against theft or damage, or you can insure them separately for around CHF 20-30 a year. Rental skis include mandatory theft insurance.

☑ SURVIVAL TIP

Take good care of your expensive equipment wherever you are, and when you must leave it unattended, mix your skis and poles with those of your friends (most people won't ski with odd skis and poles!).

Learning to Ski or Snowboard

If you're a newcomer to downhill skiing, it's worthwhile enrolling in a ski school for a week or two to learn the basics – and it's much safer than simply launching yourself off the nearest mountain, particularly for other skiers. Good skiing is all about style and technique, and the value of good coaching cannot be over-emphasised. Private and group lessons are available in all resorts, for toddlers to senior citizens. Switzerland Tourism publish an *Index of Swiss Ski Schools* (see also 🖥 www.snowsports.ch). Many ski schools also provide snowboarding classes.

If you're a complete beginner, you may like to try the French short ski (*Kurzski, ski-évolutif/ ski moderne*) method of instruction using progressively longer skis. As a learning method for adults it's highly recommended by both former pupils and experts alike. As a beginner you want to be able to turn easily and you don't want to go too fast. Short skis provide both of these advantages, plus better balance, and allow beginners to start learning parallel turns immediately. Adult beginners start on skis of around one metre in length and usually progress to 1.6m skis within a week, by which time most are making 'passable' parallel turns. The main drawback is that the *ski-évolutif* method isn't taught in many resorts outside France. A similar method is widely taught in North America, where it's called the graduated length method (GLM).

Ski Exercises

It's advisable to perform some special ski exercises for at least a few weeks before taking to the pistes. This helps to increase your general flexibility and strength, and prepares your body for the unique demands of skiing. It also ensures that you won't ache quite so much after a day on the pistes. Special ski exercise classes are held in most cities and towns in Switzerland and shown on TV. Most ski books also contain recommended exercises.

 Caution

Grossly unfit skiers are a danger to everyone – not least themselves.

Insurance

Check that your family and visitors are fully insured for ski accidents, including helicopter rescue (see page 91). If you live and work in Switzerland, you're covered for ski accidents by your compulsory employee, non-occupational, accident insurance, but this doesn't include your family members. See also **Chapter 13**.

Piste Plan

Always obtain a piste plan on arrival in a resort and check the connecting runs, so as not to get lost or take the wrong runs. In Switzerland

runs are graded as follows: blue (easy), red (intermediate) and black (difficult). In Austria and France there are green-graded runs for beginners. Unfortunately plans aren't always easy to read. There's sometimes a lot of walking between lifts and what appears on the plan to be the top of a lift, may turn out to be the bottom. Without a piste plan it's possible to end up by mistake on one of those dreaded 'north face of the Eiger' blackest-of-black runs. A piste plan also helps beginners avoid T-bars when skiing on their own, although they can be shared with another skier. Swiss resorts have mostly T-bars or chair-lifts and few button (single tow) lifts.

Clothing

In addition to proper ski clothes (jacket, trousers and gloves), you may also need thermal underwear, silk inner gloves, silk socks, woolen hats and helmets. These may not sound too fashionable or glamorous, but are more welcome than the latest ski-wear fashions on freezing cold days – if you ski badly, you look like an idiot no matter what you're wearing! A one-piece ski suit is best for beginners, as it keeps out the snow when you fall on your behind. Lightweight clothes and gloves can be worn on warmer days (gloves should always be worn to protect your hands from injury).

Après ski boots with non-slip rubber soles are essential when walking on ice or snow, and are inexpensive.

Skin & Eye Protection

Your skin and eyes need protection from the sun and glare when skiing (snow blindness is rare, but not unknown). When skiing in bright sunlight, special ski sunglasses or goggles with side protection or mirror lenses are best. You can also buy ski goggles with interchangeable lenses, for sunny and overcast days, as you may need them whether the sun is shining or not. Buy the best you can afford. A loop connected to sunglasses and hung around your neck helps prevent their loss in a fall and is also handy when you aren't wearing them. However, don't wear dark sunglasses or goggles that inhibit your vision in poor visibility, e.g. when it's snowing, as it makes it's difficult to see the bumps and dips. You can have a nasty accident if you hit an unseen bump (or a fellow skier) at speed!

It's easy to get sunburned at high altitudes, even in winter. Use a total block-out cream for your lips, nose, ears

and the rest of your face, even when it doesn't appear particularly bright. Apply often and liberally, particularly to lips.

Safety

Safety is of paramount importance in any sport, but it's particularly important when skiing, where the possibility of injury is ever present (one in every ten participants suffers an injury at some time). In recent years, skiing-related deaths and serious injuries have increased considerably as slopes have become more crowded and skiers have looked further afield for more daring and dangerous thrills. Accident insurance (see page 178) is essential when skiing anywhere! Safety brochures for skiers are available from the Swiss Bureau for the Prevention of Accidents (see **Accidents** below).

 Caution

A number of skiers die and thousands are injured each year in ski accidents in Switzerland.

Equipment

While it's unnecessary to wear the latest ski fashions, it's important to have suitable, secure and safe equipment – particularly bindings and boots. Although the latest high-tech bindings are a great help in avoiding injuries, the correct settings are vital. They should be set so that in the event of a fall, you part company with your skis before your leg (or part thereof) parts company with your body. Beginners' bindings must be set so that they release fairly easily, but not so easily that they open each time a turn is attempted. Have your skis and bindings serviced each season by a qualified ski mechanic (any ski shop can do this). If you're using hired or second-hand skis, double check that the bindings are set correctly and that they release freely in all directions. If you aren't entirely happy with hired equipment, never hesitate to request adjustments or an exchange.

Young children should wear safety helmets at all times as soon as they're able to use normal pistes and lifts. A ski helmet is obligatory if a child is in ski school (in recent years an increasing number of adults have also started wearing helmets).

Ability & Injuries

Try to ski with people of the same standard as yourself or with an experienced skier who's willing to ski at your pace, and don't be in too much of a hurry to tackle those black runs. Stop skiing and rest when you feel tired. A sure sign is when you keep falling over for no apparent reason. Most accidents happen when skiers are tired.

If you injure yourself, particularly a knee, stop skiing and seek medical advice as soon as possible. If you attempt to ski with an injury or before an injury has had time to heal, you risk aggravating it and doing permanent damage. It's better to ride down in the cable-car than on a stretcher!

Weather

Unless you're an expert skier, it's best to avoid skiing in bad weather and in poor snow conditions. When snow cover is poor or runs are icy, the danger of injury increases dramatically, particularly for beginners and intermediates who often find it difficult or impossible to control their skis. It also isn't much fun unless you're a fanatic!

Avalanche Warnings

NEVER ignore avalanche warnings (*Lawinengefahr, danger d'avalanches*), denoted by black and yellow flags or signs and warning lights, or attempt to ski on closed (*gesperrt, barré*) pistes or anywhere there's a danger of avalanches (reports are issued at tourist offices and resort websites). Avalanches on open pistes are extremely rare as overloaded slopes overlooking pistes are blasted with explosives to remove excess snow.

Don't ski or snowboard off-piste on your own or if you aren't an experienced off-piste skier; in an unfamiliar area you should hire an experienced local guide.

Each year around 25 skiers and snowboarders are killed in avalanches in the Alps, usually when skiing off-piste (although in recent years there have been a number of disasters involving chalets situated directly below mountains). You can buy a small radio transmitter, e.g. an avalanche transceiver, that helps rescuers locate you if you're buried in an avalanche (some also have a flashing light system). They're expensive, although sensible off-piste skiers consider their lives are worth the cost (they are mandatory equipment for participants in guided off-piste tours). You can also wear an ABS air balloon rucksack, which can be inflated like a car air-bag to protect you in the event of an avalanche, which are recommended by the Swiss Avalanche Research Association.

Avalanche bulletins are provided on service number ☎ 187 (CHF 0.50 plus 0.50 per minute) and the internet (🖥 www.slf.ch) for off-piste skiers and ski tourers.

Skiers who cause avalanches can be billed for the cost of rescue, damage to property and clean-up operations.

Restricted Areas

Only ski or snowboard where it's permitted. In some areas off-piste skiing is forbidden to protect plants and the wildlife habitat. Many animals are hibernating in winter and others need to preserve their precious reserves of fat to survive the winter. You won't help their chances of survival by frightening them.

Trees are planted in many areas to help prevent avalanches and are easily destroyed by careless skiers. Some areas, which are sign-posted, are designated as conservation areas for flora and fauna, and you can be fined for skiing there.

The Highway Code for Skiers & Snowboarders

As the ski slopes become more crowded, the possibility of colliding with a fellow skier has increased dramatically. Snowboarders have a reputation of being ruthless and leaving a trail of fallen skiers in their wake when speeding down the piste – snowboarders use a different line from skiers and need to take particular care. Happily, the result of most clashes is just a few bruises and dented pride, nevertheless the danger of serious injury is ever present. You cannot always protect yourself from the lunatic fringe. e.g. the crazy novice who skis way beyond his limits and the equally loony 'expert' who skis at reckless speeds with a total disregard for other skiers.

Serious head injuries can often be prevented by wearing a helmet – they are compulsory for children in ski schools – which are becoming more common for both children and adults. The following guidelines from the International Ski Federation's (FIS) Code of Conduct for skiers may help you avoid an accident:

◆ **Respect for others:** A skier or snowboarder must behave in such a way that he neither endangers nor prejudices others.

◆ **Control of speed & skiing:** A skier or snowboarder must adapt his speed and way of skiing to his own personal ability, and to the prevailing conditions of terrain and weather.

◆ **Control of direction:** A skier or snowboarder coming from above, whose dominant position allows him a choice of paths, must take a direction which assures the safety of the skier below.

◆ **Overtaking:** A skier or snowboarder should always leave a wide enough margin for the overtaken skier or snowboarder to make his turn.

◆ **Crossing the piste:** A skier or snowboarder entering or crossing a piste must look up and down to make sure that he can do so without danger to himself or to others. The same applies after stopping.

◆ **Stopping on the piste:** Unless absolutely necessary, a skier or snowboarder must avoid making a stop on the piste, particularly in narrow passages or where visibility is restricted. If a skier or snowboarder falls, he must clear the piste as quick as possible.

◆ **Climbing:** A climbing skier or snowboarder must keep to the side of the piste and in bad visibility, keep off the piste altogether. The same goes for a skier or snowboarder descending on foot.

Accidents

If you're hit by a reckless skier or snowboarder you can sue for damages or can equally be sued if you cause an accident. There's no foolproof way of avoiding accidents (apart from avoiding skiing altogether). Obey the FIS code (above) and make sure that you're well insured for both accidents and private liability (see **Chapter 13**). If you're involved in an accident or collision you should do the following:

◆ obtain the names and addresses (local and permanent) of all people involved and any witnesses;

◆ report the accident to the local police within 24 hours. This is essential if you wish to make a claim against an insurance policy or a third party;

◆ make notes and diagrams of the accident scene while it's still fresh in your mind;

◆ notify your insurers as soon as possible and forward any documentation to them.

If you suspect any equipment was at fault, e.g. a ski binding, retain it and note the precise type, size, adjustments and nature of the fault. If you work in Switzerland, your compulsory accident insurance covers you against ski accidents. However, it doesn't include cover for accidents caused by you, for which you need private liability insurance (see page 184) with a minimum insured sum of CHF 2m.

The Swiss Commission for the Prevention of Accidents on Ski-Runs and Cross-Country Trails (☎ 031 390 22 30, 🖥 www.skus.ch), publish a booklet in English entitled *Guidelines for the Conduct of Skiers and Snowboarders.*

Snow & Weather Conditions

Before you set out or plan a ski trip, it's wise to check the snow conditions and weather forecast, as it isn't much fun skiing in a blizzard, rain, freezing cold or bad visibility – or when there's very poor snow coverage. When snow cover is poor, many runs are closed, particularly those down to the valley or bottom station, and you must endure a lot of queuing and walking between lifts. Many resorts have installed snow-making machinery on runs and are able to guarantee that a limited number of runs are open. However, when snow conditions are bad in most areas, overcrowding can be horrendous.

Most resorts have websites where the latest information (*Schnee- und Pisten-bericht, bulletin d'enneigement*) is shown, including snow conditions, number of runs open, local weather (and possible a 7-day forecast), the number of lifts in operation and even webcams where you can see the conditions for yourself. Snow conditions are also available via general websites, e.g. 🖥 www.skiinfo.ch and www.myswitzerland.com.

Swiss weather forecasting is usually highly accurate – one of the best forecasts is provided by the Swiss meteorological service (🖥 www.meteoschweiz.ch).

Ski Clubs

You may find that it's worthwhile joining a ski club affiliated to the Swiss-Ski Federation (☎ 031-950 61 11, 🖥 www.swiss-ski.ch). This usually entitles you to an Swiss-Ski booklet; skiing insurance; ski-lift vouchers; hotel and other discounts; membership of your local cantonal ski association; and a subscription to the *Swiss-Ski* magazine (in German), the official organ of Swiss-Ski.

All towns, most villages and many companies have their own ski clubs, and in some cities there are also international ski clubs for expatriates. Groups of ten or more skiers usually receive a reduction on the cost of an individual day pass. A schedule of Swiss downhill skiing, cross-country and skating races (*Terminkalender Breitensport, calendrier du ski populaire*) is published annually by the Swiss-Ski Federation (see above).

Cross-country Skiing

Cross-country skiing (*Ski-Langlauf/Ski-Wandern, ski de fond/ski nordique*) doesn't have the glamorous jet-set image of alpine skiing, but nevertheless it's a popular sport in Switzerland. It appeals to both young and old, particularly those whose idea of fun is a million miles away from hurtling down a hill at 100kph (62mph), with a thousand metre drop on one side and a glacier on the other. Cross-country skiing can be enjoyed at any pace and over any distance, and therefore has great attractions for both those who aren't very fit and keen athletes. It can be exhilarating, particularly if you make the effort to learn the correct technique and persevere beyond the beginner's stage.

Cross-country skiing rates highly as a total body workout and is claimed by many to be one of the best of all forms of exercise (which is why most gyms have cross trainer machines).

Compared with alpine skiing, cross-country skiing has the advantages of cheaper equipment, lower costs, fewer broken bones and no queues. No expensive ski-lift passes are necessary, although skiers must buy a CHF 100 annual Cross-Country Pass entitling them to use over 5,500km (3,500mi) of tracks throughout Switzerland (🖥 www.loipen-schweiz. ch). Alternately, a local seasonal card can be purchased for around CHF 35 or a day pass for CHF 6 per day. Children (under 16) ski for free. Essential equipment costs as little as CHF 500 for skis, bindings, poles, boots and gloves. No special clothing is necessary apart from gloves and boots, provided you have a warm pullover and tracksuit. You can, of course, buy more expensive equipment and special clothing.

Prepared cross-country trails (classical as well as skating style), usually consisting of two sets of tracks (*Langlauf-Loipen, pistes de ski de fond*), are laid on specially prepared and sign-posted routes, where you ski in the direction of the arrows. There are cross-country ski trails in most winter ski resorts in Switzerland, Austria and Germany, although there are fewer in France and Italy. You can enjoy cross-country skiing anywhere there's sufficient snow, although using prepared trails is easier than making your own, as is usually done in Scandinavia. The total number of kilometres of cross-country trails open in Swiss resorts is shown on resort websites. Many resorts have floodlit tracks for night skiing.

An annual booklet published by Swiss-Ski, *Langlauf, Ski de fond*, is a must for all keen cross-country skiers. It contains information on all aspects of cross-country skiing (in English, French and German), a complete list of all Swiss cross-country skiing circuits, and race information. It's available free from most sports shops or by post from the Swiss-Ski Federation (🖳 www.swiss-ski.ch).

As with downhill skiing, you should try cross-country skiing with rented equipment before buying your own, as you may find that you don't like it.

SKI VARIATIONS & OTHER WINTER SPORTS

When you're bored with all those 'easy' black pistes, you may like to try something different. For information about the following winter sports, contact Switzerland Tourism (see page 211).

◆ **Bob-sleighing:** For the really brave or completely loony sensation-seeker (the famous Cresta run in St. Moritz is the world's fastest and most dangerous). Ladies aren't allowed to participate – unless they masquerade as men!

◆ **Curling:** Curling is a bit like lawn bowls on ice, except that the 'balls' (called rocks) are flat with a handle on top. Curling rinks are usually located indoors, although some resorts have outdoor rinks.

◆ **Dog sledding & horse racing:** Dog sledding and horse racing are popular in some resorts, although they generally aren't for novices. 'White Turf' horse races draw huge crowds for the traditional races on the frozen lake of St. Moritz (🖳 www.whiteturf.ch). There are also horse races in Arosa each winter.

◆ **Freestyle skiing:** A winter sport for circus acrobats and high-board divers. Involves doing a triple somersault on skis – among other things. For the brave and accomplished skier. Spectacular but can be dangerous if you land on your head.

◆ **Heli-skiing:** No, you aren't pulled along by a helicopter, but are deposited by it in inaccessible places at around 4,000m (ca. 13,000ft) from where you ski home (or get lost). For proficient off-piste skiers only. Heli-skiers in Switzerland must be accompanied by a licensed mountain guide.

◆ **Ice hockey:** A popular sport in Switzerland with both competitors (five leagues) and spectators. If only the Swiss could come up with a decent national team! (Although they did manage to beat the Canadians at the 2006 Olympic Games!)

◆ **Ice skating:** Many towns and winter holiday resorts have outdoor ice rinks open from around October to April. There are also some 90 indoor rinks, many of which are open all year round. Take extra care when skating on natural ponds and always observe warning signs. Rescue equipment (long poles) and alarms are usually prominently displayed.

◆ **Luge:** A single seat, feet-first toboggan used on a bob-sleigh run at break-neck speeds. Skeleton is a head-first (kamikaze position) version of the luge, hence the name.

◆ **Monoskiing:** Mono-skiing equipment consists of one wide ski with two normal ski bindings side by side pointing in the direction of the board. Skiers use normal ski poles and wear ski boots. It usually requires good skiing ability, although it may appeal to those who have difficulty distinguishing between their left and right feet. See also **Snowboarding** (box).

◆ **Off-piste skiing:** Off-piste skiing in deep powder snow is what most advanced skiers dream about. It can be dangerous and aspirants should be able to handle black runs with confidence. See also **Avalanche Warnings** above.

◆ **Ski-bobbing:** This is similar to bicycling on snow and sometimes called snow-biking. Provides plenty of exhilarating, down-to-earth thrills and spills. Ski-bobs can be hired in over 70 resorts, some of which have specially marked runs. However, some resorts ban them due to the danger to skiers.

◆ **Ski hang-gliding & paragliding:** If jumping off a mountain with a parachute or hang-glider (while wearing skis) is your idea of fun, these may appeal to you.

◆ **Ski-joring:** Skiers are pulled along by galloping horses at hair-raising speeds. An old 'sport' which is quite rare these days (mad horses and even madder skiers being in short supply).

◆ **Ski touring:** This involves walking uphill and skiing or snowboarding downhill. Requires good off-piste skiing ability, excellent physical condition, and special skis (skins) or snow shoes and other equipment. It should never be attempted without a guide, unless you're an expert.

Snowboarding

A sport which involves the use of a snowboad attached to the rider's feet using a special boot set into a mounted binding at right or left angles, depending on the boarder's preference. The binding doesn't release in a fall and no ski poles are used.

◆ **Snow rafting:** Participants sit in a rubber boat (or rubber tube), while it rockets down pistes at 100kph (62mph). It's best attempted on controlled and segregated slopes, where there are no trees or other obstacles (such as people). A dangerous 'sport' which is banned in many resorts.

◆ **Speed skiing:** For skiers who never got to lesson three – how to turn. Ski at up to 200kph/124mph (if you dare). Popular in France (enough said).

◆ **Telemark skiing:** The Swiss Telemark Ski Association (🖳 www.telemark.ch) was founded in 1989, since when it has enjoyed increasing popularity. Telemark is characterised by 'bending down', which is enabled by the free heel and the mobile shoe, dropping the knee and lifting the heel. Courses are provided in the larger ski resorts, but bear in mind that it isn't easy to learn.

◆ **Tobogganing & Sledding:** Many resorts have special runs reserved for tobogganing, while in others, runs may also be open to skiers. Great fun for children, both young and old (i.e. adults). Sometimes runs are floodlit during the evening. A brochure is available from Switzerland Tourism listing runs of up to 11km/7mph.

Some of the above sports are limited to a small number of resorts or are restricted to particular pistes or areas. If they don't provide enough challenges, you can always try skiing down the Matterhorn as a Japanese Kamikaze skier did in 1985 (he survived). Another Japanese (who else?) skied (he actually fell most of the way) down Mount Everest with a parachute, which was supposed to slow him down. He also lived to tell the tale and they even made a film of it – otherwise nobody would have believed it!

SWIMMING

There are heated indoor (*Hallenbad, piscine couverte*) and outdoor (*Freibad, piscine en plein air*) swimming pools in most Swiss towns, a total of around 1,000 when both public and private (e.g. hotel) pools are included (many hotel pools are open to non-residents for a small fee). Most towns and villages catering for winter sports and summer hiking have indoor swimming pools. The entrance fee is usually around CHF 7-10 and facilities may include wave machines, saunas, solariums, table tennis, mini-golf and games areas.

You can also swim at over 170 locations in Swiss lakes (*Strandbad, piscine naturelle*) from around June to September. The water temperature of the largest lakes is shown on the internet (e.g. 🖳 www.meteoswiss.admin.ch and www.wiewarm.ch – the latter site also shows opening times of both lakes and pools). There are even a few areas set aside for nude sunbathing, although men and women are usually segregated and all are hidden from prying eyes.

There are a number of large indoor swimming centres and water parks in Switzerland containing hot water pools, sulphur baths, thermal whirlpools, connecting indoor and outdoor pools, wave machines, huge water slides, solariums and saunas (some have mixed saunas). Swimming centres have restaurants and are open daily from around 10am to 10pm. The entrance fee is high, e.g. CHF 25 or more for just four hours, although they make a pleasant change from the local pool for a special day out. Spas throughout Switzerland (see page 169) have hot-spring pools where you may swim gently or relax in the water. Children aren't, however, always admitted. Most swimming pools and clubs organise swimming lessons (all levels from beginner to fish) and run life-saving courses.

WATERSPORTS

All watersports including sailing, windsurfing, water-skiing, rowing, canoeing and subaquatic sports are popular in Switzerland. This is hardly surprising as the country has over 1,600 natural lakes (totalling some 13,355,100km^2 or 330,000 acres) and 32,000km (20,000mi) of rivers. Boats and equipment can be hired on most lakes and rescue services are provided, although they aren't usually free. Instruction is available for most watersports on major lakes and in holiday centres. Unfortunately there's one small problem with sailing and windsurfing in Switzerland: a lack of wind, particularly in summer. The Urnersee and the Silvaplaner lake in Engadin are, however, known for their strong winds and also offer kite and wake-surfing.

> Being landlocked hasn't held Switzerland back in the world yachting arena, and the Swiss have won the prized America's Cup on two occasions: in Auckland in 2003 and in Valencia in 2007; they lost to the US in the 2010 final.

Rowing and canoeing are possible on most lakes and rivers. The Rotsee lake near Lucerne is the most famous Swiss rowing venue and has one of the most beautiful courses in the world. Wetsuits are recommended for windsurfing, water-skiing and subaquatic sports, even during the summer. White-water rafting is an exciting and popular sport and is taught and practised in many areas. Those who like something even more adventurous (and even wetter) may wish to try canyoning (or canyoneering), which involves negotiating canyons using a variety of techniques which may include walking, scrambling, climbing, abseiling and swimming.

You must pass a written test before you can use a motorboat with a motor size of 6kW (7.5 PS) or a sailing boat with a sail area of over 15m^2 (161ft^2). Boats must usually have a mooring and cannot be stored at home except in a garage or boathouse. Information regarding river rafting, kayaks and sailing schools is available from Switzerland Tourism.

Comprehensive information about sailing in Switzerland is available from Swiss Sailing (🖥 www.swiss-sailing.ch). If you're interested in becoming a part-owner of a sailboat in Switzerland, see Sailcom (🖥 www.sailcom.ch).

Be sure to observe all warning signs on lakes and rivers!

OTHER SPORTS

The following is a selection of other sports with a popular following in Switzerland:

Athletics

Most Swiss towns and villages have local athletics clubs and organise local competitions and sports days.

Ballet & Jazz Ballet

Hardly sports, but nonetheless excellent exercise. Dance, training and exercise classes are provided in many towns throughout Switzerland and are also organised by gymnasiums. Jazz ballet classes are also organised by Migros Club Schools (see **Day & Evening Classes** on page 118).

Billiards & Snooker

Many hotels, bars and sports clubs have billiard or snooker tables and there are a few billiards' clubs in the larger towns. English-style snooker isn't played in public clubs in Switzerland.

Bungee Jumping

If your idea of fun is jumping out of a cable car or a hot-air balloon with an elastic rope attached to your body to prevent you merging with the landscape, then bungee jumping may be just what you're looking for.

Darts

Not really a sport, darts can be played at any of the Pickwick chain of pubs (🖥 www.pickwick.ch) in Switzerland and other English- and Irish-style pubs.

Football (Soccer)

Between mid-July and mid-June, the ten football (soccer) clubs in the first division (Swiss Super League) play each other at home and away twice.

The team finishing top is crowned champions, while the bottom team is demoted to the second division (Swiss Challenge League) and the team finishing ninth has to beat the team that finished second in the Challenge League (ten teams) to stay in the Super League. Most major Swiss cities and towns have either a first or second division football team. Many are professional and of a similar standard to teams in the English or German second or third divisions. Most towns and villages have amateur football clubs for all ages and standards.

Gymnasiums & Health Clubs

There are gymnasiums and health clubs in most towns with tons of expensive bone-jarring, muscle-wrenching apparatus. Costs are around CHF 100 a month or CHF 1,000 a year, although they can be reduced by taking advantage of off-peak reductions and some health insurance companies will pay part of the membership fee. Many 1st class hotels have fitness rooms.

Gymnastics

An extremely popular sport in Switzerland – gymnastic clubs abound in all areas, even in small towns and villages.

Handball

Played indoors on a pitch similar to a five-a-side football pitch. Handball players pass the ball around by hand and attempt to throw it into a small goal.

Hockey

Called land hockey to avoid confusion with the more popular ice hockey. 'Uni-hockey' (🖥 www.swissunihockey.ch) or indoor hockey is a popular sport in Switzerland, with men's and women's National A and B leagues, as well as many amateur leagues.

Horse Riding & Racing

Popular but expensive – there are some 400 riding schools and equestrian centres in Switzerland. Some resorts organise cross-country riding holidays. For further information, contact the Swiss Equestrian Federation (🖥 www.fnch.ch). There are horse race meetings in Switzerland from March until November, with a meeting almost every weekend. For information and race dates, see 🖥 www.turf.ch.

Martial Arts

Kung Fu, Judo, Karate and other martial arts are taught and practised in most towns. There are over 300 judo clubs in Switzerland. Timid children are sometimes encouraged to learn judo to combat school bullies.

In-line Skating & Skate-boarding

Switzerland has an active rollerblading (in-line skating) community and 1,100km (700mi) of paved skating paths, including three national skating routes and eleven regional routes (see 🖥 www.skatingland.ch). Inline skaters also join in the 'slow up' events and in special Monday night skating events (see 🖳 www.nightskate.ch). Many cities and towns have skate board parks with ramps and obstacles; for further information, contact the Swiss Skateboard Association (🖳 www.swiss-skateboard.ch).

Rugby

A surprisingly popular sport in Switzerland, where there are clubs in all the major cities (yet another 'habit' they picked up from the British – along with skiing).

Shooting

Shooting ranges abound in Switzerland and shooting is particularly popular on Sunday mornings to prevent you having a lay-in. Annual target shooting is compulsory for all Swiss men as part of their military service. Most towns and villages have a local shooting federation which organises local competitions. Crossbow shooting is also popular.

Ten-pin Bowling

Ten-pin bowling centres can be found in all major Swiss cities. Some hotels and restaurants have ten-pin bowling and skittle (*Kegelbahn, jeu de quilles*) alleys, which are usually tucked away in the cellars.

Swiss Sports

The Swiss also have their own Alpine sports (including cow fighting!), which are usually incomprehensible to anyone but a Swiss mountain man. These include stone throwing (*Steinstossen* or *Steinwerfen, le lancer de la pierre*), traditional Swiss wrestling (*Schwingen, la lutte à la calotte*) and the strangest of all, *Hornussen*. In *Hornussen* a puck-like plastic object (the *Hornuss*) is placed at the tip of a curved rail planted in the soil. The striker hits the *Hornuss* with a whip-like cane around two metres in length, while the catchers (strategically placed in the field) attempt to bat it away with large wooden boards on poles before it hits the ground. *Hornussen* isn't expected to become an Olympic sport any time in the near future.

Miscellaneous

Many foreign sports and pastimes have a group of expatriate fanatics in Switzerland including cricket, American football, baseball, boccia, boules, croquet, polo and softball. For more information enquire at community and tourist offices, embassies and consulates, and social clubs.

Sport for the Disabled

Switzerland has an extensive sports programme for the disabled, organised by the Swiss Association for Handicapped Sport (*Plusport Behindertenspor Schweiz, Sport Handicap Suisse*, Chriesbaumstr. 6, CH-8604 Volketswil, ☎ 044 908 45 00, 🖳 www.plusport.ch).

17.
SHOPPING

Shopping in Switzerland is among the best in the world, although you may sometimes wonder whether the Swiss are all millionaires and just what they do with all those gold watches, diamond necklaces and fur coats. Actually millionaires make up only half the population of Switzerland – the rest are foreigners. Joking aside, it has been conservatively estimated that Switzerland has over 100,000 millionaires (including many foreigners) and the highest level of per capita accumulated wealth in the world. There are, however, a few shops that cater to the needs of poor foreigners and English is spoken in most major towns and tourist areas. Most Swiss shops accept Euros (and gold bars).

There's generally no bargaining in Switzerland, although if you plan to spend a lot of money in one store you may wish to ask for a discount (except in department stores and supermarkets). Value added tax (VAT) is always included and there are no hidden extras: the advertised price is the price you pay. Swiss shopkeepers are usually scrupulously honest and most shops will exchange goods or give refunds without question. The Swiss customer is highly critical and demands top quality, durability and after sales service – but not necessarily value for money. However, although prices may be higher than in many other countries, goods may be of superior quality and therefore comparisons aren't always valid.

Cartels are common and aren't illegal unless they're shown to be harmful. Consequently, the prices of some goods and services can be up to 50 per cent higher than in some EU countries, which makes shopping in Switzerland's neighbouring countries rewarding. Sales and prices of most goods in Switzerland are strictly regulated and prices for branded goods are often fixed to protect small shop owners. Stores can, however, sell branded goods under their own name at lower prices or sell goods at reduced prices during official sales, e.g. in January and July. Many Swiss prefer to shop in their local village or town and happily pay higher prices in return for the convenience of shopping locally (and to support local businesses).

There are large indoor shopping centres in all areas where you can do all your shopping under one roof, and cities and most large towns usually have a traffic-free shopping street or town centre. Many Swiss manufacturers provide factory shops where you can shop at generous discounts, although opening hours are limited and some shops are open only a few days a week or month.

Most shops hold sales (*Sonderverkauf/ Ausverkauf, soldes*) in January and July, when goods are available at reduced prices and if you plan to have a shopping spree, it's definitely worth waiting for the sales. Around Christmas time, storage areas are provided in many towns, where shoppers can leave their purchases free of charge (while they buy more). Some major cities, e.g. Zurich, publish monthly shopping guides. Finally, don't panic if you're pounced on by an army of shop assistants – it's just the natives way of being friendly. If you don't want their help, tell them that you're just looking and hopefully they'll go away.

For those who aren't used to buying articles with metric measures and continental sizes, a list of comparative weights and measures are included in **Appendix D**.

American Women's Clubs (see **Appendix A**) and other women's clubs are an excellent source of shopping information.

SHOPPING HOURS

Shopping hours in Switzerland are usually from around 8 or 9am to 6.30 or 6.45pm, Tuesdays to Fridays, and from 8am to between 4 and 6pm on Saturdays. On Mondays, many shops close in the morning and open from between 1 and 2pm until around 6.30 or 6.45pm, although some are closed all day. Many towns have late night shopping until 8 or 9pm on Wednesday, Thursday or Friday (in Zurich, many shops stay open until 8pm from Mondays to Fridays), and many shopping centres also have extended shopping hours. In smaller towns, all shops and businesses close for lunch, e.g. from noon until 2pm.

Local shops, for example those located in villages, close for a half or full day a week (usually Monday) and may close earlier on a Saturday, e.g. 2pm. It's customary for certain businesses to be closed on the same day; for example, most hairdressers (Friseur, coiffeur) are closed on Mondays. Shops generally close at 4 or 5pm the day before a public holiday, even when it's a late shopping day.

All shops are closed on Sundays except bakeries, some of which open from around 10am to noon. However, stores are permitted to open on six Sundays or official holidays a year, and stores are often open on a few Sundays in the run up to Christmas. Geneva and Zurich airports have shopping centres open from 8am to 8pm daily, and some motorway (Autobahn, autoroute) shopping centres are open every day of the year, with the exception of Christmas Day. In and around most main railway stations (Hauptbahnhof, gare centrale) in the main cities there are shops with extended opening times (e.g. 7am to 10pm), including Sundays and public holidays.

In recent years, Migros and Co-op have added mini-markets to their petrol stations – open seven days a week – where you can also buy fresh bread. Grocery stores near border crossings are usually open on Sundays, and shops in many tourist resorts (including the 'tourist' areas of some major cities) are open on Sundays and public holidays throughout the season.

SHOPPING CENTRES & MARKETS

There are many large modern indoor shopping centres (Einkaufszentrum, centre commercial) in Switzerland, which often have over 100 shops including supermarkets, department stores, furniture stores, restaurants, banks and a post office, plus many of the small specialist shops you would expect to find in an average town. The main attractions, in addition to the wide choice of shops, are protection from inclement weather and free parking, meaning you can simply wheel your purchases to your car (parking is expensive and difficult in most city and town centres, particularly on Saturdays). To encourage the use of public transport, some shopping centres charge a small fee for parking, perhaps offering the first hour free.

Shopping centre stores periodically issue books of discount coupons (Einkaufsbon/Bezugsschein, bon d'achat) to attract customers.

Most towns have markets (Markt/marché) on various days of the week, with Wednesdays and Saturdays the most popular. These vary from fruit and vegetable markets to flea/curiosity (second-hand goods) markets. In major cities there are markets on most days of the week. Food markets usually open around 6am and may close as early as 11am, while curiosity markets often operate from 10am to 4pm or even until 9pm in summer. Check with local tourist or information offices.

SUPERMARKETS

Many foreign foods can be found in local supermarkets (Supermarkt, supermarché) if you look hard enough, but don't overlook the many delicious local foods on offer. One of the advantages of living in central Europe is being able to sample the bewildering choice of continental food and beverages on offer. Don't despair if you cannot find your favourite foods, as there are many other delicacies available. The German, French and Italian-speaking parts of Switzerland all offer excellent regional and ethnic specialities. Most department stores sell imported foods, including Globus, Jelmoli and Manor (see **Department & Chain Stores** below), and all major towns have a variety of delicatessens and imported food shops.

However, don't expect the bewildering range and choice of convenience and packaged foods that you find in American and British supermarkets – in fact, in some regards, shopping is Swiss supermarkets is like going back 20 years when compared with UK and US stores (although this isn't necessarily a bad thing!).

Among the best value-for-money supermarkets are Aldi, Co-op, Denner Discount (particularly for wine, beer, cigarettes and perfumes – now owned by Migros), Lidl, Migros and Spar, all of which have branches throughout Switzerland. Prices in village shops are generally higher than in

mondo.ch for information) on their labels, which can be collected and exchanged for books, pictures, games, etc.

Migros offers regular customers a client reward scheme, whereby you receive a client 'cumulus' card (*Cumulus-Karte, carte cumulus*) and earn one point for each franc spent. Every three months you receive a booklet with special discount offers and vouchers worth CHF 0.01 per point collected, therefore effectively you receive 1 per cent discount on your purchases. The Co-op has a similar scheme called 'Supercard' where you collect points and benefit from discounts on specific articles in their 'Supercard' catalogue or receive a cash rebate on any item in stores. The cashier will usually ask if you would like to pay with your points (or pay part of the sum in points) if she sees that you have several francs worth of points.

Most supermarkets have a coffee bean grinding machine for customers' use. If you live in a farming community, you can buy unpasteurised milk from your local dairy by the bucket full (you supply the container). It's cheaper than buying milk by the carton from a supermarket, but it should be boiled before use. Many farms sell potatoes and other vegetables in bulk and allow you to pick your own fruit during the harvest season.

Supermarkets sell beer, soft drinks and mineral water by the crate, where you pay a deposit on the crate and bottles, which are usually returnable. Many people also have drinks delivered to their homes, rather than struggle home with heavy crates from the supermarket. Ask your neighbours about deliveries.

Teenagers must be aged 16 to buy beer and 18 to buy wine and spirits. Stores are obliged to check IDs and risk huge fines if they don't comply. The police carry out regular checks by sending under-aged teens in to buy alcohol; if they succeed the store is prosecuted and fined.

See also **Shopping Abroad** on page 250 and **Home Shopping** on page 249.

supermarkets, although many villages have a reasonably priced Volg store. The German grocery store giants Aldi (with around 130 Swiss stores) and Lidl (which has around 65 stores in Switzerland) have 'forced' the Co-op and Migros to introduce 'budget' lines (called 'Budget' by Migros and 'Bon Prix' by the Co-op).

Migros – one of the largest companies in Switzerland and a cooperative owned by its customers – generally has the lowest prices. It also has the most outlets and accounts for some 25 per cent of the total Swiss food sector. The Co-op (over 1,400 stores) has around 20 per cent of the food market, but a slightly larger share of the non-food market than Migros. Migros doesn't sell spirits, wine or tobacco (which was decreed by its founder), unless it's a rural branch with a special licence, although stores acquired by Migros such as Denner, Globus and Migrol all sell these products (for the time being at least). Migros and the Co-op operate mobile shops in some areas (ask your neighbours or enquire at your local branch). Most supermarkets do home deliveries, although you need an internet connection to place an order.

In common with many countries, most supermarkets in Switzerland provide only small plastic carrier bags, and charge from CHF 0.20-0.40 for larger, more sturdy paper bags and CHF 2.50-4.50 for quality reusable bags. You may wish to copy the Swiss and take a bag with you when shopping. Some supermarkets provide free boxes. Supermarket trolleys require a deposit of CHF 1 or 2, which ensures that most customers return them to a collection point rather than abandoning them in the car park (or taking them home). Name-brand food Items such as Gerber or Nestlé may have 'Mondo' stamps (see 🖥 www.

DEPARTMENT & CHAIN STORES

Switzerland has many excellent department (*Warenhaus, grand magasin*) and chain stores. One of the most famous and exclusive Swiss department stores is Globus (🖥 www.globus.ch), part of the Globus group which includes Herren Globus (menswear), Interio (home furnishings and furniture) and Office World – all of which have been owned by Migros (see below) since 1997. Manor (🖥 www.manor.ch) and Jelmoli (🖥 www.jelmoli.ch), including Innovation and Grand Passage, are department store chains with outlets in most Swiss cities and large towns. Manor are noted for their own-label, value-for-money clothes. Other department stores include Co-op City, Bon Genie and Loeb (Berne)

Switzerland has a number of DIY and hardware chains include Co-op Bau und Hobby, Hornbach and Obi (Migros), which in addition to hardware and household goods may also stock motoring accessories, bicycles and skis at competitive prices, and may also have a gardening centre where you can buy plants, pots, fertilizer, and garden and balcony furniture, etc.

Media Markt is a good source for inexpensive CDs and electronic equipment, while Inter Discount (🖳 www.interdiscount.ch) operate a large chain of stores selling hi-fi, video, photographic, radio, computer and other electronic equipment at competitive prices. Shop around for electronic and computer equipment, as prices for similar items vary considerably; don't forget to compare the guarantee period, which can vary from six months to two years.

Many department stores (e.g. Globus, Jelmoli, Loeb and Manor) provide account cards (store cards), some of which double as credit cards where the account balance can be repaid over a period. Card holders can take advantage of special offers and discounts. Some account cards can be used in other franchised stores and businesses, e.g. Globus and the Jelmoli J-Card.

Department stores and many smaller shops provide a free gift-wrapping service, particularly at Christmas time, and will deliver goods locally or send them by post (both within Switzerland and worldwide). Some stores have a 'Mister Minit' department, where on-the-spot shoe repairs, key cutting and engraving is done.

Migros

Migros (🖳 www.migros.ch) deserve a special mention for the high quality and range of its products (mostly own brand) and services, plus a reputation for limiting price increases. Migros stores come in three sizes, denoted by the number of Ms displayed outside:

Migros Stores	
M	Food store only
MM	Food and household goods, sometimes a restaurant
MMM	Complete department store selling food, household goods, furniture, clothes, hi-fi, electrical goods; sports equipment and often has a restaurant

Migros (plus some other stores) provide discounts on all purchases on the opening day of a new branch and on special anniversaries, plus many special offers. They also operate DIY stores, a travel agency, book and record stores (Ex Libris), furniture stores (Micasa) petrol stations and banking services (M-Bank, with ATMs in its supermarkets called M-Bancolinos), among other things. In addition to the M-card (Migros bank), Migros accepts credit and debit cards.

NEWSPAPERS, MAGAZINES & BOOKS

You may not have been much of a newspaper (*Zeitung, journal*), magazine (*Magazin/Zeitschrift, revue/périodique*) or book (*Buch, livre*) reader at home, but not being able to obtain your favourite English-language reading can be an unexpected deprivation abroad. However, newsagents in Switzerland stock among the widest selection of foreign newspapers in any country, although British and American newspapers and magazines are expensive. If you enjoy reading it's advisable to stock up on magazines and books before your arrival and during holidays abroad. However, large savings can be made by taking out subscriptions to magazines and newspapers (or reading then via the internet).

British and other European newspapers are sold at kiosks in most large towns. British daily newspapers are usually on sale at most railway stations the day after publication and at main railway stations and international airports on the day of publication. If you're hooked on British Sunday newspapers, they're available at many main railway stations and airports from around 11am on Sundays. To save a wasted journey, telephone first, as they sometimes don't arrive – if they aren't at your local railway station, they're usually also unavailable at airports. Note, however, that they are very expensive (and usually smaller).

Major foreign European newspapers are available on the day of issue in Basle, Geneva and Zurich and perhaps a day later in other cities. Some English-language daily newspapers are widely available on the day of publication including *USA Today*, the *International Herald Tribune* (printed in Zurich) and the *Wall Street Journal Europe* (printed in Frankfurt). Many English and foreign newspapers produce weekly editions including the British *International Express*, *Guardian Weekly* and *Weekly Telegraph*.

Many foreign newspapers can be purchased on subscription at a large saving on kiosk prices, although when sent airmail from within Europe, e.g. from the UK, they usually arrive a few days after publication.

English-language monthly magazines published in Switzerland include *Swiss News*, *Cream Magazine* and the *'Hello'* magazines of Basle, Berne and Zurich. Quarterlies include *AIR Magazine* and *Inside Switzerland*. Swiss news in English is also available online, e.g. Swissinfo (🖳 www.swissinfo.org.)

Most major international newspapers are available online – see 🖳 www.onlinenewspapers.com/switzerl.htm and www.world-newspapers.com/switzerland.html.

There are no national newspapers in Switzerland, but a wide variety of regional daily newspapers (over 100), weekly newspapers (over 350) and some 2,000 magazines, plus professional and specialist journals. Most cantons have an official daily or weekly newspaper or booklet containing a wealth of local information. It includes job vacancies, local and official events, meetings, church services, plus advertisements for houses and apartments (for rent and sale), small ads, restaurants and entertainment. A number of unsolicited free newspapers are delivered to homes.

There are many excellent English-language bookshops in Switzerland, including all the major cities, although the selection may be a bit limited when compared with a major bookshop in the UK or the US. However, most will order any English-language book in print at no extra cost. A small selection of English-language paperbacks is also usually available in Swiss bookshops and at news kiosks (which should all sell this book, but sadly don't!).

Book prices in Switzerland aren't fixed and many people also buy books by mail or abroad, e.g. from Amazon. Fixed prices were prohibited by the competition authority in 1999 and the Swiss voted against reintroducing price controls in a referendum in 2012.

FURNITURE & FURNISHINGS

Furniture (*Möbel, meubles*) is quite expensive in Switzerland compared with many other European countries. There is, however, a huge choice and the quality is invariably good. Exclusive modern and traditional furniture is available everywhere from a wide range of speciality home stores, although not everyone can afford the exclusive prices. At the upper end of the market is Roche Bobois (🖳 www.roche-bobois.com), with stores in Fribourg, Geneva, Lausanne and Zurich, selling designer furniture and soft furnishings, and Möbel Pfister (🖳 www.pfister.ch) with 20 stores, offering a huge choice with a wide quality and price range.

Ikea (🖳 www.ikea.com/ch) sells good quality, modern furniture for home assembly plus home furnishings, and has seven stores in Switzerland; Fly (🖳 www.fly.ch), owned by Manor, is an inexpensive but fashionable chain with 20 stores selling furniture and home accessories; while Conforama (🖳 www.conforama.ch) has around 15 stores selling furniture, home accessories, appliances and consumer electronics.

Two reasonably-priced national chains are Micasa (🖳 www.micasa.ch), part of the Migros group, which offers good value furniture (especially quality leather suites), and Manor (🖳 www.manor.ch), which is good for home furnishing and appliances. More upmarket is Interio (🖳 www.interio.ch), owned by Migros, specialising in modern designer furniture and accessories, with eight main stores (plus many smaller shops), and Globus (🖳 www.globus.ch, also owned by Migros), which is excellent for top quality home furnishings and household goods.

Note that you cannot buy furniture 'off the shelf' in most stores, particularly large items, and delivery usually takes four to eight weeks. Otto's (🖳 www.ottos.ch) is a discount chain store that also sells furniture – their inventory depends on what they can buy that's surplus, over-stock, in liquidation, etc., as they buy cheap and sell cheap. They also have a food section with many international items. Otto's have around 100 stores in Switzerland, of which 60 carry furniture. Lipo (🖳 www.lipo.ch) is another discount store selling surplus, over-stock and liquidation items, including furniture and furnishings. It has 13 stores in Switzerland (11 in northern Switzerland).

A rare exception to fixed prices is when you're buying a large quantity of furniture. Don't be reticent about asking for a reduction, as many stores will give you a 10 to 20 per cent discount. If you need to buy furniture in a hurry, bear in mind that delivery can take four to eight weeks (even from Ikea), depending on the manufacturer and supplier. Most shops don't keep much furniture in stock, and usually it's ordered direct from the manufacturer, who may deliver it to your home.

If you live near the border, shopping across the border for furniture is an option worth considering. You can also order furniture from catalogues, e.g. from France and Italy. It's also possible to rent furniture from a number of companies, such as In-Lease (☎ 041-310 7352, ⌨ www.in-lease.com, ✉ swiss@in-lease.com).

HOUSEHOLD GOODS & APPLIANCES

There are numerous stores selling home appliances and household goods in Switzerland, including many of those listed above. Among the best are Fust (⌨ www.fust.ch), owned by the Co-op, which has over 140 stores throughout the country selling cookers, washing machines, dryers, refrigerators, freezers, televisions and vacuum cleaners. Others include Conforama (⌨ www.conforama.ch), Globus (⌨ www.globus.ch), Micasa (⌨ www.micasa.ch) and Manor (⌨ www.manor.ch).

Large appliances such as cookers and refrigerators are usually provided in rented accommodation, although not always in French-speaking areas. Dishwashers are sometimes installed and private washing machines are rare in cheaper apartments. The standard width of kitchen appliances in Switzerland was traditionally less than across the rest of Europe and consequently domestic prices for Swiss-made dishwashers, washing machines and dryers were much higher than the European average (not deliberately, surely?). This is, however, no longer the case and you may also be able to tailor an older kitchen to accommodate foreign (or new Swiss) appliances.

Check the latest Swiss safety regulations before shipping white goods to Switzerland or buying them abroad, as they may need expensive modifications.

If you already own small household appliances, it's worthwhile bringing them to Switzerland as usually all that's required is a change of plug (but check first). If you're coming from a country with a 110/115V electricity supply, e.g. the US, then you'll need a lot of expensive transformers. Don't

bring a TV to Switzerland without checking its compatibility first, as TVs from the UK and the US won't work. Smaller appliances such as vacuum cleaners, grills, toasters and electric irons aren't expensive in Switzerland and are of excellent quality. Note that the Swiss generally take their lighting fixtures with them when moving home, therefore you'll need to buy these (and possibly hire an electrician to install them) in addition to buying lamps and shades.

If you need kitchen measuring equipment and cannot cope with decimal measures, you'll need to bring your own measuring scales, jugs, cups and thermometers. Foreign pillow sizes, e.g. British and American, aren't the same as Swiss sizes, and the Swiss use duvets and not blankets to keep warm in winter (besides central heating).

LAUNDRY & DRY CLEANING

All towns and shopping centres have dry cleaners (*Chemische Reinigung, nettoyage à sec/ chimique*), most of which do minor clothes repairs, invisible mending, alterations and dyeing. Express cleaning may mean a few days rather than hours, even at an outlet where cleaning is done on the premises. You usually pay in advance and it's quite expensive (better to buy washable clothes), particularly for leather and suede. Cleaning by the kilogramme with no pressing is possible in some places and much cheaper.

If you live near the French border it may be worthwhile using a French dry cleaner. Not only can they usually do the job much quicker they also charge considerably less.

There are self-service launderettes (*Wäscherei, blanchisserie*) in major towns and cities, but they're expensive at around CHF 10 to wash and dry a 5kg load. They are, however, rare in smaller towns, as (communal) washing machines are provided in most rented accommodation (the Swiss don't usually wash their dirty linen in public).

SECOND-HAND BARGAINS

Switzerland has an active second-hand (*gebraucht*, *occasion*) market, particularly in antiques, motor cars, gold and gem stones, although asking prices are generally higher than in other countries. There's a local second-hand furniture and junk store (*Brockenhaus, broccante*) in most towns, which may also have a Salvation Army (*Heilsarmee, armée du salut*) shop. These usually have restricted opening hours. Second-hand clothes shops are also popular. The Seefeld district in Zurich has a number of factory shops offering designer clothes at a fraction of the original price, and shops offering clothes of humbler (and cheaper) pedigree are available in many areas.

☑ SURVIVAL TIP

You can find bargain and second-hand goods on the internet at Glocals (🖥 www.glocals.com/classifieds/goods-for-sale), mainly for the Geneva region, Fundgrueb's Local website (🖥 www.local.ch), Gratis Inserate (🖥 www.gratis-inserate.ch) and the ubiquitous eBay (🖥 www.ebay.ch), although the Swiss prefer Ricardo (🖥 www.ricardo.ch).

There are weekly newspapers in some areas devoted to bargain hunters, including Fundgrueb (🖥 market.local.ch) and Inserate-Markt (🖥 www.inserate-markt.ch) in German-speaking areas, and Aux Trouvailles (🖥 www.auxtrouvailles.ch) in French-speaking areas. In Zug the amtsblatt (🖥 www.amtsblatt.ch) is packed with ads and if you're lucky you might even get something for free, e.g. a piano. Advertising is usually free, as advertisements are financed by newspaper sales, although you must buy a copy in order to place an advertisement. *Fundgrueb* also have a list of Swiss flea markets and fairs on their website (🖥 http://market.local.ch/de/m/fleamarkets).

The classified advertisements in local newspapers and adverts on shopping centre, supermarket and company bulletin boards may also prove fruitful. Many expatriate clubs and large companies publish monthly magazines or newsletters containing small ads, where everything from furniture to household apparatus and cars are advertised for sale. Sales are held in many towns and villages, e.g. for children's clothes and toys, usually in the spring and autumn.

FACTORY OUTLETS

Factory outlets/stores (*Fabrikläden/Fabrikverkauf, magasin d'usine*) abound in Switzerland. Sometimes they're just a small shop near the factory, e.g. Chocolat Halba 'Schoggihüsli' (🖥 www.schoggihuesli.ch), but my also consist of an entire outlet shopping centre, e.g. Fashion Fish in canton Aarau (🖥 www.fashionfish.ch).

The first outlet village in Switzerland – Alpenrheinvillage (🖥 www.alpenrheinvillage.ch) – opened in Landquart (near Chur in Graubunden) in 2009 and is open seven days a week.

A useful book is *Fabrikläden in der Schweiz 2012/13* (Factory Shops in Switzerland), published by Zeppelin, which is updated every few years.

HOME SHOPPING

Home shopping is quite popular in Switzerland and you can expect to receive some unsolicited mail-order catalogues with your junk mail. A few large department stores also publish mail-order catalogues, for example Jelmoli. Beware of some mail-order companies (e.g. selling CDs and books) who offer attractive gifts to members as an inducement to recruit new members. Prices are often high, particularly when compared with the special offers available in many shops, and it's costly to resign your membership – whether you've received any benefits or not. Make sure you know what you're signing.

Many major stores abroad publish catalogues and send goods anywhere in the world, for example Fortnum & Masons and Harrods in the UK. Many provide account facilities or payments can be made by credit card. Although many foreign mail-order companies won't send goods abroad, there's nothing to stop you obtaining catalogues from friends or relatives and ordering through them. Buying goods by mail-order from the US can result in large savings, even after paying shipping and VAT. Most mail-order companies also have websites where you can order goods.

INTERNET SHOPPING

Shopping via the internet has taken off in a big way in recent years and is now the fastest-growing form of retailing. Many Swiss companies offer internet shopping, but the real benefit comes when shopping abroad, when savings can be made on a wide range of products (you can buy virtually anything via the internet). However, when comparing prices take into account shipping costs, insurance, duty and VAT. Shopping on the internet is usually secure and even safer than shopping by phone or mail-order (in many cases the trader never even sees your credit card details). To find companies or products via the internet, simply use a search engine, e.g. 💻 www.google.ch for Swiss websites.

Online grocery shopping is provided by Co-op (💻 www.coop.ch) and Migros (Le Shop), who operate possibly the best online shop in Switzerland (💻 www.le-shop.ch). Migros offer a monthly billing service, collection from a store or next day delivery to your doorstep via the post express service and reasonable delivery fees (from CHF 7.90 up to a maximum of 15.90 depending on the value of your order) anywhere in Switzerland.

For DVDs try Cede (💻 www.cede.ch) or DVD Rental (💻 www.dvdrental.ch/en). Another useful website is 'toppreise' (💻 www.toppreise.ch – 'top prices'), a price comparison site for household electronics such as computers, TV, video, photo, etc., which shows the lowest prices. Shopping City (💻 www.shoppingcity.ch) is a website listing Swiss online shopping websites and Comparis (💻 http://en.comparis.ch) also shows price comparisons for many products and services.

If you purchase a small item by post from outside Switzerland, you may have to pay VAT (*MWSt, TVA*) at 8 per cent on delivery or at the post office on collection. Goods sent from EU countries (usually above a minimum value) should be free of local value added tax (see **Shopping Abroad** below). Gift parcels from abroad that don't exceed CHF 100 in value are exempt from VAT, but the value must be clearly marked in the customs declarations.

When you purchase a large item abroad and have it shipped to Switzerland by air freight, you should have it sent to your nearest airport. The receiving freight company will notify you when it has arrived. You must provide them with details of the contents and cost (an invoice copy) so that they can clear the goods through customs. They will deliver the goods to you with the bill for VAT and freight, payable on the spot, unless you make alternative arrangements.

The cost of air freight within Europe or even from North America is usually reasonable, however, the delivery and handling charges from a Swiss airport to your home can be as high as the air freight costs to Switzerland! If possible, it's a lot cheaper to collect goods yourself after they've been cleared through customs. Ensure that goods sent by air freight are fully insured. It's sometimes better to have goods sent by post (excluding local taxes), rather than importing them personally, when it's often a long process to obtain a refund.

SHOPPING ABROAD

Shopping abroad makes a pleasant change from all those boring Swiss shops full of luxury goods. It can also save you a lot of money and makes an enjoyable day out for the family. Don't forget your passports or identity cards, car documents, dog's vaccination documents and Euros. Most shops in border towns happily accept Swiss francs, but usually at a lower exchange rate than a bank.

Many foreigners and Swiss, particularly those living in border areas (e.g. Basle, Geneva and Lugano), take advantage of the generally lower prices outside Switzerland and do their weekly shopping abroad. Almost half the residents of Geneva – almost 40 per cent of whom are foreigners – regularly do the bulk of their shopping in France (don't forget to take some bags, as they no longer provide free paper or plastic bags), and overall around one-third of Swiss residents regularly shop abroad. Germany, France and Italy all have a lower cost of living than Switzerland.

A combination of lower prices, a favourable exchange rate and low Swiss VAT, mean that

savings can be made on many items, although savings on foodstuffs (and wine) are lower than they were before German giants Aldi and Lidl entered the Swiss market (and the Co-op and Migros introduced 'budget' lines). You can still save money when buying food abroad, although how much you save depends very much on where you shop and what you buy.

> ☑ SURVIVAL TIP
>
> Note that in all countries except Germany there are minimum purchase levels, below which you're unable to reclaim local VAT.

The best buys in Germany include electrical, electronic and photographic equipment; household appliances; computers and software; DVDs; optical goods and services; furniture; sporting goods; car parts, servicing and accessories; alcohol; and meat products. Buying a car abroad, e.g. in Germany or Italy, can also yield huge savings.

On weekdays, shopping hours are much the same as in Switzerland, except on Wednesdays, when shops usually close at 1pm. In many German towns bordering Switzerland, most shops are open until 6pm on Saturdays especially to cater for the influx of shoppers from Switzerland. Note, however, that prices may be slightly higher in border towns than in larger inland German cities.

Of course, not everything is cheaper abroad and it's wise to compare prices and quality before buying. Bear in mind that if you buy goods that are faulty or need repair, you may need to return them to the place of purchase, which could be a hassle with customs paperwork. Shops in border areas will often deliver goods to you in Switzerland, in which case you won't pay local VAT, but will be charged Swiss VAT – and they may even deliver free of charge.

Reclaiming VAT

When buying goods outside Switzerland on which you intend to reclaim foreign VAT, the procedure is as follows:

1 Obtain a receipt for your purchase and tell the shop assistant that you would like a form to reclaim the tax. The shop completes the tax reclaim form (*Ausfuhrschein/Zollschein*, *fiche d'exportation/feuille d'exportation*) and enters the tax rate and total amount to be refunded. Write your name and your Swiss

address on the form. If you wish to claim your tax refund by mail, check that the vendor will reimburse tax this way.

2 Have the form stamped by a customs official in the country of purchase before entering Switzerland. The official may want proof that you don't live in the country, e.g. a Swiss residence permit. If you're flying back to Switzerland with your purchases, e.g. from the UK, you'll need to carry them as hand luggage in order to have your tax reclaim form stamped.

3 At the Swiss customs post, present your receipt to the official and tell him what you've purchased. He will calculate the import duty and Swiss VAT to be paid, if any. Swiss customs officials sometimes query your country of residence, so make sure that you have your Swiss residence permit handy.

4 To reclaim the VAT, return the form in person to the vendor or send it by post (keep a copy of the receipt and tax form). This must usually be done within a limited period, e.g. six months for goods purchased in Germany.

Some shops in border areas will deliver goods to you in Switzerland within a certain radius, in which case you won't pay local VAT but may be charged for delivery. For expensive purchases, a shop may send someone to accompany you to the border and return your local tax on the spot, on receipt of the stamped tax reclaim form.

Duty-free Allowances

Swiss customs regulations allow duty-free purchases up to CHF 300 per person, per day, with the following restrictions:

◆ 1l/kg of butter and cream;

◆ 4l/kg of oil, fat and margarine;

◆ 5l/kg of milk, cheese, yoghurt and other dairy products;

◆ 2.5kg of eggs;

◆ 20kg of vegetables;

◆ 20kg of fruit (excluding oranges);

◆ 3l of fruit juice;

◆ 2.5kg of potatoes and potato products (including crisps!);

◆ 20kg of cereals, flour and flour-based products (bread, cakes etc);

◆ 3.5kg of meat and meat products such as sausages and poultry. This may include a maximum of just 500g of fresh or frozen meat (beef, pork, lamb, veal, goat, horse, donkey and mule!). On no account may you exceed the limit on meat imports.

Those aged over 17 may also import the following:

◆ 2l of wine or champagne under 15° proof and one litre of alcohol over 15° proof – if you import more than one litre, duty on the excess amount is likely to equal or exceed its cost;

◆ 200 cigarettes **or** 50 cigars **or** 250g of pipe tobacco (double for visitors domiciled outside Europe).

There are regulations prohibiting the importation of meats from certain countries and occasional restrictions on the import of some meats due to outbreaks of swine fever or foot and mouth disease. If in doubt, check with the Federal Veterinary Office (☎ 031-323 30 33, 💻 www.bvet. admin.ch).

At the Swiss border you must declare what you've purchased and, if asked, produce receipts to verify the place of origin and the price paid. When you exceed the permitted tax-free limit, you're liable to pay VAT (see page 208) on all your purchases, including the duty-free allowance. Customs duty on goods imported above the duty-free allowance is calculated by weight, depending on the category of goods, which is payable in addition to VAT. Swiss customs officials are usually reasonable and flexible and unless you're a big-time smuggler, will treat you fairly.

For further information, see the Swiss Federal Customs Administration website (💻 www.ezv.

admin.ch/zollinfo_privat – change the language to English and click on 'food and drink').

Never attempt to import illegal goods and don't agree to bring a parcel into Switzerland, or to deliver a parcel in another country, without knowing exactly what it contains. It could contain something illegal such as drugs.

EMERGENCY RATIONS

All residents of Switzerland are requested to keep an emergency food supply (*Notvorrat, provisions de secours*) in their nuclear shelter. The food supply includes 1 to 2kg per person of sugar, rice or pasta, oil or fat, protein rich food, carbohydrate rich food and food of your choice (if the bombs don't get you the food will!). To this must be added liquids (nine litres per person), fuel, cleaning materials, assorted extras such as medicines, rubbish sacks, spirit stove (for cooking), methylated spirits and iron tablets. Don't forget essentials such as baby food, nappies (diapers), diabetic treatments, drugs and vitamin tablets. Washing powder is also one of the essential requirements, although most shelters have no running water and no toilet facilities. You should take a radio (although reception may be impossible). Most Swiss also keep a good supply of wine in their shelters (they plan to go out with a bang!).

The necessary foods are listed in a pamphlet called *Household Reserves*, available from your community or from the Bundesamt für wirtschaftliche Landesversorgung (☎ 031-322 21 56, 💻 www.bwl.admin.ch). Foods can be stored only for a limited period and must be replaced periodically (see pamphlet).

RECEIPTS

When shopping in Switzerland, always insist on a receipt (*Quittung/Kassenbon, quittance*) and retain it until you've left the store or reached home. This isn't just in case you need to return or exchange goods, which may be impossible without the receipt, but also to verify that you've paid if an automatic alarm sounds as you're leaving the shop or any other questions arise. When you buy a large object which cannot be wrapped, a sticker should be attached as visible evidence of purchase, in addition to your receipt. In supermarkets, the cashier usually sticks your receipt to goods with sticky tape.

It's advisable to keep receipts and records of all major purchases made while resident in Switzerland, particularly if your stay is only for a limited period. This may save you time and money when you finally leave Switzerland and are required to declare your belongings in your new country of residence.

CONSUMER ASSOCIATIONS

The independent Swiss Consumers Association provides free product information and legal advice, and publishes books and monthly or bimonthly magazines in local languages, available on subscription and from news kiosks. The association has three main offices, serving the main language regions of Switzerland, plus local advisers in many areas.

◆ **French:** Fédération Romande des Consommateurs (☎ 021-312 80 06 or ☎ 0900-575 105 for advice and information, CHF 2.85 per minute, 💻 www.frc.ch).

◆ **German:** Stiftung für Konsumentenschutz (☎ 031-370 24 24 or ☎ 0900-900 440 for advice, CHF 2.90 per minute, 💻 www.konsumentenschutz.ch).

◆ **Italian:** L'Associazone Consumatrici della Svizzera Italiana (☎ 091-922 97 55, 💻 www.acsi.ch).

Another publication worthy of special mention is *Ktipp*, a German-language consumer magazine which is one of the best-selling subscription publications in Switzerland. It costs CHF. 37.50 a year (20 issues) or CHF. 69 for two years from K-Tipp (☎ 044 266 17 17, 💻 www.ktipp.ch).

18.
ODDS & ENDS

This chapter contains miscellaneous information. Most of the topics covered are of general interest to anyone living and working in Switzerland, although not all subjects are of vital importance. However, buried among the trivia are some fascinating snippets of information.

ALARMS

There are various alarms for the Swiss population in times of peace (*Alarmierung der Bevölkerung in Friedenszeiten, alarme de la population en temps de paix*), with which all residents of Switzerland should be familiar. When alarms are to be tested, announcements are made in the communities concerned. The famous Swiss underground shelter plays an important role in Switzerland's civil defence system and all new houses built in Switzerland must have one. (The Swiss have a master plan to arise from their bolt-holes after the radiation has dispersed and conquer what's left of the world!)

The following information is provided at the back of Swiss telephone directories, where it's listed in French, German and Italian. Some communities and cantons may have additional alarm signals.

General Alarm

The general alarm (*allgemeiner Alarm, alarme général*) is a continuous oscillating high frequency tone for one minute. Information is broadcast on radio DRS (frequency 103) and local radio in the Swiss national and other languages, including English. Instructions is given by the authorities on what action to take. Inform your neighbours (or ask them what's going on!).

Radioactivity Alarm

The radioactivity alarm (*Strahlenalarm, alarme radioactivité*) is an interrupted oscillating high frequency tone for two minutes. Signifies IMMEDIATE DANGER. Close all doors and windows and seek shelter IMMEDIATELY in the nearest nuclear shelter. Take emergency rations with you if they aren't already stored in your shelter, plus a transistor radio and listen for further instructions (if you can receive anything in your bunker).

Water Alarm

The water alarm (*Wasseralarm, alarme eau*) is an interrupted low frequency tone for six minutes. Warning of a danger of floods in the local area. Listen to local radio and TV for information. If you're in the danger area, evacuate IMMEDIATELY and seek high ground. There may also be local regulations concerning water alarms.

> #### All Clear
> The all clear (*ende der Gefahr, fin du danger*) is announced via radio, TV and loudspeaker vehicles.

BUSINESS HOURS

The usual business hours (*Geschäftsstunden, heures de bureau*) for offices (not shops or factories) vary, but are generally from 8 to noon and 1.30 or 2pm to 5 or 6pm, Mondays to Fridays. Many businesses close for lunch, which may extend from 11.30 or noon to 2pm, and most are closed on Saturdays. Switchboards may be unmanned (unwomaned?) at lunchtimes, during which telephones may be unanswered or be connected to an answering machine. Government offices are usually open from around 8 to 11.45am and from 2 to 4pm.

CHILDREN

There are various laws in Switzerland governing the behaviour of children in public places. Children under 16 years old, which is the legal age of sexual consent in Switzerland, aren't permitted in public places after 10pm. unless accompanied by an adult. Those under 16 aren't allowed in bars, night clubs or casinos. Switzerland is generally a safe place for children, although they should be informed of the usual dangers, such a 'talking to strangers'.

CITIZENSHIP

Obtaining Swiss citizenship (*Schweizer Nationalität/ Schweizer Staatsbürger, nationalité suisse/ citoyen suisse*) isn't easy and the application process is long-winded. However, it cannot be too difficult as some 40,000 people a year are naturalised. Following your application, an 18-month investigation is carried out to determine whether you're suitable. If you survive the inquisition you must then pass a general knowledge quiz on Switzerland – failure to answer correctly means no lovely red Swiss passport (as a consolation, a tasty chocolate Swiss passport is available from sweet shops).

To qualify for Swiss citizenship, a foreigner who isn't married to a Swiss citizen must have been a resident of Switzerland for 12 years, including three of the last five years, in order to qualify for Swiss citizenship. The number of years spent in Switzerland between the ages of 10 to 20 count double. A foreigner married to a Swiss citizen must have been married three years and have been living in Switzerland for five years, and is eligible for simplified citizenship (*erleichterte Einbürgerung, naturalization facilitée*), which in practice means a quicker citizenship process. The children of a foreigner married to a Swiss citizen have the right to Swiss citizenship.

Foreigners who receive Swiss citizenship don't automatically lose the nationality of their country of origin, as dual nationality is accepted by the Swiss, but isn't by all other countries.

CLIMATE

It's almost impossible to provide a general description of the Swiss climate, as it varies considerably from region to region (like the Swiss themselves); probably no other country in Europe has such diverse weather conditions in such a small area.

The Alps, extending from east to west, form a major weather division between the north and south of the country, and separate weather forecasts are usually given for each area. The climate north of the Alps is continental with hot summers and cold winters, although prolonged periods when the temperature is below freezing are rare during daytime (unless you live on top of a mountain).

In winter, the average daytime temperature at higher elevations is often below zero and can be freezing, although the sun can be very hot and you can get sunburned easily. In winter it usually snows everywhere at some time, even in the lowlands, although Basle gets an average of just 11 days snow per year and it rarely snows in Geneva (around nine days a year), and it usually melts within a day or two. At higher altitudes, it generally thaws by spring, except above 2,000m (6,561ft). Many areas experience heavy fog and mist, caused by temperature inversions, particularly in autumn. In winter, avalanches are common but they rarely occur in towns or villages or on ski pistes where there's extensive avalanche protection (slopes where there's a danger of avalanches are cleared by blasting). Mudslides, rockfalls and floods are a danger in some areas in spring (with the winter thaw) and in summer.

In Ticino, south of the Alps, a mild Mediterranean climate prevails and even in winter it's significantly warmer here than elsewhere in Switzerland. Spring and autumn are usually mild and fine in most areas. Generally, Switzerland has more rainfall than most other regions of Europe (although Valais is particularly dry) and the country is noted for its low humidity and lack of wind. Most areas suffer occasionally from the *foehn*, a warm oppressive south wind often blamed for headaches, fatigue, vertigo, bad tempers and other minor irritating

complaints (you can even buy a gadget to ease its unpleasant effects).

The daily weather forecast in winter includes the snowfall limit (*Schneefallgrenze, limite des chute de neige*), which is the lowest level (in metres) where snow will fall and where freezing point will occur (*Nullgradgrenze, limite du degré zéro*). Generally, Swiss weather forecasts are highly accurate. Average afternoon temperatures for the major cities in Centigrade and Fahrenheit (in brackets), are shown in the table below.

The Swiss weather forecast is available by telephone (☎ 162 – CHF 0.50 plus 0.50 per minute) in the local language, via the internet (e.g. 🖳 www.meteocentrale.ch/en and www.wetter.ch) and in daily newspapers. The pollen count (*Pollenbericht, indice de pollen*) is reported in daily newspapers and at 🖳 www.meteoschweiz.ch (under Health). Avalanche bulletins are given on telephone service number ☎ 187 (CHF 0.50 plus 0.50 per minute) and in English on the website of the Swiss Federal Institute of Snow and Avalanche Research (🖳 www.slf.ch/index_en).

A fun website for those living in northern Switzerland is 🖳 www.sonnig.ch, showing a map of webcams which allow you to find out where the sun is shining within 30-40 minutes of Zurich!

CRIME

Switzerland is a safe country in which to live or visit and has a very low crime rate – one of the lowest, if not the lowest, in the world. Violent crimes such as assault, mugging and rape are fortunately rare in Switzerland and you can safely walk anywhere, day or night. Gun crime rates are so low that statistics aren't even kept. Over half of all crimes in Switzerland are committed by foreigners (particularly violent crime and drug offences) and Swiss prisons contain a high proportion of foreigners, although most are non-residents who come to Switzerland especially to commit crimes.

Negligence is the cause of many thefts, with mopeds and bicycles being the main target. The Swiss are too trusting for their own good and often leave doors, windows and even safes open for their friendly neighbourhood thief (if you're a crook, you shouldn't be reading this). Don't leave cash, cheques, credit cards, passports, jewellery and other valuables lying around or even hidden in your home (the crooks know all the hiding places). Good locks help but may not keep the professionals out (they drill them out). It's better to keep your valuables in a home safe or a bank safety deposit box and ensure that you have adequate home contents insurance (see below). Remember to lock your car and put any valuables in the boot or out of sight, particularly when parking overnight in a public place, and look after your expensive skis and other belongings in ski resorts.

Most modern apartment blocks in Switzerland are fitted with an intercom system, allowing residents to speak to callers before giving them access to the building. In addition, most apartment doors have a spy-hole so that you can check a visitor's identity before opening the door; many homes also have armoured doors with high

City	Average Temperature °C (°F)		Rainfall mm (inches)
	January	July	
Basle	0.9 (33.6)	18.5 (65.3)	778 (30.6)
Berne	1.0 (33.8)	17.5 (63.5)	1,028 (40.5)
Geneva	1.0 (33.8)	19.3 (66.7)	822 (32.4)
Lucerne	0.2 (32.4)	17.9 (64.2)	1,545 (60.8)
Lugano	2.6 (36.7)	21.1 (70.0)	1,171 (46.1)
Sion	0.8 (33.4)	19.1 (66.4)	598 (23.5)
Zurich	0.5 (32.9)	17.6 (63.7)	1,086 (42.8)

Climate

Source: 🖳 www.meteoschweiz.ch.

security locking systems which help prevent burglaries.

There are pickpockets in major cities and tourist centres, so don't walk around with your wallet or purse on display (men shouldn't keep their wallet in their back trouser pocket). Some theft insurance doesn't cover pickpocket thefts, only robbery with violence (so tell your insurance company that you were robbed at gun point!).

ECONOMY & TRADE

Despite its limited size and lack of raw materials, Switzerland is one of the most productive, competitive and prosperous countries in the world. Swiss products are renowned for their quality, reliability and after sales service, with a strong emphasis on the refinement and finishing of products, and high quality specialisation. Switzerland's success is due to a combination of technical know-how, enterprising spirit, hard work, virtually no strikes, high investment in plant and equipment, and an overriding pro-business mentality. Like Japan, it's largely dependent on imports, particularly raw materials, semi-finished and finished products, energy sources and food. Many Swiss companies are leaders in their fields and a 'Made in Switzerland' label has a certain cachet to many buyers, who gladly pay a premium for Swiss quality, durability and reliability.

One of Switzerland's most important industries is precision mechanical and electrical engineering, which produces highly specialised equipment and tools, particularly machine tools, and textile and printing machinery. Many Swiss companies are also world leaders in the fields of life sciences (biotech, MedTech, pharmaceuticals), information and communication technologies (ICT), and micro- and nanotechnology. Other major industries include watch-making, chemicals and pharmaceuticals, tourism, and the textile and clothing industries. The Swiss food industry is also prosperous and Swiss chocolate and cheese, among other foods, are exported throughout the world (Nestlé is the world's largest food company). Despite the fact that only a quarter of Switzerland's surface area is productive, Swiss farmers produce around 70 per cent of the country's food.

It's the service sector, however, which contributes most towards balancing the budget, in particular Swiss banks and insurance companies. The tourist industry is also important and is one of the country's largest employers, providing work directly or indirectly for some 250,000 people. Tourism is Switzerland's third-largest export earner (after the machine and chemical industries)

with foreign tourists spending some CHF 15bn annually (around 3 per cent of GDP). The Swiss workforce consists of around 4.6m people or around 55 per cent of the population (55 per cent men and 45 per cent women), some 25 per cent of whom are foreigners, mostly from the EU. Around 75 per cent of people are employed in the services sector, 23 per cent in industry, trades and construction, and just 2 per cent in agriculture and forestry.

It was feared that Switzerland's rejection of European Union membership would prove an obstacle to future growth and prosperity, as few western countries are so dependent on the outside world for their economic survival. However, Switzerland has negotiated a series of bilateral trade treaties with the EU, and most EU citizens have the right to live and work freely in Switzerland (Swiss citizens have the same rights in EU countries). As a trading partner, Switzerland is the third-largest goods supplier and second-largest customer of the EU, and some 45 per cent of Swiss direct investment is in EU countries. The Swiss can therefore enjoy the benefits of EU membership without the bureaucracy and expense (nobody said the Swiss weren't smart!).

Switzerland cannot afford any kind of isolation, either with regard to energy or raw materials, or in relation to its capital and labour markets.

For this reason, it's foreign exchange system has always been based on a free market, opposition to all forms of protectionism, and a policy of low customs duties with almost no restrictions on imports. It's ranked fourth in the world for economic freedom – behind Hong Kong, Singapore and New Zealand – and first in Europe.

Agricultural products are virtually the only exception. Most food imports are subject to duties in order to protect the livelihood of Swiss farmers and ensure sufficient food production in times of need (due to their high production costs, Swiss farmers cannot compete with imports). Swiss farmers receive a large part of their income from federal subsidies, although there are regular battles over milk prices and production quotas. Despite the duties on imported food, Switzerland imports more agricultural products per capita than almost any other European country. Other important benefits of the Swiss farming policy are safeguarding the traditional Swiss way of life, particularly in mountainous regions, and the protection of the environment.

Swiss agriculture is subsidised to the tune of around CHF 500 per resident per year. However, in addition to producing food so that Switzerland isn't entirely dependent on imports, Swiss farmers do an important job caring for the countryside, thus boosting tourism.

The Swiss economy remains strong and competitive, despite the high value of the Swiss franc – which is eroding the country's competitiveness – high labour costs and ever-increasing competition. Swiss companies have, however, felt the pinch in recent years and are increasingly being forced to move production and other facilities abroad, reduce prices and shave their profit margins. The Swiss economy is among the world's most open and most competitive, and its GDP per head is the third-highest in the world, thanks primarily to high-value-added services, specialized industries, and a highly qualified workforce.

Switzerland spends more per capita on research and development, science and education than any other country, has one of the highest numbers of computers per head of any country, and is a world leader in advanced technology exports. The Swiss economy is among the world's most open and most competitive – in 2009 it knocked the US off the top spot – and its exports as a percentage of GDP are the world's highest. The Swiss have also produced (per capita) more Nobel Prize winners and registered more patents than any other country.

Switzerland was one of the few countries to avoid recession in recent years and the government has forecast growth of 1 per cent for 2012 and 1.4 per cent for 2013 (borh reduced due to a slowdown in the economy).

GEOGRAPHY

Switzerland is a landlocked country (although it has been described as the only island in the world surrounded entirely by land!) situated in the central Alpine region of central Europe, with borders with five countries: Italy (734km/456mi) to the south, Austria (164km/102mi) and the Principality of Liechtenstein (41km/25mi) to the east, Germany (334km/207mi) to the north and France (573km/356mi) to the west. Some two-thirds of its frontiers follow the natural contours of mountain ridges, lakes and rivers, with around 25 per cent of its area consisting of scenic high Alps, lakes and barren rock. It's a small country of 41,290km² (around 15,940mi²), with a maximum distance from east to west of 348km/216mi and just 220km/137mi from north to south. The Alps, mainly in the central part of the country, reach altitudes of over 4,000m (13,123ft).

Geographically, Switzerland can be divided into three main regions:

♦ The alpine massif, which includes the whole of southern Switzerland, covers some 60 per cent of the country and is home to around 20 per cent of the population. Approximately 20 per cent of the total alpine range lies within Switzerland.

♦ The central plateau (Mittelland), north of the alpine massif, consists of some 30 per cent of the land area and is where some two-thirds of the population lives.

♦ The Jura mountains in the north-west make up the remaining 10 per cent of Switzerland and around 15 per cent of the population.

The highest point in Switzerland is the Dufour Peak of the Monte Rosa (4,634m/15,203ft) and the lowest Lake Maggiore, on the border with Italy (195m/639ft above sea level). The Swiss Alps contain the crossroads formed by the St. Gotthard, Grimsel, Furka and Oberalp passes, and are the source of both the Rhine and Rhône rivers. Due to its central position, Switzerland has long been an important link in communications and transport between northern and southern Europe, a fact that has been decisive in determining the course of its history.

Communications and telecommunications are excellent and among the best in the world, with extensive motorway and rail networks with multiple connections with all its neighbours, and three major airports (Zurich, Geneva and Basle) and several minor regional airports, providing direct connections with most major international destinations.

Maps of Switzerland showing the major cities, geographical features, communications and the 26 cantons, are included in Appendix E.

GOVERNMENT

Switzerland is the most politically stable country in the world. The Swiss constitution (reviewed and updated in 2001) provides both the confederation and cantons with the system of a democratic republic, in the form of direct or representative democracy. Switzerland's foreign policy is neutral. A number of important recent referendums (e.g. EEA membership and Swiss UN troops, both of which were rejected) have shown only too clearly that the Swiss government is increasingly out of step (at least in terms of foreign policy) with its people. However, Switzerland's foreign policy isn't entirely isolationist and in 1992 it became a member of the IMF and the World Bank (it's also a member of the Council of Europe, GATT and the OECD). In 2002, the Swiss voted to become a member of the United Nations (after 57 years!).

In Switzerland, power flows upwards from some 3,000 communities (*Gemeinde, commune*), each of which has a local council or municipal authority.

A Swiss citizen is first and foremost a citizen of a community (written in his passport), which remains ultimately responsible for his welfare throughout his life. In a community, the executive is the administrative council headed by the mayor, with legislative matters handled by the municipal council. The community levies local taxes and has self-rule in all matters that aren't the responsibility of either the federal government or the canton. These include the administration of public property such as forests; water, gas and electricity supplies; bridges, roads and administrative buildings; schools (primary education); and the civil defence, fire, health and local police departments. Several communities make up a borough or county (*Bezirk, district*).

Next in line are the 26 cantons (*Kanton/ Stände, canton*) – see **Chapter 2** – six of which rank as 'half-cantons' (Appenzell-Ausserrhoden,

Appenzell-Innerrhoden, Glarus, Nidwalden, Obwalden and Uri). Each canton has its own written constitution and is in effect a sovereign state subject to federal law. The cantonal governments consist of an executive state council of five to nine members (each head of a department) and a legislative grand council of varying size, depending on the canton. Each canton is responsible for its own civil service; citizenship; church matters; education; finances and income tax; labour department; land usage; law and order; libraries; public health; public transport; roads; stock exchange supervision; and water and electricity supply.

The federal government is directly responsible for the armed forces; civil, criminal and industrial law; currency; customs and federal taxes; fishing, forestry and hunting (shared with the cantons); foreign policy; hydroelectric and nuclear power; monetary controls; pensions; post and communications services; and railways. Legislative power is exercised by the federal assembly (*Bundesversammlung, Assemblée Fédérale*), consisting of two chambers of equal status:

◆ **The Council of States** (*Ständerat, Conseil des Etats*) comprises 46 representatives of the cantons. The 20 'full' cantons have two representatives each and the six half-cantons one each.

◆ **The National Council** (*Nationalrat, Conseil National*), is elected for a four-year term and consists of 200 direct representatives of the people. The number of members allocated to each canton depends on their size and population, e.g. Zurich has 34 seats, while the half cantons of Appenzell-Ausserrhoden, Appenzell-Innerrhoden, Glarus, Nidwalden, Obwalden and Uri have just one seat each.

Both chambers hold four regular sessions a year, each of three weeks duration, and bills must be debated and passed by both chambers. Members aren't professional politicians and hold other jobs, although most are self-employed or high-ranking corporate executives with the time and money to serve as part-time politicians. Politicians are paid around CHF 70,000 a year.

Traditionally, relatively few federal politicians have been women (possibly because they've only had the right to vote since 1971), although this is changing; in 2009 almost 30 per cent of *Nationalrat* members, 22 per cent of *Ständerat* members and three of the seven federal councillors were women. (In 2010, the President of Switzerland was a woman, and both chambers majority, rather than indulging in petty squabbling and party politics (are you listening UK and US?).

However, Swiss politics are also terminally boring for most foreigners, although the EU issue injected a modicum of interest in recent decades and the Swiss are beginning to debate issues with some passion (and often vote the opposite way in referendums from what their elected representatives recommend).

> If you're an insomniac, you can find out more about Swiss politics at 🖳 www.socio.ch/poli.

LEGAL ADVICE

Many towns and all major cities offer free or inexpensive legal advice for foreigners in English and other languages. Advice encompasses both criminal and civil law, e.g. the interpretation of house rental or purchase contracts. Ask your community or local information office for the address of your nearest legal office (*Notariat, Étude de notaire*). With regard to divorce, Swiss private international law applies only when either spouse is a Swiss citizen or has been residing in Switzerland for more than two years.

If you have reason to complain about faulty goods or bad service (admittedly rare) and your initial attempts at redress fall on deaf ears, try writing a letter in English to the manager or managing director. This often has surprisingly positive results (see also **Consumer Associations** on page 253). Even when dealing with government bureaucrats or officials, you can be successful if you protest loudly and long enough. The Swiss usually submit meekly to all rules and regulations, and therefore bureaucrats are often cowed when faced with an assertive foreigner. Legal advice and services may be provided by your embassy or consulate in Switzerland, including, for example, an official witness of signatures (Commissioner for Oaths).

MILITARY SERVICE

If you work in Switzerland, you may notice that your Swiss male colleagues have a habit of disappearing for a few weeks every few years. They aren't entitled to more holidays than foreigners, but are simply doing their military service (*Militärdienst, service militaire*). Switzerland has a 'citizen' army of part-time soldiers and can muster over 200,000 men at

Berne

– *Nationalrat* and *Ständerat* – were also presided over by women.) The misogynist men of half canton Appenzell-Innerrhoden steadfastly refused to give women the right to vote in community and cantonal elections, until being overruled by the federal government in 1990.

The federal assembly elects the seven federal councillors (comprising the federal executive), who serve for four years and head the departments of foreign affairs; the interior; justice and police; defence and sport; finance; economics and environment; and transport and energy (including communications). Re-election of federal councillors is permitted. Each year the assembly elects a councillor as president of the confederation (who remains anonymous to everyone but his/her spouse). The highest judicial authority is the Federal Supreme Court, which sits in Lausanne and consists of 30 members elected by the federal assembly.

The Swiss system of democracy, although not perfect, is among the best devised. Almost everyone is represented through proportional representation (with the notable exception of the 1.8m foreigners who comprise around 23 per cent of the population). Local communities and cantons have real powers that cannot be usurped or vetoed by the federal government, and all important decisions must be decided by the people through referendums. The system functions well because politicians of all parties work together for the greater benefit of the arms in 48 hours to defend the homeland (only brigade commanders and above and instructors are full-time professionals, a total of just 4,000, plus around 1,000 part-time personnel).

However, don't be concerned as foreign residents aren't liable for military service. If you become a Swiss citizen, military service depends on your age and whether you've already served in a foreign army (if you have, you won't be trusted and will be exempt). You'll probably be unaware of it as a foreigner, but success and promotion in the army often opens the door to position and power in Swiss industry, government and finance. The Swiss army was cut by around a third in the last decade from 600,000 to 400,000 and has since been cut to just 120,000 active (see below) soldiers, 80,000 reserves and 20,000 recruits.

All Swiss males must serve at least 260 days from the age of 19, when they undergo a basic 21-week training course, after which they become 'active' troops. Most ranks (soldiers and non-commissioned officers/NCOs) must complete a number (around six) of 19-day refresher courses, usually once a year, and remain on 'reserve' until the age of 35, when military service ends (the exception being senior officers, who serve until they're 50). Senior NCOs and officers undergo additional periods of training. The total length of military training is around one year and includes annual target practice when not on active duty. Military service isn't compulsory for women, although they can volunteer to serve in the women's military service.

To speed up mobilisation in the event of a war, Swiss soldiers keep their uniforms, gas masks, arms and, until recently (2007), even ammunition at home – a sure-fire recipe for civil war in less disciplined countries. It was estimated in 2006 that 300 deaths a year were attributed to army weapons (including suicide) and there was also a wave of murders using army rifles in 2006-07, which led to a public outcry and the end of issuing soldiers with live ammunition to keep at home.

An unusual feature of the Swiss armed forces is that in peace time they have no general, one being appointed only in the event of a threat of war.

Anyone who's unfit for military service must serve in the auxiliary services, e.g. the civil defence or ambulance service. In 1991, Switzerland finally recognised the status of conscientious objectors, prior to which anyone who refused to serve in the army was imprisoned. An alternative civil service (390 days) has now been established for those who object to military service on religious or moral grounds.

Swiss citizens living abroad aren't liable for military service, but are required to pay a military exemption tax (*Militärpflichtersatz, taxe d'exemption du service militaire*) of a percentage of their salary, even if they never intend to return to Switzerland. The tax also applies to anyone excused service on medical, moral or religious grounds. Swiss employers usually pay employees their full salary while they are doing their military service, except in extreme circumstances when they're unable to do so.

Although the majority of Swiss proclaim that they loathe military service, whenever the question of abolishing conscription or the army is raised in a referendum, they vote to retain it. However, in 1989, almost 36 per cent voted to abolish the army, which shocked the complacent military and political establishment to the core, although in a second referendum in December 2001, only 23 per cent voted to abolish the army. However, fears in military circles that a future referendum could prove terminal have led to a reduction in the length of military service and the number of personnel.

In 1994, the Swiss voted against allowing their troops to volunteer for UN peacekeeping missions. The army has been reformed twice over the last decade, with one of the goals being the reduction of costs. Switzerland's annual defence budget is over CHF 4bn – a lot of money for a country without an enemy in the world and which hasn't fought a foreign campaign since

Swiss guard, Rome

1515! There are, however, plans to slash the military budget in the coming years by reducing manpower, putting equipment and vehicles into storage, and closing military camps.

PETS

If you plan to bring a pet (*Haustier, animal domestique*) with you to Switzerland, check the latest regulations beforehand and ensure that you have the correct documents, not only for Switzerland but for all the countries that you must pass through to reach Switzerland, e.g. if you're travelling by road. If you need to return prematurely, even after a few hours or days, to a country with strict quarantine regulations, your pet could be put into quarantine.

Swiss Regulations

There's generally no quarantine period for animals in Switzerland, although all dogs and cats over five months old must have an international health certificate stating that they've been vaccinated against rabies (*Tollwut, rage*). You must have an official letter stating that your pet was in good health before the vaccination, which must have been given at least 30 days and not more than one year before entering the country. Certificates are accepted in English, French, German and Italian. A dog or cat must also be microchipped or have a tattoo.

Dogs and cats under five months of age may be imported from many countries, i.e. most European countries (except Turkey and the former USSR states), Australia, Canada, New Zealand and the USA, without a rabies vaccination, but a veterinary attestation of their age and good health is required.

Dogs and cats from countries that don't require rabies vaccinations (e.g. Australia and New Zealand) can be imported without a vaccination certificate. Swiss residents aren't allowed to import dogs with cut ears or cropped tails, although those coming to live in Switzerland can import such dogs when they enter the country. Dogs and cats arriving by air at Swiss airports are examined on arrival. If they don't have the required documentation or fail the examination, they're kept at the airport until the owner arranges a return flight, which must be done within ten days, otherwise the animal will be put to sleep. Dogs and cats from Malaysia and cats from Australia are subject to additional regulations.

Birds (except canaries) need a special import licence, obtainable from the Federal Veterinary Office (see box), and are quarantined until it's established that they don't have parrot fever (psittacosis). Rabbits also need special permission and must undergo a quarantine period of around 15 days, but guinea-pigs, golden hamsters, rats, mice, aquarium fish and canaries may be imported without a health certificate. An import licence and a veterinary examination is required for some domestic animals, e.g. horses. Dangerous animals (e.g. poisonous snakes, man-eating tigers, etc.) require a special import licence.

For the latest regulations concerning the importation or keeping of pets in Switzerland, contact the Federal Veterinary Office (Bundesamt für Vetrinärwesen, Office Vétérinaire Fédéral, ☎ 031-323 30 33, 🖥 www.bvet.admin.ch).

British Regulations

The Pet Travel Scheme (PETS – now under the auspices of the EU pet passport scheme), replaces quarantine for qualifying cats and dogs. Under the scheme, pets must be micro-chipped (i.e. have a microchip inserted in their neck), be vaccinated against rabies, undergo a blood test and be issued with a health certificate (passport). In the UK, EU pet passports are issued only by Local Veterinary Inspectors (LVI), while in other EU countries passports can be issued by all registered vets. Allow plenty of time, as they can take months to be issued.

The scheme is restricted to animals imported from rabies-free countries and countries where rabies is under control, which includes most European countries plus many non-European countries including Australia, Canada, New Zealand and the USA (see the website below for a complete list).

Pets exported from Britain must travel by sea via any major British ferry port, by train via the Channel Tunnel or via all current and future UK and EU airports utilised by Easyjet. Only certain routes and carriers (listed on the website of the Department for the Environment, Food and Rural Affairs/DEFRA – 🖥 www.defra.gov.uk/wildlife-pets/pets/travel/pets) are licensed to carry animals. Contact DEFRA for further information (☎ 0870-241 1710, ✉ pettravel@ahvla.gsi.gov.uk).

British pet owners must complete an Application for a Ministry Export Certificate for dogs, cats and rabies susceptible animals (form EXA1), available from DEFRA at the above address. DEFRA will contact the vet that you've named on the form, who will perform a health inspection. You'll then receive an export health certificate, which must have been issued no more than 30 days before your entry into Switzerland with your pet.

General Information

Switzerland is now officially rabies-free, and dogs no longer require a rabies (*Tollwut, rage*) vaccination unless they travel to countries outside Switzerland, when they must have had a rabies vaccination at least six weeks before travelling and thereafter every two years. A vaccination for distemper (*Staupe, morve/maladie carré*) is also recommended every two years, but isn't mandatory.

A dog needs a licence when it's six months old, available from your local community office or the dog control office in major cities, on production of its international health certificate. Owners now require private liability insurance (see page 184) in all cantons before a dog licence is issued. A card is issued by the insurance company, which must be produced when applying for a licence.

Licences must be renewed annually (the date varies depending on the community, which will make an announcement in local newspapers) and cost between CHF 60 and 180 a year depending on your community. If you have two or more dogs, the cost of licences can be astronomical in some areas. Owners of unlicensed dogs are fined. If you move home within Switzerland, you must re-register your dog in your new community, but you aren't required to pay the dog tax again if you've already paid in your previous community.

All dogs must be microchipped, and dogs arriving from abroad must have this done within ten days and be registered with the Animal Identity Service (☎ 031-371 35 39, 🖥 www.anis.ch). If the ownership changes, the owner moves home or the dog dies, it must be reported to ANIS. If a dog's found lost or roaming the streets, it's taken to an animal shelter (*Tierheim, refuge pour animaux*) and the owner is notified (through the microchip data).

If you plan to leave a pet at a kennel or cattery (*Tierpension, pension pour animaux*), book well in advance, particularly for school holiday periods. Dogs left at kennels must be inoculated against kennel cough (*Zwingerhusten, toux canine*), and all vaccinations must be registered with your veterinary surgeon (*Tierarzt, vétérinaire*) and listed on your pet's international health certificate.

Dogs must be kept on a lead (*an der Leine, être tenu en laisse*) in all public places. There are special areas and parks where dogs are allowed to roam free. Owners of dogs that foul public footpaths may be fined, so take a small shovel and plastic bag with you when walking your dog (no joke!). In some 75 per cent of communities there are special green containers (Robidog) about the size of a garbage can, which are for the disposal of dog waste (they also dispense plastic bags which can be used as gloves).

Brackets or hooks are provided outside many shops and in shopping centres, where you can secure your dog by its lead while shopping (most shops and public buildings such as post offices don't allow entry to dogs). When dogs are prohibited, it may also be shown by a round sign with a red border and a white background with a black image of a dog in the centre. Dogs require half-price tickets on public transport and are (surprisingly) admitted to many restaurants.

Since September 2008, new dog owners have been required to attend dog-owner classes and dogs must also attend dog obedience school.

Miscellaneous Information

Note also the following:

♦ Some apartments have regulations forbidding the keeping of dogs, cats and/or other animals.

♦ Most major cities and towns have veterinary hospitals (*Tierspital, hôpital pour animaux*) and a veterinary surgeon is usually on 24-hour call for emergencies. Ask the telephone operator (☎ 1811) for the number.

♦ A brochure about the keeping of dogs is published by some cantons.

♦ In some cantons you require special permission to keep a dog of a potentially dangerous breed, e.g. American Staffordshire Terrier, Bull Terrier, Dobermann, Dogo Argentino, Fila Brasileiro, Japanese Tosa, Pitbull Terrier, Staffordshire Bull Terrier and Rottweiler, and crosses of these breeds.

♦ A new federal law requires all dog bites to be reported to the police, and it's now mandatory to have liability insurance for your dog in all cantons.

♦ The death of a dog or horse must be reported to your community and your vet (there may be a special department). Your community or vet will arrange to collect and cremate the body for a fee, as you aren't permitted to bury a large dead pet in Switzerland; burying cats and other small pets is generally acceptable. You can also have a pet cremated privately and keep the ashes.

♦ If you take your dog to some countries, e.g. Italy, it must wear a muzzle.

if you need one you usually need to phone or visit the local police station. The large number of foreigners in Switzerland take their cue from the Swiss and are generally law-abiding – which is just as well, as their meal-ticket (residence permit) can easily be cancelled.

POPULATION

The estimated population of Switzerland in mid-2012 was around 7.95m, excluding those with short-term resident permits and asylum seekers. Around 1.8m (23 per cent) of the total are foreigners. Switzerland is one of the world's most cosmopolitan countries with foreign residents from some 200 different countries and one of the highest ratios of foreigners to natives of any European country. Germans and Italians are the largest foreign communities, each comprising around 16 per cent (of the total number of foreigners), followed by the Portuguese at around 13 per cent. Some two-thirds of foreign residents are from EU/EFTA countries. The canton of Geneva has the highest proportion of foreign residents at around 45 per cent.

The population density of around 190 inhabitants per km^2 – living in an area of 41,290km^2 (some 15,950mi^2) – is one of the highest in the western world. When the uninhabited areas are excluded, the average population density rises to over 250 people per km^2. This figure reaches over 400 inhabitants per km^2 in the central plateau, which incorporates the main centres of population. In 2012, the canton of Basle City had about 5,000 inhabitants per km^2, Geneva 1,600 and Zurich 800. The city of Geneva has over 11,500 inhabitants per km^2, making it one of the most densely populated cities in the western world.

Over 50 per cent of the population live in urban areas, although less than 25 per cent live in cities with 30,000 inhabitants or more. The largest Swiss cities are Zurich (population 380,000), Geneva (188,000), Basle (170,000), Lausanne (130,000) and Berne (126,000). In sharp contrast to the cities, the population density is only around 27 inhabitants per km^2 in canton Graubunden and 60 in canton Valais.

REFERENDUMS

Direct democracy, as practised in Switzerland, results in numerous national referendums, meaning that the people have a direct say in all important (and many insignificant) decisions. Referendums are also held at the canton level, although their use varies from canton to canton.

Bernese Mountain Dog

◆ Dogs and cats may travel on public transportation. Cats and small dogs (no larger than 30cm/12in at the shoulder) can be transported in a cage or basket when they travel free, otherwise they require a half fare ticket and must remain at your feet.

POLICE

Switzerland has no uniformed federal police force (*Polizei, police*), as law and order is the responsibility of the cantons and police uniforms vary from canton to canton. Besides cantonal police, Switzerland also has city and town police, and a non-uniformed federal police force. All police are armed, efficient and courteous, particularly when giving you a speeding ticket. Law enforcement is generally strict, particularly for any number of trivial offences, but generally fair.

There are a significant number of foreigners living and working illegally in Switzerland, and you can be stopped by special plain clothes police and asked for your passport or identity card at any time, particularly if you're driving a car with foreign registration plates.

You rarely find a policeman on the streets in towns or cities unless he's directing traffic (another indication of the low crime rate) and

The voting age is 18 for federal elections, but varies for cantonal elections.

The following kinds of national referendums are held in Switzerland:

♦ **Obligatory referendum:** A change or addition to the constitution proposed by the federal government.

♦ **Optional referendum:** A change in the law demanded by a minimum of 50,000 voters nationwide or by eight cantons.

♦ **Popular Initiative:** A new article or change in the constitution registered by a petition signed by 100,000 voters.

A change in the legislation requires a majority vote by the electorate, while a change in the constitution must be approved by a majority of the votes cast by the people and a majority of the Council of States (canton representatives). The decision of the voters is final at all levels (communal, cantonal and federal), although provided the requirements are met, an issue can be put before the voters repeatedly, perhaps couched in different terms.

Many people believe that Switzerland has too many referendums and that it's too easy to call one. Voting isn't compulsory and the turnout is often low, e.g. between 30 and 50 per cent), unless a particularly important or controversial issue is at stake (political apathy is rife in Switzerland). Turnout is highest in Schaffhausen, which may have something to do with the fact that people are fined CHF 3 if they don't vote! Of the 70 per cent of the population eligible to vote, only some 40 per cent actually vote (around 30 per cent of the population). Votes are usually decided by something over half of the votes cast, i.e. 15 per cent of the population or 25 per cent of eligible voters.

A foreigner will usually be unaware that a referendum is taking place, unless the issue is of national interest and widely publicised. Recent referendums have involved banning Minarets, joining the UN, abolishing the army and limiting the foreign population, all of which are unique, these questions having been put to the people of no other country. Foreigners seldom have voting rights in Switzerland, irrespective of how long they've been residents (particularly when the Swiss are voting on whether to throw them out!).

Foreigners in the French-speaking region of Switzerland enjoy the right to vote at the local and sometimes cantonal level, but this is rarely the case in German-speaking Switzerland.

RELIGION

Around 42 per cent of the Swiss population are Roman Catholics, some 35 per cent Protestants, 8 per cent other religions (e.g. old Catholic, Jewish, Islamic and Hindu) and 15 per cent have no religion. Besides local Protestant and Catholic church services conducted in local languages, there are English churches and English-language services in all major cities, e.g. Catholic, Anglican, Church of England and International Protestant. There are also bible study groups in many areas and Jewish, Islamic, Greek Orthodox and other religious centres in the major cities. In major cities, services are often held in languages other than the local Swiss language. In addition to the established mainstream religions, Switzerland is also home to some 600 religious movements, cults and pseudo-religious organisations.

The curriculum of Swiss state schools includes compulsory religious education, which may be segregated by denomination when the class entails more than simple bible study. Parents can, however, request that their children are excused from religious education classes. Although the Swiss constitution includes freedom of conscience and belief, certain radical sects are banned. Contact your community, tourist, or information office for information regarding local places of worship and service times.

SMOKING

Many Swiss are extremely anti-smoking and health conscious, although almost a third of the population smokes. Smoking isn't permitted in cinemas, theatres, public transport, enclosed areas of railway stations, many public buildings (e.g. post offices), and doctor's and dentist's waiting rooms. In 2006, Ticino was the first canton to forbid smoking in public buildings and in 2007 it prohibited smoking in all restaurants and bars (unless there's a separate, enclosed room for smokers).

In Canton Geneva, where the strictest anti-smoking laws in Switzerland were passed in summer 2008, the vote was overturned by the Federal Tribunal because the canton enforced the ban before the cantonal parliament had a chance to adopt a formal law! A national anti-smoking law came into effect on 1st May 2010, making it illegal to smoke in public places, including restaurants without an enclosed smoking area. By the end of 2009, 18 cantons had passed anti-smoking legislation, 15 of which have stricter rules than the national legislation.

However, two-thirds of Swiss voters rejected a proposal to tighten a smoking ban in indoor workplaces and public spaces – to the relief of hotels and restaurants – in a referendum in 2012 (of the 26 cantons, only Geneva voted slightly in favour).

Smoking is still possible in restaurants smaller than 80m² termed 'smoking' restaurants (do they serve smoked salmon?). In recent years, a number of websites have appeared where you can find a smoke-free restaurant (see ⌨ www.eatsmokefree. ch or www.rauchfreigeniessen.ch) or a smoke-free hotel room (⌨ www.rauchfreischlafen.ch).

SOCIAL CUSTOMS

All countries have their own particular social customs and Switzerland is no exception. As a foreigner you'll probably be excused if you accidentally insult your host, but you may not be invited again. The following are a few Swiss social customs:

◆ When you're introduced to someone you should use the formal form of address (Sie, vous). Don't use the familiar form (du, tu) or call someone by their Christian name until you're invited to do so. Generally the older or more important person, e.g. your boss, will invite the other person to use the familiar form of address and first names (usually after around 50 years' acquaintance in Switzerland). Younger people are much less formal.

◆ After you've been introduced to a Swiss, address him or her as Mrs. (Frau, Madame) or Mr. (Herr, Monsieur) followed by his or her family name and shake hands without gloves (unless it's 20°C below freezing). When saying goodbye, it's a formal custom to shake hands again.

◆ It's customary to say good day on entering a small shop and goodbye on leaving. Even the checkout cashier in a supermarket may do this (usually apathetically).

◆ If you're invited to dinner, take along a small present of flowers, a bottle of (good) wine or chocolates. If you take flowers, there must be an odd number and you should unwrap them before presenting them to your hostess. Flowers can be tricky, as to some people, carnations mean bad luck, chrysanthemums are for cemeteries and roses signify love. Maybe you should stick to plastic, silk or dried flowers – or perhaps a nice bunch of weeds.

◆ Don't arrive late for an invitation and don't overstay your welcome – your host will probably fall asleep around 9pm or earlier, which is your cue to leave.

◆ The Swiss say good appetite (en Guete, bon appétit) before starting a meal. If you're offered a glass of wine, wait until your host has made a toast (Prost/zum Wohl, santé) before taking a drink. If you aren't offered a (another) drink, it's time to go home (another clue is that your hosts may open all the windows to 'air' the apartment).

◆ A good guest never helps with anything, as this might imply that your hosts cannot cope.

◆ It's customary to telephone in advance before dropping in on a Swiss family, unless they're relatives or close friends. Privacy is respected in Switzerland.

◆ You should always introduce yourself before asking to speak to someone on the telephone and don't telephone at meal times or after 9pm.

◆ If you're planning a party, it's polite to notify your neighbours (so they don't call the police to complain about the noise too early).

◆ If you do a Swiss a favour, he usually feels obliged to repay you with a gift. The habit of doing favours for nothing is generally un-Swiss and a Swiss may expect you to reciprocate if he does you a favour.

♦ Although the Swiss are usually formal in their relationships, their dress habits, even in the office, are often casual. Depending on where you work, employees may be allowed to wear jeans or shorts (in summer) with sandals or clogs. You aren't usually expected to dress formally for dinner, but you shouldn't wear jeans unless it's a barbeque.

♦ Sunday is a day of peace when the Swiss won't tolerate noise, e.g. electric drills, hammering or loud music (somebody ought to inform the church bell-ringers and shooting ranges). The general Sunday working law (see **Sunday Working** on page 36) even prohibits the glorious Sunday pastimes of car washing and gardening. If you're fortunate enough to have a garden, you may sit, but not work in it on a Sunday. Washing your clothes on a Sunday is also forbidden, at least in a communal washing machine, as is hanging out clothes to dry. Go for a hike – like the Swiss!

TIME DIFFERENCE

Like most of the continent of Europe, Switzerland is on Central European Time (CET), which is Greenwich Mean Time (GMT) plus one hour. The Swiss change to summer time in spring (usually the end of March) when they put their clocks forward one hour; in autumn (fall), usually the last weekend in October, clocks are put back one hour for winter time (spring forward, fall back). Time changes are announced in local newspapers and on radio and TV. The international time difference in winter between Switzerland and some major world cities is shown below.

The precise time can be obtained by calling the 'speaking clock' on ☎ 161 (CHF 0.50 per call) or via the internet, e.g. 🖳 www.worldtimeserver.com/current_time_in_CH.aspx. The approximate time in Switzerland is also shown on TVs and computers.

TIPPING

In Swiss hotels and restaurants, a service charge of 15 per cent is included in all bills and tipping (*Trinkgeld, pourboire*) isn't necessary (Americans please note!). However, it's customary to leave a little extra change after a meal or to round up the price when paying for something small, like a coffee. In most major cities and towns, including Basle, Berne, Geneva and Zurich, a 15 per cent service charge is included in taxi hire costs. A service charge is always included in the price of hairdressing.

No tipping is generally the rule, although there are a few exceptions, notably railway and hotel porters, wash and cloakroom attendants, and garage petrol pump attendants, e.g. when they clean your windscreen or check your oil. People do, of course, reward good service and if you intend to become a regular customer somewhere it often pays to sweeten the staff. Large tips are, however, considered ostentatious and in bad taste (except by the recipient!).

TOILETS

Last, but not least, when you need to go to the little girls' or boys' room, you'll find Switzerland has the cleanest and most modern public toilets in the world. Some even have revolving, self-disinfecting seats, automatic bidets, automatic soap dispensers, taps and hand dryers, and possibly even individual, fresh, cotton towels (free of charge). Public toilets are found everywhere and are generally free, although those located at some railway stations and motorway stops may cost from CHF 0.20 to 2. Toilet humour is frowned upon, so don't write on the walls!

In recent years, 'Hygiene Centres' (with showers, make-up tables, baby changing tables and hygiene products) have been installed at railway stations in Basle, Berne, Geneva, Lausanne, Lucerne, Thun and Zurich.

TIME DIFFERENCE					
SWITZERLAND	**LONDON**	**JO'BURG**	**SYDNEY**	**AUCKLAND**	**NEW YORK**
12 noon	11am	1pm	10pm	12 midnight	6am

Lucerne

19.

THE SWISS

Who are the Swiss? What are they like? Let us take a candid and totally prejudiced look at the Swiss people, tongue firmly in cheek, and hope they forgive my flippancy or that they don't read this bit (which is why it's hidden away at the back of the book).

The typical Swiss person is scrupulously honest, narrow-minded, industrious, pessimistic, boring, hygienic, taciturn, healthy, insular, tidy, frugal, sober, selfish, spotless, educated, insecure, introverted, hard-working, perfect, religious, rigid, arrogant, affluent, conservative, isolated, private, strait-laced, neutral, authoritarian, formal, responsible, self-critical, unfriendly, stoical, materialistic, a part-time soldier, impatient, ambitious, intolerant, unromantic, reliable, conscientious, obstinate, efficient, square, enterprising, humourless, unloved (too rich), obedient, liberal, thrifty, stolid, orderly, staid, placid, insensitive, patriotic, xenophobic, courteous, meticulous, inventive, prejudiced, conventional, intelligent, virtuous, smug, loyal, punctual, egotistical, serious, bourgeois, cautious, dependable, polite, reserved, shy, law-abiding and a good skier.

You may have noticed that the above list contains 'a few' contradictions, which is hardly surprising as there's no such thing as a typical Swiss. Apart from the many differences in character between the French, German, Italian and Romansch speakers of Switzerland, the population encompasses a potpourri of foreigners from all corners of the globe. Inevitably when you're sure you have the Swiss neatly labelled and pigeonholed, along comes another friendly, humorous and fun-loving Swiss who ruins all your preconceptions. Nevertheless, I refuse to allow a few misfits to spoil my argument...

With 'all' the above traits, it will come as no surprise to discover that the Swiss aren't always the best companions with whom to share a deserted island. On the other hand, the characteristics that often make the Swiss so solemn and serious are the bedrock of the country's political and financial stability. A revolution or two may make life more exciting, but would do little for the economy or the strength of the Swiss franc.

The Swiss are rather uncommunicative and tend to meet everything foreign with reserve, the general consequence of which is an innate distrust of foreigners (unless you're a tourist). It's difficult to become close friends with a Swiss (even for other Swiss) and they rarely start a conversation with strangers. In fact, the Swiss have taken the art of non-conversation to new heights. Rumour has it that the French and Italian-speaking Swiss are more open, less stressed and more friendly than their German-speaking countrymen, although most foreigners notice little difference. In fact, social contact of any kind between the Swiss and most foreigners is rare, and the vast majority of foreigners in Switzerland count few Swiss among their friends. This is particularly true in cantons such as Geneva, where over 40 per cent of the population are foreigners and the rest are split between Swiss from other parts of Switzerland and locals. Surprisingly, some foreigners actually marry Swiss citizens, although they usually meet abroad.

The Swiss have reluctantly opened their borders to EEA nationals, but many are now (understandably) having second thoughts, as they are being over-run by Germans in their Panzer cars who take all the best jobs.

The Swiss love their guest worker (*Gastarbeiter*, *travailleur étranger*) as only those who know they're superior can (we all need someone to look down upon). It's so convenient to have someone to blame for your troubles (and to do all the dirty manual jobs), whether it's unemployment, crime, pollution, housing shortages or social problems – the guest worker makes a useful scapegoat. Even Swiss with foreign names find themselves the victims of xenophobia.

You may be unaware that you have Swiss neighbours – except when they complain. They won't welcome you when you move into a new house or apartment and if you can speak the local language, it's up to you to invite them round for coffee and introduce yourself. Don't expect your neighbours to drop round for a cup of sugar; the Swiss are much too reserved to do such a thing, and in any case they never run out of anything. Only close friends or relatives call on each other without making appointments.

In business, the Swiss are even more formal. After many years, colleagues may still address each other as Herr Zürcher or Madame Guisan, using the formal *Sie* or *vous* form of address. Young Swiss are, however, less formal than their parents. The Swiss aren't so strict with foreigners and if you speak to them in English, you may find yourself on first name terms after a relatively short period. You can get away with a lot by being an eccentric foreigner (at least I hope so), as we're all a little strange to the Swiss.

To many foreigners, the Swiss don't appear to be the merriest of people. This is often difficult to understand considering the beautiful country they inhabit (inhibit?), and the high standard of living and quality of life they enjoy. Switzerland has been unkindly referred to by some foreigners as a robotic paradise (or 'land of the living dead'), where many people lack spontaneity and soul, are devoid of a sense of fun and zest for life, and are afraid to open their hearts for fear of looking foolish. This may in part be due to the fact that only some 15 per cent of Swiss consume alcohol daily – it's enough to make anyone dull!

There's no truth in the rumour that laughter is forbidden, although you may sometimes wonder if there's a tax on humour! The Swiss don't even laugh when you tell them they have no sense of humour. It may come as a big surprise that the Swiss have their very own book of jokes in English called, *Tell me a Swiss Joke* – and the pages aren't blank. Of course, all the jokes could be borrowed (joke!)? Maybe their lack of humour is all the fault of a local wind called the *Foehn*, which gives people headaches and

makes them grumpy. Of course not all Swiss lack a sense of humour, although the minority that don't are usually foreigners masquerading as Swiss or Swiss who have worked abroad and been corrupted by foreigners. Life is taken seriously in Switzerland and if foreigners followed their example perhaps they too would be rich! Many Swiss, particularly among the ultra-conservative German-speakers, believe it's sinful to be lazy, to retire early or to enjoy yourself.

The Swiss are very, very careful with their money. There's over CHF 10,000bn deposited in Swiss banks (although not all Swiss owned) and the Swiss are second only to the Japanese in savings per capita. Maybe they've worked out a way of taking it with them or have ATMs in heaven (all Swiss go to heaven). Alternatively, Hoffman La Roche may have discovered the secret of eternal life. It's no coincidence that the Swiss are pioneers in cellular therapy, rejuvenation and revitalisation. Their meanness is the one characteristic that they deny most vehemently, but then nobody likes to be thought of as a penny-pincher. Be wary if a Swiss invites you to dinner as he may split the bill with you (or leave you to pick up the tab). To be fair (who's trying to be fair!), although the Swiss don't believe in wasting money, it's rumoured that they're gracious and generous hosts in their own homes – if only you could get an invitation!

The Swiss don't approve of flaunting their wealth or their poverty, which officially doesn't exist. Incredibly, over 500,000 inhabitants of Switzerland are considered to live below the official poverty level (probably all foreigners), although most of Switzerland's 'poor' would be considered wealthy in many third world countries. The little old man sitting next to you on the tram could easily be one of the more than 250,000 millionaires in Switzerland. 'If you've got it, flaunt it' isn't the Swiss way of doing

things. In fact, modesty is taken to extremes; for example if a Swiss tells you that he's a fair skier, it usually means he's not quite as good as the world champion (he may even **be** the world champion).

The Swiss are very law-abiding (except regarding speed limits). Any Swiss loitering in town at 3am is more likely to be waiting for the green light to cross the road than preparing to rob a bank. In fact anyone out at 3am is probably a foreigner preparing to rob a bank, as all Swiss will have been in bed since early evening. The Swiss slavishly follow all rules and regulations and delight in pointing out your transgressions: they're world leaders in robotics – there are over 5m in Switzerland (Ouch!).

In Switzerland, rules (however trivial) certainly aren't made to be broken, and if you use the 'in' door to exit, or park an inch or two outside a parking space, it will be quickly brought to your attention by an upstanding Swiss citizen. Solzhenitsyn left Switzerland, where he arrived after deportation from Russia, complaining that Swiss bureaucracy was worse than Russia's (even the usually placid Swiss were taken aback by this pronouncement). In Switzerland, everything that isn't illegal is forbidden; everything else is compulsory. Switzerland is often described as a benevolent police state and heaven help anyone who steps out of line.

The Swiss like everything to be spotless and are obsessed with cleanliness (it being next to godliness). They employ an army of guest workers to clean up after them and not only vacuum clean their tunnels and footpaths, but scour the streets between villages. Swiss streets are so clean you could eat off them and are cleaner than the average kitchen hand in some countries.

Swiss banks (colloquially known as laundromats) even launder dirty foreign money so their citizens won't become contaminated.

Switzerland isn't exactly a land of milk and honey for the dedicated career woman, who's considered something of an eccentric. Most Swiss men think that a women's place is in the home, particularly the kitchen (not the bedroom judging by the low birth-rate). What they think of women politicians is unprintable! They don't think much of politics and politicians in general – but then who does? Swiss women didn't obtain the right to vote until 1971 and Swiss marriage laws, which were heavily biased in the husband's favour, were finally revised in January 1988 to give a wife equal rights with her husband (after 81 years). Swiss women are among the least emancipated in Western Europe and the majority appear to like it that way. The Swiss are slow to make changes, both individually and as a nation. However,

they're usually quick to embrace new technology, particularly when it will make them rich(er).

The Swiss have enjoyed the good life for so long that they've forgotten what it's like to live in the real world. However, Switzerland's seemingly permanent prosperity and stability is occasionally threatened by worldwide recessions, such as happened in the early '90s and the financial crisis in 2008, when even the sober Swiss bankers had to go cap in hand to the government to bail them out. Among the country's biggest concerns are unemployment; drug addiction; asylum seekers and refugees; the environment; provision for the elderly (pensions); relations with the EU; crime; the cost of housing; and taxation – not necessarily in that order. Many Swiss are fearful of what the future may hold – the only certain thing is that (like everyone else) they must adapt to the challenges of the 21st century and can no longer afford to live in cloud cuckoo (clock) land.

Despite their idiosyncrasies, most foreigners could learn a lot from the Swiss, who excel in many things. They're excellent skiers, the world's best hoteliers and have the best public transport in the world. They're also the world's most prolific flag flyers and best *hornussen* players. In business, they're among the world's best bankers and insurance salesmen, and are renowned for the quality of their products, from precision machinery and watches, to cheese and chocolate. Switzerland is the most ordered and stable (financially and politically) country in the world. If we turned the operation of the world economy over to the Swiss, the rest of us could relax and organise the parties.

The Swiss political system is a (boring) model of democracy, where co-operation and compromise are preferred to obstruction and obstinacy (members of the Swiss Radical Party are actually liberals). Swiss politicians even ask the opinion of the Swiss people when important issues are at stake. It hardly seems credible, but the Swiss could give politicians a good name – not only can you believe them most of the time, but even the government's statistics are usually accurate. Finally, despite the famous words of a former British Chancellor of the Exchequer, most inhabitants of Zurich are of average height and bear little resemblance to gnomes. They do, however, have lots of treasure.

The Swiss are a nation of diverse peoples who don't always see eye to eye, although generally Switzerland is an outstanding example of unity in diversity. However, nothing is guaranteed to bring the Swiss closer together than being made fun of by a bloody foreigner! (Pssst! Don't Tell the Swiss, but William, their national hero, didn't exist.)

20.

MOVING HOUSE OR LEAVING SWITZERLAND

When moving house or leaving Switzerland, there are numerous things to be considered and a 'million' people to be informed. The checklists contained in this chapter are intended to make the task easier and may even help prevent an ulcer or nervous breakdown – provided of course you don't leave everything to the last minute!

MOVING HOUSE WITHIN SWITZERLAND

When moving house within Switzerland the items mentioned below should be considered:

♦ You must usually give your landlord at least three months notice before vacating rented accommodation (refer to your contract). If you don't give sufficient notice or aren't terminating your contract on one of the approved moving dates, you'll need to find someone to take over your apartment (see **Terminating the Lease** on page 65). This also applies if you have a separate contract for a garage or other rented property, e.g. a holiday home, in Switzerland. Arrange a date with your landlord for the handover.

☑ SURVIVAL TIP

When terminating a contract your letter must be sent by registered post to reach your landlord by the last day of the month at the latest.

♦ Inform the following:

– your employer – and 'book' your free day off which you're entitled to under Swiss employment law;

– your present community eight days before moving house and your new community within eight days of taking up residence (see **Registration** on page 53);

– your electricity, gas, water and telephone (fixed, mobile, internet) companies, e.g. cancel your fixed-line phone at your present address and register for a new number at the new address;

– radio/TV (☎ 0844-834 834, 🖳 www.billag. ch);

– your insurance companies (for example health, car, house contents and private liability); banks, post office, stockbroker and other financial institutions; credit card and hire purchase (credit) companies; lawyer and accountant; and local businesses where you have accounts;

– your Social Security office (AHV/AVS) if you're self-employed;

– your family doctor, dentist and other health practitioners. Health records should be transferred to your new doctor and dentist, if applicable.

– your family's schools. If applicable, arrange for schooling in your new community. Try to give a term's notice and obtain a copy of any relevant school reports or records from your children's current schools.

– all regular correspondents, subscriptions, social and sports clubs, professional and trade journals, and friends and relatives. Give or send them your new address and telephone number. You can obtain a free moving (*Umzug/démanagement*) info pack from post offices containing free address change postcards and discount coupons. Arrange to have your post redirected by the post office (see **Change of Address** on page 84).

– your canton's motor registration office within 14 days of moving if you have a Swiss driving licence or a Swiss-registered car. If you're moving to a new canton, you'll receive a refund of your road tax from your previous canton. You're required to re-register your car in a new canton within 14 days and to return your old registration plates to your former canton's motor registration office.

– your local consulate or embassy if you're registered with them.

◆ Return any library books or anything borrowed.

◆ If you're moving cantons, arrange to settle your income tax liability in your present canton (see **Chapter 14**).

◆ If applicable, book a kennel for your dog and re-register it in your new community (see **Pets** on page 263).

◆ Arrange shipping for your furniture and belongings (or transportation if you're doing your own move).

◆ Arrange for a cleaning company and/or decorating company for your house or apartment, if necessary (see **Contract Termination** on page 65).

◆ If applicable, ensure the return of your deposit from your landlord.

◆ Cancel the milk and newspaper delivery.

◆ Note the readings on your gas, electricity and water meters.

☑ SURVIVAL TIP

Ask yourself (again): 'Is it really worth all this trouble?'

LEAVING SWITZERLAND

Before leaving Switzerland for an indefinite period, the following items should be considered in addition to those listed above.

◆ Give notice to your employer, if applicable.

◆ Check that your and your family's passports are valid.

◆ Check whether there are any special entry requirements for your country of destination, e.g. visas, permits or vaccinations, by contacting the relevant embassy or consulate in Switzerland. An exit permit or visa isn't required to leave Switzerland, but if you intend to return and want to retain your right to residence, you should obtain an 'assurance of resident permit' or 'authorisation of absence' (see **Leave of Absence** on page 48).

◆ You may qualify for a rebate on your income tax and federal old age and survivors insurance. Your employer and community will assist you with these. Tax rebates are normally paid automatically.

◆ Your private company pension contributions will be repaid in full (see **Company Pension Fund** on page 177). Before your pension fund repays your funds, you must provide a statement from your community office stating that you've de-registered and are leaving Switzerland.

◆ Arrange to sell anything that you aren't taking with you (e.g. house, car and furniture) and to ship your belongings. Find out the exact procedure for shipping your belongings to your country of destination. Check with the local embassy or consulate of the country to which you're moving, as special forms may need to be completed before arrival. If you've been living in Switzerland for less than a year, you're required to re-export all imported personal effects, including furniture and vehicles (if you sell them, you may need to pay duty).

◆ If you have a Swiss registered car that you plan to take with you, you can retain your Swiss registration plates for up to one year or until your Swiss insurance expires. When you re-register your car abroad, your Swiss registration plates must be returned to your former canton's motor registration office or can be destroyed, in which case you must provide official proof. If you don't return them, the Swiss authorities won't be pleased – and have long memories.

◆ Pets may require special inoculations or may need to be placed in quarantine for a period (see page 263).

◆ Contact your telephone company well in advance to recover your telephone deposit, if applicable (see **Moving or Leaving Switzerland** on page 91). Don't forget to cancel your mobile phone contract, but not until after you have got another one!

◆ Arrange health, travel and other insurance (see **Chapter 13**).

- Depending on your destination, you may wish to have health and dental check-ups before leaving Switzerland. Obtain a copy of your health and dental records and a statement from your health insurance company stating your present level of cover.

- Terminate any Swiss loan, lease or hire purchase (credit) contracts and pay all outstanding bills (allow plenty of time as most Swiss companies are slow to respond).

- Check whether you're entitled to a rebate on your road tax, car and other insurance. Obtain a letter from your Swiss motor insurance company stating your no-claims bonus.

- Sell or let your house, apartment, car or other property.

- Check whether you need an international driving licence or a translation of your Swiss or foreign driving licence for your country of destination.

- Give friends and business associates in Switzerland an address, telephone number and email address where you can be contacted.

- If you'll be travelling or living abroad for an extended period, you may wish to give someone 'power of attorney' over your financial affairs in Switzerland so that they can act on your behalf in your absence. This can be for a fixed period or open-ended and can be limited to a specific purpose only. **You should, however, take legal advice before doing this.**

- Buy a copy of *Living and Working in XXXXX* before leaving Switzerland. If we haven't published it yet, drop us a line and we'll get started on it right away!

Gute Reise/Bon voyage!

APPENDICES

APPENDIX A: USEFUL ADDRESSES

Embassies

Embassies are located in the capital Berne, while many countries also have consulates and missions in Basle, Geneva and Zurich (plus some other towns). Embassies and consulates are listed in telephone directories under *Konsulate, consulat/ambassade* and on the website of the Federal Department of Foreign Affairs (⌨ www.eda.admin.ch/eda/en/home/reps/forrep.html), where you can also find details of Swiss embassies abroad (⌨ www.eda.admin.ch/eda/en/home/reps.html). A selection of embassies in Berne are listed below.

> Embassy visiting hours vary considerably and all embassies close on their national holidays as well as on Swiss public holidays. It's therefore advisable to check the business hours before visiting.

Argentina: Jungfraustr. 1, CH-3005 Berne (☎ 031-356 43 43).

Austria: Kirchenfeldstr. 77-79, PO Box 266, CH-3005 Berne (☎ 031-356 52 52, ⌨ www.bmeia.gv.at).

Belgium: Jubiläumsstr. 41, PO Box 150, CH-3000 Berne 6 (☎ 031-350 01 50, ⌨ www.diplomatie.be/bernfr).

Bosnia-Herzegovinia: Thorackerstr. 3, CH-3074 Muri b. Berne (☎ 031-351 10 51, ⌨ www.ambasadabih.ch).

Brazil: Monbijoustr. 68, PO Box 1004, CH-3000 Berne 23 (☎ 031-371 85 15).

Bulgaria: Bernastr. 2, CH-3005 Berne (☎ 031-351 14 55, ⌨ www.bulembassy.ch).

Canada: Kirchenfeldstr. 88, PO Box, CH-3000 Berne 6 (☎ 031-357 32 00, ⌨ www.canadainternational.gc.ca/switzerland-suisse).

Chile: Eigerpl. 5, CH-3007 Berne (☎ 031-370 00 58).

China: Kalcheggweg 10, CH-3006 Berne (☎ 031-352 73 33, ⌨ www.china-embassy.ch).

Colombia: Dufourstr. 47, CH-3005 Berne (☎ 031-351 17 00, ⌨ www.emcol.ch).

Croatia: Thunstr. 45, CH-3005 Berne (☎ 031-352 02 75).

Czech Republic: Muristr. 53, CH-3000 Berne 31 (☎ 031-350 40 70, ⌨ www.mzv.cz/bern).

Denmark: Thunstr. 95, CH-3000 Berne 31 (☎ 031-350 54 54, ⌨ schweiz.um.dk).

Egypt: Elfenauweg 61, CH-3006 Berne (☎ 031-352 80 12).

Finland: Weltpoststr. 4, PO Box 11, CH-3000 Berne 15 (☎ 031-350 41 00, 🖥 www.finlandia.ch).

France: Schosshaldenstr. 46, CH-3006 Berne (☎ 031-359 21 11, 🖥 www.ambafrance-ch.org).

Germany: Willadingweg 83, PO Box 250, CH-3000 Berne 15 (☎ 031-359 41 11, 🖥 www.bern.diplo.de).

Greece: Weltpoststr. 4, PO Box 246, CH-3000 Berne 15 (☎ 031-356 14 14).

Hungary: Muristr. 31, PO Box 216, CH-3006 Berne (☎ 031-352 85 72).

India: Kirchenfeldstr. 28, PO Box 406, CH-3000 Berne 6 (☎ 031-350 11 30, 🖥 www.indembassybern.ch).

Indonesia: Elfenauweg 51, CH-3006 Berne (☎ 031-352 09 83, 🖥 www.indonesia-bern.org).

Iran: Thunstr. 68, PO Box 227, CH-3000 Berne 6 (☎ 031-351 08 01, 🖥 www.iranembassy.ch).

Ireland: Kirchenfeldstr. 68, CH-3005 Berne (☎ 031-352 14 42, 🖥 www.embassyofireland.ch).

Israel: Alpenstr. 32, CH-3000 Berne 6 (☎ 031-356 35 00, 🖥 www.embassies.gov.il/bern).

Italy: Elfenstr. 14, CH-3006 Berne (☎ 031-350 07 77, 🖥 www.ambberna.esteri.it).

Japan: Engestr. 53, CH-3000 Berne 9 (☎ 031-300 22 22, 🖥 www.embjapan.ch).

South Korea: Kalcheggweg 38, PO Box 28, CH-3000 Berne 15 (☎ 031-356 24 44).

Lebanon: Thunstr. 10, CH-3074 Muri b. Berne (☎ 031-950 65 65, 🖥 www.ambassadeliban.ch).

Libya: Tavelweg 2, PO Box 633, CH-3000 Berne 31 (☎ 031-350 01 22).

Liechtenstein: Willadingweg 65, CH-3000 Berne 15 (☎ 031-357 64 11, 🖥 www.bern.liechtenstein.li).

Luxembourg: Kramgasse 45, PO Box 619, CH-3000 Berne 8 (☎ 031-311 47 32).

Macedonia: Kirchenfeldstr. 30, CH-3005 Berne (☎ 031-352 00 02).

Malaysia: Jungfraustr. 1, CH-3005 Berne (☎ 031-350 47 00, 🖥 www.kln.gov.my/web/che_berne/home).

Mexico: Weltpoststr. 20, CH-3015 Berne (☎ 031-357 47 47, 🖥 www.sre.gob.mx/suiza).

Monaco: Hallwylstr. 34, CH-3005 Berne (☎ 031-356 28 58).

Morocco: Helvetiastr. 42, CH-3005 Berne (☎ 031-351 03 62).

Netherlands: Seftigenstr. 7, CH-3007 Berne (☎ 031-350 87 00, 🖥 www.zwitserland.nlambassade.org).

Nigeria: Zieglerstr. 45, PO Box 574, CH-3000 Berne 14 (☎ 031-384 26 00).

Norway: Bubenbergplatz 10, PO Box 5264, CH-3001 Berne (☎ 031-310 55 55).

Pakistan: Bernastr. 47, CH-3005 Berne (☎ 031-350 17 90, 🖥 www.swisspak.com/web/peb).

Philippines: Kirchenfeldstr. 73, CH-3005 Berne (☎ 031-350 17 17, 🖥 www.philembassyberne.ch).

Poland: Elfenstr. 20a, CH-3006 Berne (☎ 031-358 02 02, 🖥 www.berno.polemb.net).

Portugal: Weltpoststr. 20, CH-3015 Berne (☎ 031-352 86 68).

Romania: Kirchenfeldstr. 78, CH-3005 Berne (☎ 031-352 35 22, 🖥 www.berna.mae.ro).

Russia: Brunnadernrain 37, CH-3006 Berne (☎ 031-352 05 66, 🖥 www.switzerland.mid.ru).

Saudi Arabia: Kramburgstr. 12, CH-3006 Berne (☎ 031-352 15 56, 🖥 www.embassy-saudi.com/switzerland-bern.html).

Serbia: Seminarstr. 5, CH-3006 Berne (☎ 031-352 49 96).

Slovakia: Thunstr. 63, CH-3006 Muri b. Berne (☎ 031-356 39 30, 🖥 www.mzv.sk/bern).

Slovenia: Schwanengasse 9, CH-3011 Berne (☎ 031-310 90 00).

South Africa: Alpenstr. 29, CH-3000 Berne 6 (☎ 031-350 13 13, 🖥 www.southafrica.ch).

Spain: Kalcheggweg 24, PO Box 99, CH-3000 Berne 15 (☎ 031-350 52 52).

Sweden: Bundesgasse 26, CH-3001 Berne (☎ 031-328 70 00, 🖥 www.swedishembassy.ch).

Thailand: Kirchstr. 56, CH-3097 Liebefeld (☎ 031-970 30 30, 🖥 www.thaiembassybern.org).

Turkey: Lombachweg 33, PO Box 34, CH-3000 Berne 15 (☎ 031-359 70 70).

Ukraine: Feldeggweg 5, CH-3005 Berne (☎ 031-352 23 16).

United Kingdom: Thunstr. 50, CH-3005 Berne 15 (☎ 031-359 77 00, 🖥 www.ukinswitzerland.fco. gov.uk).

Uruguay: Kramgasse 63, CH-3011 Berne (☎ 031-311 27 92).

USA: Sulgeneckstr. 19, CH-3007 Berne (☎ 031-357 70 11, 🖥 www.bern.usembassy.gov).

Government

Central Compensation Office (OASI/DI): Av. Edmond-Vaucher 18, CH-1200 2 Geneva (☎ 022-795 91 11, 🖥 www.avs-ai-international.ch).

Federal Aliens Office: Quellenweg 6, CH-3003 Berne-Wabern (☎ 031-325 11 11, 🖥 www.bfm. admin.ch).

Federal Office for Migration (FOM), Free Movement of Persons and Emigration, Quellenweg 6, 3003 Berne-Wabern (☎ 31-325 11 11, 🖥 www.bfm.admin.ch).

Federal Office for Social Insurance: Effingerstr. 20, CH-3003 Berne (☎ 031-322 90 11, 🖥 www.bsv.admin.ch).

Federal Veterinarians Office: Schwarzenburgstr. 155, CH-3003 Berne (☎ 031-323 30 33, 🖥 www.bvet.admin.ch).

Head Customs Office: Monbijoustr. 40, CH-3003 Berne (☎ 031-322 67 43, 🖥 www.zoll.admin.ch).

State Secretariat for Economic Affairs (SECO), Labour Directorate, Effingerstrasse 31, 3003 Berne (☎ 31-323 25 25, 🖥 www.eures.ch/www.job-area.ch).

Swiss Broadcasting Corporation (SRG): Giacomettistrasse 1, CH-3000 Berne 31 (☎ 031-350 91 11, 🖥 www.srg.ch).

Swiss Bureau for the Prevention of Accidents: Hodlerstra. 5a, CH-3011 Berne (☎ 031-390 22 22, 🖥 www.bfu.ch).

Switzerland Tourism (ST): PO Box 695, CH-8027 Zurich (☎ 0800-100 200 30/044-288 11 11, 🖥 www.myswitzerland.com).

Swiss Radio International: Giacomettistr. 1, CH-3000 Berne 15 (☎ 031-350 92 22, 🖥 www.swissinfo.org).

Miscellaneous

The Automobile Club of Switzerland (ACS): Wasserwerkgasse 39, CH-3000 Berne 13 (☎ 031-328 31 11, 🖥 www.acs.ch).

British Swiss Chamber of Commerce: Bellerivestr. 209, CH-8008 Zurich (☎ 044-380 03 08, 🖥 www.bscc.ch).

English Teachers Association, Switzerland: ETAS Administration, Rue de l'Hôpital 32, CH-1400 Yverdon (☎ 024-420 32 54, 🖳 www.e-tas.ch).

Health.ch AG, Dorfstr. 24, 8700 Küsnacht (☎ 043-541 15 21, 🖳 www.doctor.ch). Internet site with lists of doctors, dentists, pharmacies and clinics throughout Switzerland.

Mobility Carsharing Schweiz: Gütschstr. 2, Postfach, CH-6000 Lucerne 7 (☎ 0848-824 812, 🖳 www.mobility.ch).

Pro Infirmis Schweiz: Postfach, CH-8032 Zurich (☎ 044-388 26 26, 🖳 www.proinfirmis.ch).

Pro Senectute Schweiz: Lavaterstr. 60, Postfach, CH-8027 Zurich (☎ 044-283 89 89, 🖳 www.pro-senectute.ch).

REGA Administration und Secretariat: Rega Center, PO Box 1414, CH-8058 Zurich Airport (☎ 044-654 37 37, 1414 in an emergency or +41 333 333 333 if your mobile phone doesn't have a SIM card from a Swiss network provider, 🖳 www.rega.ch).

STA Travel: Ankerstr. 112, Postfach 8026, CH-8004 Zurich (☎ 058-450 40 00, 🖳 www.statravel.ch).

Swiss Accidents and Insurance (SUVA): Fluhmattstr. 1, Postfach 4358, CH-6002 Lucerne (☎ 041-419 51 11, 🖳 www.suva.ch).

Swiss-American Chamber of Commerce: Talacker 41, CH-8001 Zurich (☎ 043-443 72 08, 🖳 www.amcham.ch).

Swiss Camping Association: Bahnhofstr. 5, CH-3322 Schönbühl (☎ 031-852 06 26, 🖳 www.swisscamps.ch).

Swiss Hotel Association (SHV): Monbijoustr. 130, PO Box, CH-3007 Berne (☎ 031-370 41 11, 🖳 www.swisshotels.ch).

Swiss Red Cross: Rainmattstr. 10, CH-3001 Berne (☎ 031-387 71 11, 🖳 www.redcross.ch).

Swiss Youth Hostels: Schaffhauserstr. 14, CH-8006 Zurich (☎ 044-360 14 14, 🖳 www.youthhostel.ch).

Touring Club of Switzerland (TCS): CH de Blandonnet 4, PO Box 820, CH-1214 Vernier (☎ 041-22 41 72 520, 🖳 www.tcs.ch).

Transport Club of Switzerland (VCS): Stock Str. 41, PO Box, CH-3360 Herzogenbuchsee (☎ 0848-611 611, 🖳 www.verkehrsclub.ch).

APPENDIX B: FURTHER READING

One of the most useful Swiss publications for anyone seeking information about anything in Switzerland is Publicus, the *Swiss Year Book of Public Life* (Schweizer Jahrbuch des Öffentlichen Lebens, Annuaire Suisse de la vie publique), also available on CD-ROM. It contains the addresses and telephone numbers of federal and canton government departments, charitable organisations, embassies and much more, and is available from Schwabe & Co. AG, Steintorstr. 13, PO Box, CH-4010 Basle (☎ 061-278 95 65, 🖥 www.publicus.ch).

In the lists on the following pages, the publication title is followed by the author's name and the publisher's name (in brackets). Some titles may be out of print, although you may still be able to find a copy in a Swiss bookshop or a library.

Economy & Government

The Referendum – Direct Democracy in Switzerland, Kris W. Kobach (Dartmouth)

Switzerland In Europe, Christine Trampusch (Routledge)

Target Switzerland: Swiss Armed Neutrality in World War II, Steven Halbrook (Da Capo Press)

The Swiss and the Nazis: How the Alpine Republic Survived the Shadow of the Third Reich, Steven Halbrook (Casemate)

Hiking & Climbing

The Bernese Alps: A Walking Guide, Kev Reynolds (Cicerone)

Walking in Switzerland, Clem Lindenmayer (Lonely Planet)

Walking Switzerland the Swiss Way, Marcia & Philip Lieberman (Mountaineers Books)

Walking in the Alps, Kev Reynolds (Cicerone Press)

Walking in the Engadine – Switzerland: 100 Walks and Treks, Kev Reynolds (Cicerone Press)

Miscellaneous

Asterix in Switzerland, René Goscinny and Albert Uderzo (Asterix)

Buying or Renting a Home in Switzerland, David Hampshire & Anne-Marie Travers (Survival Books)

The Expat Jobseeker's Guidebook To Switzerland, Tomasz Meissner (CreateSpace)

Hoi – Your Swiss German Survival Guide, Sergio J. Lievano and Nicole Egger (Bergli Books)

Swiss Me, Roger Bonner (Bergli Books)

Swiss Watching: Inside the Land of Milk and Honey, Diccon Bewes (Nicholas Brealey)

Swisscellany, Diccon Bewes & Mischa Kammermann (Bergli)

Switzerland – You Danced In My Heart, Charmiene Maxwell-Batten (lulu.com)

Ticking Along with the Swiss, Patricia Highsmith, Stanley Mason et al (Bergli)

Village Life in Switzerland, Sophia Duberly Delmard (Forgotten Books)

The Xenophobe's Guide to the Swiss, Paul Bilton (Oval)

Travel & Tourism

DK Eyewitness Travel Guide: Switzerland (Dorling Kindersley)

Frommer's Switzerland (John Wiley & Sons)

Insight Guides Switzerland (APA Insight Guides)

Karen Brown's Switzerland: Charming Inns & Itineraries, Clare & Karen Brown (Karen Brown's Guides)

Let's Go Austria & Switzerland (Macmillan)

Michelin Green Guide To Switzerland (Michelin)

Michelin Red Guide Switzerland (Michelin)

The Rough Guide to Switzerland, Matthew Teller (Rough Guides)

Switzerland, Nicola Williams (Lonely Planet)

Switzerland By Train, Barbara Ender-Jones (JPM Publications)

Switzerland Without a Car, Anthony Lambert (Bradt)

APPENDIX C: USEFUL WEBSITES

This appendix contains a list of some of the many websites dedicated to Switzerland. Websites about particular aspects of life and work in Switzerland are also mentioned in the relevant chapters.

Business

British Swiss Chamber of Commerce (☐ www.bscc.ch).

Chambers of Commerce & Industry (☐ www.cci.ch/en/map.htm).

Doing Business (☐ www.doingbusiness.org). Provides objective measures of business regulations and their enforcement.

Infonautics Business Directory (☐ www.swissdir.ch). Index of *Swiss Business*, Companies, Hotels and Tourism.

Osec, Business Network Switzerland (☐ www.osec.ch). The umbrella organisation for the promotion of exports, imports and investments, as well as the promotion of Switzerland as a business location.

Swiss-American Chamber of Commerce (☐ www.amcham.ch).

Swiss Banking (☐ www.swissbanking.ch). Swiss Bankers' association website where the Swiss banking system is explained.

Swiss Business Hub USA (☐ www.swissbusinesshub.org). Trade Commissions of Switzerland to the US.

Swiss Business School (☐ www.sbs.edu). One of the world's leading business schools (situated in Zurich).

Swiss Firms (☐ www.swissfirms.ch/en). Promotes member companies of the Swiss Chambers of Commerce and supports them in their daily business activities.

Swiss Network (☐ www.swissnetwork.com). Portal for business and investments in Switzerland.

Education & Families

All for Kids (☐ www.allforkids.ch). Fun learning and creative products in English for families in Switzerland.

Bilingual Middle School (☐ www.bilingual-middleschool.ch). German-English primary school in Zurich.

CRUS (☐ www.crus.ch/information-programme/study-in-switzerland.html?L=2). Information about study in Switzerland from the Rectors' Conference of Swiss Universities.

Educa (☐ www.educa.ch). Covers all levels of the Swiss education system.

Education in Switzerland (☐ www.about.ch/education/index.html). Information about the Swiss school system.

English Teachers Association Switzerland (☐ www.e-tas.ch).

Geneva Association of Private Schools (🖥 www.agep.ch/eng).

Gymboree (🖥 www.gymboree.ch). Play, music & arts' classes for infants to five years with classes in Basle, Geneva and Zurich.

International School of Central Switzerland (🖥 www.isocs.ch). New international school located in Cham, Zug.

International Schools in Switzerland (🖥 http://switzerland.english-schools.org).

ISW International School Winterthur (🖥 www.iswinterthur.ch). International school offering the International Baccalaureate (IB) examination.

Lake Geneva Swiss Private Schools (: www.avdep.ch/default.cfm).

The Learning Place (🖥 www.thelearningplace.ch). Language school in Zug.

Mothering Matters (🖥 www.mmjournal.com). Devoted to parenting in Switzerland.

Swiss Education Group (🖥 www.swisseducation.com). The leading Swiss provider of hotel management schools.

Swiss Federation of Private Schools (🖥 www.swiss-schools.ch).

Swiss International School (🖥 www.international-school.ch). Zurich North international school is an IB World School that offers students an international education in the English language.

Swiss University (🖥 www.swissuniversity.ch). The portal of Swiss universities for those planning to study in Switzerland.

Finance & Mortgages

Comparis (🖥 www.comparis.ch/hypotheken). Insurance and mortgage comparisons online.

Credit Suisse (🖥 www.credit-suisse.com/ch/en). Credit Suisse in English.

Homegate (🖥 www.homegate.ch). Mortgage rate comparison (French/German only).

Swiss Banking (🖥 www.swissbanking.ch). Swiss Bankers' Association website where the Swiss banking system is explained.

Swiss Cantonal Banks (🖥 www.kantonalbank.ch/e/index.php). An association of 24 Swiss cantonal banks offering a wide range of banking services and mortgages.

Swiss Federal Banking Commission (🖥 www.finma.ch/archiv/ebk/e/index.html).

Union Bank of Switzerland (🖥 www.ubs.com). UBS in English.

Zurich Insurance (🖥 www.zurich.ch/site/en.html). Zurich insurance and mortgages.

Government

Directory of Administrative Authorities (🖥 www.ch.ch/verzeichnis/index.html?lang=en#). Federal, cantonal and communal authorities.

Federal Government (🖥 www.admin.ch). The website of the Swiss government with links to all state departments.

Federal Office of Housing (🖥 www.bwo.admin.ch).

Federal Office for Migration (🖥 www.bfm.admin.ch). Provides information about work and residence permits.

Swiss Embassies (🖳 www.eda.admin.ch/eda/en/home/reps.html). Contact details and links to Swiss embassy websites.

Swiss Emigration (🖳 www.swissemigration.ch). Information about living and working in Switzerland.

SwissInfoDesk (🖳 www.nb.admin.ch). Information about Switzerland from the Swiss National Library (NL).

Swiss Parliament: Federal Assembly (🖳 www.parlament.ch/e/pages/default.aspx).

Swiss Parliament: Federal Council (🖳 www.admin.ch/br/index.html?lang=en).

The Swiss Portal (🖳 www.ch.ch). A wealth of practical information provided by the Swiss government.

Swiss Statistics (🖳 www.bfs.admin.ch/bfs/portal/en/index.html).

Swisstopo (🖳 www.swisstopo.admin.ch). Swiss Federal Office of Topography.

Living and Working

Anglo Info (🖳 http://geneva.angloinfo.com). Everything you need to know about life in and around Geneva.

Anglo Swiss Clubs (🖳 www.angloswissclubs).

Auris Relocation (🖳 www.aurisrelocation.com). Swiss specialist relocation company.

Basel Expats (🖳 http://baselexpats.com). Local and general info for expats.

Crown Relocation (🖳 www.crownrelo.com). A division of the Crown Worldwide Group established in 1965.

English Forum (🖳 www.englishforum.ch). English-language community forum.

Expats in Switzerland (🖳 www.expatinch.com). Wide range of useful information.

Geneva Info (🖳 www.geneva.info). Geneva information for expats.

Geneva Lunch (🖳 http://genevalunch.com). Community 'newspaper' for the Lake Geneva region.

Geneva Welcome Centre (: www.cagi.ch). Website of CAGI, which helps find accommodation **for international civil servants,** members of permanent missions, consulates, NGOs and their families.

Glocals (🖳 www.glocals.com). Social networking website. Began life as 'genevalocals', but now covers the whole of Switzerland.

Jobs in Switzerland (🖳 www.jobsinch.com). Website of Tomasz Meissner, author of *The Expat Jobseeker's Guidebook To Switzerland.*

Keller Relocation (🖳 www.keller-swiss-group.com). Removals and relocation for the whole of Switzerland and worldwide.

Know it All (🖳 www.knowitall.ch). The ultimate guide to daily life for English-speakers in the Geneva, Vaud and neighbouring French areas.

Local (🖳 www.local.ch). Find regional information at a glance, e.g. phone numbers, events and classifieds, anywhere in Switzerland.

Lucerne4you.ch (🖳 www.lucerne4you.ch). Information for expats in Lucerne including with a free monthly newsletter and regular events

Migros Online (🖳 www.leshop.ch). Shop at Migros from the comfort of your home (in English).

Survival Books (🖥 www.survivalbooks.net). Publisher of *Living and Working in Switzerland* and *Buying or Renting a Home in Switzerland*.

Swiss Association of Relocation Agents (🖥 www.sara-relocation.com).

SwissConnex (🖥 www.swissconnex.ch). A portal that links to many sites covering health, tourism, sports and business.

Switzerland is Yours (🖥 www.switzerland.isyours.com). Micheloud & Cie's website offering financial and immigration services for newcomers.

Taxation (🖥 www.taxation.ch). Swiss taxation website.

XpatXchange (🖥 www.xpatxchange.ch). Excellent one-stop site for English-speaking expats in Switzerland.

Zug4you (🖥 www.zug4you.ch). Information for expats in the Canton of Zug, including the local daily news in English website thezugpost.ch (www), a monthly newsletter and organized events if you sign up (free)

Zurich4you (🖥 www.zurich4you.ch). Information for expats in the Canton of Zurich, monthly newsletter and regular organized events.

Zurich Expats (🖥 http://zurichexpats.com). Info for expats living and working in Zurich.

Media

24 Heures (🖥 www.24heures.ch). Leading French-language magazine.

Annonce 24 Heures (🖥 http://annonces.24heures.ch). Small ads website.

Basler Zeitung (🖥 www.baz.ch). The online version of *Basler Zeitung*, covering mainly the northwest of Switzerland. In German, but with many articles are translated into English.

Berner Zeitung (🖥 www.bernerzeitung.ch). Berne's leading newspaper (German).

Bergli Books (🖥 www.bergli.ch). Specialist Swiss publisher of books about Switzerland and the Swiss for expatriates.

Blick (🖥 www.blick.ch). Switzerland's leading tabloid newspaper (in German).

Cosmopolis (🖥 www.cosmopolis.ch/english/archives.htm). Current affairs and culture magazine.

The Economist (🖥 www.economist.com/countries/switzerland). English business magazine Contains interesting in-depth articles about Switzerland.

Gourmet World (🖥 www.gourmet-verlag.ch). German-language food magazine.

Hello Switzerland (🖥 www.helloswitzerland.ch). Swiss culture, politics, tourism and events – free quarterly magazine published by Network Relocation.

Le Temps (🖥 www.letemps.ch). Leading French-language newspaper.

Marmite (🖥 http://marmite.ch). Food and drink magazine in German.

Le Matin (🖥 www.lematin.ch). Popular French-language newspaper.

News (🖥 www.news.ch). Excellent news website (German only).

Neue Zürcher Zeitung (🖥 www.nzz.ch). The leading national newspaper in Switzerland, mainly Zurich focused (German).

Swissinfo (🖥 www.swissinfo.org). National and international news provided by Swiss Radio International.

Swiss News magazine (⌨ www.swissnews.ch). Swiss monthly news and events magazine for expats.

Swiss Newspapers Online (⌨ www.onlinenewspapers.com/switzerl.htm). The most comprehensive list of Swiss national and regional newspapers in A-Z order.

Swiss Style (⌨ www.swissstyle.com). Swiss lifestyle magazine published by Anglo Info (see **Living and Working** above**)**.

Swiss Television (⌨ www.srgssrideesuisse.ch/en). Switzerland's national radio and television company.

Swisster (⌨ www.swisster.ch). News website dedicated to the English-speaking expatriate community in Switzerland.

Tribune de Genève (⌨ www.tdg.ch). Geneva's leading newspaper.

Zeitung (⌨ www.zeitung.ch). Index of Swiss newspapers published in German.

Miscellaneous

About Switzerland (⌨ www.about.ch). General information about Switzerland.

Comparis (⌨ www.comparis.ch). Provides interactive comparisons of insurance premiums, telephone and bank charges (etc.).

Dignitas (⌨ www.dignitas.ch). The Swiss organisation that assists those with terminal or incurable illnesses to end their lives with dignity.

Directories (⌨ www.directories.ch). Swiss online telephone book.

Eat Smoke Free (⌨ www.eatsmokefree.ch). A directory of Swiss restaurants that are non-smoking or that have separate dining rooms for non-smokers.

English Forum (⌨ www.englishforum.ch). A forum for English speakers throughout Switzerland.

Feiertagskalender (⌨ www.feiertagskalender.ch). Lists public holidays for each canton.

Health.ch AG (⌨ www.doctor.ch). Lists of doctors, dentists, pharmacies and clinics throughout Switzerland.

History (⌨ www.hls-dhs-dss.ch/index.php). Historical dictionary of Switzerland.

Meteo Swiss (⌨ www.meteoswiss.admin.ch). Swiss weather from the Federal Office of Meteorology and Climatology

My Swiss Alps (⌨ www.myswissalps.com). Everything you ever wanted to know about the Swiss Alps.

Presence Switzerland (⌨ www.presence.ch). Information about Swiss history, geography and society.

REGA (⌨ www.rega.ch). Swiss air rescue service.

Ricardo (⌨ www.ricardo.ch). Switzerland's most popular auction site.

Search (⌨ www.search.ch). Search engine for Swiss websites.

Sociology in Switzerland (⌨ www.socio.ch). Website of the Sociology Institute of Zurich (University of Zurich) containing a wealth of media and political links.

Swiss Airports (⌨ www.airport.ch). Swiss airports portal.

Swiss Red Cross (⌨ www.redcross.ch).

Swiss Ski (⌨ www.swiss-ski.ch). Website of the Swiss Ski Federation.

Swissworld (💻 www.swissworld.org). Provides information about Switzerland's history, the political system, culture and society – and on the history of chocolate production in Switzerland.

Tel.search.ch (💻 http://tel.search.ch). The electronic phone book.

Traveling (💻 www.traveling.ch/index2.php?title=city). A useful index of Swiss towns/cities with links to their websites.

Wikipedia (💻 http://en.wikipedia.org/wiki/Switzerland). Wikipedia pages for Switzerland.

Yoodle (💻 www.yoodle.ch). Swiss search engine.

Property Rental & Purchase

Alle Immobilien (💻 www.alle-immobilien.ch). Buy or rent property (English version).

Anibis (💻 www.anibis.ch/c/15). Classified property ads in French (Suisse romande).

Anzeiger (💻 www.anzeiger.ch). Buy or rent property – browse by canton. German only.

Comparis (💻 www.comparis.ch/immobilien/intro.aspx). One of Switzerland's leading websites for buying and renting property. English version.

Dream Chalet (💻 www.dreamchalet.nl). Dutch website for Swiss property investors.

Geneva Immobilier (💻 www.geneveimmobilier.ch). Geneva association of around 30 real estate agents.

Global Property Guide (💻 www.globalpropertyguide.com/Europe/Switzerland). Useful information about Swiss real estate for investors.

Haus Forum (💻 www.haus-forum.ch). The largest house-building database in Switzerland.

HEV Immo (💻 www.hev-immo.ch/hev/home/estate/index.htm). Property sales by the Hauseigentümerverband Schweiz.

Homegate (💻 www.homegate.ch). Comprehensive database of apartments and houses for rent or sale. English version.

Home Styling by Ursula (www.homestyling-by-ursula.ch).

Immobilienmakler (💻 www.die-immobilienmakler.ch). Find a real estate agent anywhere in Switzerland.

Immo Click (💻 www.immoclick.ch). Buy or rent property (French/German only).

Immo Galaxy (💻 www.immogalaxy.ch/e). Largest real estate agent in Ticino.

ImmoMarkt Schweiz (💻 www.immomarktschweiz.ch). Property sales by 15 cantonal banks.

Immo-Net (💻 www.immo-net.ch). Buy or rent property (French/German only).

Immo Scout (💻 www.immoscout24.ch). Buy or rent a home (English version).

Immo Search (💻 http://immo.search.ch). Buy or rent property (French/German only).

In-lease (💻 www.in-lease.com). Furniture rental services.

Rent Law (💻 www.mietrecht.ch). Everything you need to know about tenancy law (in German).

Swiss Architects (💻 www.swiss-architects.com). Find a local architect.

Swiss Property (💻 www.swissproperty.co.uk). Swiss property sales for investors.

Swiss Getaway (💻 www.swissgetaway.com). Swiss property specialist for foreign investors.

Swiss Real Estate Association (🖳 www.svit.ch). The professional body for Swiss real estate agents.

Tenants' Associations (German-speaking cantons, 🖳 www.mieterverband.ch, French–speaking cantons, 🖳 www.asloca.ch, Italian-speaking Ticino, 🖳 www.asi-infoalloggio.ch).

USPI Geneva (🖳 www.uspi-ge.ch). Union of real estate agents in Geneva.

WG Zimmer (🖳 www.wgzimmer.ch/home.cfm?land=CH&lang=D). Switzerland's largest flatshare website.

Travel & Tourism

The Automobile Club of Switzerland (🖳 www.acs.ch). Motoring organisation.

Inforoute (🖳 www.inforoute.ch). Up-to-date traffic information on Swiss motorways, alpine passes and tunnels.

Mobility Carsharing Schweiz (🖳 www.mobility.ch). Enjoy the benefits of car use without the costs and hassles of ownership.

Museumspass (🖳 www.museumspass.ch). A portal providing access to information about museums in Switzerland.

My Switzerland (🖳 www.myswitzerland.com/en). Swiss national tourist office website with comprehensive information and links to accommodation, transport, sports facilities, events etc.

Out and About (🖳 www.outandabout.ch). Leisure guide for the greater Zurich area.

STA Travel (🖳 www.statravel.ch). Student travel agent with travel shops throughout Switzerland.

Swiss Hotel Association (🖳 www.swisshotels.ch).

Swiss International Air Lines (🖳 www.swiss.com).

Swiss Railways (🖳 www.sbb.ch). Train schedules and personalized timetables.

Swiss Travel System (🖳 www.swisstravelsystem.com). Travel passes for visitors.

Switzerland.com (🖳 www.switzerland.com). Wealth of general information about Switzerland from Switzerland Tourism.

Touring Club of Switzerland (🖳 www.tcs.ch). Motoring organisation.

Youth Hostels (🖳 www.youthhostel.ch). List all youth hostels in Switzerland, with an online reservation system.

APPENDIX D: WEIGHTS & MEASURES

S witzerland uses the metric system of measurement. Those who are more familiar with the imperial system will find the tables on the following pages useful. Some comparisons shown are only approximate, but are close enough for most everyday uses.

In addition to the variety of measurement systems used, clothes sizes often vary considerably with the manufacturer – as we all know only too well! Try all clothes on before buying and don't be afraid to return something if, when you try it on at home, you decide it doesn't fit (most shops will exchange goods or give a refund).

Women's Clothes									
Continental	34 36	38	40	42	44	46	48	50	52
UK	8	10	12	14	16	18	20	22	24 26
US	6	8	10	12	14	16	18	20	22 24

Pullover's											
	Women's						Men's				
Continental	40	42	44	46	48	50	44	46	48	50	52 54
UK	34	36	38	40	42	44	34	36	38	40	42 44
US	34	36	38	40	42	44	sm	med		lg	xl

Men's Shirts									
Continental	36	37	38	39	40	41	42	43	44 46
UK/US	14	14	15	15	16	16	17	17	18 -

Men's Underwear						
Continental	5	6	7	8	9	10
UK		34	36	38	40	42 44
US		sm	med		lg	xl

sm = small, med = medium, lg = large, xl = extra large

Children's Clothes

Continental	92	104	116	128	140	152
UK		16/18	20/22	24/26	28/30	32/34	36/38
US		2	4	6	8	10	12

Children's Shoes

Continental	18 19 20 21 22 23 24 25 26 27 28 29 30 31 32
UK/US	2 3 4 4 5 6 7 7 8 9 10 11 11 12 13
Continental	33 34 35 36 37 38
UK/US	1 2 2 3 4 5

Shoes (Women's & Men's)

Continental	35	36	37	37	38	39	40	41	42	42	43	44	45	46.5	47.5
UK	2	3	3	4	4	5	6	7	7	8	9	9	10	11	12
US	2.5	3.5	4.5	5.5	6.5	7.5	8.5	9.5	10.5	11.5	12.5

Weight

Imperial	Metric	Metric	Imperial
1oz	28.35g	1g	0.035oz
1lb*	454g	100g	3.5oz
1cwt	50.8kg	250g	9oz
1 ton	1,016kg	500g	18oz
2,205lb	1 tonne	1kg	2.2lb

Area

British/US	Metric	Metric	British/US
1 sq. in	0.45 sq. cm	1 sq. cm	0.15 sq. in
1 sq. ft	0.09 sq. m	1 sq. m	10.76 sq. ft
1 sq. yd	0.84 sq. m	1 sq. m	1.2 sq. yds
1 acre	0.4 hectares	1 hectare	2.47 acres
1 sq. mile	2.56 sq. km	1 sq. km	0.39 sq. mile

Capacity			
Imperial	**Metric**	**Metric**	**Imperial**
1 UK pint	0.57 litre	1 litre	1.75 UK pints
1 US pint	0.47 litre	1 litre	2.13 US pints
1 UK gallon	4.54 litres	1 litre	0.22 UK gallon
1 US gallon	3.78 litres	1 litre	0.26 US gallon

An American 'cup' = around 250ml or 0.25 litre.

Length			
British/US	**Metric**	**Metric**	**British/US**
1in	2.54cm	1cm	0.39in
1ft	30.48cm	1m	3ft 3.25in
1yd	91.44cm	1km	0.62mi
1mi	1.6km	8km	5mi

Temperature	
°Celsius	**°Fahrenheit**
0	32 (freezing point of water)
5	41
10	50
15	59
20	68
25	77
30	86
35	95
40	104
50	122

Temperature Conversion

Celsius to Fahrenheit: multiply by 9, divide by 5 and add 32. (For a quick and approximate conversion, double the Celsius temperature and add 30.)

Fahrenheit to Celsius: subtract 32, multiply by 5 and divide by 9. (For a quick and approximate conversion, subtract 30 from the Fahrenheit temperature and divide by 2.)

NB: The boiling point of water is 100°C / 212°F. Normal body temperature (if you're alive and well) is 37°C / 98.6°F.

Power			
Kilowatts	Horsepower	Horsepower	Kilowatts
1	1.34	1	0.75

Oven Temperature		
Gas	Electric	
	°F	°C
-	225–250	110–120
1	275	140
2	300	150
3	325	160
4	350	180
5	375	190
6	400	200
7	425	220
8	450	230
9	475	240

Air Pressure	
PSI	Bar
10	0.5
20	1.4
30	2
40	2.8

APPENDIX E: MAPS

The map opposite shows the 26 Swiss cantons (listed in alphabetical order below). Cantons Appenzell Inner-Rhodes, Appenzell Outer-Rhodes, Basle-Town, Basle-Country, Nidwalden and Obwalden rank as half-cantons and have only one seat in the Council of States (all other cantons have two seats). The letters in brackets are the official canton abbreviations, as shown on vehicle number plates.

Aargau/Aargovia (AG)

Appenzell Inner-Rhodes (AI)

Appenzell Outer-Rhodes (AR)

Berne (BE)

Basel-City (BS)

Basel-Country (BL)

Fribourg (FR)

Geneva (GE)

Glarus (GL)

Grisons/Graubunden (GR)

Jura (JU)

Lucerne (LU)

Nidwalden (NW)

Obwalden (OW)

Neuchâtel (NE)

St. Gallen (SG)

Schaffhausen (SH)

Solothurn (SO)

Schwyz (SZ)

Ticino (TI)

Thurgau (TG)

Uri (UR)

Valais (VS)

Vaud (VD)

Zug (ZG)

Zurich (ZH)

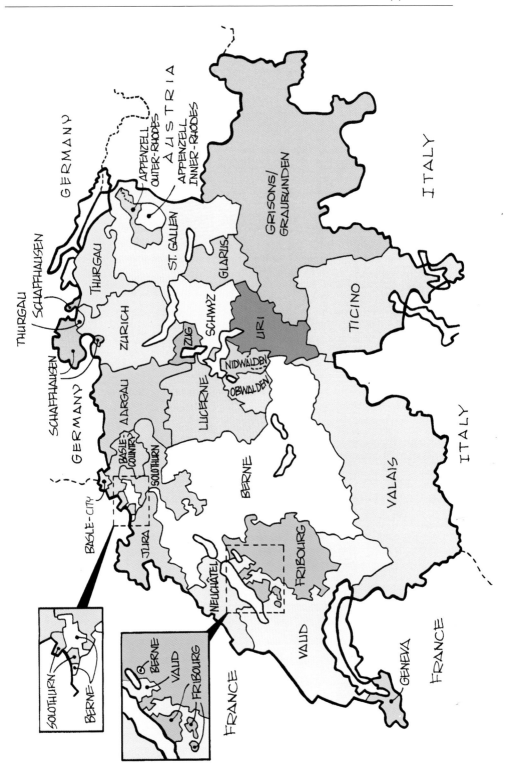

Physical:

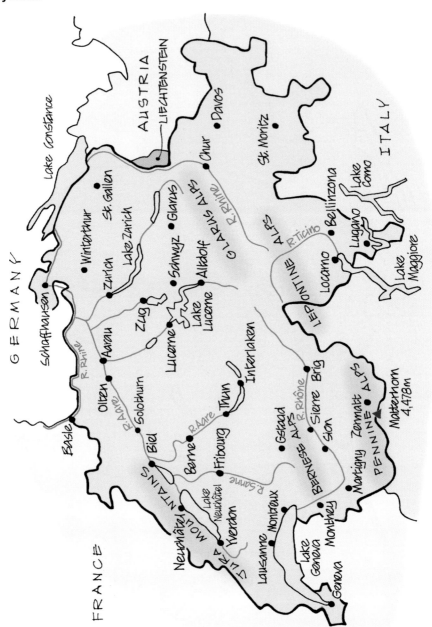

Major Roads:

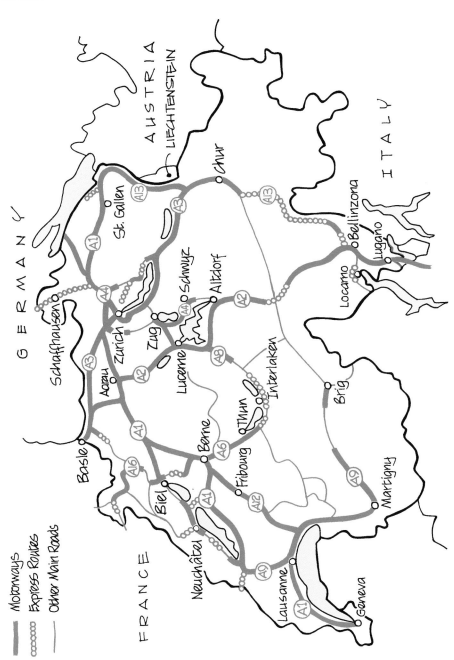

Railways & Airports:

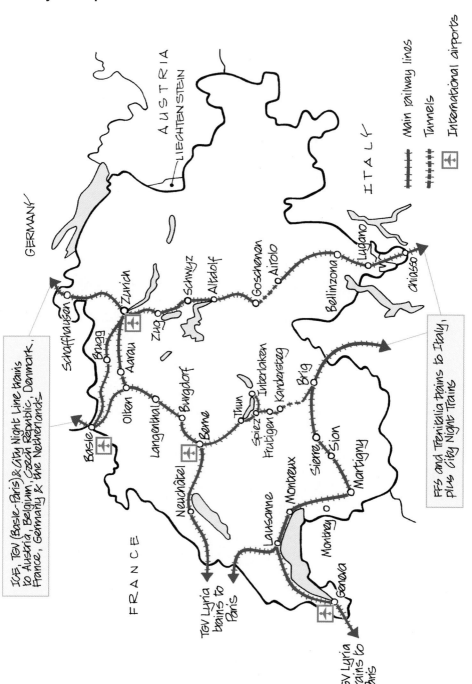

INDEX

Who Are We?

Survival Books was established in 1987 and by the mid-'90s was the leading publisher of books for people planning to live, work, buy property or retire abroad.

From the outset, our philosophy has been to provide the most comprehensive and up-to-date information available. Our titles routinely contain up to twice as much information as other books and are updated more frequently. All our books contain colour photographs and most are printed in full colour. They also contain original cartoons, illustrations and maps.

Survival Books are written by people with first-hand experience of the countries, cities and the people they describe, and therefore provide invaluable insights that cannot be obtained from official publications or websites, and information that is more reliable and objective than that provided by the majority of unofficial websites.

Survival Books are designed to be easy – and interesting – to read. They contain a comprehensive list of contents and index and many also have extensive appendices, including useful addresses, further reading and useful websites to help you obtain additional information, as well as other useful reference material.

Our primary goal is to provide you with the essential information necessary for a trouble-free life or property purchase and to save you time, trouble and money.

We believe our books are the best available – they are certainly the best-selling. But don't take our word for it – read what reviewers and readers have said about Survival Books at the front of this book.

Most of our books are available as Paperbacks, Kindle and eBooks. Order your copies today by visiting www.survivalbooks.net

Our Living and Working guides are essential reading for anyone planning to spend a period abroad – whether it's an extended holiday or permanent migration – and are packed with priceless information designed to help you avoid costly mistakes and save time, trouble and money.

Living and Working guides are the most comprehensive and up-to-date source of practical information available about everyday life abroad. They aren't, however, simply a catalogue of dry facts and figures, but are written in a highly readable style – entertaining, practical and occasionally humorous.

Our aim is to provide you with the comprehensive information necessary for a trouble-free life. You may have visited a country as a tourist, but living and working there is a different matter altogether; adjusting to a new environment and culture and making a home in any foreign country can be a traumatic and stressful experience. You need to adapt to new customs and traditions, discover the local way of doing things (such as finding a home, paying bills and obtaining insurance) and learn all over again how to overcome the everyday obstacles of life.

All these subjects and many, many more are covered in depth in our Living and Working guides – don't leave home without them.

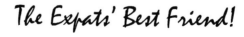

The Expats' Best Friend!

London's Hidden Secrets: A mini series of three guides to the city's quirky and unusual sights that most visitors and even residents don't get to visit.

London's Secret Walks: A walking book with a difference, taking you off the beaten track to visit London's hidden and 'secret' sights.

London's Secrets: a new series including Museums & Galleries, Parks & Gardens and Pubs & Bars, with more to come.

Retiring in France: Everything a prospective retiree needs to know about one of the world's most popular retirement destinations.

Running Gîtes and B&Bs in France: An essential guide for anyone planning to invest in a gîte or bed & breakfast business.

Shooting Caterpillars in Spain: The hilarious and compelling story of two innocents abroad in the depths of Andalusia in the late '80s.

Sketchbooks series: A series of beautiful sketchbooks with walks, including Cornwall, the Cotswolds, the Lake District and London.

Where to Live in London: The only book published to help newcomers choose the best area to live to suit both their lifestyle and pocket.

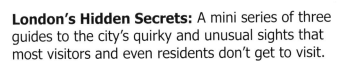

For a full list of our current titles, visit our website at www.survivalbooks.net

PHOTO

CREDITS

NOTES

NOTES

London's Secrets

LONDON'S HIDDEN SECRETS

ISBN: 978-1-907339-40-0, £10.95

Graeme Chesters

A guide to London's hidden and lesser-known sights not found in standard guidebooks. Step beyond the chaos, cliches and queues of London's tourist-clogged attractions to its quirkier side.

Discover its loveliest ancient buildings, secret gardens, strangest museums, most atmospheric pubs, cutting-edge art and design, and much more: some 140 destinations in all corners of the city.

LONDON'S HIDDEN SECRETS VOL 2

ISBN: 978-1-907339-79-0, £10.95

Graeme Chesters & David Hampshire

Hot on the heels of London's Hidden Secrets comes another volume of the city's largely undiscovered sights, many of which we were unable to include in the original book. In fact, the more research we did the more treasures we found, until eventually a second volume was inevitable.

Written by two experienced London writers, LHS 2 is for both those who already know the metropolis and newcomers wishing to learn more about its hidden and unusual charms.

LONDON'S SECRET WALKS

ISBN: 978-1-907339-51-6, £11.95

Graeme Chesters

London is a great city for walking – whether for pleasure, exercise or simply to get from A to B. Despite the city's extensive public transport system, walking is also often the quickest and most enjoyable way to get around – at least in the centre – and it's also free and healthy!

Many attractions are off the beaten track, away from the major thoroughfares and public transport hubs. This favours walking as the best way to explore them, as does the fact that London is a visually interesting city with a wealth of stimulating sights in every 'nook and cranny'.

320 PAGES, PRINTED IN COLOUR

LONDON'S SECRETS: PARKS & GARDENS

ISBN: 978-1-907339-93-6, £10.95

Robbi Atilgan & David Hampshire

London is one the world's greenest capital cities, with a wealth of places where you can relax and recharge your batteries. Britain is renowned for its parks and gardens, and nowhere has such beautiful and varied green spaces as London: magnificent royal parks, historic garden cemeteries, majestic ancient forests and woodlands, breathtaking formal country parks, expansive commons, charming small gardens, beautiful garden squares and enchanting 'secret' gardens. Not all are secrets, of course, but many of London's most beguiling green spaces are known only to insiders and locals.

So, whether you're a nature lover, horticulturist or keen amateur gardener, or just looking for somewhere for a bit of peace and quiet or a place to exercise or relax, you're sure to find your perfect spot in London. **Published Summer 2013.**

LONDON'S SECRET PLACES

ISBN: 978-1-907339-92-9, £10.95

Graeme Chesters & David Hampshire

London is one of the world's leading tourist destinations with a wealth of world-class attractions: amazing museums and galleries, beautiful parks and gardens, stunning palaces and grand houses, and much, much more. These are covered in numerous excellent tourist guides and online, and need no introduction here. Not so well known are London's numerous smaller attractions, most of which are neglected by the throngs who descend upon the tourist-clogged major sights. What London's Secret Places does is seek out the city's lesser-known, but no less worthy, 'hidden' attractions.

LONDON'S SECRETS: MUSEUMS & GALLERIES

ISBN: 978-1-907339-96-7, £10.95

Robbi Atilgan & David Hampshire

London is a treasure trove for museum fans and art lovers and one of the world's great art and cultural centres, with more popular museums and galleries than any other world city. The art scene is a lot like the city itself – diverse, vast, vibrant and in a constant state of flux – a cornucopia of traditional and cutting-edge, majestic and mundane, world-class and run-of-the-mill, bizarre and brilliant.

So, whether you're an art lover, culture vulture, history buff or just looking for something to entertain the family during the school holidays, you're bound to find inspiration in London. All you need is a comfortable pair of shoes, an open mind – and this book!

LONDON'S SECRETS: PUBS & BARS

ISBN: 978-1-907339-93-6, £10.95

Graeme Chesters

British pubs and bars are world famous for their bonhomie, great atmosphere, good food and fine ales. Nowhere is this more so than in London, which has a plethora of watering holes of all shapes and sizes: classic historic boozers and trendy style bars; traditional riverside inns and luxurious cocktail bars; enticing wine bars and brew pubs; mouth-watering gastro pubs and brasseries; welcoming gay bars and raucous music venues. **Published Summer 2013.**

320 PAGES, PRINTED IN COLOUR

LIVING & WORKING IN
FRANCE

Living and Working in France, first published in 1993 and now in its 10th edition, is the most accurate, comprehensive and up-to-date book available about daily life – and is essential reading for newcomers. What's it really like Living and Working in France? Not surprisingly there's a lot more to life than baguettes, berets and boules! This book is guaranteed to hasten your introduction to la vie française, irrespective of whether you're planning to stay for a few months or indefinitely.

PRINTED IN COLOUR!

Topics include:

◆ How to find a job with a good salary and conditions

◆ How to obtain a residence or work permit

◆ How to avoid and overcome problems on arrival

◆ How to find your dream home

◆ How to make the most of post office and telephone services

◆ How to get the best education for your family

◆ How to make the best use of public transport and much, much more.

Packed with comprehensive, up-to-date, accurate information, facts and figures, and 'insider' tips, all written and presented in the 'easy to read and understand' style for which Survival Books are famous. Our books will save you weeks or months of research, answer hundreds of questions – including many you hadn't even thought of – and help you avoid problems and save money!

Buy your copy today at www.survivalbooks.net

Survival Books – The Francophiles' Best Friend

LIVING & WORKING IN
GERMANY

Living and Working in Germany, first published in 2000 and now in its 4th edition, is the most comprehensive book available about daily life – and is essential reading for newcomers. What's it really like Living and Working in Germany? Not surprisingly there's a lot more to life than bier, bratwurst and beetles! This book is guaranteed to hasten your introduction to the German way of life, irrespective of whether you're planning to stay for a few months or indefinitely.

PRINTED IN COLOUR!

Topics include:

♦ How to find a job with a good salary and conditions

♦ How to obtain a residence or work permit

♦ How to avoid and overcome problems on arrival

♦ How to find your dream home

♦ How to make the most of post office and telephone services

♦ How to get the best education for your family

♦ How to make the best use of public transport and much, much more.

Packed with comprehensive, up-to-date, accurate information, facts and figures, and 'insider' tips, all written and presented in the 'easy to read and understand' style for which Survival Books are famous. Our books will save you weeks or months of research, answer hundreds of questions – including many you hadn't even thought of – and help you avoid problems and save money!

Buy your copy today at www.survivalbooks.net

Survival Books – The Expatriates' Best Friend

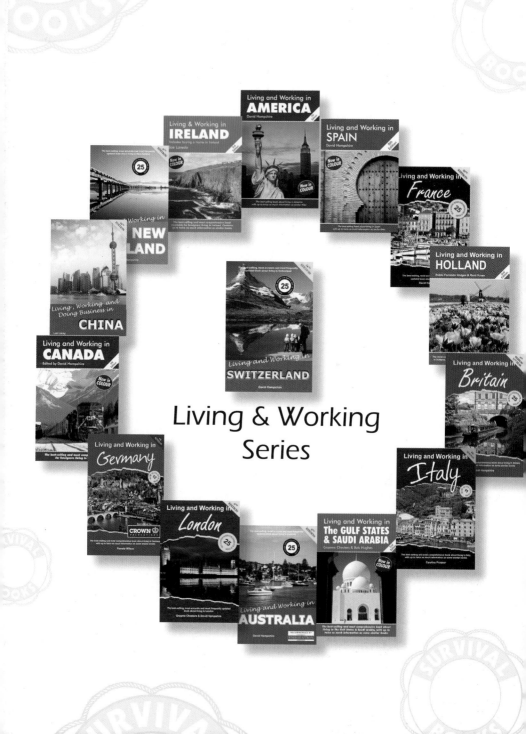

Living & Working
Series